MORTAL THOUGHTS

Mortal Thoughts

Religion, Secularity & Identity in
Shakespeare and Early Modern Culture

BRIAN CUMMINGS

OXFORD
UNIVERSITY PRESS

OXFORD
UNIVERSITY PRESS

Great Clarendon Street, Oxford, OX2 6DP,
United Kingdom

Oxford University Press is a department of the University of Oxford.
It furthers the University's objective of excellence in research, scholarship,
and education by publishing worldwide. Oxford is a registered trade mark of
Oxford University Press in the UK and in certain other countries

British Library Cataloguing in Publication Data
Data available

ISBN 978–0–19–967771–9

Printed in Great Britain by
CPI Group (UK) Ltd, Croydon, CR0 4YY

1007294754

For Freya

Preface

This book, while a study of literature, philosophy, and art of the past, is about a number of issues of contemporary importance. First, it considers how secularization has been a key component in the explanation of the emergence of modernity. Since the nineteenth century and even to the present day, it has been assumed that we are modern because we have become secular. This idea is currently under threat from a number of sides. The secularity of modern society is much less apparent than it was a generation ago; politics is becoming more rather than less self-consciously adapted to religious concerns. At the same time, cultural theorists question whether secularization, far from a historical explanation, was an ideological aspiration, one very particular to the twentieth century, and a very Western anxiety at that.

Secondly, this book considers the apparent paradox that while secularization is no longer a concept favoured in the social sciences that attempt to describe the modern condition, it is still a time-honoured cliché among cultural historians in describing the transition to that supposed condition in early modernity. In particular, early modern culture is commonly understood in terms of a debate over identity and subjectivity, and that debate (while the object of flourishing and diverse scholarship) is founded on a presupposition that pre-modern culture was predominantly (and distinctively) religious. Intriguingly, renewed interest in the last decade in the religious culture of the sixteenth century has not threatened this presupposition, indeed it could be said to have reinforced it. For example, the so-called 'religious turn' in early modern literary studies has endorsed a view that the 'religious' as a sphere was (as it were) intrinsically communal, bodily and even implicitly nostalgic.

Shakespeare, as ever, is at the centre of these debates about cultural iconography. While once he was the apostle of individualism and modernity, now he is found equally attractive as a carrier of the sacramental community of the body social. Shakespeare keeps playing his part as the actor of our cultural fantasies. My book participates in this process but also suggests some further questions for us to ask about the past and the present. It disputes whether modernity, or the literary, is secular, but in rejecting such mantras it also questions whether identity, as a concept, really is opposed to bodily or communal principles; whether 'religious' (as in 'religious turn') is any more useful a term than 'secular'; whether the problem of human identity indeed challenges either of these simplifications; and whether the early modern always has to be valued only insofar as it helps us to explain the modern.

It focuses, chapter by chapter, on a variety of ideas and genres that have been used in the past to explain either identity or cultural change. As in studies of Renaissance subjectivity from Burckhardt onwards, the visual arts form a continuous focus of interest as well as literary genres; just as the book alternates freely between questions of representation in culture and questions of philosophy. The chapters, while following a logical order and a kind of chronology, are not to be read as a single thesis but more as separate case studies that are cumulatively suggestive. Identity and mortality form common threads. What it is to be human, and how a life is framed by its ending, are issues that cross religious confessions, and interrogate the sacred and secular divide. I am interested in the pressure posed to questions of identity by ideas of finitude and contingency, and the ways in which religious change is often poised around the anxieties this creates. This also challenges conventional divisions between kinds of literary and artistic endeavour. Forms of incipient life writing (and life drawing) are here treated alongside philosophical speculation, alongside visual or dramatic representation. I try to be faithful to the demands of particular genres but make no apology for the framing of questions outside of generic propriety. While Shakespeare dominates the middle chapters, other writers—Thomas More, John Foxe, John Donne, and John Milton—all of whom have frequently been used to characterize a spirit of the age, are the centrepiece of others; and Montaigne appears throughout. The graphic art of Albrecht Dürer—who among art historians has had a similar iconic function to Shakespeare—bookends the whole.

Like a person, this book has had a particular life that has made it what it is. While an idiosyncratic project, it has emerged through very special forms of collaboration. Writing it was made possible by a Major Research Fellowship between 2009 and 2012 from the Leverhulme Trust. I cannot thank the trustees enough for the generosity and imagination with which they undertake sponsorship of intellectual activity. The Leverhulme name has come to be synonymous with the highest ideals in academic life. In my case, an initial aim to convey one of the last remaining mysteries of Shakespeare studies—the place of religion—has been enabled to link to a larger question about the cultural concept of religion altogether.

As well as creating time to think and write, an inadvertent benefit of the Leverhulme Research award was that it freed me from the constraints of space in order to take up a Visiting Fellowship at the Centre for Advanced Studies at Ludwig-Maximilians-Universität in Munich. This was an inspiration for a number of personal and professional reasons. The Centre is a creative home for intellectual exchange and a testimony to the benefit of conducting research in companionship, where ideas flow. It also gave me the wonder of a different geographical perspective—at the Catholic heart of the European phenomenon which also fostered the German Reformation; and also, serendipitously, of an intellectual context—a stone's throw from the last home of Max Weber in Seestraße, a villa in Schwabing next to the Englische Garten, where the walls talk a distinctive form of *wissenschaftliche* idealism.

I often feel I wrote the book in Munich even when I was not there. Professor Dr Andreas Höfele first asked me to Munich in 2005 (to give a paper which is the origin of Chapter 2) as part of the Sonderforschungsbereich on 'Pluralization and Authority in the Early Modern Period'. During my Fellowship in Munich I was able to be a formal associate of the project as it went through its last rites, in which I gave a paper that became Chapter 6. Meanwhile, Dr Sonja Asal asked me to give a lecture at the Centre for Advanced Studies (now Chapter 7). Andreas has been an enlightened and supremely genial presence in all my thinking for the book. At the same time, others have provided a context and creative spur for many of the threads: Gabriel Josipovici, Maggie Boden, and Andrew Hadfield in Sussex; Martin van Gelderen and Kevin Sharpe at the European University Institute in Fiesole and the Herzog August Bibliothek in Wolfenbüttel, where we joined together respectively at a Winterschool and a Summer School (for which I thank all the participants); David Daniell at the Tyndale Society; Giles Mandelbrote and Hugh Cahill at Lambeth Palace Library; Helen Cooper, Andrew Taylor, and Eamon Duffy for inviting me to give talks in Cambridge; James Simpson, Stephen Greenblatt, and Barbara Lewalski for similar occasions at Harvard; likewise Margreta de Grazia and Bronwyn Wallace at Penn; David Kastan—when he was there—and Molly Murray at Columbia; Jim Kearney, both at Yale and UCSB; Andrew Lynch and Chris Wortham at the University of Western Australia; Terence Cave, Vincent Gillespie, and Susan Brigden in Oxford; Philip Schwyzer at Exeter; and Jerome de Groot in Manchester. Versions of papers were also given at the Society for Renaissance Studies in York, and the Renaissance Society of America. A version of Chapter 2 was published in *Renaissance Studies*, 23 (2009), 463–85; of Chapter 3 in Tara Hamling and Richard L. Williams (ed.), *Art Re-Formed: Re-Assessing the Impact of the Reformation on the Visual Arts* (Newcastle: Cambridge Scholars Publishing, 2007), 183–200; and of Chapter 4 in *English Literary Renaissance*, 27 (1997), 197–232; I am grateful to the publishers for permission to reprint.

Jacqueline Baker has been a fabulous editor to work with, and Jenny Townshend and Rachel Platt at OUP helped in all kinds of ways. Sandra Assersohn searched zealously for reproductions of the images and never blanched at my fussiness. Among many friends who have done so much to help in the years I worked on the book I single out as ever Gabriel Josipovici, Margreta de Grazia, Eamon Duffy, James Simpson, Jim Kearney, Tom Fulton, David Kastan, Andrew Hadfield, Jenny Taylor, Lindsay Smith, Penny McCarthy, Lalage Neal, Claudia Richter, Isabel Karremann, Björn Quiring, Tobias Döring, Claudia Ölk, Tom Betteridge, Peter Marshall, Alex Walsham, Peter Lake, and not least the late and wonderful Kevin Sharpe. My mother, Sheila Cummings, died as I was finishing the book: my father Wesley, my brother David, and my sons Thomas and Daniel have looked after me through that time, as they have at all others. The book is dedicated to the person without whom not: Freya Sierhuis, Fellow of the Centre for Advanced Studies at LMU, who shared all the ideas as we collaborated in Munich; took me on a rail trip to Dürer's house in Nuremberg, as well as to the mountains to forget about Shakespeare; and even suggested the title of this book.

Brian Cummings

York, November 2012

Contents

List of Illustrations   xiii

Introduction: Secularization & Identity   1

1 The Mortal Self   19
   Dürer & Montaigne

2 The Reformed Conscience   67
   Thomas More

3 The Writer as Martyr   92
   Cranmer & Foxe

4 Public Oaths & Private Selves   133
   More, Foxe, & Shakespeare

5 Soliloquy & Secularization   168
   Shakespeare

6 Hamlet's Luck   207
   Shakespeare & the Renaissance Bible

7 Freedom, Suicide, & Selfhood   236
   Montaigne, Shakespeare, Donne

8 Soft Selves: Adam, Eve, & the Art of Embodiment   278
   Dürer to Milton

Bibliography   327
Primary Sources   327
Secondary Sources   337
Index   349

List of Illustrations

Cover Image

Albrecht Dürer, *Nude Self-Portrait* (1503?), pen, ink and brush against a black ground on green paper, Schlossmuseum, Weimar, Germany/The Bridgeman Art Library

1   Albrecht Dürer, *Nude Self-Portrait* (1503?); pen, ink, and brush. Schlossmuseum, Weimar, Germany/ The Bridgeman Art Library   26

2   Albrecht Dürer, *Head of the Dead Christ* (1503); charcoal. British Museum Sloane 5218-29 © The Trustees of the British Museum   28

3   Albrecht Dürer, *Coat of Arms* (1523); woodcut. British Museum 1895-1-22-745 © The Trustees of the British Museum   31

4   Albrecht Dürer, *Coat of Arms with a Skull* (1503); engraving. British Museum 1895-9-15-359 © The Trustees of the British Museum   33

5   Andrea Mantegna, *Entombment with Four Birds* (c.1465); engraving. © RMN-Grand Palais (Musée du Louvre)/ Thierry Le Mage   36

6   Andrea Mantegna, *Descent into Limbo* (c.1470); pen, brown ink, and wash. Paris, École Nationale Supérieure des Beaux Arts inv. 189. Photograph: Jean-Michel Lapelerie   37

7   Giovanni Antonio da Brescia, *Descent into Limbo* (1490s); engraving. Boston, Museum of Fine Arts Harvey D. Parker Collection P 1006. Photograph © 2013 Museum of Fine Arts, Boston   38

8   Pieter Claesz, *Vanitasstilleven met schedel, horloge, konische roemer en boek* (1630); oil on panel. The Hague, Royal Cabinet of Paintings, Mauritshuis   42

9   Albrecht Dürer, *Self-Portrait* (1484); silverpoint. Vienna, Graphische Sammlung Albertina, 4839/The Bridgeman Art Library   52

10 Albrecht Dürer, *Portrait of the Artist's Mother* (1514); charcoal. Berlin, Staatliche Museen zu Berlin, Kupferstichkabinett/ Giraudon/The Bridgeman Art Library   54

11 Montaigne's annotation in MS hand, Titus Lucretius Carus, *Titi Lucretii Cari De rerum natura libri sex* Parisiis, et Lugduni habentur [Paris & Lyons]: In Gulielmi Rouillii, et Philippi G. Rouillii Nep. ædibus, via Jacobæ sub concordia, 1563 [i.e. 1564?], p. 251. Reproduced by kind permission of the Syndics of Cambridge University Library/ Montaigne 1.4.4   65

12 John Foxe, *Actes and Monuments of these latter and perrilous dayes* (London: Iohn Day, 1563), 'The burning of the Archbishop of Cant[erbury] D[octor] Tho[mas] Cranmer in the town dich at Oxford, with his hand first thrust into the fyre, wher with he subscribed before'. Oxford, Bodleian Library, Douce F subt.3. fo. 1503   111

13 John Foxe, *Actes and Monuments of these latter and perrilous dayes* (London: Iohn Day, 1563), 'Tho. Bilney being in prison, diuers tymes proueth the fire with hys finger'. Oxford, Bodleian Library, Douce F subt.3. fo. 466   123

14 John Foxe, *Actes and Monuments of these latter and perrilous dayes* (London: Iohn Day, 1563), 'The sharpe burning of Thomas Tomkyns hand, by cruel Boner hym selfe, who not long after burnt also hys body'. Oxford, Bodleian Library, Douce F subt.3. fo. 1101   126

15 John Foxe, *Actes and Monuments of these latter and perrilous dayes* (London: Iohn Day, 1563), 'The burning of Rose Allins hands by Syr Edmond Tirryll, as she was goyng to fetche drynke for her Mother, lying sycke in her bed'. Oxford, Bodleian Library, Douce F subt.3. fo. 1706   131

16 Rubens, *Death of Seneca* (*c.*1610); oil on panel. München, Alte Pinakothek; Bayerische Staatsgemaeldesammlungen BPK, Bildagentur für Kunst, Kultur und Geschichte, Berlin © 2012. Photo Scala, Florence   264

17 Albrecht Dürer, *Adam and Eve* (1504); engraving. British Museum 1868-8-22-167. © The Trustees of the British Museum   279

18 Albrecht Dürer, *Apollo and Diana* (1501–4); pen and ink. British Museum Sloane 5218–183. © The Trustees of the British Museum   286

19 Albrecht Dürer, *Study for the Figure of Eve* (1504); pen and ink. British Museum Sloane 5218–182. © The Trustees of the British Museum   288

20 Hans Baldung Grien, *Fall of Man* (1511); chiaroscuro woodcut. British Museum 1845-8-9-922. © The Trustees of the British Museum   292

21 Hans Baldung Grien, *Adam and Eve* (1519); woodcut.
Staatliche Museen zu Berlin SPK, Kupferstichkabinett
Rosenwald Collection 1943.3.925   295

22 Lucas van Leyden, *Fall of Man* (*c.*1530); engraving.
Washington, DC, National Gallery of Art, Rosenwald
Collection 1943.3.5611   312

23 Hans Baldung Grien, *Death and a Woman* (1515);
chiaroscuro drawing. Firenze, Gabinetto Disegni e Stampe
degli Uffizi; La Morte e una donna, inv. 1046E (IN12203)   315

24 Hans Baldung Grien, *The Bewitched Stable Groom* (1544–5);
woodcut. British Museum 1895-1-22-239. © The Trustees
of the British Museum   317

25 Rembrandt, *Adam and Eve* (1638); etching. Washington,
DC, National Gallery of Art, Rosenwald Collection
1943.3.7102   319

Introduction
Secularization & Identity

One of the key principles in the formation of a history of modern identity is that it was the result of an inevitable process of secularization. Such an assumption is so strong as to be unconscious; but it is also part of the formal structure of the concept. From Jakob Burckhardt—who first originated the historical principles of 'The Development of the Individual' and 'The Discovery of the World and of Man'[1] as definitive moments in the emergence of European civilization or modernity—to Charles Taylor—who followed *Sources of the Self* (1989) with the equally monumental *A Secular Age* (2007)—cultural historians and theorists have formulated such ideas as not only related but *necessarily* related:

> The social orders we live in are not grounded cosmically, prior to us, there as it were, waiting for us to take up our allotted place; rather society is made up of individuals, or at least for individuals.[2]

Individualism, in this guise, arises at the same time as—is perhaps a result of—what Max Weber called *Entzauberung* or 'disenchantment'.[3] 'The fate of our times is characterized by rationalization and intellectualization and, above all, by the "disenchantment of the world".'[4] Weber borrowed this resonant phrase from Friedrich Schiller and used it repeatedly, almost as a mantra, to cover the character of modernity in all its guises, from

---

[1] The phrases 'Entwicklung des Individuums' and 'Die Entdeckung der Welt und des Menschen' are chapter headings in *Die Kultur der Renaissance in Italien* (1860).

[2] *A Secular Age* (Cambridge, Mass.: Harvard University Press, 2007), 540.

[3] The phrase *Entzauberung der Welt* ('disenchantment of the world') originates in Weber's late lecture given in Munich in 1918 and published in 1919, 'Wissenschaft als Beruf': 'Das aber bedeutet: die Entzauberung der Welt. Nicht mehr, wie der Wilde, für den es solche Mächte gab, muss man zu magischen Mitteln greifen, um die Geister zu beherrschen oder zu erbitten', *Gesammelte Aufsätze zur Wissenschaftslehre*, ed. Johannes Winckelmann (Tübingen: J. C. B. Mohr, 1985), 594.

[4] 'Science as a vocation', *From Max Weber: Essays in Sociology*, ed. H. H. Geerth and C. Wright Mills, new edn. (London: Routledge, 2009), 155.

political economy and the natural sciences to the exigencies of German academic life.[5]

Weber incorporated both liberal political ideals and an Enlightenment view of history to identify a philosophical progression in a linear direction towards technological rationalization.[6] He did not regard this as of universal benefit. Disenchantment involved a retreat from 'sublime values' (*die sublimsten Werte*) in public life towards alternatives Weber clearly viewed with some misgiving: 'the transcendental realm of mystic life' or else 'the brotherliness of...personal human relations' (p. 155). This has transferred itself also into the artistic world:

> It is not accidental that our greatest art is intimate and not monumental, nor is it accidental that today only within the smallest and intimate circles, in personal human situations, in *pianissimo*, that something is pulsating that corresponds to the prophetic *pneuma*, which in former times swept through the great communities like a firebrand, welding them together. (p. 155)

Any renewed attempt at monumentality in art he saw doomed to monstrosity. With something like a prophetic energy of his own, Weber in Munich in 1918 predicted that any attempt 'intellectually to construe new religions without a new and genuine prophecy' (p. 155) would result in something still worse.

Weber's concept of 'disenchantment' has had a very wide and influential currency. This legacy to the interpretation of cultural history could be summarized in the following way. In a modernized, secularized society, such as now dominates in the West, scientific knowledge is valued more highly than religious belief, and rationalism dominates over mysticism in determining social processes and decisions. Weber saw the two as going hand in hand: as the sacred gives way to the secular, so the prophetic cedes to the personal, the intimate. Individualism is seen in this model as a by-product of the disillusioning of man from either subjection to divine agency or incorporation in the world of spirits or demons. Placing man at the centre of the universe, the cliché goes, involved dethroning God. Yet just as powerfully, secularization can be seen as a by-product of this idea of the individual. We are secular to the extent that we live in a society conceived via individualized agency. It is not too much to see in this powerful nexus of ideas the mainstay of the emergence of the social sciences at the beginning of the twentieth century as a new hegemony in political and ethical explanation.

---

[5] H. H. Geerth, 'The Man and his Work', in *From Max Weber*, 51.
[6] Geerth, 'A Philosophy of History', *From Max Weber*, 51.

Weber's 'disenchantment' has been joined in this respect to Henri Hubert and Marcel Mauss's concept of 'désacralisation'.[7] Here the technical use of this word in Hubert and Mauss has been reapplied later with articulate vigour. Hubert and Mauss were concerned with analysing the ritual processes by which a communication is made between the worlds of the sacred and the profane.[8] A broader historical revaluation of the term has used it to describe how the ritual processes by which ordinary objects were once consecrated with extraordinary powers are subverted by the social rationalization of such actions as mere 'magic' or 'superstition'. This is further related to a third seminal moment in the modern social sciences: Émile Durkheim's concept of *anomie*, in which the individual is unmoored from the ties that bind a society and the moral forces by which our ancestors lived.[9] The decline of religion is once again seen an essential part of this process:

> religion extends over an ever diminishing area of social life. Originally, it extended to everything: everything social was religious—the two words were synonymous. Then gradually political, economic and scientific functions broke free from the religious function.[10]

Thus disenchantment is related structurally to the idea of individualization in societies.

By the middle of the twentieth century, the idea of 'secularization' had gained such a powerful meaning both in cultural history and in sociological terminology that it had acquired its own history. Secularization was an old word—used within Catholic Europe to describe the process by which a priest re-entered secular society, or after the Reformation to mean the appropriation of ecclesiastical lands and property into the control of the state or individuals empowered by the state. The new coinage of the word, however, was ideologically and often emotionally charged. In one direction, especially in 'progressive' contexts, it meant nothing less than the liberation of human ideas as well as institutions from a religious yoke. However, 'secularization' is by no means always a term of praise. In the opposite regard, it could be taken (according to a more conservative philosophical bent) as the process by which society was losing its moral guard. This is its currency among some theologians, such as Josef Ratzinger. Yet among other Christian commentators the term was even welcomed, as allowing a more liberalized or disestablished view of religion itself. What-

---

[7] *Essai sur la nature et la fonction du sacrifice* (1898).

[8] *Sacrifice: Its Nature and Function*, trans. W. D. Halls (Chicago: University of Chicago Press, 1964), 57.

[9] *De la division du travail social* (1893).

[10] *The Division of Labour in Society*, trans. W. D. Halls (London: Macmillan, 1984), 119.

ever the disagreements about its value, in fact, there was nonetheless a kind of consensus of historical factuality: this was the state of things at the end of the twentieth century. In this context, a value neutral definition could be attempted:

> By secularization we mean the process by which sectors of society and culture are removed from the domination of religious institutions and symbols.[11]

In the modern west, Peter Berger concluded, in a seminal study in 1967 of religion in contemporary social thought, an increasing proportion of people looked on the world (and themselves) as outside of the limits of religious interpretation.[12] Taylor puts it with stark simplicity: 'We live in a secular age'.[13]

This book both challenges the historical assumptions that lie behind the idea of secularization and questions the boundary between the religious and the secular on which it is based. It is an essay in literary history rather than in contemporary philosophy, but it does share some assumptions with many recent voices which have questioned the idea of secularization. Included among these are Taylor, who believes that the secular idea was transformed after the Second World War, and that in the contemporary world there is 'an unheard of pluralism of outlooks, religious and non- and anti-religious, in which the number of possible positions seems to be increasing without end' (p. 437). Yet in some ways in making this analysis Taylor attributes even more power to the sense that once upon a time things were very different, and that history in relation to religion shows a distinctive regressive pattern which has only recently been disturbed. Central to the pattern of change is the Renaissance and its view of the individual. My argument is that the historical picture of secularization has been determined largely by the ideological investment in the idea of a secular modernity. In place of this I search for an explanation of early modern identity which is not in thrall to modern secularization. This is not to say either that there are no versions of secularity in the early modern period—clearly there are—or that there is not a peculiar attention to concepts of personhood. But a different picture can be drawn of the relation of problems of the self to problems of religion. In the process, we can see how, both in the past and in our own society, the secular and the religious,

---

[11] Peter L. Berger, *The Social Reality of Religion* (Harmondsworth: Penguin University Books, 1973), 113.

[12] Berger, *The Social Reality of Religion*. First published in the USA as *The Sacred Canopy* (1967).

[13] *A Secular Age*, 1.

far from being incommensurate, intersect in creative and profound ways.

Beneath the surface of the grand narrative of secularization there were always obvious tensions. Weber's term *Entzauberung* is only rather dubiously translated as 'disenchantment'. The verb *entzaubern* means to 'break a spell', literally to undo an enchantment, and does not have the connotations of disappointment and cultural disillusion possessed by the English equivalent. In that sense, Weber was appealing to a historical movement within Christianity itself. The Protestant Reformation believed itself to be reinvigorating as much as reinventing religion by doing away with what it saw as 'magic': 'And surely, if a man will but take a view of all poperie, he shall easily see, that the most part is meere Magique', wrote William Perkins in the 1590s.[14] Whereas the stereotyped view of secularization is of a movement decisively *away* from religion, Weber—the most important formative theorist of religion in the early twentieth century—famously considered even the definition of religion to be as yet beyond him.[15] Durkheim recognized that Christianity was itself the origin of the idea of the individual as moral sovereign which gave rise to the possibility of *anomie*; and he studied Calvinism as a case study of the break-up of moral community wholes into individualized fragments.[16] All the more peculiar has been the fate of the word 'désacralisation'. Hubert and Mauss, far from identifying a progression or descent from sacralization to desacralization, considered the two concepts to be in a necessary tension within any act of sacrifice, and perhaps in any human ritual: a two-way interface between the separation and the incorporation of the individual within the group.

Most misunderstood of all in this respect is the phrase that has come to symbolize and summarize the whole concept: Friedrich Nietzsche's 'Gott ist tot'. Routinely extracted from *Also sprach Zarathustra* as a kind of call-to-arms of secular discontent, or radical post-Christian *jouissance*, 'God is dead' is originally found in the voice of the Madman in *Die fröhliche Wissenschaft* (1882), and is a statement full of philosophical and historical irony, deeply couched in metaphors stolen from Lady Macbeth:

> God is dead. God remains dead. And we have killed him. How shall we comfort ourselves, the murderers of all murderers? What was holiest and mightiest of all that the world has yet owned has bled to death under our knives: who will wipe this blood off us? What water is there for us to clean

---

[14] *A golden chaine: or The description of theologie containing the order of the causes of salu-ation and damnation, according to Gods word* (Cambridge: John Legate, 1600), 51.

[15] *Wirtschaft und Gesellschaft* (1922).

[16] *Division of Labour in Society*, 228; on Calvinism, see *Le Suicide* (1897), discussed in Chapter 7.

ourselves? What festivals of atonement, what sacred games shall we have to invent? Is not the greatness of this deed too great for us? Must we ourselves not become gods simply to appear worthy of it?[17]

Nowhere here is there an idea of religion as casually thrown off or emptied out into a new secular utopia. 'Come you spirits | That tend on mortal thoughts', to quote Lady Macbeth again.[18] The profound angst of getting rid of God is part of the philosophical struggle, not the prelude to its possibility; and Nietzsche's point is more human enfeeblement than empowerment through the dethroning of God.

Indeed, some of the most creative intellectual energy over the idea of 'secularization' can be seen to have come from within theology. The idea of 'demythologization' was developed not as a response outside theology but as a new way of understanding the New Testament, in the work of Rudolf Bultmann. In the 1950s, deliberately paradoxical terms such as 'secular theology' and even 'secular Christianity' were developed to accommodate a response to the anxious demands of the secular within religion in the post-war years. Dietrich Bonhoeffer's phrase, 'religionless Christianity', forged in the war, became the banner for a fractured form of theology which tried to make sense of twentieth-century history.[19] The 'death of God' became itself a form of theological concept in the 1960s.[20]

However, it may be that the idea of secularization has had a power in the twentieth century, and beyond, that transcended its internal logic. Its attraction is precisely its explanatory generalization. It has come to stand for a cultural moment, a cultural philosophy bound up with modern human experience. The idea of a godless world has corresponded to a sense of the forces of a new history of existential alienation but also scarcely imaginable material suffering: the trenches of Flanders, the holocaust, the nuclear bomb.[21] Secularization in this context has become inexorably linked to other trends in contemporary thought, whether in forms of philosophical pessimism or in varieties of existentialism and postmodernism. Here there are strong ironies of transmission, particularly when we consider secularization in relation to ideas of selfhood. For

---

[17] *The Gay Science*, trans. Walter Kaufmann (New York: Vintage Books, 1974), § 125.

[18] *Macbeth*, 1.5.40–1. Quotations from Shakespeare (unless otherwise noted) follow the *Arden Shakespeare*, using the online edition (*The Shakespeare Collection*), citing act, scene, and line numbers: <http://shakespeare.galegroup.com>, accessed 6 December 2012.

[19] *Letters and Papers from Prison*, ed. Eberhard Bethge (London: SCM Press, 1972).

[20] John Robinson, *Honest to God* (London: SCM Press, 1963) is a popular example, discussed in John D. Caputo and Gianni Vattimo, *After the Death of God* (New York: Columbia University Press, 2007), 92.

[21] Jeffrey W. Robbins, 'Introduction' to *After the Death of God*, 2.

the connection between individualism and secularization has been taken for granted even when the autonomy of selfhood has come under philosophical attack. While Nietzsche mythologized the death of God, he ironized the spirit of modernity. In similar vein, Michel Foucault relentlessly satirized the apotheosis of individualism yet saw it as part of the cultural spillage of post-Christianity. It has therefore seemed natural to find allies for secularization in Nietzsche and Foucault even as they are used for consciously avant-garde academic revisionism. A case in point is the turn on the self in Stephen Greenblatt. Greenblatt recognized the 'resolutely dialectical' processes which determined what Burckhardt and Michelet had described as *the* turning point in the history of identities, and embraced the human technologies of the Reformation as part of this complexity; but he still traced within this what he called 'a shift from the Church to the Book to the absolutist state'.[22] Greenblatt, following Nietzsche and Foucault, no longer saw Burckhardt's 'The Development of the Individual' as a liberation, but the new enslavement was still remorselessly disenchanting and desacralized. Even in its obverse and postmodern form, the history of individualization is a secularizing history.

Here the idea of the Renaissance comes peculiarly into focus. The Renaissance was already indentified by Nietzsche as a heroic effort of the human spirit to break free from the suffocating influence of Christianity. In Burckhardt, Nietzsche's older colleague at Basel, the thesis that the Renaissance was intricately connected both with a rejection of religion and a new concept of selfhood found its definitive statement in 1860:

> In the Middle Ages both sides of human consciousness—that which was turned within as that which was turned without—lay dreaming or half awake beneath a common veil. The veil was woven of faith, illusion, and childish prepossession, through which the world and history were seen clad in strange hues.[23]

The key word here is 'common': only in the Renaissance, and specifically in Italy, Burckhardt declares, did this 'veil' first 'melt away'. Mankind only then first conceptualized itself in 'an *objective* treatment' derived from a political consideration of the State (p. 81). Of equal force was a move inwards:

> The *subjective* side at the same time asserted itself with corresponding emphasis; man became a spiritual *individual*, and recognized himself as such (p. 81)

[22] *Renaissance Self-Fashioning: More to Shakespeare* (Berkeley and Los Angeles: University of California Press, 1980), 8.
[23] *The Civilization of the Renaissance in Italy*, trans. S. G. C. Middlemore, 2nd edn. (Oxford: Phaidon Press, 1981), Pt. II, p. 81.

Burckhardt's prose at this point now reads a little jejune. In the last three generations, his book has undergone many revisionist attacks. His thesis on the rise of the individual has been rewritten by New Historicism after Greenblatt. But his idea of secularism and the Renaissance is more persistent, not least in Greenblatt's own later work, such as *The Swerve*.[24]

Within the cultural history of the early modern period, it is not too much to say that Shakespeare has an iconic role in this narrative. That this should be the case in literary study is natural enough, and within English-speaking countries it is explicable in general terms. Yet even Burckhardt, a Swiss writing about Italy, makes Shakespeare's drama one of the seminal episodes in his idea of the emergence of the statehood of the individual. The place of Shakespeare within this historiography is both submerged and structural, however. He is not the originator of any such ideas, but that is almost the point; he is the symptom, the cultural sign of change: 'all Europe produced but one Shakespeare', Burckhardt says; 'such a mind is the rarest of Heaven's gifts'.[25] Shakespeare is both an agent of change—heralded as the first truly modern author, in his charismatic self-presence; and its observer in action—the creator of the symbolic imaginary identities of human character, Hamlet and so on. It does not much matter that nobody particularly believes in the historical veracity of such claims. The claims are too big to want verification. They confirm who we are. And just as implicit as Shakespeare's relationship to individuality is his ownership of a self-determining secularity:

> What piece of work is a man, how noble in reason, how infinite in faculties,
> in form and moving how express and admirable, in action how like an angel,
> in apprehension how like a god: the beauty of the world, the paragon of
> animals—and yet, to me, what is this quintessence of dust?[26]

For Burckhardt, it was Shakespeare's non-religious status which explained the full range of his historic significance in the emancipation of the cultural power of what we call *Personlichkeit*, 'personhood' or 'identity'. Shakespeare could not have existed under a Spanish viceroy, or the Roman Inquisition, or even in England at the time of the religious revolution a generation later (p. 191).

Secularization and the idea of art have a special relationship. The *Oxford English Dictionary's* first reference to 'secularization' in its generic sense is from the *Fine Arts Quarterly* for 1863 (only three years after Burckhardt): 'With this secularization of the art, painting rapidly threw off the conventionalism

---

[24] *The Swerve: How the World became Modern* (New York: W. W. Norton, 2011).
[25] *Civilization of the Renaissance*, 191.
[26] *The Tragedy of Hamlet, Prince of Denmark*, 2.2.303–8.

of the cloister.'[27] Art is taken to be religion's antithesis, and also its usurper. Once religion is thrown off, new gods are needed, and art takes on the transcendence that has been left behind. We live in 'The age of the world picture', Heidegger stated in 1938: art comes to be 'an expression of human life [*Lebens*]'.[28] This is the distinctive condition of modernity: an age which represents the world to itself. Again, the connection with an idea of consciousness is not a coincidence. It is derived from Hegel: this is what makes human historical consciousness unique, in that it 'makes the individual comprehend himself as a person, in his uniqueness as a universal in himself'.[29] The nexus of religion and art, modernity and consciousness is very tight here. It does not seem an exaggeration to say that such formulations underlie the formations of the modern historical disciplines of art and literature. In both, the Renaissance had a central role in the early development not only of a suitable syllabus but also a conceptual framework.

Secularity was understood to be the inaugural moment of literature's formation, a defining aspect of its identity. Literature was held to be a fundamentally secular form, and its emergence was explained in terms of the transition from a religious culture. 'Secularism is conceived to be the inaugural moment of literature's formation, a defining aspect of its identity', Gauri Viswanathan has written.[30] In the book that provided the manifesto for the emergence of English Literature as a primary subject in the new humanities at the end of the nineteenth and the beginning of the twentieth centuries, Matthew Arnold's *Culture and Anarchy*, this transference of values is taken as axiomatic:

> Religion says: *The kingdom of God is within you*; and culture, in like manner, places human perfection in an *internal* condition, in the growth and predominance of our humanity proper, as distinguished from our animality.[31]

Dover Wilson, who edited Arnold, was also the doyen of English Shakespearians in the mid-century. The historiography of English Renaissance literature naturalized the secularizing narrative of culture as an object of

---

[27] *OED*, SECULARIZATION, n. 2. Second edn., 1989; online version December 2011. <http://www.oed.com>, accessed 22 February 2012.

[28] Martin Heidegger, 'The Age of the World Picture', *The Question Concerning Technology and Other Essays*, trans. William Lovitt (New York: Harper and Row, 1977).

[29] Georg Wilhelm Friedrich Hegel, 'Reason in History', General Introduction to *The Philosophy of History*, trans. Robert S. Hartman (Indianapolis: Bobbs-Merrill, 1953), III.3.a.

[30] Gauri Viswanathan, 'Secularism in the Framework of Heterodoxy', *PMLA*, 123.2 (March 2008), 466.

[31] *Culture and Anarchy*, ed. John Dover Wilson (Cambridge: Cambridge University Press, 1971), 47.

human study. The Elizabethan theatre, projected as a transformation of the drama of the miracle plays of the Middle Ages, and perhaps even (in a more residual sense) the energies of the sacred rituals of the church themselves, was an iconic example of this secularization. Shakespeare again held the key.

While secularization as a concept has preoccupied historians, sociologists, and theologians for decades, it is only in recent years that literary theory has taken notice of one of its own determining tenets. The irony is that this has happened long after the secularization thesis had in other areas come under increasing attack. Not surprisingly, since Weber had such a seminal role in its origination, it was the German-speaking world which first produced a critique. Hans Blumenberg's *Die Legitimät der Neuzeit* (1966), which originated in a lecture to the Seventh German Philosophy Congress of 1962, indeed coincided with the most confident expression of the idea of secularization in English, such as in Peter Berger's *The Sacred Canopy*. Blumenberg was involved in a complex reappraisal of the concept of modernity in Heidegger or Adorno as a kind of aberration and delusion or (in Adorno's terms) a 'negative dialectic'. He was also taking up a radical stance in relation to Karl Löwith's *Meaning in History* (1949), which deconstructed the modern idea of 'progress' as a fallacy, created by its secularized versions of medieval Christian ideas, and leaving it in a state of philosophical 'illegitimacy'.[32]

The subtlety and intellectual force of Blumenberg's argument is still apparent fifty years later, and has in some ways still not been fully absorbed. It begins with an acknowledgement of the way that secularization is difficult to define objectively because it is something that is never in view from the outside. *Säkularisierung* intrinsically refers to an 'age'—our age, that is—in that it contains within itself the Latin term *saecula*. Its whole purpose is to tell us where we have come from, and yet it already presupposes where we are. Secularization, Blumenberg asserts, contains within itself a complex ideological register of ideas of loss, transformation, and crisis.[33] Yet these are not emotions from which we have escaped and emerged, as in the teleological metaphor of secularization as process. In this sense, Blumenberg rejects the idea of modernity as an overthrowing of theological values: those theological values are still being assimilated. Yet he also rejects the idea, promulgated with vigour by Carl Schmitt in relation to the concept of 'political theology'—of secularization as an

---

[32] Robert M. Wallace, 'Progress, Secularization and Modernity: The Löwith/Blumenberg Debate', *New German Critique*, 22 (1981), 63–79.
[33] *The Legitimacy of the Modern Age*, trans. Robert M. Wallace (Cambridge, Mass.: MIT Press, 1983), 4–5. Wallace's translation is based on the 2nd edn. of the German original (Frankfurt: Suhrkamp, 1973–6).

expropriation of Christian concepts in modern form—such as Schmitt's own example of the modern doctrine of the state as a secularized theological concept.[34]

In a central part of his book, Blumenberg embarks on something of an astonishing satire of what he calls 'the rhetoric of secularizations' (p. 103). He describes a series of 'rhetorical effects and hyperboles', beginning with a savage characterization of Schmitt's concept of public law as a 'stage god'. He shows how secularization as an intentional style simultaneously invokes the sacred as a false idol and then takes on its aura. It creates metaphors of boundary while trying to make a stake on both sides of this boundary. The 'renaissance' he sees as an iconic example of this style, 'which frequently makes literary appearances in vestments of sacral ideas of rebirth and the related cult symbols' (p. 105). One of his funniest examples is Heinrich Heine's description of Shakespeare, whose dramas are 'the worldly gospel', and who was born 'in the northern Bethlehem that was called Stratford-upon-Avon'.[35]

Beyond the literary bravura of Blumenberg's critique is a revaluation both of history and of philosophy. To resist the temptation to see one epoch as a transformed—whether etiolated or revolutionized—pastiche of another is to restore both a sense of the urgency of the present and the investment of the present in history. The last statement of *Legitimacy of the Modern Age* is 'History knows no repetitions of the same; "renaissances" are its contradiction' (p. 596). This question then leaves open what we might do when we have abandoned the framework of secularization. This present study involves an attempt to retrace back through history to see how the period of the Renaissance might look if we take away the secularizing narrative of 'renaissance'. As such, it joins in the increasingly widespread dissent towards the idea of secularization in a number of fields.

Most spectacular of these is in sociology. This is spectacular because, as we have seen, sociology's own foundations are located in a theory of secularization. However, secularism no longer appears as the historically determined fate of modernity. There are modern political states which are conspicuously religious; and there are secular states which are desecularizing as we speak (the United States may be one of them).[36] If secularization is not inevitable, the concomitant anxiety (and evidently it is felt to be an anxiety) is whether it was ever true. If modernity is not a highway

[34] Blumenberg, *Legitimacy of the Modern Age*, 92.

[35] Heine, *Shakespeares Mädchen und Frauen*, in *Sämtliche Schriften*, ed. K. Briegleb (Darmstadt: Wissenschaftliche Buchgesellschaft, 1968–), iv. 173.

[36] Peter Berger (ed.), *The Desecularization of the World: Resurgent Religion and World Politics* (Grand Rapids, Mich.: Eerdmans, 1999).

to secularity, what does that make us think of the original location of religion? While this question is being asked urgently in the contemporary world, it also raises difficult questions about history, both the history of religion narrowly conceived, and more widely, in the way that the emerging redundancy of religion has been written into a history of how modernity came about in the first place.

In the field of literature, the turn against secularization has been particularly sharply felt in post-colonial studies. Views have polarized around the supposed incommensurability of religious beliefs and secular values, especially as perceived in relation to Islam. This has resulted in the question being openly asked, 'Is critique secular?' Talal Asad and Saba Mahmood have asked whether the assertion of secularity has not been framed in such a way as to prejudice arguments about law and justice according to westernized tenets.[37] Judith Butler's response in the same volume makes a spirited defence of the post-Enlightenment heritage of the secular in forming what she calls 'the sensibility of critique'.[38] Gauri Viswanathan has suggested a more wide-ranging challenge to what she sees as a secularized orthodoxy in literary theory and its own historicization. She questions the way that literary history has been constructed to confirm this orthodoxy, and especially a 'periodization inherent in narrativizing the decline of religious culture in these terms, with the Enlightenment as a pivotal transition point'.[39] In such a history, religious literature is turned into evidence of the same phenomenon, since 'religious traces are no more than a historical reminder of a displaced worldview' (p. 467).

This places once again a peculiar burden on those periods associated with pivotal transition. The Renaissance once more comes into view, especially because of the way that in literary history the Renaissance formerly eclipsed the Reformation as an engine of historical explanation. During most of the twentieth century, the Reformation was a mere footnote in literary history, part of the narrative which saw the Renaissance as the literary inheritor of the waning of a medieval religious world view. There was considerable irony in this. Ever since Weber, the Reformation had played a key role in the idea of secularization. The idea of 'disenchantment', as we have seen, was a part of the Protestant polemic of Luther, Zwingli, and Calvin, and enthusiastically pursued by English puritans. Magic has played a complex role in ideas of secularization from the beginning.

---

[37] *Is Critique Secular? Blasphemy, Injury, and Free Speech*, Townsend Papers in the Humanities (Berkeley and Los Angeles: University of California Press, 2009).

[38] 'The Sensibility of Critique: Response to Asad and Mahmood', in *Is Critique Secular?*, 101.

[39] 'Secularism in the Framework of Heterodoxy', 467.

On the one hand, historians of medieval popular culture such as Anton Gurevich have used popular religious magic as a way of suggesting that medieval Christianity was less orthodox and homogeneous than in the secularizing thesis which saw it as awaiting a revolution. On the other hand, Keith Thomas's *Religion and the Decline of Magic* (1971), for long a dominant book in the field, used the disenchantment thesis to suggest an inevitable historical process of change.

Historians have reacted in complex ways to this inheritance. Eamon Duffy's *Stripping of the Altars* (1992) turned upside down the suggestion in Gurevich and elsewhere that popular religion could be distinguished so easily from orthodox religion. In the opposite direction, it also fought vociferously against Thomas's idea of decline. Yet Duffy himself, in a strange dynamic, upholds some of the secularizing thesis in his view of the Protestant Reformation. For he sees the Reformation as an attack both on ritual and on community, and in the process confirms the view in Weber of an opposition between religion as magic and religion in its rationalized, intellectualized form. The Reformation in Duffy is constantly characterized as doctrinal and discursive, a religion of the head at odds with a religion of the body. In the process, he also resurrects the old ghost of the religion of individualism rejecting and replacing communal belief and tradition.

Everywhere, and not least in literary history, there is renewed interest in the history of early modern religion.[40] Yet we could ask if the model of religion that has been used in various forms of revisionism and 'the religious turn' is quite the right one. The task that is often set out for us is how to reframe an existing argument once religion is put back into the equation. In doing this, we are in danger of repeating the old secularizing paradigm even as we claim to shift it. In an odd way, religion in modern meaning has come to be constructed in terms of its opposite. If the secular is a concept that came into being in opposition to religion, the paradoxical result is that in reimagining the religious in a self-consciously 'secular age', we think of it as whatever is left outside the realm of secularity: religion, if you like, is the 'non-secular'. Yet if religion and secularity turn out instead to have had porous boundaries all along, everything we describe in historical writing via the assumption of a dialectic between the religious and the secular has to be removed and rethought. The realm of the religious includes many things that we think of in secular terms. And yet at the same time we should be wary of re-describing this in terms of

---

[40] A survey of these developments, in turn highly influential in its own right, is: Ken Jackson and Arthur F. Marotti, 'The Turn to Religion in Early Modern English Studies', *Criticism*, 46.1 (2004), 167–90.

the modern sense of 'religious', for then we re-infect the argument with a concept of the radically non-secular. 'To rethink the religious is also to rethink the secular and its truth claims', suggests Mahmood; but we could also reverse this to say that to rethink the secular means to rethink the religious.[41] The religious, perhaps, is not quite as 'religious' as we thought, and intersects with the world in its totality, not in some hermetically sealed sphere all of its own.

One aspect of this is that religion since the nineteenth century has been thought of in 'private' terms. Religion is conceived as a set of personal beliefs. For a person to be religious, we assume that that person sees the world from the point of view of believing such beliefs. This itself can be seen as a fall-out of the secularization thesis. Berger has written that 'privatized religion' is one of the features of the secularized world view.[42] Viswanathan notes how this relegation of religion to private belief has also narrowed the view of religious ideas, producing a particularly vexed relationship with ideas of gender and sexuality.[43] The modern world is determined by individual consciousness and intentions, we say; so religion is one subset of such intentions, privately adhered to. It is then given special privileges, in a strained and often volatile fashion, in relation to private and especially sexual ethics. This is the way in which religion, in the West, has been re-accommodated within a political theory of society. Freedom of religious belief is just one in a set of vital personal freedoms; and society functions only to the extent that it can tolerate these freedoms in another person. In this way, a liberal non-religious system both allows for the religion of others, yet also defines the practice of religion on its own terms.

Shakespeare, again, is exemplary of the difficulties here. While for almost all of the twentieth century he was idolized as a secular author, so that attempts to place him within a religious framework were marginalized and often regarded as maverick or bizarre, in the last ten years there has been a volte-face. Yet it could be said that this has still been conducted according to a modern and yet outdated conception of religion as a practice. Shakespeare's religion has been recovered along the lines of a personal belief system. The overwhelming motivation has been biographical—and the always murky and fragile documents of Shakespeare's biography have been pored over to prove his affiliation, mainly to Catholic doctrine and belief. Yet before we can assess religion in Shakespeare, still less Shakespeare's

[41] Mahmood, 'Religious Reason and Secular Affect: An Incommensurable Divide?', in *Is Critique Secular?*, 65.
[42] Berger, *Social Reality of Religion*, 137.
[43] 'Secularism in the Framework of Heterodoxy', 475.

own religion, we need to reassess how religious and other impulses relate in pre-modern conditions.

This brings us once again to the complex that joins secularization with personal identity. For if we do not believe in secularization, what happens to the history of individualism? It is the contention of this book that the history of the self in the early modern period has been falsely constructed on an assumption of emerging secularism. We write as if an idea of the self could only come into being as a result of an emptying out of a religious framework. Instead, I look to see what happens if we do not make this assumption. I am not arguing that thereby everything changes; still less that we find the religious framework restored. On the contrary, in the life-stories and ideas I describe, religion is in flux, within the broad set of influences that go by the name of the European Catholic and Protestant Reformations: but these fluxes are fundamental to concepts of the self, not a passing irrelevance. The reconstruction of self after the sixteenth century happens as much through the reinterpretation of religious ideas as by an overturning of them.

The method of the book is to engage with a series of key concepts in the formation of identity, all of which are understood to have undergone fundamental change in the Renaissance, and in the past have been subject to a secularizing analysis, but which are here revealed as part of a more complex cultural history. These concepts, which each occupy a chapter are, in turn: the 'self-portrait' in art and literature; the formation of political 'conscience'; martyrdom and political execution; public identity and space and the invention of the 'private'; self-address and the dramatic soliloquy; chance and contingency in the formation of identity; suicide and ideas of personal and political freedom; selfhood and embodiment. These chapters engage with a series of authors ranging from More to Foxe, from Shakespeare to Milton, from Montaigne to Donne. The construction and performance of identity is analysed through its language, rhetorical figuration, and conceptual space, involving newly ambiguous forms of literary subjectivity. As in Burckhardt onwards, in this book the visual arts form a continuous focus of interest as well as literary genres; just as the book alternates freely between questions of representation in culture and questions of philosophy.

In some cases, as with the discussion of the 'self-portrait' in Albrecht Dürer and Michel de Montaigne, interpretation centres on the extravagantly improvisatory representation of the self in artistic and literary form. The concept of subjectivity is fictive here, yet it also relates to the embodiment of the artist in direct and physical ways: Dürer and Montaigne intercalate their representational selves with their own autographs, archives, and artefacts in ways that complicate the idea of identity as self-sufficient. In other chapters, as with the narrative of the last years of Thomas More in Chapters 2 and 4, the materials considered include letters and personal remains, and the articulation of selfhood is made lifelike and realistic. Here, and in the records of other political prisoners in Chapter 3, taken from the work of John Foxe, we seem to be looking less at autobiographical self-portraits as at unmediated self-representations. Yet the boundaries turn out to be permeable, just as they are between the archival records Foxe uses and the techniques of dramatic monologue and visual iconology he (and his printer John Day) employ to render the personhood of the martyr. These chapters reveal a radically modern ambiguity about personal autonomy and political ideology, in which the idea of the 'internalization' of religion and of political identity is exposed in a peculiarly externalized fashion. This is a key to ways in which religious subjectivity enmesh with ideas that we associate in modernity with the writer or reader as prisoner of conscience.

In the central chapters of the book (4 to 6), it is a natural step to move from self-presentation and the narrative of selfhood to fictional drama. Here we are dealing with aesthetic readings of the record of human inwardness, as traced especially by Shakespeare. Yet the distinction is also not absolute, since Shakespeare draws on materials from life, from the articulation of selfhood in public and private rituals, and since these rituals are also acts of rhetorical self-presentation and literary formation. These chapters focus on particular speech acts (oaths in Chapter 4, soliloquies in Chapter 5) or else on particular conceptual formations (privacy in Chapter 4, chance and luck in Chapter 6) to reconfigure the relationship between religion, secularity, and identity. Shakespeare's iconic status as a figure on the cusp of modernity through secularization is invoked in order to question it, but the issues of personal truth and inward self-reflection are recognizably still with us. *Mortal Thoughts* attempts to put this history within a new shape.

The final chapters (7 and 8) both return to Montaigne and Shakespeare and move onwards chronologically into the mid-seventeenth century. The book here takes a more openly metaphysical and philosophical direction, concentrating directly on the human body, its experience, and interpretation, in chapters on suicide (7), and birth, embodiment, and materialism (8). These chapters consider new developments in philosophy from late humanism towards the Enlightenment, but once again rewrite the psychological and sociological turn implied by secularization.

The chapters do not form a continuous narrative either chronologically or conceptually. They form instead stand-alone essays which nonetheless share a perspective and an argument. At the heart of the book is the idea of mortality. Each of the chapters is based around the moment of facing death and the afterlife. This is not surprising. In one direction, the key change of emphasis implied in the idea of radical secularity is the absence of a concept of the afterlife. In another, the trials of religious faith embodied in the Reformation brought with them renewed anxiety and uncertainty over identity as the individual faced the threat of death. Both kinds of existential crisis examine the fate of the individual in an imagined eternity. Mortality is the place where arguments about identity and arguments about religion and secularity come together.

The changing culture of early modern death has been the subject of much new writing in the last twenty years, whether in terms of the controversy over the medieval cult of the saints; or changing practices in Christian ritual and burial; or doctrines of salvation in terms of either sanctification or predestination; or the imagination or treatment of the physical remains at death; or the revival of Lucretius and the theory of mortalism (the death of the individual incorporated in the death of the body). This book builds on such studies while also suggesting a different frame of reference. The focus is not on death and its anthropology as such, so much as on the philosophical consequences of the realization of mortality itself as a boundary for the self. This context for the book crosses over the confessional divides between Catholic and Protestant, as it does between Christian and pagan.

This concern is philosophical, but the method employed here is as much aesthetic as doctrinal. The locus of attention is subjective experience. It raises attention to the language in which subjectivity is understood. This is partly because of its focus on literary and other artistic productions. But the method of the book might be likened to what in the work of Reinhard Koselleck has been called *Begriffsgeschichte* or 'conceptual history'.[44] However, unlike Koselleck, while it deals with the complex history of words such as 'conscience', 'sincere', 'private', 'solitude', 'luck', 'suicide', or 'passion', it does not frame this as an independent scholarly discipline. The words are a way into mental self-presentation. Perhaps in this sense, what is offered is what Blumenberg called a 'metaphorology' of history.[45] Can the images used by minds in the past tell us more about the hopes and cares, passions and anxieties that regulate an era, than their

---

[44] Koselleck, *Begriffsgeschichten: Studien zur Semantik und Pragmatik der politischen und sozialen Sprache* (Frankfurt am Main: Suhrkamp, 2006); Koselleck's work has been translated in a number of forms, e.g. *The Practice of Conceptual History: Timing History, Spacing Concepts*, trans. Todd Samuel Presner (Stanford, Calif.: Stanford University Press, 2002) and *Futures Past: On the Semantics of Historical Time*, Studies in Contemporary German Social Thought (New York: Columbia University Press, 2004).

[45] *Paradigms for a Metaphorology*, trans. Robert Savage (Ithaca, NY: Cornell University Press, 2010).

carefully elaborated systems of thought? *Mortal Thoughts* opens out new approaches to authorship; the narrative first person; dramatic dialogue; the invention of the soliloquy; and the subjective space of the interpreting spectator or reader, by investigating a series of personal narratives: of conscience and of martyrdom; of good and bad faith; of oaths made at the moment of execution; of chance and providence; of suicide and freedom; and of material being and nothingness. Its philosophical centre is an idea of the self less as a fixed place ready for Renaissance 'discovery', so much as of a fragile space which both invokes, and threatens, the very possibility of imaginative autonomy or what it is to be human. It therefore transcends the narrow division of religious and secular to suggest a more open-ended approach to the history of identity.

1

The Mortal Self

Dürer & Montaigne

'C'est moy que je peins', the author declares to the reader, 'it is myself that I portray'.[1] So Michel de Montaigne announces famously in his Preface, 'Au lecteur', to the *Essais*. He comes before us in all his 'defects' ('mes defauts'), showing 'ma forme naïfve', a pun in French only half-caught in English by 'my natural form'. He appears to us without concealment or deception, ingenuous and artless, and yet also frank and natural, as a person in his native habitat. As if to redouble his honesty, he divests himself even of the sophistications of his own culture. He wishes indeed that he could come to his reader *without* culture, without any presentiment of civilization, unmediated by law, habit, or custom:

> Had I been placed among those nations which are said to live still in the sweet freedom of nature's first laws, I assure you I should very gladly have portrayed myself here entire and wholly naked. (Frame, p. 2)

'Je t'asseure que je m'y fusse très-volontiers peint tout entier, et tout nud' (*Essais*, 27). Montaigne removes the last barrier between self and book, and between book and reader. There is nothing else here, no one else beside me. And then, with a characteristic throw-away insouciance and self-deprecation, he tells the reader no more frivolous book could be imagined. It is all vanity: 'So farewell'. There is no reason to read on.

In Montaigne, 'reading and thinking' converge in what Richard Regosin calls 'the book of the self', which is coterminous with 'le moi' in the *Essais*.[2] Yet Montaigne in 1580 also spoke beyond and over the head

---

[1] 'It is myself that I portray'; 'Au lecteur', *Les Essais*, 27. All citations from the *Essais* are by volume, essay, and page number using the new Bibliothèque de la Pléiade edition: Montaigne, *Les Essais*, ed. Jean Balsamo, Michel Magnien, and Catherine Magnien-Simonin (Paris: Gallimard, 2007). The English translation is by Donald M. Frame, originally published in 1943, taken from *The Complete Works*, trans. Donald M. Frame (New York: Everyman's Library, 2003), 2.

[2] Richard L. Regosin, *The Matter of My Book: Montaigne's Essais as the Book of the Self* (Berkeley and Los Angeles: University of California Press, 1977), 93.

of his readers towards the subject of selfhood in modernity.[3] His claim, 'je suis moy-mesme la matiere de mon livre' (*Essais*, 27), has been repeated countless times as an inaugural moment in what is commonly assumed to be a quintessentially modern movement. 'Our modern notion of the self is related to, one might say constituted by, a certain sense (or perhaps a family of senses) of inwardness', says Charles Taylor in *Sources of the Self: The Making of the Modern Identity* (1989). If one version of this 'radical reflexivity' is represented by Descartes, who 'situates the moral sources within us', and who, through the *cogito*, gives us a 'quite self-sufficient certainty',[4] Montaigne, Taylor asserts, yields up a form of inwardness which is equally all-encompassing but radically uncertain:

> Rather than objectifying our own nature and hence classing it as irrelevant to our identity, it consists in exploring what we are in order to establish this identity, because the assumption behind modern self-exploration is that we don't already know who we are. (p. 178)

We no longer go inward in order to find God; but only in the hope that there, at last, or at least, we might find some consolatory order or meaning in our lives.

---

[3] Books I and II were first published in 1580 as *Essais de Messire Michel Seigneur de Montaigne, Chevalier de l'Ordre du Roy, et Gentilhomme Ordinaire de sa Chambre* (Bordeaux: Simon Millanges). An expanded edition appeared in 1588, adding a third volume as well as revising the first two (*Essais de Michel Seigneur de Montaigne: cinquiesme edition, augmentee d'un troisieme livre et de six cens additions aux deus premiers* (Paris: Abel L'Angelier)). Montaigne's own working copy of the 1588 edition (the 'Bordeaux Copy') was filled with extensive manuscript additions in his own hand. The different states of the text are conventionally referred to as 'A', 'B', and 'C' texts. In 1595 a posthumous edition appeared, prepared by Marie de Gournay, incorporating the 'Bordeaux Copy' readings along with further changes: *Les Essais de Michel Seigneur de Montaigne: édition nouvelle, trouvee apres le deceds de l'autheur, reveuë et augmentee par luy d'un tiers plus qu'aux precedentes impressions* (Paris: Abel L'Angelier). A full description of the early editions can be found in R. A. Sayce and David Maskell, *A Descriptive Bibliography of Montaigne's Essais 1580–1700* (London: Bibliographical Society, 1983); for the editions up to 1595, see pp. 1–35. The edition used here is based on the 1595 text (see n. 1); it has been compared also with the text based on the 'Bordeaux Copy' in *Oeuvres complètes*, ed. Albert Thibaudet and Maurice Rat, Bibliothèque de la Pléiade (Paris: Gallimard, 1962). Sometimes, as a point of interest, the first English translation by John Florio, published in 1603, is also cited, here using *Essays vvritten in French by Michael Lord of Montaigne, Knight of the Order of S. Michael, gentleman of the French Kings chamber: done into English, according to the last French edition, by Iohn Florio reader of the Italian tongue vnto the Soueraigne Maiestie of Anna, Queene of England, Scotland, France and Ireland, &c. And one of the gentlemen of hir royall priuie chamber* (London: Melchior Bradwood for Edward Blount and William Barret, 1613). References to translations will be included in the text, cited either from Frame or Florio.

[4] *Sources of the Self: The Making of the Modern Identity* (Cambridge, Mass.: Harvard University Press, 1989),143 and 156.

NAKED WRITING

Such declarations are never, however, quite what they seem. Montaigne does not come to us unmediated by either culture or landscape or language, as his own admission tells us. Felicity Green has criticized the modernist preoccupation with a certain version of the self that is projected back onto Montaigne. Taylor's distinction between sincere self-presence and an alternative world of social performance failing to live up to that essential being does not, Green argues, conform to Montaigne's own, very different sense of self as 'freedom'.[5] Nor does Montaigne write, exactly, whatever his promise, in 'my natural form'. What would naked writing be like? Montaigne knows that he is not giving us this, and he knows that we know it, too. Ian Maclean comments how Montaigne's concept of 'le moi' as a *tabula rasa*, an empty page waiting to be written, is prone to 'une telle instabilité foncière'.[6] Naked writing would be written in a language with no apparent characteristics, it would speak from the heart to the heart, directly from self to self. We have a word for this in the twentieth century, which we call 'stream of consciousness', just as we refer to something we call 'free verse'. Yet these are, we know, affectations of literary style, something we put on in imitation of naked mental states. Beyond this, there is the psychological phenomenon known as 'automatic writing', writing without consciousness of the content, a phenomenon largely confined to the occult and the practice of spiritual mediums, as in Hélène Smith's claim in the nineteenth century to convey messages from Mars written in a Martian language, a claim unsurprisingly disputed by the psychologist Théodore Flouroy in *From India to the Planet Mars*, where he showed the origins of Smith's language in sources forgotten from her childhood, an effect for which he coined the term cryptomnesia.[7]

Perhaps in some neurologist's dream there exists a cognitive machine which could make my thoughts coterminous with yours, rendering a language in which naked writing could occur. But for Montaigne it is rather a figure of speech, albeit a favourite one: history, he said, should be written 'nue et informe'.[8] It is a way of expressing to the reader his desire for the closest possible relationship between writing and being,

---

[5] Green, *Montaigne and the Life of Freedom* (Cambridge: Cambridge University Press, 2012), 2–3.

[6] Ian Maclean, *Montaigne philosophe* (Paris: Presses Universitaires de France, 1996), 75.

[7] Théodore Flournoy, *From India to the Planet Mars: A Study of Somnambulism with Glossolalia*, trans. Daniel Vermilye (New York: Harper, 1901), 193.

[8] 'Des livres', II.x.438 ('naked and unformed', Frame, p. 368).

and for that matter between writer and reader.[9] Indeed, in Montaigne's promise to show himself as he is, 'en ma façon simple, naturelle et ordinaire' (*Essais*, 27), he is using almost exactly the terms of classical rhetoric for a figure known as παρρησία (*parrhesia*). Quintilian defined this as *oratio libera*, 'free speech': 'The same may be said of Free Speech, that which Cornificius calls Licence [*licentia*], and the Greeks παρρησία (*parrhesia*). For what is less "figured" than true freedom?'[10] In its simplest form, indeed, Quintilian says this figure arises from 'sincere feeling' and is not figurative at all in the sense he usually means. But in other cases we use the style of simple speech in a 'fictitious' way, one where we employ the appearance of naturalness to convince our interlocutor of our point of view. Parrhesia, we should realize, is not at all a straightforward way of speaking. Its use within rhetorical theory and literary practice is constituted by what Freya Sierhuis has called the 'parrhesiastes-game': a 'figure of speech that entailed speaking the truth boldly and straightforwardly, while at the same time vindicating this straightforwardness'; a double-bluff, perhaps, in which the declaration of honesty is both a rhetorical simulation of honesty and yet not necessarily therefore a denial of honest intention.[11]

Montaigne, it could be said, has it both ways here. His ingenuousness is not purely disingenuous; his artifice is candid. For no speech is wholly natural or simple, and no language unmediated. His language of the self is an approximation, not quite as he is in his own skin, we might say, so much as how he might appear to us in an old favoured shirt, some faded soft linen garment of the colour of the earth of his native Bordelais. His shirt sweats as he does; it takes on the tincture of his blood and his tears; it is secreted with the odours and tastes of his hidden passions and creaturely comforts. This is how he characterizes what is for him 'la philosophie morale'.[12] Others describe an exemplary life, but Montaigne eschews this 'richer stuff': 'Chaque homme porte la forme entiere, de l'humaine condition' ('Each man bears the entire form of man's estate', III.ii.845; Frame, p. 740). He names himself, 'Michel de Montaigne', as the centre of his enquiry, not out of narcissism or vainglory, but as the only proper subject of his reasoning study of the mind and emotions at work.

---

[9] Regosin, *The Matter of My Book*, 85.

[10] Quintilian, *Institutio oratoria*, 9.2.27; ed. and trans. Donald A. Russell, Loeb Classical Library, 5 vols. (Cambridge, Mass.: Harvard University Press, 2001), iv. 48–9.

[11] 'The Rhetoric of Religious Dissent: Anti-Calvinism, Satire and the Arminian Controversy in the Dutch Republic', *Renaissance and Reformation Review*, 12 (2010), 307–27; this ref. p. 316.

[12] 'Du repentir', *Essais*, III.ii.845.

In this way, however, we should distinguish Montaigne from other declaratory statements of the 'radical reflexivity' described by Taylor. Among the most frequently quoted of these is the 'Oration on the Dignity of Man' by Pico della Mirandola, where God tells Adam:

> Definita caeteris natura intra praescriptas a nobis leges cohercetur. Tu, nullis angustiis cohercitus, pro tuo arbitrio, in cuius manu te posui, tibi illam prefinies. Medium te mundi posui, ut circumspiceres inde comodius quicquid est in mundo. Nec te celestem neque terrenum, neque mortalem neque immortalem fecimus, ut tui ipsius quasi arbitrarius honorariusque plastes et fictor, in quam malueris tute formam effingas.[13]

> The nature of all other beings is limited and constrained within the bounds of laws prescribed by us. Thou, constrained by no limits, in accordance with thine own free will, in whose hand we have placed thee, shalt ordain for thyself the limits of thy nature. We have set thee at the world's centre that thou mayest from thence more easily observe whatever is in the world. We have made thee neither of heaven nor of earth, neither mortal nor immortal, so that with freedom of choice and with honour, thou mayest fashion thyself in whatever shape thou shalt prefer.[14]

On the contrary, Montaigne's self is a self of limits. But these limits are not self-imposed: they are what define the human. Above all, the human is a creature that is mortal. Nothing could be further from Montaigne's philosophical foundations than Pico's beguiling phrase *neque mortalem neque immortalem*, for the first and foremost given of human life is mortality. It is only within the constraint of mortality that human free will (*libero arbitrio*) can be articulated; it governs the whole meaning of what it is for life to be *volontaire*.

Far from being a state of perfection, mortality is defined as imperfection. Indeed this is its correct logical category, as it has no permanent state; it is a state of flux, of in between, at best a coming into being. Montaigne does not portray being itself, Michael Screech comments, but 'only his becoming-and-passing-away'.[15] This idea permeates the *Essais*, and reaches its fruition at the conclusion of the 'Apologie de Raimond Sebond':

> de façon, que ce qui commence à naistre, ne parvient jamais jusques à perfection d'estre. Pour autant que ce naistre n'acheve jamais, et jamais n'arreste, comme estant à bout, ains depuis la semence, va tousjours se changeant et muant d'un à autre. (II.xii.640)

---

[13] Pico della Mirandola, *Oratio de hominis dignitate* (Bologna: Benedetto Faelli, 1496), § 5, fo. 132ʳ⁻ᵛ.

[14] *The Renaissance Philosophy of Man*, ed. E. Cassirer, P. O. Kristeller and J. H. Randall, Jr. (Chicago: University of Chicago Press, 1948), 225.

[15] M. A. Screech, *Montaigne and Melancholy* (London: Duckworth, 1983), 81.

> So that what is beginning to be born never arrives at the perfection of being;
> forasmuch as this birth is never completed, and never stops as being at an
> end, but from the seed onward goes on ever changing and shifting from one
> thing into another. (Frame, p. 554)

Mortality is never a state, in that it never achieves completion, or else only
in its own finitude, at which point it ceases to be what made it what it
is.

   This imperfection in ontological terms is then reflected in human
nature. Like any natural being, the human creature is defined by its im-
perfections. Hence Montaigne's typical reference to himself in the Preface
'Au lecteur' in terms of his physical defects and idiosyncrasies. In a literal
sense, these physical characteristics constitute himself. He is different
from others to the extent that he has these particular faults and blemishes.
Yet he also revels in physical descriptions of the human as especially im-
perfect. This indeed is the true sense of the naked self:

> Certes quand j'imagine l'homme tout nud (ouy en ce sexe qui semble avoir
> plus de part à la beauté) ses tares, sa subjection naturelle, et ses imperfec-
> tions, je trouve que nous avons eu plus de raison que nul autre animal, de
> nous couvrir. (II.xii.509)

> Indeed, when I imagine man quite naked, yes, even in that sex, which seems
> to have the greatest share of beauty, his blemishes, his natural subjection,
> and his imperfections, I think we had had more reason than any other
> animal to cover ourselves. (Frame, p. 433)

The most ill-favoured creature of all, the *turpissima*, is the ape; and no
animal more resembles man. *Turpa* was also the standard term for the sexual
organs. In a classic Montaigne joke, he adds in an aside that there is no
better way to cool human lust than to reveal the male body in all its glory:

> Vrayement c'est aussi un effect digne de consideration, que les maistres du
> mestier ordonnent pour remede aux passions amoureuses, lentiere veue et
> libre du corps qu'on recherche. (II.xii.510)

> Truly it is also a fact worthy of consideration that the masters of the craft
> order as a remedy to amorous passions the entire and open sight of the body
> that we pursue. (Frame, p. 433)

The passions, Aristotle says, change our judgements and make us prone to
pleasure and pain.[16] In Montaigne, paradoxically, the human body is the
antidote to passion. The natural state of man is bodily shame.

---

[16] *Rhetoric*, II.1.1378ᵃ; ed. and trans. John Henry Freese, Loeb Classical Library, repr.
edn. (Cambridge, Mass.: Harvard University Press, 1994), 173.

AT DEATH'S DOOR

The visual image has this seeming advantage over writing, that it can reveal the artist truly naked. Albrecht Dürer's three-quarter length nude self-portrait (Fig. 1) (now in the Graphische Sammlungen in Weimar), drawn in ink and brush (using both black and white for body colour) against a prepared black background on green tinted paper, is among the most enigmatic and yet semantically loaded of all that artist's works.[17] While the artist's monogram was added only later and by another hand, its authenticity is not in doubt. However, the subject was not identified until little more than a century ago, and it was formerly regarded merely as a nude study. 'Ein neues Selbstbildnis Dürers' was announced by Franz Roh only in 1916, a fact that seems amazing in view of the all-consuming fame of the pre-eminent German artist in the nineteenth century, and the collectability of his self-portraits since the seventeenth.[18] Yet it is not altogether surprising. Dürer's nude self-portrait is half a millennium ahead of its time: there are no other examples in western art until Egon Schiele in the early twentieth century, who may himself have been influenced by the recent discovery.[19] When the nude image of Dürer was first opened out to the world of connoisseurship it inevitably posed questions of form, style, and intention which were unresolvable, and perhaps still are. It is not clear how the sketch was accomplished. Murano glassmakers did not begin making body-length mirrors with glass backing until the later sixteenth century.[20] In all likelihood any mirror known to Dürer was a highly polished metal disc small in proportions; seeing himself naked was a task of the imagination.

Naked the artist stands before the viewer, but who is the more disturbed, him or me? He stands seemingly alone, unembarrassed and self-absorbed, except that the expression in his eyes fully recognizes the presence of the viewer, in an exchange that is frank and awkward at the same time. Have I caught him unawares, or has he entered into my space, aware that I am already there? He is not posing. His weight is on his rear leg, as if in movement; his muscles are caught in their own business, with

---

[17] Winkler 267; Dürer's drawings are here referred to using the catalogue by Friedrich Winkler, *Die Zeichnungen Albrecht Dürers*, 4 vols. (Berlin: Deutscher Verein für Kunstwissenschaft, 1936–9).

[18] *Reportorium für Kunstwissenschaft*, 39 (1916), 10–15.

[19] Egon Schiele's 1910 nude self-portrait in coloured chalk is discussed in Heinrich Schwartz, 'Schiele, Dürer and the Mirror', *Art Quarterly*, 30 (1967), 210–23. Although Rau in 1916 was the first scholar formally to identify the Dürer as a self-portrait, the idea had already been suggested by Rudolf Wustmann in 1906.

[20] *At Home in Renaissance Italy*, ed. Marta Ajmar-Wollheim and Flora Dennis (London: V & A Publications, 2006), 54.

Fig. 1. Albrecht Dürer, *Nude Self-Portrait* (1503?); pen, ink, and brush.

no hint of show or affectation; his hair is bundled in a net, a state of déshabille suggesting that he is on his way either to or from sleep. In that way, the image, while placing the body of the artist on self-conscious and permanent display, also seems unconcerned by my presence as onlooker. I am eavesdropping rather than prying or ogling. I am entering the private world of another self; or else, alternatively, he is pressing his private self into my consciousness.

Who was the image for, and when was it made? As Joseph Leo Koerner has pointed out in the most intricate study of the work, 'colour-ground drawings in the period were generally autonomous, collectible works', and Dürer pioneered the idea of the artist's drawings as art works of high value.[21] But if so, no commission or sale is known, and as Koerner also remarks, the self-portrait also looks 'wilfully incomplete' (p. 242). The image below the artist's right elbow is jaggedly cut off, as are his legs below the knees, while on the other side Dürer has not filled in the black background beyond the outline of his torso, and his left arm is entirely missing. The moulding in ink of the chest is an astonishingly detailed creation, with a sheen and finish announcing its own virtuosity, but the rendition of the face is by contrast improvisatory and as if sketched in haste.

The self-portrait has been dated to around 1503, but the reasons have more to do with creating a context for Dürer's other works than for understanding this one on its own terms. Erwin Panofsky linked it to an annotation, in Dürer's handwriting, found on a drawing of a head of the dead Christ.[22] Like the 'Drawing of a Suffering Man' of the same year, the Christ has been linked by Stephanie Porras to an idea of *Autonomie*: a linkage between 'artistic creation', the 'suffering subject' and 'biographical presence'.[23] As is often the case with Dürer, the image of the head of Christ (Fig. 2) bears his manuscript gloss at two different stages: once, in charcoal, the monogram and the date 1503; and second, in a barely visible postscript, 'Dis[z] angsicht hab ich uch erl…gemacht (?) in meiner Kranckheit ('This face I…made in my sickness').[24] Dürer's habit of

---

[21] *The Moment of Self-Portraiture in German Renaissance Art* (Chicago: University of Chicago Press, 1997), 242; Koerner cites the series of drawings known (from their similar background paper) as the 'Green Passion' (Winkler 302–14) as a comparison.

[22] Erwin Panofsky, *The Life and Art of Albrecht Dürer*, 4th edn. (Princeton: Princeton University Press, 1955), 90.

[23] 'künstlerischer Schöpfung, leidendem Subjekt und biographischer Präsenz'; Stephanie Porras, '"ein freie hant": Autonomie, Zeichnen und der junge Dürer', in Daniel Hess and Thomas Eser (eds.), *Der frühe Dürer* (Nuremberg: Verlag des Germanischen Nationalmuseums, 2012), 529.

[24] Winkler 272. Transcription from *Albrecht Dürer 1471 bis 1528: Das gesamte graphische Werk*, 2 vols. (Munich: Rogner & Bernhard, 1970), vol. i: *Handzeichnungen*, 309. The first word could read 'Die 2', ('the two') referring to this drawing and one of the same year of a 'suffering man' (Winkler 271).

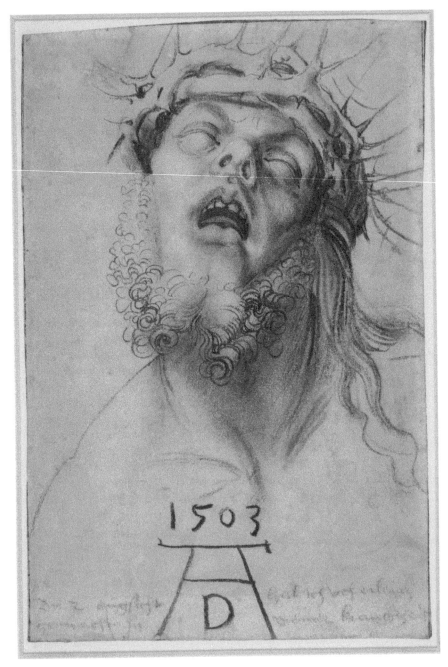

Fig. 2. Albrecht Dürer, *Head of the Dead Christ* (1503); charcoal.

commenting retrospectively on the sheets of his earlier work, frequent in his drawings (especially of very personal and familial pieces) and sometimes found in his painting (as in his portrait of his master Michael Wolgemut) has perhaps been taken too literally by art historians committed to the establishment of authorial provenance. Dürer's scribal memory of his career—in the case of the fabulous silverpoint drawing of the child Albrecht (Fig. 9) now in the Albertina in Vienna (the primal scene of his life and work) added conceivably thirty or forty years later—may not be altogether trustworthy, even if it is not part of a conscious fabrication.[25] Dürer's self-construction, like Montaigne's, was a lifelong project, staggeringly self-conscious in its design and layered meaning. More than this, his self-image has been articulated by others, ever since the earliest collecting of his work, as an iconic image of the artist in person. His startling oil panel in the Alte Pinakothek in Munich, dated 1500, as if in a jubilee of his own existence, has been dubbed 'the moment' of self-portraiture. It evokes an idea of 'the modern replacement of love of God with love of self'.[26]

So self-conscious has the presence of Dürer in the history of self-representation become, that this last remark is in fact made only ironically by Koerner. He points out that the image is not self-authorized, but is a conscious pastiche of the artist in the pose of Christ, front on, love revealed as flesh. Even this Christomorphic identification, Koerner argues, is as old as art history as a discipline. The first comparison of Dürer's self-portrait with the Holy Face by Jan van Eyck was made in 1876, in one of the first monographs on the artist's work; it was realized in some form even in the seventeenth century.[27]

Dürer's self-image is thus never to be taken at face value, but rather as a commentary on his own mind and body, or a philosophical essay on the subject of memory and identity. Still, it is easy to sympathize with Panofsky's desire to authenticate the nude self-portrait. Finding the record of an outbreak of plague (that mainstay of early modern biography) in Nuremberg in 1503, and seeing the coincidence with the head of the Dead Christ drawn 'in my sickness', as well as the shockingly graphic charcoal head of the 'suffering man' (Winkler 271, also in the British Museum) of the same year, Panofsky placed the nude self-image squarely in the context of a morbid illness:

> The convalescent painter looks at his emaciated body and still haggard face with the same mixture of fatigue, apprehension and dispassionate curiosity with which a farmer might take stock of his crops after a bad storm. (p. 90)

---

[25] Winkler 1; the image and inscription are discussed in Giulia Bartrum, *Albrecht Dürer and his Legacy: The Graphic Work of a Renaissance Artist* (London: British Museum Press, 2002), 79.

[26] Koerner, *Moment of Self-Portraiture*, 40.

[27] Koerner, *Moment of Self-Portraiture*, 72.

Panofsky may be guilty of a certain romantic sentimentalism here. The so-called 'emaciated body' is the envy of many another male, and the face is 'haggard' only with a degree of imagination. Yet Dürer's interest in his own body in sickness as well as in health is attested by a later drawing from around 1512, in which the artist is shown pointing to a place in his abdomen. At the top of the page Dürer writes that here is where the yellow spot is, and here is where it hurts.[28] Whether or not the nude self-portrait is so precisely autobiographical, Panofsky's sense of 'apprehension and dispassionate curiosity' catches with beautiful sensitivity the combination of intense self-reflection and ambiguity, properly speaking the uncanny, which the image possesses. This is no ordinary self-portrait, even by the most prolific of auto-artists.

However mesmerizing the body, a different clue to the meaning of the image is to be found rather in the seemingly opaque semantic register of the black background. The starkness of the matt ground clearly acts visually to define the figure in the foreground, and is a fundamental of technique. Yet the way that the body threatens or even transgresses the limits of the black space suggests that he is crossing a threshold between one physical space and another, a feeling accentuated by the way the rippling muscles of his torso imply movement forwards and at a diagonal angle right across the viewer's perspective. The inference of the image, indeed, is that the figure is passing through a doorway towards the viewer.

There is an additional significance to the door here which has escaped the voluminous commentary on the artist and his self-image. Dürer's father, the goldsmith Albrecht the elder, had moved from Ajtós near Gyula in Hungary to Nuremberg in 1455.[29] The Dürer family name was a translation of the Hungarian word *ajtó*, *die Tür* ('door') in German, and appeared originally in writing as 'Thurer' or 'Turer'. The coat of arms on the reverse side of Dürer's earliest portrait of his father shows a gateway with open doors, possibly a barn door as an allusion to his ancestors' trade, since they were cattle breeders.[30] Verbal play through iconography was endemic in humanist image-making: Dürer's pupil Hans Baldung portrayed himself in green costume after his nickname 'Grien'.[31] A woodcut by Dürer dated 1523 (Fig. 3) prints this coat of arms of the doorway

---

[28] Koerner, *Moment of Self-Portraiture*, 177.
[29] Panofsky, *Life and Art of Albrecht Dürer*, 4.
[30] This portrait is now in the Uffizi.
[31] Koerner, *Moment of Self-Portraiture*, 423–4. An example is the *St Sebastian Altarpiece*, a painting in oil on wood now in the Germanisches National Museum, Nürnberg.

Fig. 3. Albrecht Dürer, *Coat of Arms* (1523); woodcut.

surmounted by a winged helmet and a bust of a young black man.[32] The helmet and wings, and the cocked angle of the coat of arms, repeat the design of an earlier engraving, the 'Coat of Arms with a Skull', where Death as a wild man greets a young woman while holding a staff bearing a heraldic blazon of a skull.[33] Colourfully, it is sometimes called the 'Coat of Arms of Death' (Fig. 4). Dürer's woodcut of his personal arms of the doorway, meanwhile, was a large image, and Giulia Bartrum surmises it may have been used as a label to mark his belongings.[34] Dürer's drawing for this also survives.[35] In 1527 (the year before the artist's death) Mathes Gebel produced a medal with the coat of arms of the door on one side and a portrait of the artist on the reverse.[36]

Even if the suggestion of a framed open door behind the self-image of the naked artist is not a verbal joke, however, the impression of liminal space is essential to its effect. The ghostly highlights which surround his body only accentuate this; they suggest a powerful source of light, perhaps a candle, in the room he is walking into, the room in which the viewer, too must stand. As for an open doorway, this is a standard aspect of the iconography of classical Roman grave sculpture. Figuring the passage from life to death as a door is so universal as to be proverbial. Wilpert, in his monumental study of palaeo-Christian sarcophagi, surmised that the symbolic motif of a door as the boundary between life and death is so widespread as to be called neither pagan nor Christian, but human.[37] In the Old Kingdom of Egypt, tombs bore fake doors in relief in order to imitate death as well as real ones to close off the artefacts of the necropolis. In a similar way, from the earliest times in ancient Italian tombs, a sculpted door doubled between the entrance to the tomb and the entrance to the world of the dead.[38] In later Roman art its symbolism was all the more powerful. The grave itself, on a roadway outside the city, conforming to Roman cultic law that graves should be outside the civic space, was often figured as a house.

The tomb was liminal literally but also figuratively: the dead live elsewhere, poised on the borderland of still living mortals. They lie just beyond view. This symbolic value was easily transferred from monuments

---

[32] *Das druckgraphische Werk*, 258; Dürer's woodcuts and engravings are here referred to using the catalogue by Rainer Schoch, Matthias and Anna Scherbaum, *Albrecht Dürer: Das druckgraphische Werk*, 3 vols. (Munich: Prestel Verlag, 2001–4). See also the description in Bartrum, *Albrecht Dürer*, catalogue no. 9, p. 85.

[33] *Das druckgraphische Werk*, 37; Bartrum, *Albrecht Dürer*, cat. 83, p. 148.

[34] Bartrum, *Albrecht Dürer*, 85.

[35] Winkler 941.

[36] Bartrum, *Albrecht Dürer*, cat. 10, p. 85.

[37] G. Wilpert, *I sarcofagi cristiani antichi*, 3 vols. (Rome: Ponteficio Istituto di Archeologia Cristiana, 1928–36), i. 143.

[38] J. M. C. Toynbee, *Death and Burial in the Roman World* (London: Thames and Hudson, 1971), 17.

Fig. 4. Albrecht Dürer, *Coat of Arms with a Skull* (1503); engraving.

and tombs to the literature and art of death more widely. E. H. Haight distinguished a variety of meanings in classical poetry between the closed door representing death, the open door as representing eternal life, and in between, ambiguously, a door left ajar as figuring some kind of hope without certainty.[39] Britt Haarløv, in the most extensive study of the open door motif, suggests that this distinction is too rigorous.[40] The door has multiple associations, and varied forms, which both convey a complex set of meanings and yet also resonate in ways that make those meanings further unsettle each other. At one and the same time, the doorway left visibly ajar both suggests temporality—motion towards and away—and, in its emptiness, figures the unknown. Death is unknowable as well as inevitable. It is the uncertain frame within which life is lived.

Haarløv's study shows numerous examples both of the door standing alone, with a variety of techniques in relief to indicate its openness or closedness, and also of the door as framing either a supernatural being as guardian of the door, or else a human figure figuring the soul between life and death. The former motif is more common in sarcophagi, the latter in crematorial urns. A sarcophagus of the Four Seasons from the third century has a central relief representation of a door clearly ajar, one door standing out from the other and with a visible space between.[41] In some funereal urns, the figure framed by the door is naked, and the door behind is fully open, a mysterious vacuum.[42] These symbolic techniques were the subject of close study in the Renaissance, as part of its project of uncovering ancient modes of meaning. Iconography was carried over into Renaissance monumental sculpture in tomb construction, and was also widely applied across the visual arts. The classical meaning of the open doorway was therefore a familiar visual language to Italian humanist artists such as Andrea Mantegna.

Dürer came into direct contact with these traditions in his first visit to Venice in 1494–5; but he did not need to travel to Italy to find such things. Hartmann Schedel, author of the Nuremberg Chronicle, produced a large book of 'Antiquities', illustrated with drawings of classical monuments by himself and a pupil of Wolgemut.[43] Perhaps in emulation, Dürer worked on similar encyclopaedic projects when he returned to Wolgemut's workshop from Italy. At around the same time, whether

---

[39] E. H. Haight, *The Symbolism of the House Door in Classical Poetry*, 152.

[40] *The Half-Open Door: A Common Symbolic Motif within Roman Sepulchral Sculpture* (Odense: Odense University Press, 1977), pp. 9–10.

[41] Front of Sarcophagus with the Four Seasons (detail), middle 3rd century CE; Rome, Capitoline Museum, MC1185.

[42] Haarløv, *The Half-Open Door*, cat. I,7.

[43] Panofsky, *Life and Art of Albrecht Dürer*, 31.

before or after his departure for Italy has been debated since Panofsky, he worked on several drawings copying mythological engravings by Mantegna. One of these is of the Death of Orpheus; Mantegna also treated this theme in a fresco in the Camera degli Sposi at Mantua.[44] It is well known that Dürer's own fame grew more through his engravings than his paintings; it is less widely realized that his knowledge of Italian art was received also primarily through printed works. It was an engraving, not the fresco, which Dürer copied. Mantegna was a master and an innovator in all two-dimensional media, and his prolific work with engraving was also in turn disseminated all the more widely by his own imitators before and after his death. Thus a beautiful *Entombment with Four Birds*, from around 1465 (Fig. 5), in which Christ's body is laid in a sarcophagus by Mary and a group of apostles, was copied faithfully and accurately from Mantegna's prototype by Giovanni Antonio da Brescia sometime between 1500 and 1504; and in another version by another artist in 1515.[45] The figures of the saints are etched against the stark black background of the opening of the cave, like a door in a classical grave. Another engraving of the Entombment shares the same motif—the human body etched against a black space which frames him.

This motif is repeated in even more startling style in a series of works entitled *Descent into Limbo*, on which Mantegna and his school, his peers, and admirers worked for a period of around thirty years. A drawing by Mantegna in pen and brown ink with brown wash may be as early as 1465. Another now in Paris (Fig. 6) is from around 1470.[46] A tempera painting over a drawing on vellum by Giovanni Bellini dates from the late 1470s; and an exquisite tempera on wood by Mantegna from the early 1490s.[47] In between, images which received a much wider dissemination, perhaps crossing the Alps, are two states of an engraving sometimes attributed to Mantegna, and close in composition to the second of the drawings and another, again faithfully copied from Mantegna's engraving by Giovanni Antonio in the 1490s (Fig. 7).[48] While composed with rigorous architectural structure and concentration of meaning, the images are replete, we could say stuffed, with mythological and biblical iconography. An angel trumpets from above the entrance to hell; devils, cast as brilliant classicized grotesques, flutter away in a hideous fuss of resentment at

[44] Panofsky, *Life and Art of Albrecht Dürer*, 32.

[45] *Andrea Mantegna*, ed. Jane Martineau (Milan: Electa, 1992), cat. 29–31, pp.183–8.

[46] *c.*1468; Pen, ink, and brown watercolour on vellum; Paris, École Nationale Supérieure des Beaux Arts, inv. 189.

[47] For a description of the full range of these images, see *Andrea Mantegna*, cat. 65–71, pp. 259–72.

[48] *Andrea Mantegna*, cat. 67 a and b, cat. 68.

Fig. 5. Andrea Mantegna, *Entombment with Four Birds* (*c.*1465); engraving.

Fig. 6. Andrea Mantegna, *Descent into Limbo* (*c.*1470); pen, brown ink, and wash.

Fig. 7. Giovanni Antonio da Brescia, *Descent into Limbo* (1490s); engraving.

Christ's intrusion. The good thief stands in a stylized statuesque pose as a doorman bearing an enormous and abstracted cross. On the other side of the opening, a naked Adam and Eve represent the vast numbers of souls caught in hell before the coming of Christ, some way between the guilt of original sin and the innocence of patriarchs who never knew the incarnation and therefore cannot be so completely to blame for their eternal state. In some versions, as an image of the inclusion of the viewer in the meaning of the image, the features of a head of a fool with cap and bells can be made out in the rock to the side of the headstone.

Yet for all its allusion and teeming meaning, the subject is cast by Mantegna and his followers with an unmistakeable air of the unfathomable and the mysterious. This enigma is centred on the figure—and the action—of Christ. First, in all versions, and with an emphasis that turns upside down the whole iconographic cult of Christ seen head on, full face, is that instead here he walks away and with his back towards us. In *De Pictura*, Leon Battista Alberti discussed how *istoria* or narrative in painting could be achieved obliquely, referring to an example mentioned in Pliny of an antique depiction of the *Immolation of Iphigenia*.[49] Here the artist showed the nature of the overwhelming grief of a father at his daughter's death at his own hand by refusing to show his face to us, and 'let his most bitter grief be imagined, even though it was not seen'.[50] David Ekserdjian has argued that this reference in Alberti was highly significant to Mantegna.[51] The radical decision to remove Christ's face withholds his emotion from us, whether at the horrors of hell which face him, or at his own ambiguous mortality. Is Christ, in the intermission between Good Friday and Easter, emerging already from death, or is he going further in? This feature of the iconography of *The Descent into Limbo* dovetails with the presentation of the doorway into hell. Indeed the lightless opacity of the opening once more frames the human body, as in Dürer's self-image, and holds it in stillness and ambiguous meaning. In both images, as in Alberti's recommendation, obliquity is a key to the representation of death. The back of Christ's form, in full sunlight, contrasts in negative against the realm of death in night-time shadow. While the portal of hell is a massive architectural archway, the blocks of stone a third of a

---

[49] The account is in Pliny, *Epistolae* XXXV.73–4; Alberti's source is more likely a rhetorical treatise where Pliny is quoted, such as Quintilian, *Institutio*, II.xiii.13; or Cicero, *Orator*, xxii. 74; ed. and trans. H. M. Hubbell, Loeb Classical Library (London: Heinemann, 1962), 360.

[50] Alberti, *On Painting*, Book II; trans. John R. Spencer (New Haven: Yale University Press. 1970), 77. Alberti's work dates to 1435–6.

[51] David Ekserdjian, 'The Descent into Limbo', in *Andrea Mantegna*, ed. Martineau, pp. 258–9.

human height, the door itself, half hidden by Christ's cowering figure as
he stoops to enter, seems awkwardly small, while in its position in the
perspective centre it confronts us with its liminality. The naked dead can
be seen groping upwards from inside, below our point of view, as if trying
to get out. The door itself, seemingly too large for the frame, lies shattered
in front, as Christ, death's conqueror, but for the moment still its uncertain prisoner, strides across it, hesitant, yet walking the wrong way, towards death, to meet the unknown.

It is not impossible Dürer saw a version of this image, which was commonly known and admired. Giovanni Antonio made copies of Dürer's
engravings (including his St Jerome with the skull in 1497), as well as
Mantegna's, and worked in the same circles.[52] Whether Dürer knew this
particular Mantegna at the time of the self-portrait or not, the symbolism
of the two images is shared. Christ goes one way into the void, while
Albrecht the artist emerges in the opposite direction, from darkness into
our light (see Fig. 1). Koerner describes the naked artist, aptly, as 'a creature of flesh and blood already betraying marks of fallenness and mortality' (p. 239). Yet he also calls it, betraying perhaps our contemporary
neuroses more than Dürer's, an 'unprecedented spectacle of narcissistic
self-display' (p. 242). If Koerner, reading Freud back into Dürer's drawing, makes the artist's genitals the centre of the image—'the seat of his
male creative powers' (p. 246)—he also sees in Freud another framing
language of melancholia and mourning.

While recognizing the drawing's abiding melancholy, and its proleptic
mourning of the self which now is but one day will not be, I would prefer
to see in the image an alternative iconography of death, one that has been
less in evidence lately but which was well known in classical times, was
acutely present in the consciousness of the sixteenth century, and which
is coming into view again in the twenty-first. It is of death not as a fact of
decomposition or a presence of morbidity in the flesh, or even the fear of
these things, but as a process or a condition between states, a process
which in that sense both frames and defines the living being between one
form of non-life and another. Like Mantegna's Christ in limbo, Dürer as
naked artist is an exercise in flamboyant chiaroscuro. The left side of his
chest, drawn in white colour with intense realism, shimmers with light;
while his right side, his muscles protruding with the effort of his own
motion, begins to merge into the shade behind him. Meanwhile his face,
more scratchily drawn, is also half in the dark. His genitals cast their own
shadow; but their presentation seems matter-of-fact rather than narcissistic

---

[52] *Andrea Mantegna*, 443.

or flagrant. Dürer presents himself to us *as he is*. He is half in light, and half already in shadow. He is a figure caught in his own time, a time which eludes him and bypasses him even as it catches him, belatedly or seemingly immortally, in our presence; as it catches every viewer in every time in his or her own moment. The image reflects, in short, on the condition of mortality itself. His body exists, and by this very fact, it perishes. And in that state of suspended consciousness it takes us with it.

REFLEXIVITY & REFLECTIVITY

This is not a book on death as such. Studies of high quality on this topic, and especially of its place in Renaissance visual culture and literature, abound. My object is neither the representation, nor the culture, nor the ritual of death. Its subject is rather mortality, the condition of finitude which encompasses human life. However, I do not mean by that, either, the *vanitas* tradition which preoccupied poets as well as painters in the Renaissance. Dürer's 1507 *Allegorie des Geizes* in oil on limewood of a half-naked old woman with a sagging breast and a bulging sack of coins, painted on the reverse of a *Portrait of a Young Man* (in the Kunsthistorisches Museum in Vienna), shows his mastery of this iconography. The comparison of youth and age implicit in the two sides of the panel, and the virtuoso display of the verisimilar in showing hair, skin, teeth, and muscle in advanced decrepitude, are each a study in the perishability of human fortune and even the bare embodiment of the human being. Once again, this is a symbolic tradition Dürer shares with Venetian painters, such as Giorgione, who painted *Col tempo*, also figured as an old woman, in the same decade. The celebrated engraving *Melencolia I*, with its numerous symbolic references to time, is often taken as an early landmark in *vanitas* topoi, and its companions in Dürer's summa of the techniques of engraving in 1513–14, *Ritter, Tod und Teufel* (*The Knight, Death and the Devil*), and *St Jerome in his Study*, are also replete with images of death. The skulls in his repeated engraved images of St Jerome look forward to the *vanitas* as genre painting, one of the stylistic reference points of northern European painting in the next two centuries. The scriptural sentiment from Ecclesiastes, *Vanity of vanities; all is vanity*, is the ground-note for a complex interplay of visual signs. Pieter Claesz's *Vanitasstilleven met schedel, horloge, konische roemer en boek* (1630), today in the Mauritshuis in The Hague (Fig. 8), may be taken to summarize these topoi: a human skull dominates the scene, with another human bone along its back to frame it; it sits on a pile of paper with a quill pen on top of a book, with the pages all beginning to fray with age; an elaborate and expensive

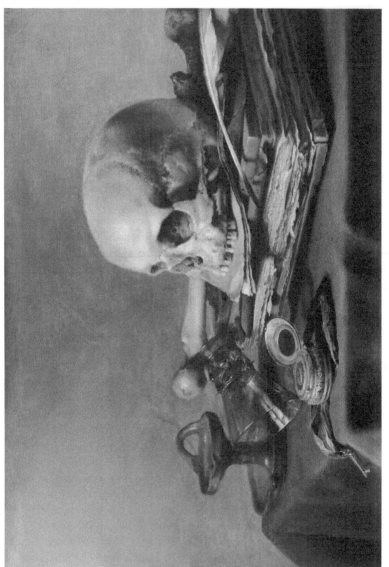

Fig. 8. Pieter Claesz, *Vanitasstilleven met schedel, horloge, komische roemer en boek* (1630); oil on panel.

timepiece sits in the foreground, surrounded by a ribbon holding the key to wind it when it has run out; behind the watch, a glass has fallen, about to shatter; while to one side, seemingly forgotten, is an oil-lamp holder— where if the viewer looks carefully, the wick, entirely spent, is just visible, and a wisp of smoke catches its dying breath as it merges into thin air behind the skull.

Mortal Thoughts is a study of human mortality and identity in the visual and verbal imagination of northern Europe from the early six-teenth to the late seventeenth century. At its centre lies a series of essays on Shakespeare, not so much as a culmination as a symptom of a certain way of thinking and feeling. The topics do not form an exact chronol-ogy or other form of logic. Their interaction is more meditative and interactive with the materials on display. At the heart of this methodol-ogy is the presence of the viewer and reader and spectator, especially this particular viewer and reader, as an intrinsic part of the imaginative sub-ject. This idea requires some explanation. Human embodiment and its subjective experience is central to the concerns expressed here. How-ever, it is not the perishable material condition of skin, flesh, and bone in the *vanitas* still life which will obsess me, however much they will come into view. Rather, it is the sense in Claesz's exquisite limpid surface of the evanescence of material experience itself. Claesz not only captures the material presence of the objects so lovingly represented—the strange mixture of transparency and opacity in the glass, the ethereal material trail of smoke—but also their transience. The still life is life caught in its momentariness. And yet in its material representation in a visual form—a quality equally found in a poem or an essay or a play—this passingness becomes itself objectified. The subject of the painting is as much the temporality of the objects as their material form; it is mortal-ity rather than merely death.

This could be said to be an interest that is philosophical rather than material. But it is philosophical in a very specific sense. I do not wish to develop here a theory of mortality or of subjective experience, although both of these questions will often subtend themselves. Instead, I see the experience of viewing Dürer's self-portrait or of reading Montaigne or of watching *Hamlet* not as an exercise in philosophy but as, if you like, an example of the moment of philosophy. This idea has several meanings. One is that, as in Montaigne's whole conception of the *Essais*, philoso-phy—or as he prefers to call it (as a verb) 'philosopher'—itself occurs in time. The central theme of this book is not only the idea of mortality, but that the thinking being is mortal, and even more so, that thought is itself bound up with mortality. My concern is with the moment of philosophy in the precise sense that philosophizing is a temporal and temporary form of thinking. In getting it right we feel both the pleasure of the moment, in a glimpse of understanding, and we apprehend a sense of its disappearance, a realization that illumination is brief and transitory. Understanding is not a noun but the participle of a verb: it is something we do rather than have, and in doing it we lose it as soon as we capture it. Second, thinking is mortal in that it is bound by our impermanence and incompleteness. Subjective knowledge is prone to error and bafflement. Thomas Nagel has written about the way that 'the recognition of our contingency, our finitude, and our containment in the world' has been used in modern philosophy to undergird certain kinds of relativism, and instead objects that we should counter this 'with an ambition of transcendence, however limited may be our success in achieving it'.[53] Contingency and finitude are inherent to philosophy, he says. But could we find a way of understanding this outside the realm of epistemology? Montaigne's sense of contingency in thinking is not only an exercise in scepticism: perhaps, indeed, it makes scepticism something more than we think it is. Montaigne invites the reader, Maclean remarks, 'to fill in the interstices of the text'.[54] In this sense, the 'developable text' of the *Essais*, and the reception of the reader, are a prime part of Montaigne's sense of philosophy as 'speculative writing'. That is, scepticism is not a new doctrine or set of ideas, but an attitude towards thinking itself, and more precisely towards the thinking person. It is not ideas which are subject to the sceptical frame, but the self that thinks, and therefore the act of thinking.

There are also two other ways in which the knowledge of the self that is discussed in this book may be called *philosophical* in this specific temporal sense that is bound by a sense of its own limits. One is the idea of the work of art or literature as intrinsically reflexive. The meanings I discuss involve intense self-scrutiny. Montaigne holds that reflexivity is the condition peculiar to the human.[55] Dürer's work is haunted, as is well known, by the presence of the artist. Self-portraiture was a fascinating new genre of its time, but as Koerner has written at length, it also becomes—perhaps is from the beginning—a discourse on the nature of the artist and of the nature of art. The self-portrait is not my prime object, either in visual terms or in the examination of autobiographical writing. But I am interested in the way that the very act of writing involves reflecting upon the self. It is useful here to bear in mind a distinction made by Jerrold Seigel in *The Idea of the Self* between what he calls 'reflexivity' and

---

[53] Thomas Nagel, *The View from Nowhere* (New York: Oxford University Press, 1986), 9.

[54] Maclean, 'Le Païs au delà: Montaigne and Philosophical Speculation', in I. D. McFarlane and Ian Maclean (eds.), *Montaigne: Essays in Memory of Richard Sayce* (Oxford: Clarendon Press, 1982), 128.

[55] Maclean, *Montaigne philosophe*, 76.

'reflectivity'.[56] Something is 'reflexive', he says, when 'it simply doubles or reinforces its origin'. The most basic example is the image in a mirror. However, 'reflectivity' involves a further stage or layer of thinking, what Seigel calls 'the ingredient of intellectual self-awareness in selfhood'. We pay attention to the world in such a way that makes us think also and at the same time of the status of such mental contents in our own minds. This could be called a phenomenological approach, except that in addition to considering the ways in which any objective thinking about the world involves a subjective point of view, it also has an extra layering of self-reference in that it includes reflecting on the nature of that interrelationship. No element of self-reflection, in this context, is unmediated.

Seigel comments that it is often difficult to say which type of thinking is which. But there are also many places where we confuse one with the other in less productive ways. Dürer's self-portraits, for instance, and autobiography altogether, are sometimes treated as if they are only 'reflexive' in the base sense: that is, that they are formed by, and represent to us, a moment of self-reflection. But they also, in Seigel's sense, involve forms of thinking of a 'second order' kind: they not only perform the function of the mirror, they encourage intense scrutiny of the relation between subject and object, and of the nature of subjective experience. *Mortal Thoughts* is about 'reflectivity' in this second meaning. While the mirror image often leaves the impression of a relationship between self and thinking that is passive and instinctive, 'reflectivity' is a complex examination of our role as agents. It involves the world as well as ourselves, the world in ourselves and ourselves in the world.

In that sense, finally, we can also see that self-reflection need not be bound to a single consciousness. Dürer's self-portrait is subjective but it is also intersubjective. It is not produced for the artist's consumption alone—even though it appears that Dürer habitually collected examples of his own self-image and kept them to himself.[57] In the very act of creation, however, he creates a dialogue with another subjective position, even if in the first instance it is his own. Montaigne's Narcissism, Antoine Compagnon remarks, is always characterized by a grammatical doubling.[58] Doubling, in the act of self-reflection, is repeated and is mimetic. Like the effect of two mirrors at an angle to each other, whereby the image is repeated into infinity, the image sets up its own gloss, so that we watch ourselves in the act of watching ourselves. Every time another viewer

---

[56] *The Idea of the Self: Thought and Experience in Western Europe Since the Seventeenth Century* (Cambridge: Cambridge University Press, 2005), 12.

[57] Jeffrey Chipps Smith, 'Albrecht Dürer as Collector', *Renaissance Quarterly*, 54.1 (Spring 2011), 1–49, this ref. p. 6.

[58] Antoine Compagnon, *Nous Michel de Montaigne* (Paris: Éditions de Deuil, 1980), 147.

looks at the image, it is also, by virtue of the same process, not Dürer's own body only that she or he is looking at. Our embodiment is bound up in the image as well as his. Yet when another person is looking (especially, in the case of the nude self-image, when that person is a woman), there is also the simultaneous sensation of difference as well as likeness. It is within this complex set of relational meanings that this book attempts to find new ways of figuring the experience of human imagining.

HISTORIES OF SELFHOOD

This book also includes a dialogue between the self of the artist or author and the self of the viewer or reader in another sense. My subject is not only the dialogue between self and self, but between past self and present self. Histories of the self are legion. Yet the relationship between the idea of selfhood and the idea of intellectual or cultural history is much closer than we recognize. In the first place, ever since *Geistesgeschichte* or *Kulturgeschichte* began to be written in the mid-nineteenth century, one of its main objects has been to identify a moment in history in which the self became central. Ever since Jakob Burckhardt's *Die Kultur der Renaissance in Italien* of 1860—has there ever been a more seminal study of a cultural era?—there has been a war of ownership over the rise of human subjectivity:

> When this impulse to the highest individual development was combined with a powerful and varied nature, which had mastered all the elements of the culture of the age, then arose the 'all-sided man'—'l'uomo universale'—who belonged to Italy alone.[59]

More ink has been spilt on identifying the first springs in human thought of self-consciousness than is strictly conscionable. The boundary between the Middle Ages and the Renaissance is the place where such a moment has been most actively sought. Burckhardt's view of *Der Mensch des Mittelalters*, and the corresponding awakening of *Personlichkeit* in the Renaissance, is one that refuses to go away.

Burckhardt's cultural analysis is carefully presented in narrative terms, as a chronological development. His main verbs authoritatively present the emergence of subjectivity as historical fact. Yet there is an alternative way of reading his account, magisterial and ardently written that it is. There is more than one aspect to this. First of all, modernity itself is identified

---

[59] Burckhardt, *Die Kultur der Renaissance in Italien*, 2 vols., 11th edn. (Leipzig: E. A. Seeman, 1913), i. 147; trans. S. G. C. Middlemore, 2nd edn. (Oxford: Phaidon Press, 1981), 84.

with the idea of selfhood. And since modernity is felt to be a peculiar and transcendent condition, a state of mind that is by definition distinctive, the whole effort of historiography is to uncover the process by which modernity emerged. The second vital aspect of this is the way that the Renaissance has been used to construct this concept of cultural struggle and revolution. The Renaissance and the Enlightenment have this distinguishing feature that they are perhaps the only major historical eras that are identified in cultural, rather than political, imperial, or military, terms. Each is used to explain modernity, but it could be said that the argument is always circular, since the identification of subjectivity as the major concern of each movement is not in any way an accident. Before Burckhardt, the very word 'renaissance' was something of a neologism. It was to some degree invented to conjure into being the very thing that needed explaining.

This is, perhaps, to put the argument too crudely. Yet even today, 150 years after Burckhardt's book, the same cultural explanations are repeated. And the same boundary period of 'early modernity' is used to solve, or at least to justify, the nature of the query of emergence. Seigel's book is sub-titled 'Thought and Experience in Western Europe since the Seventeenth Century', and combines intense philosophical analysis with a teleological picture of intellectual history to explain it. Taylor, more self-consciously, models the concept of selfhood as historical, one 'which had a beginning in time and space and may have an end'.[60] Having come into being, the dominant logic of inwardness expresses what it feels like to be modern: 'the unconscious is for us within, and we think of the depths of the unsaid, the unsayable, the powerful inchoate feelings and affinities and fears which dispute with us the control of our lives, as inner' (p. 111). This provides us all the more with the need to historicize the self. For other-wise, we are left with the assumption that modernity is the only way of thinking and experiencing:

> when a given constellation of self, moral sources, and localization is *ours*, that means it is the one from *within* which we experience and deliberate about our moral situation. It cannot but come to *feel* fixed and unchallenge-able, whatever our knowledge of history and cultural variation may lead us to believe (p. 111)

Taylor then goes on to give a narrative which will be familiar to anyone who has read any book on the history of subjectivity—Augustine as a kind of innocent precursor of a movement which springs up with the Renaissance moment of self-consciousness and then is definitively under-stood and conceptualized by Descartes. Oddly, this history is presented

---

[60] *Sources of the Self*, 111.

by Taylor not as a cliché but as a history of repression, as if we had forgotten how it was that we came to be how we are.

Of course, it is not as if a counter-argument does not exist. Indeed, as Seigel notes, the idea of the fixity of the 'modern identity' has been under attack virtually since Burckhardt himself. Not the least figure in this is Burckhardt's admirer, Nietzsche. Throughout the twentieth century, a series of philosophical and artistic movements proclaimed that 'modernity had given or was giving place to a new condition'.[61] Claude Lévi-Strauss and Maurice Merleau-Ponty were followed in the 1960s by wave upon wave of intellectual movements associated with analyses that were by turns philosophical, literary, and historical, associated with Roland Barthes, Michel Foucault, and Jacques Derrida. Eventually a name for this condition was found: the 'postmodern'. Yet all the time, however uncomfortable with the idea of modernity, these new movements continued to believe wholeheartedly in the *history* of modernity and its foundation in early modernity. There was instead a repeated appeal to a frozen moment of new challenge in which the old order was undermined. But the old order itself remained oddly unchallenged: indeed it is the necessary precondition for revolutionary change that there should be an established old order.

In fact, the historiography of the Renaissance moment of the self is nowhere near as established as we like to think. Every new generation of Renaissance scholars muses at the credulity of the general culture on this question, while announcing its own analysis as the first moment of revisionism. Yet revisionism began a long time ago. It is over sixty years since Panofsky wrote about the sudden emergence of the Renaissance as an 'old theory': 'Much has been done to explode the old theory according to which the Renaissance came in with a bang, so to speak'.[62] My own approach will not be to claim yet again the banner of sceptical rethinking or debunking. Burckhardt has been buried often enough. More interesting is the question of why he keeps on returning. No other academic book has remained so long in print as *Die Kultur der Renaissance in Italien* as if it were still today a current monograph. This is because it still does work for us, even when we wish to deny it. For this reason, my aim is not a sceptical rewriting of the claim of the historical emergence of selfhood but an understanding of a mirror process between history and modernity. The idea of reflexivity in the sixteenth and seventeenth centuries can be used as a form of reflectivity on the present. Rather than see Montaigne as a precursor of modernity, then, he can be seen as a mirror in which we choose to see ourselves. Yet this will also, I hope, reclaim the artists of

---

[61] *The Idea of the Self*, 4.   [62] Panofsky, *Life and Art of Albrecht Dürer*, 33.

the past as our contemporaries, rather than as interesting only as prophets of their supersession by us.

However, there are certain more specific ways in which I will make some revisionist claims. This can be considered in relation to some of the characteristic recent writing on the body in Renaissance studies, but it also adumbrates some of the central claims of the idea of selfhood. The fascination with death in the sixteenth century has been said to be characterized by 'its startling physical presence'.[63] Yet, here, as I have said, I will be more interested in thinking about its liminal metaphysical status. It will be as a category of uncertainty—perhaps *the* category of uncertainty, that I will consider it as a boundary condition for selfhood. Mortality sets the limits of the self, but just as importantly, it defines the self as having limits. Second, what has been called 'the new death' in the sixteenth century has been hailed by Michael Neill as part of a 'secularizing process' (p. 3).

This is over and again the distinctive claim made for the historical significance of the Renaissance self. Here it will be questioned whether this secularizing claim is ever justified except as an assertion reflecting more on ourselves and our own condition. Let us take as an example the self-portraits of Dürer. On the one hand they appear to proclaim, at the very same moment as Pico's *Oration on the Dignity of Man*, an idea of the human body as the self-referential point of its own diagnosis. And yet, as many iconographic studies have shown, Dürer's most famous self-image, the iconic full-frontal of his face and upper body now in the Alte Pinakothek in Munich, is modelled on the conventional image of Christ. Whereas the convention in portraits was sideways on, Christ was face on. Dürer repeatedly presented the iconography of the man of sorrows as a kind of self-portrait, and vice versa. Is this a secularizing process? Only if we force Dürer to step out of his own century into ours. It is the same when we consider the nude self-portrait. The nude human body preoccupied Dürer in a series of preparatory drawings and trial prints leading towards the bravura copper engraving of *Adam and Eve* in 1504 (Fig. 17), an image which became one of the (as it were) copyright icons of Dürer's European fame. He experimented with the naked male and female both in idealized and realistic vein and in a number of iconographic modes, including classical as well as biblical (I return to this in Chapter 8). He also made exercises in rendering hands and arms and other body parts. The nude self-portrait therefore plays a part in this *Kunstwerk* of the human form. But Dürer makes no distinction between the biblical and the classical frame of reference. The nude could be Apollo or Adam interchangeably.

---

[63] Michael Neill, *Issues of Death: Mortality and Identity in English Renaissance Tragedy* (Oxford: Clarendon Press, 1997), 3.

Rather in the same way as in my previous study, *Grammar and Grace*, this book puts the Reformation back into literary and artistic culture. What happens when, instead of disallowing the religious as part of the framing of human identity, we allow it to have its natural voice? It is more a polemical assertion to leave this out than to leave it in. I do not make any special claim for this; rather, it seems to me odd to do anything else. Dürer, More, Montaigne, Shakespeare, Donne, and Milton are artists whose work is produced in the scope of the Reformation, not despite it.

WRITING & DYING

One of the most characteristic of all the *Essais*, I.xix, begins with the morbid statement, 'Cicero dit que Philosopher ce n'est autre chose que s'aprester à la mort' (I.xix.82) ('Cicero says, that to philosophize is nothing but to prepare for death', Frame, p. 67).[64] The statement calls forth from Montaigne an equally characteristic moment of self-glossing. What does he mean? The gloss is divided in two, the second part of which has tended to be the paraphrase that his readers have taken from his epigrammatic opening sentence. He breaks off his first gloss to say: 'Ou bien, c'est que toute la sagesse et discours du monde se resout en fin à ce point, de nous apprendre à ne craindre point à mourir' (I.xix.83) ('Or else it is because all the wisdom and reasoning in the world boils down finally to this point: to teach us not to be afraid to die', Frame, p. 67). This sentiment, while terse and moralistic, might also be taken to be both conventional and consolatory. Montaigne, and just as importantly his anticipated readers, are steeped in Stoic moral philosophy. Stoicism teaches the control of the will and the reason in order to suppress the violence and overmastery of human passions, above all fear, and above all fears, the fear of death. If we can only learn not to fear death, we can learn to live well.

However, the very gravity and sheer reasonableness of this sentiment has worked to occlude the much stranger text that precedes it. This is because the first gloss to the essay's title, 'That to philosophize is to learn to die' is both difficult formally to comprehend, and also (by extension) difficult to take in, still less to accept:

> C'est d'autant que l'estude et la contemplation retirent aucunement nostre ame hors de nous, et l'embesongnent à part du corps, qui est quelque apprentissage et ressemblance de la mort. (I.xix.82)

---

[64] The Bordeaux copy (followed by Frame) numbers the essay I.xx.

This is because study and contemplation draw our soul out of us to some extent and keep it busy outside the body; which is a sort of apprenticeship and semblance of death. (Frame, p. 67)

This is a far harder saying than the admittedly morose opening of the essay leads us to believe. Philosophy—or more precisely, the practice of philosophy, the French verb *philosopher*, 'to philosophize'—is not only a didactic exercise in teaching us ('apprendre') to die, it is an action which 's'aprester à la mort', it prepares us, it makes us ready, in that it presages death itself. Philosophy is a rehearsal for death, it even imitates death.

As such it appears a striking or even extravagant figure of speech. Yet its resonance comes from the way that it expresses something deeper than this. The act of consciousness which is embodied in philosophy—what we might call the reflective moment of considering ourselves outside of ourselves—is a form of escape from our own boundaries. Montaigne's attitude to Stoic moral philosphy is therefore ambiguous, summed up in his alternating (we might say inconsistent) uses of the words *constance* and *inconstance*.[65] In the moment of self-recognition, we retire the spirit inside us from what surrounds it. Formally, Montaigne's own text performs this act for him, in front of us. His essay separates itself from him and acts as a proxy for him—and, in that act of separation, imitates his death. Writing itself, in Montaigne's analysis, escapes the limits of the body to represent himself in other terms. It appears, in effect, to escape his own mortality by giving him a life beyond the body. Yet in that escape he also rediscovers his limits. In his writing he realizes his own death.

In the last years of his life, Dürer re-examined his own works, and attempted to take possession of them anew, by supplying them with annotation in his own handwriting. The most celebrated example of this is the silverpoint engraving of himself as an adolescent (Fig. 9). An inscription is added in the top right corner of the folio. Scholarship has dated this annotation to sometime in 1522 or after, by which time Dürer was around 50 years old.[66] The inscription reads: *Dz hab Ich aws eim spigell nach | mir selbs kunterfet Im 1484 Jar | Do ich noch ein Kint was | Albrecht Dürer.* ('This I drew myself from a mirror in the year 1484 when I was still a child. Albrecht Dürer').[67] The happenstance of the writing has been taken for the most part as a lucky dip for scholarship. The provenance of the drawing is certified and signed by the artist. The account of himself as a boy prodigy also accords with other autobiographical fragments by

---

[65] I. D. McFarlane, 'The Concept of Virtue in Montaigne', in McFarlane and Maclean (eds.), *Montaigne*, 94.
[66] Smith, 'Dürer as Collector', 38.   [67] Bartrum, *Dürer and his Legacy*, 79.

Fig. 9. Albrecht Dürer, *Self-Portrait* (1484); silverpoint.

Dürer, such as when he recounts his father's hopes that he will follow him into the goldsmith's trade, and the problems the young Albrecht had in persuading Albrecht the elder that his talent as a painter was sufficient for him to try another skill for a living.[68] More sophisticated readings, as in Koerner's book, juxtapose this precocious moment of autobiographical self-recognition with the art of self-portraiture itself.[69] A drawing of Albrecht the elder has been adduced by some scholars, including Koerner, as an early example of the self-portrait by the father himself.[70] Others, myself included, find it more likely to be a portrait by the son of the father. In that sense, I would prefer also to see the image as the younger artist's self-image *in* the image of his father, a proleptic sense of son turning into father, Albrecht into Albrecht, swapping places and stepping into the dead father's shoes. Either way, the extraordinary output of Dürer the younger, in portraits of himself, and of his family (brothers and mother and wife as well as his father) and indeed of his master Michael Wolgemut the Nuremberg artist—attests to his sense of the self.

Yet the inscriptions tell another story still. They have an air of self-authorization but yet also of lingering retrospect. On Dürer's oil portrait of Wolgemut on panel, now in the Germanisches Nationalmuseum, Nuremberg, there are two layers of annotation. First he states simply that he painted his teacher in the year 1516. Then he adds later 'and he was eighty-two years old and lived until 1519, when he passed away on St Andrew's day, before the sun went up'. What moves Dürer to record the year and even the date and hour of mortality of his master, in a second layer of inscription? True, as Jeffrey Chipps Smith comments, the information 'documents his intentional autobiographical recordkeeping' (p. 40). Yet it also marks an ambiguous attitude to the mortality of the master and his pupil. When painted, his master was still living, although he bears the clear indications of age. If we did not know the identity of the sitter, we might be tempted to place the brilliant rendition of the sunken eyelids and the reddened pupils as a *vanitas* painting within the genre of the *col tempo*. The inscription, however, while giving the painting a personal quality of empathy, also makes its own sign *col tempo*. The sitter is now dead; the painting has taken on a new meaning, a memento of the once living, now given back to us, rather than a reminder to the living of the inevitability of death. The artist's handwriting, meanwhile, both declares his still living presence in collecting and framing the painting, but also

---

[68] The evidence both of the portraits and of Dürer's notebooks has been reassessed with great skill by Thomas Eser in Hess and Eser (ed.), *Der frühe Dürer*, 261–3.

[69] Koerner, *Moment of Self-Portraiture*, 35–6.

[70] Winkler 3; Koerner, *Moment of Self-Portraiture*, 43.

Fig. 10. Albrecht Dürer, *Portrait of the Artist's Mother* (1514); charcoal.

figures forth the inevitability of his own ending. He survives for the moment; but no one can survive his own handwriting for ever. Handwriting is a sign at once of life and of mortality.

It is an obvious enough point that Dürer reserves his handwritten marginal notes on his own drawings and paintings for the most personal items in his collection. A drawing of his wife is inscribed 'mein Agnes'.[71] The man of sorrows of 1504, we recall, bears the witness to his own illness (see Fig. 2). The charcoal sketch of his mother Barbara again bears two stages of inscription (Fig. 10): the first gives a date of composition—'On March 19, this is Albrecht's mother when she was sixty-three years old'. Later he adds, 'vnd ist versciden Im 1514 Jor am erchtag vor der crewtzwochen vm zwey genacht' ('and she died in the year 1514 on rogation Tuesday at two in the night').[72] Fixing the date of death of his mother is a ritual act, confirmed by the use of the Christian calendar in recording it (as also in Wolgemut's portrait); but like any record of death in a family book or bible it has a double meaning in relation to the writer. All deaths in the family prefigure our own.

This applies with all the more force to the image of himself as a child rediscovered and reclaimed in old age. Whenever he drew it (perhaps we do not need to believe verbatim his own act of piety in expressing astonishment at the precocity of his youth) the inscribing of the drawing completes a circle. It is an act both memorial and prophetic, both awestruck by his own talent and conscious of his increasingly nearing mortality. But even if it were not so personal a gesture of self-presentation, his act of writing bears witness to the capacity of writing to declare its own incipient desuetude. Ink and pencil carry the trace of the person in a new bodily form. They continue the life of the person beyond the bounds of the person's own body. Yet like the body of the person they also are perishable and finite.

Who, in addition, is the writing for? It is addressed to Dürer as an aide-mémoire perhaps, but he also must have known (and intended even) that these marks would be there to guide some future interlocutor as well. And since the items were kept in his personal collection, Dürer seems to be leaving the inscriptions as a kind of last will and testament, to be seen by the testator only in the event of death. By the time the handwriting sees the light of day in the point of view of the future reader, Dürer will be dead and gone. That Dürer and his circles were thinking in this way can be seen from the epitaph for Dürer's tomb, written by his friend the humanist Willibald Pirckheimer, still visible in Nuremberg today: *Quicquid Alberti Dureri mortale fuit, sub hic conditur tumulo* ('whatever was mortal

---

[71] Winkler 151; now in the Albertina, Vienna.
[72] Winkler 559; Smith, 'Dürer as Collector', 40.

of Albrecht Durer is covered by this tomb'. Hans Baldung Grien kept a physical memento in the shape of a lock of hair, handed down from owner to owner and now in the Albertina alongside a huge collection of auto-graph drawings. But even if this was not his intention, and part of his own cult of mortality and the artist, writing has this status of bearing the sign of mortality.

Montaigne, too, had this sense of the ambiguous permeability of his own handwriting, to which he added this peculiarly self-conscious phil-osophy of the act of writing. A copy of the last edition (of 1588) pub-lished during his lifetime of the *Essais* was owned by Montaigne and copiously annotated in his hand.[73] He deleted text, revised words, cor-rected and added at will; in the margins and in the body of the text, he created multiple typographical variants, word substitutions, punctuation alterations, and rhetorical changes. On a few pages his writing merges with and responds to other annotations by Mlle de Gournay, while they were together in Paris between June and December 1588.[74] More exten-sive ameliorations of the *Essais* were added by Montaigne at his home between the end of 1588 and 13 September 1592 (the date of his death) which invade the blank space of the margins of the printed work and take on a new life of their own. By the time he finished, the work was a third longer than the original of 1588; the new text was incorporated in the posthumous edition of 1595. The autograph copy itself was discovered in the nineteenth century and is now known as the 'Bordeaux copy'.[75] It is a vital textual record of Montaigne's work, and one of the most precious authorial holographs in existence. It shows the mind of the author at work, his writing in its most electric immediacy. But Montaigne himself seems to have been aware also of its special status in relation to his own existence. He regarded the text of the Bordeaux copy as an extension of his own body. He called the longer additions 'allongeails', a neologism of his own. The verb *allonger* means to stretch out, to linger. The verb is a common metaphor of mortality, of the desire to stretch out one's mortal coil.[76] It is a beautiful bodily metaphor for his handwriting and its rela-

---

[73] The 'Exemplaire de Bordeaux' is described in Sayce and Maskell, *Descriptive Bibliog-raphy*, 16–17. The first edition of 1580 contained two books of essays. The revised second edition, complete with Book III, was published in 1588: *Essais de Michel Seigneur de Mon-taigne: cinquiesme edition, augmentee d'un troisiesme livre et de six cens additions aux deus premiers* (Paris: Abel L'Angelier, 1588).

[74] Sayce and Maskell, *Descriptive Bibliography*, 17.

[75] The 'Exemplaire de Bordeaux' (EB) or 'Bordeaux copy' exists in an online edition: *The Montaigne Project: Villey edition of the Essais with corresponding digital page images from the Bordeaux Copy*. [ARTFL Project / Montaigne Studies, University of Chicago.] <http://www.lib.uchicago.edu/efts/ARTFL/projects/montaigne>

[76] 'Je veux qu'on agisse, et qu'on allonge les offices de la vie, tant qu'on peut', I.xix.91.

tionship to the printed text. Montaigne was writing himself into immortality but he was also, he clearly felt, prolonging his existence by the sheer effort and act of writing. The Bordeaux copy of his book, like his body, he called a 'bundle of so many disparate pieces'. He wanted to keep writing for as long as possible: with a wry comment on his own limits, he expressed the desire to keep writing 'as long as there is ink and paper in the world'. But he also knew he could not stretch out his writing indefinitely. Death, and the paradox of organic generation which is bound up in its own end, is central to Montaigne's concept both of his own body and the body of his work.[77] The *Essais* are mortal as much as he is.

Like Dürer, Montaigne writes his own person into his project. His body is the subject of the essays just as Dürer's body is the subject of his art. His body expresses his own finitude. In the essay on death, he creates a synecdoche for his project in a poignant declaration of his mortal condition, and therefore also the conditionality of his selfhood:

> Je nasquis entre unze heures et midi le dernier jour de Febvrier, mil cinq cens trente trois: comme nous contons à cette heure, commençant l'an en Janvier. Il n'y a justement que quinze jours que j'ay franchi 39. ans. (I.xix.86)

> I was born between eleven o'clock and noon on the last day of February 1533, as we reckon time now, beginning the year the first of January. It is only just two weeks ago that I passed the age of thirty-nine years. (Frame, pp. 69–70)

He continues, wryly, 'il m'en faut pour le moins encore autant' ('I need at least that many more'. He wants to go on living, so he goes on writing. But the essay must end sometime. The essay becomes a form of its own argument: a preparation for death as he realizes the simultaneity of the act of writing and the condition of mortality:

> Ce que j'ay affaire avant mourir, pour l'achever tout loisir me semble court, fust-ce oeuvre d'une heure. Quelcun feuilletant l'autre jour mes tablettes, trouva un memoire de quelque chose, que je vouloys estre faite après ma mort: je luy dy, comme il estoit vray, que n'estant qu'à une lieue de ma maison, et sain et gaillard, je m'estoy hasté de l'escrire là, pour ne m'asseurer point d'arriver jusques chez moy. Comme celuy, qui continuellement me couve de mes pensées, et les couche en moy: je suis à toute heure preparé environ ce que je le puis estre: et ne m'advertira de rien de nouveau la survenance de la mort. (I.xix.89–90)

> To finish what I have to do before I die, even if it were one hour's work, any leisure seems short to me. Someone, looking through my writing tablets the other day, found a memorandum about something I wanted done after my death. I told him what was true, that although only a league away from my

---

[77] Compagnon, *Nous Michel de Montaigne*, 179.

house, and hale and hearty, I had hastened to write it there, since I could not be certain of reaching home. Since I am constantly brooding over my thoughts and settling them within me, I am at all times about as well prepared as I can be. And the coming of death will teach me nothing new. (Frame, p. 73)

He is writing both before and after death: the last sentences were added in his last revision, after 1588. More than any other writer, perhaps, he involves the reader in this process of exchange, making the death of the reader as much his subject as the death of the author. Montaigne comments that he would like to die without knowing it, to be caught by surprise by death while planting his cabbages; his readers, maybe, wonder if they will die while reading his book, kept equally unawares of mortality by their own displacement within his book.

ANOTHER SELF

The apotheosis of Montaigne's scepticism is found in II.xii, the 'Apologie de Raimond Sebond'. The essay is a classic example of the problem of interpreting early modern thinking about religion and the limits of human knowledge. Ostensibly it is a defence of Christianity, yet it is also a thorough examination of the possibility of a non-revealed and self-authorizing understanding of truth. Perhaps it is best understood as being in the character of a double bluff, an argument which is always providing the best case for the other side. Can we know anything for certain? The question is posed with equal rigour on both sides of the equation—so that the work has been hailed both as a defence and a rejection of theology ever since.

Sebond's *Theologia naturalis*, also known as the *Liber creaturarum*, the 'book of creatures', written in the early fifteenth century—and which Montaigne had earlier translated—set out to show the limits of human knowledge. It did so by setting out a concatenated series of principles which interlock, but which are easy to misinterpret when seen in isolation. Sebond claimed to be able to educate the laity in the understanding of both God and the world without access to the university disciplines. This was what in turn attracted Montaigne—a form of knowledge without recourse to a prior form of authority and without the claim of esoteric expertise. Yet the claim does not mean quite what it seems to. Sebond states that God gives knowledge to mankind in two forms, or 'Books'.[78] The second, holy scripture, is authoritative. But it is not open to all: only the clergy have the wisdom to interpret it correctly. For this reason, it can be misinterpreted, for instance by heretics.

---

[78] Regosin, *The Matter of My Book*, 71–4.

The first 'book' is 'the book of all creatures', that is the book of nature. It is common to all, given by God to man at creation. It consists of letters and words and sentences, like scripture, and like scripture it contains all truth. Indeed, the two books contain the same truth—since God cannot contradict himself in giving out the truth even in different forms. Unlike the second book of scripture, this first book is common to all creatures and can be understood by the whole of mankind; and it cannot yield misinformation. However, at the fall of man in the garden of Eden, man lost the ability to read the book of nature correctly.

This is a highly complex theory of knowledge, although it appears to be simple. It is based on a multi-faceted interpretation of the meanings of 'nature' in the Aristotelian corpus.[79] In fact, every aspect of 'knowledge' is subject to caveat and counter-clause. Natural knowledge is unmediated, it needs no teacher and no explanation, since it is a natural language available through the senses. Yet after the Fall it is a lost form of knowledge, cut off from immediate apprehension; although there is a further caveat that those enlightened by God can reclaim it. For Montaigne, this idea is useful because it shows that nature reveals the same truths as divine revelation.[80] Yet he also acknowledged that nature could not be read properly without enlightenment from God beforehand. Later commentators, in the seventeenth and eighteenth centuries, sometimes confused this with one of two contradictory positions. Some felt it showed that Montaigne was an ancestor of fideism—that there is no rational defence of Christianity since knowledge of God depends on revelation which can only be believed in, not known. Or else, contradictorily, that he is a precursor of deism: that nature anticipates divine knowledge because the world works according to divine principles which it naturally reveals.

In Montaigne's careful appropriation and reimagining of Sebond's system, knowledge, reason, experience—and in some sense revelation, too—are linked in mutually dependent relationship. It is not possible to pull one part out and make it subject to the others. It is in this light that we have to understand his attraction to arguments from scepticism. The passage towards modernity has given scepticism a particular role in the history of ideas: a progression from one set of ideas to another, prompted by a sceptical crisis. Yet scepticism for Montaigne is not a doctrine but a method, or even a cast of thinking or perhaps a way of life. Terence Cave calls the sceptical argument of the 'Apologie' a description of meaning as

---

[79] Maclean, *Montaigne philosophe*, 64.

[80] Ann Hartle, 'Montaigne and Skepticism', in Ullrich Langer (ed.), *The Cambridge Companion to Montaigne* (Cambridge: Cambridge University Press, 2005), 187–8.

'the product of the reader's subjective awareness rather than an essence residing in the text'.[81] In his successive rewriting of the 'Apologie', Montaigne quoted more and more from Sextus Empiricus and his *Pyrrhonian Hypotyposes*, a book first published by Henri Estienne in 1562 in Greek, and in 1567 in Latin.[82] This work appears in no other of the *Essais*. Did he resort to it here in some personal crisis? Or was it a practical method for dealing with the matter in hand?

Similar questions surround the multiple citations from Lucretius in the 'Apologie'. Lucretius, too, has been commandeered to support the case that Montaigne is setting out a sceptical argument about truth and the Christian religion. However, as Michael Screech argues, 'Epicureanism is flatly opposed to Pyrrhonist scepticism'.[83] Lucretius does not expose truth to sceptical undermining, but instead undergirds truth with a principle of certainty derived from sense impressions.

It is here that the argument about subjectivity comes to a crux. On the one hand no knowledge can be certified save by the self: we can prove nothing from reason without it being tested on individual experience. And yet experience itself is prone to an equal caveat: it proves nothing to anyone else. If this intellectual deconstruction has been taken as the ultimate vindication of Montaigne as sceptic, we run into the problem that the last thing Montaigne sets out to prove is some new doctrine of relativism. And if we take the concentration of knowledge in the person as the ultimate vindication of the self, the self unbound, the only repository of knowledge and therefore the new divinity, then we run into the problem that Montaigne's view of the self is as sceptical as his view of knowledge. Indeed the two are the same thing. Knowledge freed to the realm of the self is also knowledge limited to the realm of the self. The self is a region of limits rather than freedom.

If this seems like a self-contradiction, or self-cancellation, then it may be because we have been looking for the wrong object, the one that modern secularization wishes to find. While the object of enquiry in the 'Apologie' has been taken to be an epistemological one, Montaigne's interest may be more strictly personal. The *Essais* are not a philosophical theorem or epistemological *summa*. Montaigne follows Sebond's argument that the natural world provides its own truth. He delights in the idea that this form of truth might still be hidden from us. He is content

---

[81] Terence Cave, 'Problems of Reading in the Essais', in McFarlane and Maclean (eds.), *Montaigne*, 161.

[82] Montaigne's principal source for Sextus Empiricus was the Latin edition of 1569; see Maclean, *Montaigne philosophe*, 48–50.

[83] Introduction to *An Apology for Raymond Sebond*, trans. M. A. Screech (London: Penguin Books, 1987), p. xxiv.

at the sceptic's dissatisfaction with ideas of proof. And he uses Lucretius' paradigm of sense-based data to justify his own project of investigating, as far as possible, as far as the limitations of his own body will allow, the natural philosophy contained within his own experience. But he is far from offering this new philosophy as overthrowing others. Least of all does he wish to see off the Christian religion.[84] He uses the idea of 'natural theology' to permit his own level of enquiry; and if someone feels he has gone too far, he can always appeal to revelation as the final arbiter. There is no evidence of his idea of the self as representing a secularizing thesis: he probably would have regarded such a case as blasphemous. But he is intrigued by the idea of exposing every idea to a test of doubt, to being open to as many possibilities as feasible.[85] But these are possibilities not certainties. He is content to have discovered the limits of his own knowledge and experience; there is no other knowledge or experience he can discover the limits to: 'Si ce que nous n'avons pas veu, n'est pas, nostre science est merveilleusement raccourcie' (II.xii.473) 'If what we have not seen does not exist, our knowledge is marvellously shrunk' (Frame, p. 401).

His world of knowledge is precisely linked to the limits of his own body, not only to what he can see with his eyes, but to what is within the purview of his eyesight. This is not an argument of the power of empiricism so much as one of the limitations of contingency, the contextualization of circumstance peculiar to himself. Mortality is therefore the condition of inevitable error, he says, quoting from Seneca, *De ira*:

> *Inter cætera mortalitatis incommoda, et hoc est, caligo mentium: nec tantum necessitas errandi, sed errorum amor* (II.xii.473)[86]

> *Among other human infirmities is this one also, mental fog, and yet not so much the need to err, as the love of errors.* (Frame, p. 401)

Knowledge is limited and uncertain in the same way as mortal life and bodily experience is limited and uncertain. His body, after all, is made only of corruptible stuff, it is *Corruptibile corpus*. 'Nous voilà au rouet'— we are going round in circles: 'Puis que les sens ne peuvent arrester nostre dispute, estans pleins eux-mesmes d'incertitude, il faut que ce soit la raison: aucune raison ne s'establira sans une autre raison, nous voylà à reculons jusques à l'infiny' (II.xii.638). ('Since the senses cannot decide our dispute, being themselves full of uncertainty, it must be reason that does so. No reason can be established without another reason: then we go retreating back to infinity'; Frame, p. 552).

---

84 Hartle, 'Montaigne and Skepticism', 200.
85 Screech, *Montaigne and Melancholy*, 16–17.   86 *De ira*, II.9–10.

If the first impulse of the 'Apologie' is an appeal to empiricism, to the objective validation of arguments based on natural experience, the conclusion of the 'Apologie' is the failure of empiricism, in the retreat of natural experience into the subjective aporia of solipsism. The senses do not give access to natural objects themselves but only to their own impressions of them. Ideas based on these impressions do not represent the properties of the objects but of the mind that apprehends them. Montaigne has painted himself into a corner:

> Finalement, il n'y a aucune constante existence, ny de nostre estre, ny de celuy des objects: Et nous, et nostre jugement, et toutes choses mortelles, vont coulant et roulant sans cesse: Ainsin il ne se peut establir rien de certain de l'un à l'autre, et le jugeant, et le jugé, estans en continuelle mutation et branle. (II.xii.639)

> Finally, there is no existence that is constant, either of our being or that of objects. And we, and our judgement, and all mortal things go on flowing and rolling unceasingly. Thus nothing certain can be established about one thing by another, both the judging and the judged being in continual change and motion. (Frame, p. 553)

Mortal judgement is flawed and partial. It gives only a point of view; and that point of view is always in motion, as the viewer is a moving body in time. Still worse, the point of view is finite, as the body is finite. Reason passes as life itself does.

This brings Montaigne to a final theological turn: for he does not end the essay in a stock descent into radical scepticism. God is the only thing that 'is'. All natural things are either born, being born, or dying: they are temporary and transient. God alone has *esse*, true being. 'Nous n'avons aucune communication à l'estre, par ce que toute humaine nature est tousjours au milieu, entre le naistre et le mourir' ('We have no communication with being, because every human nature is always midway between birth and death'). This passage, borrowed closely from Amyot's Plutarch, brings him to one final quotation from Lucretius:

> mutat enim mundi naturam totius aetas[87]

Every human being is on the point of non-existence. Yet this also conveys to every human being its own unique existence. Life is fleeting and contingent, yet in this condition discovers its own peculiarity and particularity. Indeed it is the singularity of the condition of the writer Montaigne

---

[87] *De rerum natura*, V.826: 'Time changes the nature of the whole world'; *Titi Lucreti Cari De rerum natura libri sex*, ed. and trans. Cyril Bailey, 3 vols. (Oxford: Clarendon Press, 1947), i. 474–5.

which gives value to his writing: for the fleetingness of writing itself is a record of experience as it is lived. He is dying, and therefore he writes.

Nowhere does Montaigne quote more from Lucretius than in the essays 'That to philosophize, is to learn how to die' (I.xix) and 'An apology of Raymond Sebond' (II.xii). In December 1989, Montaigne's own copy of Lucretius was discovered by chance. It is of the famous edition by Denis Lambin. Inside its covers, Montaigne is found scribbling in the margins his responses to the text of the poet in the act of reading. Indeed, he records the date when he finished reading it, 16 October 1564, and his age at the time, 31 years old. As in the Bordeaux copy of the *Essais*, these marks are more than a reader's reactions. They are the marks of his mortality, his mortal thoughts. Writing is of the moment, it follows the trace of the momentariness of a life, it records its own finitude in the making. Montaigne seems to have loved this sense of transience in the mortal act of inscription. But in this transience he also finds his own existence. 'Pensiez vous jamais n'arriver là, où vous alliez sans cesse? encore n'y a-il chemin qui n'aye son issue' ('Did you think you would never arrive where you never ceased going? Yet there is no road but has its end'), he wrote in I.xix.96 (Frame, p. 80). Such a thought is not morbid, it is not an image of corrupt or decaying flesh. It is a way of capturing life on the move.

As well as marginal notes (Fig. 11), his copy of Lucretius also carries within it the burden of further reflection. Some citations he collects in the fly leaves, as if to give them more weight and gravity, as if to tie them to some place of permanence in the endpapers of his consciousness. One of these brings us to what Screech, who edited the annotations, has called the most personal of moments of self-reflection. Indeed, at first its significance passed even Screech by. Montaigne cited Book III, lines 854 and following:

nam cum respicias inmensi temporis omne
praeteritum spatium, tum motus materiai
multimodi quam sint, facile hoc adcredere possis,
semina saepe in eodem, ut nunc sunt, ordine posta
haec eadem, quibus e nunc nos sumus, ante fuisse.
nec memori tamen id quimus reprehendere mente[88]

Book III was always the most personal of books to Montaigne: it is the book which attends to mortality and the uselessness of the fear of dying. It was dangerous material in the sixteenth century because it taught the mortality of the soul as well as the body. Every body is made up of atoms which occupy

[88] 'For when you look back over all the lapse of immeasurable time that now is gone, and think how manifold are the motions of matter, you could easily believe this too, that these same seeds, whereof we now are made, have often been placed in the same order as they are now; and yet we cannot recall that in our mind's memory'; *De rerum natura*, ed. Bailey, i. 346–7.

space: that space is inherently finite. A body which exists outside space simply does not exist. Yet its materialism could also be viewed in another way. In denying the possibility of the person occupying any other space or time than that of the mortal body, it also asserts the uniqueness of that experience. The fragility of time is also the preciousness of the moment.

For a second Lucretius also imagines what for him is the impossible: that the self could be reassembled in another space or time. Lambin describes this figure of speech in Lucretius as an *anthypophora*—asking a question and then immediately answering it, but in the process leaving the lingering sense of alternative possibilities in the world. In literary terms it is the equivalent of an irony, the maintenance of two (possibly contradictory) positions at one and the same time. No wonder Montaigne admired the textual pleasure of this moment. Lambin commented:

> hunc igitur respondet non esse incredibile, si retro spectemus praeteriti temporis spatium immensum, & si consideremus materiae motus varios, & multiplices, primordia rerum, ex quibus constat hodie homo aliquis singularis, eodem ordine & olim posita fuisse, quo nunc sunt ordine collocata: & posthac eodem collocatum iri.

> Lucretius therefore replies that if we look back over the immense expanse of time past, and if we consider the many and multifarious movements of matter, it is not unbelievable that the basic elements of which any one man is made today were, long ago, placed in the same order as that in which they are assembled now, and will be assembled hereafter.[89]

But, Lambin notes, Lucretius answers his own question in the negative, suppressing the thought even as it occurs to him: it would still not be the same man, as each life would be individually distinct. Yet it is enough to have caught Lambin's imagination: 'from the matter of a particular man could be born another man many centuries later who would be, in a way, a second him', *qui sit quodam modo idem alter.*[90] The self imagines itself in another self. From this suggestion, Montaigne's own mind takes off. In his own handwriting (Fig. 11) he adds:

> Vt sunt diversi atomorum motus non incredibile est sic conuenisse olim atomos aut conuenturas ut alius nascatur montanus

> Since the movement of the atoms are varied, it is not unbelievable that atoms once came together—or will come together again in the future—so that another mountain be born.[91]

---

[89] M. A. Screech, *Montaigne's Annotated Copy of Lucretius: A Transcription and Study of the Manuscript, Notes and Pen-Marks* (Geneva: Librairie Droz, 1998), 135.

[90] Screech, *Montaigne's Annotated Copy of Lucretius*, 135.

[91] Screech, *Montaigne's Annotated Copy of Lucretius*, 134.

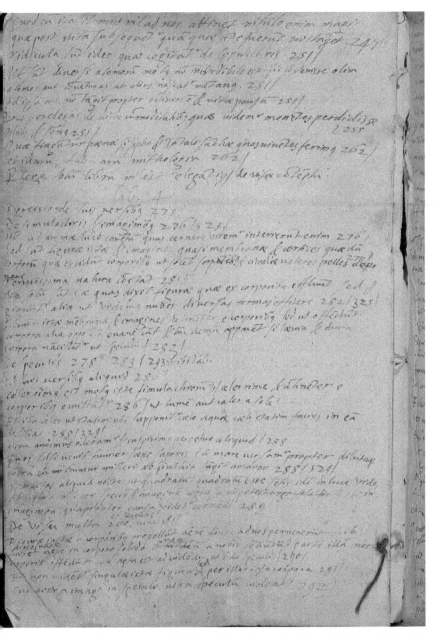

Fig. 11. Montaigne's annotation in MS hand, Titus Lucretius Carus *Titi Lucretii Cari De rerum natura libri sex* Parisiis, et Lugduni habentur [Paris & Lyons]: In Gulielmi Rouillii, et Philippi G. Rouillii Nep. ædibus, via Jacobæ sub concordia, 1563 [i.e. 1564?], p. 251.

At first Screech did not think more of the line, until he saw the concealed pun in *montanus*.[92] Another mountain might arise: another Montaigne might be born. In this pun, Montaigne realizes the singularity of his life. In the writing out of his name, he captures, for a moment, himself in life. Just like Dürer in the door between two rooms, Montaigne is mortal but he is present amongst us who live after him.

---

[92] 'It could, after all, have meant *mountain*. At that stage I would not let it mean anything else. Let it mean that for a while'; Screech, *Montaigne's Annotated Copy of Lucretius*, 11.

2

The Reformed Conscience
Thomas More

There is no figure in the early modern period, perhaps no one in the English-speaking world, who is more identified with an ideal of personal conscience than Thomas More. His imprisonment in the Tower in 1534 and interior struggle up to his ultimate trial and execution in July 1535 have become part of modern political consciousness, cited at will as an example of the individual's rights in relation to the overpowering and arbitrary assertion of the interests of the state.[1] More is an icon of private rights against public good, individual freedom against tyranny, conscience against the letter of the law. As victim of the state he creates a near perfect case of conscience, a philosophical exemplum that, even if it had no relation to the historical record, would show us with peculiar accuracy the shape of our own paradoxical relationship to human legal institutions.

And yet here, immediately, we encounter a contradiction. For the figure of More in the public imagination is almost completely at variance with the view of historians. While it is not in dispute that he died a heroic death at the hands of an intransigent political state, there exists now a revisionist consensus among specialists in the field that the ideal for which he died is quite different from the ideal for which he is remembered. This creates a peculiar controversy about the principle of conscience. If politicians, in Europe and America, following the extraordinary charisma of the play and film *A Man for All Seasons* by Robert Bolt, still blithely cite More as an apostle of liberal thought, historians have grown used to dismissing such a view as idle and idealized anachronism. The commonplace assumption of Morean scholars now is that More's view of conscience is very different from a modern view of the autonomy of the individual self. The most concise and incisive summary of this analysis can be found in Anthony Kenny's study of 1983. He isolates a quotation from Bolt's play in which the character playing More says, 'what matters to me is not whether it's

---

[1] The modern account of the life which first gave rise to this view is R. W. Chambers, *Thomas More* (London: Jonathan Cape, 1935).

true or not but that I believe it to be true, or rather not that I *believe* it, but that *I* believe it'.[2] This is a travesty of More's own position, Kenny argues. Conscience for More is not independent of truth values, indeed conscience is itself a kind of truth condition. Just as God enables the church in general to know the truth of God's revelation through its accordance with the teaching of tradition, so the individual human is guaranteed access to this truth through the mediation of his conscience in accordance with the teaching of the church. But this does not mean that a man always does right in following his conscience. For some men are in the wrong, for instance all heretics are. A heretic is still a heretic when he follows his conscience, and the state has no obligation to protect him, indeed it must pursue and examine him. Fundamentally, then, what matters to More is 'whether it's true or not' and *not* whether he believes it or not. In Kenny's summary, for More 'true conscience is simply the right appreciation of God's law'.[3] Marvin O'Connell has recently formulated this even more powerfully and suggestively, in an epigrammatic riposte to Bolt: 'Conscience for More was the right to be right, not the right to be wrong.'[4]

PRISONER OF CONSCIENCE

A struggle to identify the true meaning of More's 'conscience' goes back to the first reports of More's execution and particularly to the early lives of More written in the mid-century. This emerges especially in the account of More's trial reported by the historian, biographer, and religious controversialist Nicholas Harpsfield. Harpsfield was born in 1519 and was therefore too young to have been an eyewitness to any of the events in question. His first connection with the story of More came probably in Oxford in the 1540s where he became a protégé of William Roper, More's son-in-law. When he went into exile under Edward VI in 1550, he resided at Louvain with Antonio Bonvisi, who had been one of More's closest friends.[5] Here he also associated with other family and friends of More including John Clement and William Rastell.[6]

---

[2] *A Man for All Seasons* (New York: Vintage, 1962), 52–3.

[3] Kenny, *Thomas More* (Oxford: Oxford University Press, 1983), 93–7.

[4] Marvin O'Connell, 'A Man for all Seasons: An Historian's Demur', *Catholic Dossier*, 8.2 (March–April 2002), 16–19.

[5] Thomas S. Freeman, 'Harpsfield, Nicholas (1519–1575)', *Oxford Dictionary of National Biography* (Oxford: Oxford University Press, 2004) <http://www.oxforddnb.com/view/article/12369>, accessed 11 February 2008.

[6] The Morean presence in Louvain is reported in full in Nicholas Sanders, *De origine et progressu schismati Anglicani* (1585), fos. 123–4.

Harpsfield's *The Life and Death of Sir Thomas More* was probably writ-ten largely in exile. It was only finished, however, perhaps as late as 1557, by which time Harpsfield was a key member of the Marian regime and Archdeacon of Canterbury. At this point the *Life* became some kind of companion to Rastell's edition of *The workes of Sir Thomas More in the Englysh tonge*, in which Harpsfield may also have played a part. The *Workes* were published in 1557, but history intervened before the *Life* could emerge in print, although its finished state can be seen from its survival in eight manuscripts. Even in this brief summary, both the *Life* and the *Workes* must therefore be seen as part of a controversial effort, a sophisti-cated apologetics in which More is rehabilitated and reappropriated to fit a new political history of the Henrician period. Neither book should be seen, as some More scholars used to, as a mere source for understanding More. Harpsfield's *Life*, in particular, shows how More has a different meaning in exile in the early 1550s from the counter-Reformation tri-umph of the mid-1550s. This was to change once again after the Catholic movement went underground again in 1558. More's family returned to Louvain and it was there in 1564 that More's Latin works were published. Harpsfield himself spent most of the rest of his life in prison in the Fleet, where he nonetheless succeeded in writing a rebuttal in detail of large parts of Foxe's *Actes and Monuments* or 'Book of Martyrs'; Foxe, in turn, presented Harpsfield as one of the most virulent of the Marian persecu-tors, just as he rewrote More as a fabricator, a torturer, and a hypocrite. In death, as much as in life, More's final acts are an acute index of the con-flicts of the Reformation.

Harpsfield made a declaration of conscience a central episode in More's trial. Here, as it finally becomes clear to More himself that he is to be condemned in any case, come what may, he does what in public he has been so careful thus far not to do, to speak what is in his mind:

> I will nowe in discharge of my conscience speake my minde plainlye and freely touching my Inditement and your Statute withall.[7]

It is surely the clarity of this sentence that lies behind Bolt's portrayal in the 1960s. Most striking of all is the assimilation of an idea of 'conscience' with an ability to 'speake my minde plainlye and freely'. More here appears to place his conscience in contradistinction to the dictates of statute or of state authority. Whatever the revisionist force of Kenny and O'Connell, there appears to be at least some textual basis for the alternative view.

---

[7] Nicholas Harpsfield, *The Life and death of Sr Thomas More, knight, sometimes Lord high Chancellor of England*, ed. Elsie Vaughan Hitchcock, Early English Text Society (London: Oxford University Press, 1932), 193.

However, an understanding of the meaning of 'conscience' is complicated by the mediating presence of Harpsfield's own controversial intentions, and the variety of his sources. For much of his account, Harpsfield depends on the memoir written by Roper twenty years after More's death, probably as an aid for Harpsfield's work but published separately in 1626 as the most authentic of the early lives. This central statement does not appear in Roper, and Harpsfield adapted it from a source that was newly available to him, a Paris newsletter of August 1535: 'je veulx librement parler de vostre statut pour descharger ma conscience'.[8]

The resonance that the word 'conscience' has for Harpsfield is a conflation of many instances in the sources that he compiled of More's life in the lead up to the indictment. One is the wonderful contempt More shows for the king's solicitor, Master Rich, who had been employed to entrap him; a man, he says, whom he knew well enough as never to entrust him with any matter of consequence, one commonly esteemed as a liar and a dicer: is it likely then, 'that I would vnto him vtter the secretes of my conscience touching the kinges supremacie' (p. 190)? This passage is taken directly from Roper.[9] Another, placed earlier in the *Life*, Harpsfield takes from the final letters between More and his daughter Margaret (Roper's wife) which were also given a most prominent position as the last elements in the English *Workes* of 1557. Here More is quoted as replying to the Commissioners appointed to enforce the Oath of Succession. He did not 'condemne the conscience of any other man', but 'my conscience so moueth me in the matter' that although he would not explicitly deny the succession, he could not swear the oath as given to him. But he assured the Commissioners that he did not refuse the oath 'onely for the grudge of his conscience, or for any other phantasie' (p. 167).[10]

These citations of the word 'conscience' reveal how Harpsfield is constructing a picture of More's conscience from a range of idioms and modulations of tone. The phrase 'grudge of conscience' comes from a different register from 'the secretes of my conscience', still more from the incipient idea of a 'free' conscience. It is evident that More's concept of 'conscience' requires some unravelling. Even though we might recognize where Bolt

---

[8] The newsletter is preserved in 8 MSS in the Bibliothèque Nationale de France, Paris; it is edited by Hitchcock as an appendix to Harpsfield, *Life*, 254–66. Extracts are translated in *A Thomas More Sourcebook*, ed. Gerald Wegemer and Stephen Smith (Washington, DC: Catholic University Press, 2004), 352–5.

[9] William Roper, *The Life of Sir Thomas Moore, knighte*, ed. Elsie Vaughan Hitchcock, Early English Text Society (London: Oxford University Press, 1935), 88.

[10] See the letter from More to Margaret Roper in *The vvorkes of Sir Thomas More Knyght, sometyme Lorde Chauncellour of England, wrytten by him in the Englysh tonge* (London: John Cawod, John Waly and Richard Tottell, 1557), 1428–30.

acquired the idea that More is appealing to a 'free conscience', it is not at all synonymous with the modern definition of 'freedom of conscience' as in Article 18 of the United Nations *Universal Declaration of Human Rights*.[11] Here we may begin to posit that More uses 'conscience' in more than one way, that he understands more than one meaning by it.[12] More describes his indictment as 'directly repugnant to the lawes of God and his holye Churche' and that 'no temporall Prince' may claim this power over him.[13] Yet conscience in these terms is not an arbitrary act of will, it is an inference drawn from an independently verifiable system of reasoning. The authority of the law is not questioned by reference to a solipsistic intuition of disagreement, but by reference to an alternative and superior form of authority. The law of the land is subject to 'the lawes of God and his holye Churche', before which it must always withdraw. In this sense, the law of the land is not absolutely binding: not because conscience represents a higher value, but because conscience in this case follows a higher value, making the secular law in this case 'insufficient to charge any christian man' (p. 193).

Rather than proclaim the autonomy of his conscience as an independent source of inviolable integrity, More provides as 'proufe' of his position its conformity with the larger part of Christendom. Whereas Lord Chancellor Audley presents him at the trial as a lone voice of stubborn defiance against the general view of the bishops, the universities, and all the learned men of England, More replies that it is the English view that is in the isolated minority. If he joins the voice of the dead to the living, the numbers are all the more on More's side:

> But if I should speake of those that are already deade, of whom many be nowe holy Saintes in heauen, I am very sure it is the farre greater part of them that, all the while they liued, thought in this case that way that I thinke nowe; and therefore am I not bounden, my Lorde, to conforme my conscience to the Councell of one Realme against the generall Councell of Christendome. (pp. 195–6)

He is bound to follow his conscience not because his conscience, willy-nilly, outweighs the views of all others, but because, after all, his conscience brings with it the authority of an overwhelming burden of other,

---

[11] Office of the United Nations High Commissioner for Human Rights (1993-07-30). <http://www.unhchr.ch/tbs/doc.nsf/0/9a30112c27d1167cc12563ed004d8f15?Opendocu ment>, accessed 11 February 2008.

[12] C. S. Lewis, *Studies in Words*, 2nd edn. (Cambridge: Cambridge University Press, 1967), 202: 'We should all agree it was for *conscience'* sake that Sir Thomas More refused to take the Oath of Supremacy. But in how many different senses?'

[13] Harpsfield, *Life*, 193; based on Roper, *Life*, 92.

like, opinion. More, at this point, is less like Bolt's 'hero of the self' (what matters is 'that *I* believe it') than an advocate of demographic calculus.

SCHOLASTICISM & SYNDERESIS

So far, we might wish to go so far as to say that far from being radically modern, More's understanding of conscience is carefully orthodox and conservative. 'Conscience' is not some early modern neologism, arising out of the pressure of Reformation controversy to confront the complexity of modern political consciousness, as in the fashionable cliché. Conscience was a staple topic in scholastic theology. It was discussed in Peter Lombard's Sentences, and from there found its way into standard commentaries and university syllabuses. There are elaborate treatments in Bonaventure and in Aquinas. The Latin word *conscientia* derives not from theological or scriptural sources in Hebrew but is a literal translation of a Greek legal term: συνείδησις.[14] Literally this means knowledge 'with someone', that is 'knowledge about someone', something that can be used to witness for or against that person.[15] Since in areas of public knowledge this would be largely redundant, the word usually implies access to privy secrets, something I know about you which is unknown to others and so can be used in evidence.

The modern sense of 'conscience' clearly derives from a process that philosophers of language call 'reflexivization': being privy to one's own secret.[16] This idea seems to be unknown in classical Greek, for example in Aristotle, indeed it might have struck Aristotle as rather odd: how can I *not* know the things that only I know, furthermore how could I *not* know *that* I know them. If now via Freud we sometimes find it hard to think of things about ourselves that we *do* know that we know (certainly things that it is worth knowing), it is worth remembering how counter-intuitive the early conceptualization of conscience may have felt. The origins, in relation to a theory of modern political conscience, are certainly obscure. Peter Lombard first began thinking about conscience in a quite different sphere from what we might expect, that is, as a solution to a problem of the human will (*voluntas*) in relation to original sin. He was puzzled by a famously intractable, indeed wildly paradoxical, phrase

[14] Timothy C. Potts, *Conscience in Medieval Philosophy* (Cambridge: Cambridge University Press, 1980), 2.

[15] Lewis, *Studies in Words*, 181–2 ('Conscience and Conscious').

[16] Potts, *Conscience in Medieval Philosophy*, 3.

of St Paul in Romans 7: 'non enim quod volo bonum hoc facio sed quod nolo malum hoc ago' ('For I do not do what I want, but do what I do not want').[17] Does this mean that I can want in two different and contradictory ways at once, or that I can want and not want *the same thing* at the same time, that I might have two different kinds of will? The Sentences discuss various options, one of which interests us here. Peter makes use of an incidental detail in Jerome's *Commentary on Ezekiel*. Even though mankind is made in sin, there is always a spark (*scintilla*) of reason left in us, which could not be extinguished even in Cain, which always wants what is good and hates what is bad.[18] A man doing something that is wrong, and wanting to do it, thus always has inside him a little flash of conscience, a little bit of him which does not want to do it after all.

From such small sparks great matters are born. This passage in the Sentences was highly influential, perhaps especially because it also provided a solution to a problem in the theology of grace. If God has made us in sin, how do we ever wish for the good, and how can we ever do good, how can we ever come into grace?[19] The answer is that, whereas we are subject to an overwhelming desire for and attraction towards sin, and before grace are always ruled by sin even through our own choice, when grace comes this subjection is destroyed and the other instinct, the spark of conscience, is freed and helped by grace actively to desire the good.

When later writers returned to Jerome to find help, they found there a discussion of a highly complex passage in Plato's *Republic* which distinguished between different parts of the soul in order to explain contrary rational and appetitive impulses.[20] In the thirteenth century it became commonplace to divide conscience into two different processes: *synderesis* and *conscientia*. *Synderesis* was used for the spark of conscience itself; *conscientia* was a secondary, higher and more complex rational process. In Thomas Aquinas, *synderesis* is a natural, innate disposition to understand ethical premises. Just as by hearing or by sight aural or visual perceptions strike us without us having to do anything, so *synderesis* enables us to be struck by the truth of ethical principles without thinking about it. Strictly speaking, indeed, *synderesis* can

---

[17] *Sententiae in IV libris distinctae*, ii. dist. 39 c. 3; Bonaventuran edn., 2 vols. in 3 parts (Rome: Collegii S. Bonaventurae, 1971), i/2. 556. A translation is given in Potts, *Conscience in Medieval Philosophy*, 93.

[18] Jerome, *Commentary on Ezekiel*, 1.7; *Patrologia Latina*, 25.22; *Corpus Christianorum Series Latina*, 75.12.

[19] *Sententiae*, ii. dist. 39 c. 3; Bonaventuran edn., i/2. 556.

[20] *Republic*, iv (435A–441C and 580D–583A); ed. and trans. Paul Shorey, Loeb Classical Library, 2 vols. (London: Heinemann, 1963), i. 374–404 and ii. 370–80.

never be mistaken: not because the disposition is itself perfect, but because the truth is always true.[21] Similarly, *synderesis* itself cannot be extinguished because it is constitutive of rationality. The ability to formulate necessary (a priori) thoughts is fundamental to the possibility of reason.[22]

Nevertheless, of course, it is possible for a person to make bad judgements and to do wrong things. This is where *conscientia* comes in. For *conscientia* is not the spark of conscience itself, it is a reasoning process on the basis of this spark. It is perfectly possible that a person will make a false reasoning in this case: that is what happens with heretics, for instance. Thus while a mistake cannot be made by *synderesis*, Thomas says that it can by *conscientia*.[23] If someone (as it were) builds a false conclusion upon a *synderesis*, and feels this as her *conscientia*, she will experience this as binding, and not be able to do otherwise; which does not mean that she is right to do so. For, with better education, she will see that her *conscientia* is out of line with her *synderesis*—which of course is infallible. So rather than encouraging such a person to act in accordance with her conscience (which, indeed, she will do, necessarily, whatever we do) we should disabuse her of the false premiss or induction which has led her to mistake her true conscience.

Yet by this stage *synderesis* was a concept of some complexity. Whereas Aquinas carefully limited the idea to a habit of the intellect, Bonaventure argued that it was a habit of the natural will.[24] This indeed better explained its occurrence in Lombard's *Sentences*, but it also led to new and difficult questions: was *synderesis* innate or acquired, was it inextinguishable, what was its relation to conscience and to natural law? It also enabled *synderesis* to become part of a rather different tradition in mystical writing, where it is praised as the summit of the human soul, a connection with the divine, described through a variety of extravagant metaphors.[25] In fourteenth-century theology, this mystical strain results in a heady mix of ideas. Jean Gerson in *De theologica mystica* calls it 'an appetitive power of the soul' and 'a virginal part of the soul, or a natural stimulus to good, or the apex of the mind'.[26]

---

[21] Aquinas, *De veritate*, 16.2.
[22] Potts, *Conscience in Medieval Philosophy*, 49.
[23] Aquinas, *De veritate*, 17.2.
[24] Robert A. Greene, 'Instinct of Nature: Natural Law, Synderesis, and the Moral Sense', *Journal of the History of Ideas*, 58 (1997), 186.
[25] Greene, 'Instinct of Nature', 188.
[26] Steven E. Ozment, *Homo Spiritualis* (Leiden: E. J. Brill, 1969), 62; also cited in Robert A. Greene, 'Synderesis, the Spark of Conscience, in the English Renaissance', *Journal of the History of Ideas*, 52 (1991), 195–219 (200).

SPIRITUAL VERSUS TEMPORAL

This is the background against which historians understand More's insistence at his trial that in following his conscience he is following a principle of truth, the truth of the church. *Synderesis* acts, as it were, as a guarantee of truth. The assumption in Kenny and O'Connell is that More kept this view consistently throughout the early 1530s, as More carried out his own investigations into the consciences of his religious enemies, and then as the political tide changed, through his trial and personal agony. This is also the view of Josef Ratzinger, now Benedict XVI, erstwhile Prefect of the Office of the Congregation for the Doctrine of the Faith. In a 1991 essay on 'Conscience and Truth' presented to the bishops in Texas, Ratzinger states a classic problem with the modern liberal view of conscience. What if someone follows his conscience to commit a terrible evil? Is there no limit to conscience? It is not difficult to imagine Ratzinger's reply to this rhetorical question. He asserts that the modern doctrine of the autonomy of subjectivity enshrined in the inviolability of conscience brings not liberation but enslavement. He reassesses the possibility of an alternative doctrine of conscience which allows for its conformity to a principle of authority and truth. He revisits and reaffirms the scholastic distinction between *synderesis* and *conscientia*, and Aquinas's particular version of epistemology and ontology. And in the process he cites the example of Thomas More, with these stinging words of eulogy: 'for whom conscience was not at all an expression of subjective stubbornness or obstinate heroism'.[27]

Ratzinger is perhaps guilty here of a theologian's instinct that everybody thinks in a theological way. Intellectual historians can be guilty, too, of fitting a concept into a hermetically sealed philosophical tradition. However, 'conscience' reaches into many areas of human discourse. My aim in the remainder of this chapter is to try to understand some of the complexity of the word in the sixteenth century, to consider how many different contexts for the word (including theological) were colliding in new ways in the wake of the Reformation, and to ask whether such changes are reflected in More's own usage. How far, we could begin by asking, is the scholastic background on *synderesis* the right context for understanding More on conscience? The word is found in Britain in

---

[27] 'Conscience and Truth', Presented at the 10th Workshop for the American Bishops, Dallas, Texas (February 1991), section 2; published in pamphlet form as *Conscience and Truth* (Braintree, Mass.: Pope John XXIII Medical-Moral Research and Education Center, 1991). See also Ratzinger's earlier essay, 'Conscience in its Age', collected in *Church, Ecumenism and Politics* (New York: Crossroads, 1987), 165–79.

insular Latin sources. In French, the fourteenth-century poet Guillaume de Deguileville allegorized it as a disembodied creature with a human head. 'Synderesis' assists Satan in haranguing the human soul after death, using the submerged Old Testament metaphor of the biting (the 're-morse') of conscience.[28] From here, 'sinderesis' begins to appear in the English language in the late fourteenth century, for instance in a religious allegory of 1390 entitled *The Abbey of the Holy Ghost*.[29] The fifteenth-century monk and poet, John Lydgate, translated de Deguileville on more than one occasion; at one point he adds a gloss to explain the inkhorn term *synderesis*: it is the higher part of reason, by which 'A man shal best discerne | His conscience to governe'.[30]

The scholastic sense is certainly preserved in sixteenth-century Eng-land. Sir Thomas Eliot, in *Bibliotheca*, his Latin–English dictionary of 1538, defined 'Synteresis' as 'the pure parte of conscience'.[31] There is thus a theological and a moral background to thinking about 'conscience' available to More. But more directly relevant to his mind, something not properly acknowledged in Kenny and O'Connell in their treatment of conscience in More, is the context of law. A source which was certainly known to More was Christopher St German's *Doctor and Student*. A first edition of the First Dialogue may have existed as early as 1523 and a copy is extant from 1528.[32] It was immensely popular: twenty-one editions of the First and Second Dialogues were printed before 1600; it was first translated into English in 1530. St German published his writing anony-mously. While his authorship of *Doctor and Student* was an open secret, later works such as *The Division between the spirytualitie and temporaltie* of 1532 were more carefully concealed.[33] These later treatises were rigorously confuted by More in works such as the *Apology* of 1532, just before his own crisis hit him. It is obvious why these works concerned More: they constituted an attack on the primacy of canon law and an assertion of the supremacy of parliamentary power. As such, More's polemic was a premon-ition of the arguments he was to need himself in 1534. On the other

---

[28] Greene, 'Synderesis, the Spark of Conscience', 202.

[29] Later printed in *The Abbaye of the holy ghost* (London, 1497), A2ᵛ. The *Middle English Dictionary* gives two other references to 1400–25.

[30] *The Pilgrimage of the Life of Man, Englisht by John Lydgate, from the French of Guil-laume de Deguileville*, ed. F. J. Furnivall and Katherine B. Locock, 2 vols. (London: Early English Text Society, 1899), i. 130.

[31] *Bibliotheca Eliotae Eliotis librarie* (London: Thomas Berthelet, 1542), n.p.

[32] The complex printing history of *Doctor and Student* is described by T. F. L. Plunkett and J. L. Barton in the Introduction to their edition of the work, Selden Society, no. 91 (London, 1974), pp. xiv and lxix–lxxvi.

[33] J. B. Trapp, 'Introduction' to *The Apology, Complete Works of Thomas More*, 15 vols. (New Haven: Yale University Press, 1963–97), ix, p. xlvii.

hand, St German's legal challenges were just the kind of ammunition sought by Thomas Cromwell, who may have had some hand in promoting them.

More never identified St German as his authorial opponent, and he may not have known that the *Division* and *Doctor and Student* were by the same hand. He could have seen where *Doctor and Student* was heading in this regard; but he would also have seen, fine legal counsel that he was, that this was a legal classic in the making.[34] St German was a senior contemporary and a professional colleague, and *Doctor and Student* was a lifelong synthesis of complex ideas. The book stood on the cusp of profound legal developments, some of which More objected to but many of which he was part of. At the same time, St German was careful at this stage not to antagonize on all fronts, for instance he defended the punishment of heretics. Above all, the significance of *Doctor and Student* was the emphasis it gave to a definition of equity. Legal historians regard this as of crucial importance, ensuring 'that the strictly medieval conception of equity had a longer life in England than in any other country in Europe'.[35] The key term for St German in developing an idea of equity is the legal concept of 'conscience'. 'Conscience' was the guiding light in the English law court charged with reflecting the interests of justice or equity against the strict letter of the law.[36] That court was the court of Chancery, which was accused by common lawyers at this time of aggregating to itself ever more intrusive powers of interpretation.[37] St German was the progressive intellectual notorious for defending these new powers; and the Lord Chancellor who had been appointed in 1529 was, of course, Sir Thomas More. As a common lawyer himself (the first to be appointed to lead the Chancery for centuries) More was expected by some to defend the common law; but More turned out, in this respect, to be a friend of the new order.[38] This context thus brings us into the heart of More's involvement in the idea of 'conscience'. It also shows us how the word was already prone to new pressures and new meanings on the eve of the Henrician crisis.

---

[34] Trapp, 'Introduction', l.

[35] William Holdsworth, *A History of English Law*, 17 vols. (London: Methuen, 1903–72), iv. 279.

[36] Timothy S. Haskett, 'Conscience, Justice and Authority in the Late-Medieval English Court of Chancery', in Anthony Musson (ed.), *Expectations of the Law in the Middle Ages* (Woodbridge: Boydell, 2001), 158.

[37] The steady rise in the work of Chancery began in the fifteenth century and was increased under Wolsey. See J. A. Guy, *The Public Career of Sir Thomas More* (Brighton: Harvester Press, 1980), 37–8.

[38] Guy, *Public Career*, 42.

Doctor and Student is a paradoxical work in that while it was regarded as radical in its day and had radical effects, its arguments were based on medieval principles which were beginning to look old-fashioned. Part of this is what has been called 'the first and last serious and sustained subscription to the theory of synderesis in English'.[39] St German defined it as follows:

> Sinderesis is a naturall power of the soule | & is euer in the hyghest parte therof | mouynge and sterrynge it to good | and abhorrynge euyll. And therfore sinderesis neuer synneth nor erryth. And this sinderesis our Lorde put in man to the intent that the ordre of thynges shuld be obseruyd.[40]

St German has researched his topic in Aquinas and Gerson, and quotes and paraphrases from them liberally; in the process he reaches back to the prose of Jerome, in saying that *synderesis* 'maye not hollye be extyncted neyther in man ne yet in dampned soules' (fo. xxiii*v*).[41] Nonetheless, in words that are highly significant for More, he argues that *synderesis* is not quite inextinguishable. It can be:

> lette for a tyme eyther thorughe the darkenesse of ygnoraunce | or for vndyscrete delectacion | or for the hardnes of obstynacye | fyrste by the darkenes of ygnoraunce sinderesis maye be lette that it shall not murmure agaynst euyll bycause he byleuyth euyll to be good | as it is in herytykes the which when they dye for the wykednes of theyr errour byleue that they dye for the verye trouth of the fayth. (fo. xxiii*v*)

This is a crucial qualification, since it militates against the ambiguity of what is to come. A law based on *synderesis* could be hard and fast, watching out only for manifest error. 'Conscience', on the other hand, 'may somtyme erre and somtyme not erre' (fo. xxv*r*). Law has to adjust accordingly. It has to choose between good and bad conscience: 'the moste parfyte knowlege of any lawe...foloweth the most perfyte the most pure and the moste beste conscyence' (fo. xxvi*v*). *Synderesis* deals with 'vnyuersall principle that neuer erryth', but conscience has to make the best of it as it can, for it is possible to err in good conscience. St German concludes on an optimistic but uncertain note:

> Therefore I pray the that thou wylt alwayes have a good conscyence & if thou haue so | thou shalt alwayes be mery | & if thyn owne herte reproue the not thou shalt alwayes haue inwarde peace. (fo. xxvii*v*)

---

[39] Greene, 'Synderesis, the Spark of Conscience', 208.

[40] *Hereafter foloweth a dyaloge in Englysshe, bytwyxt a Doctour of Dyuynyte, and a student in the lawes of Englande of the groundes of the sayd lawes and of conscyence* (London?: Robert Wyer, [1530?]), fo. xxiii*v*.

[41] Greene, 'Synderesis, the Spark of Conscience', 207–8.

If the prayer is unsuccessful, however, we have to trust instead to the capacity of the law to relent from the hard letter of the law which *synderesis* would require, and to make due allowance for the vagaries of conscience. It is this principle which he calls 'Equytye', a principle which he says 'is temperyd with the swetnes of mercye' (fo. xxviiiⁱ). Conscience is thus claimed in St German as a term of adjustment, of flexibility in relation to the individual case. The reasoning process related to is intrinsically prudential and circumstantial. This is at some variance with the scholastic tradition in theology which reserves to conscience a priori powers of discrimination between truth and falsehood.

CONSCIENCE & THE REFORMATION

It is clear now that the idea of 'conscience' was undergoing some struggle in the 1520s in the law. In the meantime, new instincts about conscience were stirring within theology. Indeed, among the Protestant reformers in Germany, things were moving very quickly. Martin Luther, as often, is poised between old and new worlds. As a lecturer on the Sentences, he knew the scholastic context of conscience well, much better than More.[42] An avid reader of Gerson, he allowed for *synderesis* in his early work, but by the time of the Theses of 1517, he had moved on.[43] Perhaps Luther saw intuitively a problem of conscience in relation to grace. Peter Lombard discussed two different views on this; one that he accepts, which says that the 'spark of conscience' is like a preparation for grace, so that when grace comes it has something to work on. The other view holds that there is only one will, which defected by sin turns out only to want what is evil, until grace comes. By 1517 Luther had rejected the idea of a 'spark' (*scintilla*) of goodness left in man. After 1519, the word *synderesis* makes no further appearance in his work.[44]

At the same time, however, Luther was forced to do some new thinking on the legal and moral ramifications of conscience. With that creative energy that is characteristic of his early years, he applies the word with scholarly familiarity mixed with disruptive theological imagination. In 1521 Luther, already excommunicated by Papal Bull, faced a secular ban

---

[42] The fullest discussion of Luther's lectures on the Sentences in Erfurt in 1509 remains Paul Vignaux, *Luther, commentateur des Sentences* (Paris: Vrin, 1935), especially Part One, 'En lisant Pierre Lombard', 5–44.

[43] See Michael G. Baylor, *Action and Person: Conscience in Late Scholasticism and the Young Luther* (Leiden: E. J. Brill, 1977), 119–56.

[44] Baylor, *Action and Person*, 173–208 ('The Disappearance of the *Synteresis*').

throughout the empire: he was just as much at risk of losing his life as More in 1534. In a personal letter to Emperor Charles V, written in his own hand, he concluded: 'As long as my conscience is captive to the Holy Scriptures, which have furnished evidence for all my books, I cannot recant if I am not proven wrong'.[45] Here he appears to break the chain which in Aquinas links conscience to an argument in ethics, about how ethical commands are apprehended in the brain. Perhaps he is influenced here by the later scholastic tradition, which in Gerson calls *synderesis* the *recta ratio* or *superior pars rationis*.[46] With alarming ingenuity, Luther makes a link between conscience and intellectual affirmation, with the mental function which registers assent to something. Commenting on Psalm 4: 6 in 1518, he explicitly disavows *synderesis* as a moral guide and asserts instead: 'faith is the first principle of all good works'.[47] Conscience becomes associated with faith, with identity, rather than with ethics and behavioural psychology.

Assent, of course, can be given to many things: in Luther's case, he gives it to what he believes to be in scripture, rather than to the authority of the Pope. Heiko Oberman argues carefully that Luther's apocryphal statement at the Diet of Worms, 'Here I stand, I can no other', is not an assertion of freedom of conscience—rather as Kenny does of More.[48] Oberman is perfectly correct that in Luther conscience is neither neutral nor autonomous. Yet Luther has gone a long way there. He has made conscience a matter of a person's fundamental beliefs—what defines her as a person—and he has directly questioned the right of any outside authority (ecclesiastical or secular) to compel those beliefs. Perhaps, however, here as elsewhere, ideas are moving so quickly that Luther is not keeping pace with developments in an equal balance. In some places he gets ahead of himself; in others he reins himself back. It would not be surprising if we found similarly inconsistent responses in England, perhaps even in More.

For this is a completely different context for conscience than anything in Aquinas. This only goes to highlight two questions, which caused Aquinas great difficulty, and which despite much care he failed to resolve. One is whether a mistaken conscience is binding; and the other is whether conscience can be a mitigating factor in law. This is the background against which we can see St German's principles of equity developing. Yet

[45] *D. Martin Luthers Werke, kritische Gesamtausgabe: Briefwechsel*, 18 vols. (Weimar: Böhlau, 1930–85) WA Br. 2.307–10.
[46] Greene, 'Synderesis, the Spark of Conscience', 200.
[47] Baylor, *Action and Person*, 177.
[48] Heiko A. Oberman, *Luther: Man Between God and the Devil* (New Haven: Yale University Press, 1989), 204.

while the law responded to new challenges in one way, in theology similar questions were just as contentious. Late scholasticism produced new forms of argument on these questions, but continued to assert the possibility of erroneous conscience. Luther himself before 1517 argued that it was not always right to follow conscience, since conscience could be weak and foolish.[49] The key question on this score in England after Luther's condemnation in 1521 was how to deal with heresy. St German himself, as we have seen, was keen to establish his orthodoxy on this point. More, meanwhile, was highly familiar with the response within the church. He knew well the earliest response to Luther in English in the *Sermon against the pernicious doctrine* in 1521, where John Fisher shows the scholastic view absolutely intact. Luther feels something in his conscience but he is wrong:

> these heretykes, all be it they had grete redynes in scryptures and were fell wytted men and depely resoned, and had also pretens of vertuous lyfe and had a grete zeele thynkyng in theyr conscyence that they were bounden to do asmoche as they dyd, yet were they disceyued.[50]

Conscience in Fisher is a faculty which can remind us of the truth that we have forgotten but it is not in itself a condition of truthfulness. Conscience indeed is volatile and unpredictable; he characteristically describes its symptoms as the 'frettynge and gnawynges' (p. 247) of a troubled mind. If a person is addicted to a false doctrine, however, his conscience is not a help but a hindrance, it reinforces his mistaken apprehension that he is in the right.

This presumably is the light in which Fisher saw a new language of conscience emerging in the work of English evangelicals such as William Tyndale, after Luther's example. The most extended treatment is in *The Obedience of a Christen Man* in 1528. Tyndale, in a passage that we may not find completely logical, is attempting to justify obedience to the king as temporal power while questioning obedience to the Pope as spiritual power. Here Tyndale quotes an obvious scriptural authority, Romans 13, where Paul enjoins every soul to submit itself to the higher powers, what Tyndale coins, in a phrase that still has resonance, 'the powers that be'. God is the only true power, so 'the powers that be' *must be* ordained by God. Paul continues:

---

[49] Lectures on Romans (1515–16), *D. Martin Luthers Werke, kritische Gesamtausgabe*, 68 vols. (Weimar: Böhlau, 1883–1999) WA 56.499.10; see Baylor, *Action and Person*, 146–7.

[50] *English Works of John Fisher, Bishop of Rochester: Sermons and Other Writings, 1520–1535*, ed. Cecilia A. Hatt (Oxford: Oxford University Press, 2002), 95.

> Wherfore ye must neades obeye | not for feare of vengeaunce only: but also because of conscience.[51]

'Because of conscience' translates what in the Vulgate is *propter conscientiam*. The Greek word is συνειδήσις. A duty which is proper to the king and which is recommended by conscience does not apply to the Pope, however. The Pope, Tyndale says, 'has usurped the right of the emperor' (fo. xxxviiiᵛ), something which is in fact 'contrarie unto all conscience'. Tyndale returns specifically to Fisher's sermon against Luther and reverses its argument. Even if we fear to disobey the Pope on account of fear of vengeance, we must do so, 'because of conscience':

> First because of thine awne conscience. For though thou be able to resiste | yet shalt thou never have a good conscience | as longe as Gods worde | lawe and ordinaunce are agenste the. (fo. xiiʳ)

Second, he says, because of 'thy neibours conscience'. Even if we obtain licence ourselves, we will trouble the consciences of our neighbours, and where is the Christian love in that? What good conscience can there be in setting the conscience of one Christian against another?

It is in many ways a confused passage, and at some points it produces a very odd reading of Paul. Yet it nonetheless provokes a newly political register in the word 'conscience' itself. The Pope has broken into the temple of God, Tyndale says later, 'that is to saye | in to the herte and consciences of men' (fo. xxxixʳ). In particular, he has forced them to swear oaths, and thereby to 'forsware them selfes' against conscience. The issue of oaths, and particularly of *ex officio* oaths, was to transfix the question of religious and political allegiance for the next century and a half, and will be discussed fully in Chapter 4.[52] The procedure of the oath forces the question of what conscience is held to be, and what the limits of the law are in enquiring into it. In the next section of the *Obedience*, Tyndale argues passionately for such limits. Justice should show restraint, it should not 'breake vp in to the consciences of men | after the ensample of Antychristes disciples and compel them ether to forswere them selves by the allmightie God and by the holy Gospell' (fo. liiʳ). A man should not be forced to swear on the Gospel and thus to forswear himself; he should not be forced to testify against himself. The law has no business enquiring into men's souls. What a man believes is a private matter, a matter of secret conscience:

---

[51] Tyndale, *The obedience of a Christen man and how Christen rulers ought to governe* ([Antwerp: Maarten de Kaiser, 1528]), fo. xiiʳ.

[52] On the history of *ex officio* oaths, and More's attitude to them before and after his trial, see Chapter 4.

Let yᵗ which is secrete to God only | where of no profe can be made ner lawfull wittnesse broughte | abyde vnto the cominge of the lorde which shall open all secretes. (fo. lii^v)

In the *Answer to Sir Thomas More* in 1530, Tyndale applied a general argument to the swearing of oaths: 'Notwithstondinge | the trueth is | that no iudge ought to make a man swere agenst his wyll'.[53]

BEFORE THE LAW

More's reaction to such questions in the immediate aftermath of *Doctor and Student* was straightforward enough, in that his preoccupation in 1529 was with the conscience of Protestants. Whatever retrospective consternation defenders of More have felt, the apostle of freedom of conscience here follows St German in denying a legal defence of conscience to heretics. In Book III of *A Dialogue Concerning Heresies*, which deals at large with Tyndale's arguments in *Obedience*, More takes up the case of Thomas Bilney. A view is raised that Bilney was forced into an abjuration without first confessing to the fault. He has perhaps been compelled to act against conscience:

For yf they had forced hym thereto | they had in my mynde done hym playne and open wronge | because it might be yᵗ he sayd and sware true. And then shoulde they haue forced hym agaynst hys conscyence | to say of hym selfe vntrue. And that sholde they do not only clene agaynst ryght | but also wythout necessyte.[54]

At this point the Author turns the tables with an improvisatory mastery of his own. Bilney has denied his own part in heresy but his words belie him. It is simply not possible to take what he says as an accurate reflection of what in all conscience he thinks:

though he styll sware the contrary | must it not nedes be yᵗ in his denyenge in vertue of his othe | the thynges which they coulde not but byleue true | they must nedes therwith byleue hym all yᵗ whyle to lye & be periured? (vi. 277)

[53] *An Answere vnto Sir Thomas Mores Dialoge*, ed. Anne M. O'Donnell and Jared Wicks, *The Independent Works of William Tyndale*, iii (Washington, DC: Catholic University of America Press, 2000), 148; *An Answer to More*, ed. Henry Walter, Parker Society (Cambridge: Cambridge University Press, 1850), 147.

[54] *A Dialogue Concerning Heresies*, ed. Thomas Lawler, Germain March'Adour, and Richard Marius, *Complete Works of Thomas More*, 15 vols. (New Haven: Yale University Press, 1963–97), vi. 276.

Bilney's conscience (in More's clever parody of it) fails a test of truth: his *conscientia* is an inaccurate reflection of his *synderesis*; his conscience betrays him rather than vindicates him.

In More's view, indeed, the heretical version of conscience was a travesty of its proper function as a predicate of the truth conditions of God's revelation. The conscience of the heretic was the direct opposite, a guarantor of falsehood, a machine for lying. So at least it appeared in June 1529, when John Rastell printed the *Dialogue*. But by October More had become Lord Chancellor. Meanwhile, the ravages of heresy were getting worse: hot on the heels of Tyndale's *Obedience* came Simon Fish's *Supplication to the Beggars*. The wedge that St German was beginning to drive between temporal and spiritual authority in *Doctor and Student* was becoming an open wound in the *Division* and a host of other works that follow it such as *Salem and Bizance*. More felt compelled to answer what he considered to be a disastrous development. He was now fighting a literary war on all fronts—against Tyndale on scripture and the sacraments, against Fish on the clergy, against the *Division* in defence of canon law. At this point, as the stakes are raised, More refers to 'conscience' for the first time using the first person pronoun: 'for chargyng of myn owne conscyence'.[55] In all areas of his controversies, the word 'conscience' occurs with ever greater frequency as an index of the problems he is facing.

Yet if anything the word does not narrow but rather broadens in scope as a result of this controversial pressure. The precise analytic tool of *synderesis* is left behind. As More begins to wrestle with the politics of Cromwell's incipient reforms, indeed, it is not theology which he turns to—a factor which has perhaps led the analysis of More's conscience in Kenny or O'Connell or even Ratzinger a little astray. In any case they see too pure a line between Aquinas and More, forgetting the later scholastic developments of Gerson (or, in a perverted way, the very late scholastic Luther). Here we need to recall the day-to-day business life of More after 1529. He was in charge of the courts of Chancery and Star Chamber, and he pursued this role energetically. In the thirty-one months of his office, litigation in Chancery, already on a steep rise, reached a new height, hearing around 900 cases a year.[56] The largest proportion of these cases was, as before, property disputes, and the next largest commercial suits. The role of the Chancellor was to arbitrate in exceptional cases, to prevent an injustice that might occur through the strict application of the law, and to insist that obligations were carried out. He was able to do this because Chancery 'was a court of conscience, and respondents there

---

[55] *The debellacyon of Salem and Bizance* (London: William Rastell, 1533), fo. lxiv.
[56] Guy, *Public Career*, 50.

could be coerced into doing whatever conscience required'.[57] The prominence of conscience was unique to Chancery: it was the operation of justice in person, the person of the Chancellor, whose conscience deliberated right on a case-by-case basis. The language of conscience had developed in this specialized arena for centuries. To take a pair of more or less random fifteenth-century cases, a tenant in Farnham in Surrey, deprived of his house and livelihood, petitioned the court that this was 'a matere of conscience'.[58] In Southwark, the Commons disputed the right of 'vntrywe lyvers and people with owte consciens' to pursue their livelihood in the Stews.[59] More heard such suits on a daily basis. His practice, as summarized by John Guy, was scrupulously lacking in innovation and even cautious. He was no radical intellectual here: indeed his aim seems to have been to shore up the traditional authority of the Chancellor's 'judicial conscience'.[60]

By a curious irony, More's practice as a lawyer conformed more and more to the ideals set out in St German's *Doctor and Student*, even as he was about to be embroiled in confuting and debellating St German's more extreme treatises. Yet he was beginning to apply the principles of conscience and equity more widely than in the practical business of Chancery. He was doing so precisely in contradiction of St German's urge towards the separation of temporal and spiritual law, and the increasingly stark assertion of the primacy of a single, unified state apparatus of judicial authority. All of this was taking place as More saw with increasing clarity how his own conscience was being compromised by the matter of the king's determination to marry Anne Boleyn. In this process, the king, assisted by the bureaucratic genius of Cromwell, was siding inexorably with St German's new imagination of English law. On 15 May 1532 the English bishops surrendered their ancient liberties and delivered the *Submission of the Clergy* to the king.[61] The day afterwards, More met with the king in the garden of York Place and resigned his office.

It was another two years before More was imprisoned. To trace the vicissitudes of his personal crisis is a business that has consumed whole books. It is here that we can also see the conflict in the word 'conscience'

[57] J. H. Baker, *An Introduction to English Legal History*, 3rd edn. (London: Butterworths, 1990), 119.
[58] London, The National Archives, TNA SC1/44/12. After 1432. Letter of Henry Beaufort, Bishop of Winchester, to the Chancellor; transcribed in *An Anthology of Chancery English 1417–1455*, ed. John H. Fisher, Malcolm Richardson, and Jane L. Fisher (Knoxville, Tenn.: University of Tennessee Press, 1984), 157.
[59] London, The National Archives, TNA SC8/277/13830 Petition of Commons concerning the stews of Southwark; *Anthology of Chancery English*, 232.
[60] Guy, *Public Career*, 79.
[61] Richard Marius, *Thomas More* (London: Weidenfeld and Nicolson, 1993), 415.

coming to a head. Opinion on this matter has tended to divide between
identifying some inevitable move towards modernity—the birth of a distinctively liberal political consciousness—or else insisting on More's con-
servatism, his alignment with scholastic ethics. Yet it may be better to see
the situation as more mixed.

Perhaps it is possible to perceive a shift in the meaning of conscience
in the English language between the 1520s and the 1550s. If so, More
stands on both sides rather than on one, and this divergence of meaning
begins to infect More's lexis and praxis. If we return to the mixed idioms
of conscience noted in Harpsfield's life above, we find they have different lexical affiliations. The phrase 'the grudge of his conscience' relates
to More's anxiety that he sounds to the Commissioners like an old grouch,
nagging away at his own private concerns. This idiom is decidedly old-
fashioned, leaning back to the 'worm of conscience' that is a staple of
medieval allegorizing (Lydgate uses the word in translating de Deguileville).[62] St German, too, refers to the 'scruple or grudge of conscience' (fo.
xxiv[r]).[63] Pusillanimity is one of the seven causes St German lists of error
in conscience (fo. xxvi[r]). With an astonishing form of self-knowing wit,
More devotes a chapter to the problems of a pusillanimous conscience
in *A Dialogue of Comfort against Tribulation*, written with a piece of
charcoal in prison in 1534 but not printed until the Marian restoration.
In the *Dialogue*, an overburdened conscience is figured as a worrisome
teenager, 'a verye tymerous daughter, a sely wretched Gyrle and euer
puling, that is called scrupulosytie or a scrupulous conscience'.[64] Dancing on the wire, More creates a careful critique of the problem of conscience while risking a joke about his own notoriously fastidious tendency
to scrupulosity.

The phrase used against the appalling Rich and remembered by Roper,
meanwhile, 'the secretes of my conscience', has perhaps an even stranger
progeny and resonance. For here, More's disputes with evangelical writers
proved a prophetic commentary on *his* own trial a few years later. It may
even be that More's extraordinary powers of ventriloquism—his ability to
hear the words of his opponents and understand them or even internalize
them more fully than they did themselves—affects his own usage. For it is
Tyndale who explicitly and frequently refers to conscience as a secret
temple, or perhaps prison-house, a place where God alone can go and God

---

[62] Greene, 'Synderesis, the Spark of Conscience', 205.

[63] *OED*, GRUDGE, n. 2.

[64] *A dialoge of comfort against tribulacion* (London: Richard Tottell, 1553), H3[r]; *A Dialogue of Comfort against Tribulation*, ed. Leland Miles (Bloomington: Indiana University
Press, 1965), 91.

alone can know him. More turns this round to his own circumstances—not at all, of course, because he sees any affinity between Tyndale's conscience and his own—but because the word begins to channel a new kind of energy under the pressure of the appalling scrutiny applied by the Henrician Reformation, on both sides of the confessional fence. While this is not at all the same as saying that More changes his mind, it does not seem at all surprising to find More responding to this change.

Perhaps we could summarize this by seeing how More continues to concur with the widespread medieval social belief in the idea of conscience as the watchword of moral life, perhaps best expressed in the beautiful middle English phrase 'Aзenbite of Inwit', the 'prick of conscience', the natural resources of human remorsefulness. Yet he also recognizes the force of the theological argument that conscience can be wrong. In a similarly complex way he was capable of applying the principle of equity that in some circumstances a good judge may discriminate in the interest of justice against the application of the strict letter of the law, while also being aware of the scholastic argument that conscience is the guarantor of truth if rightly applied in sacred contexts of divine law. In the late 1520s he was actively committed to applying such principles with the strongest rigour of juridical power in the extermination of falsehoods which he felt were threatening the destruction of the fabric of society as well as the authority of the church. Yet in the 1530s he became equally conscious that such principles might be reapplied to the radical, we might say emergency view, that in extreme conditions an idea of personal and private conscience could be used to protect exactly these same ultimate truths against the intrusions of a newly empowered secular state.

In the topsy-turvy world of Tudor politics, this insight of More proved to have lasting value. As religion turned and turned again, it was this idea of 'the inwarde and secrete courte of conscience' which appealed to the Elizabethan recusant exiles, such as Robert Persons and Thomas Stapleton, as they struggled for means to oppose the equally intrusive regime of Henry's daughter.[65] Stapleton wrote a new life of More as part of *Tres Thomae*, his trio of Thomases, the apostle, the Canterbury martyr, and the Chelsea lawyer.[66] More's final agony is modelled on Christ, and More's trial is explicitly called his *passio*. It is also consciously directed at the English situation in the 1580s. More, like the Jesuits, is exposed to a 'bloody question'. Stapleton presents More as carefully delineating the limits of what

---

[65] The phrase comes from Stapleton, *A counterblast to M. Hornes vayne blaste against M. Fekenham* (Louvain: John Fowler, 1567), 444; see also Stefania Tutino, *Law and Conscience: Catholicism in Early Modern England, 1570–1625* (Aldershot: Ashgate, 2007), 17.

[66] *Tres Thomae* (Douai: Borgard, 1588).

the state can ask of him, and evincing his own loyalty in relation to those limits. Where More is exposed to question beyond those limits, he pleads silence, and asserts a sacrosanct seal of secret conscience around that silence. Persons, too, constructs an idea of religious conscience with all the theological and juridical learning he can muster. For a time he espoused a position of religious toleration. But there are limits: at no point does Persons allow 'conscience' to apply to Protestants. He is as far from modern liberalism in this respect as More.

Yet despite the necessary and salutary revisionism of historians in relation to Bolt's More, I want to suggest that the language and epistemology of conscience is ambiguated and etiolated in More himself. Formally no doubt he agreed with Giovanni Pietro Carafa, created Cardinal the year after More's death, and later Pope Paul IV: Catholics must flee from freedom of conscience as a viper in their midst. Liberty or freedom of conscience only becomes a common phrase after More's death, first in the Marian martyrs, then among the recusants in the 1560s and 1570s.[67] A formal response is different from one that is felt along the pulse, however. Only in the full complexity of his last trial and punishment did More come to understand the full complexity of the pressures that were now at work in his own time on the location and meaning of conscience.

The depth and emotion of his usage *de profundis* enters into a new phenomenological plane. For when compelled to swear his own oath, More somehow yearned for a moment of free declaration for himself:

> But sith standinge my conscience, I can in no wise doe it, and that for the instruction of my conscience in the matter, I haue not slightly loked, but by many yeres studied and aduisedly considered, and neuer could yet see nor heare that thing, nor I thinke I neuer shall, that could induce mine owne minde to thinke otherwise than I doe, I haue no maner remedie, but God hath geuen me to the straight, that either I must dedlie displease hym, or abide any worldly harme that he shall for mine other sinnes, vnder name of this thinge, suffer to fall vpon me.[68]

It is difficult not to detect in this a version of the Lutheran turn ('I...neuer could yet see nor heare that thing...that could induce mine owne minde to thinke otherwise than I doe'). It is possible also that here More, like

---

[67] The term 'fre conscience' appears in Tyndale, *A compendious introduccion, prologe or preface vn to the pistle off Paul to the Romayns* [Worms: P. Schoeffer, 1526], B5ʳ, and then in biblical translation (for instance in the Great Bible (1539), Isaiah 44). The phrase 'libertie of conscience' appears in Nicholas Ridley, *Certen godly, learned, and comfortable conferences, betwene...Rydley...Latymer during the tyme of their emprysonmentes* ([Strasbourg: heirs of W. Rihel], 1556), A3ʳ.

[68] *The Correspondence of Sir Thomas More*, ed. Elizabeth Frances Rogers (Princeton: Princeton University Press, 1947), 516.

Luther, begins the slow historical process of abandoning the distinction between *synderesis* and *conscientia*.

Something is happening here, which is difficult to trace using the ordinary methods of intellectual or literary history. It has something to do with the way that in a particular period—such as the Henrician Reformation—a conflux of forces, theological, legal, and political, makes a language even of great subtlety and longevity undergo unpredictable shifts of movement. It also has something to do with when a writer of great sensitivity is exposed to this language in a special way and becomes acutely conscious of it. The quotation here comes from perhaps the most beautiful of all More's late English writings, strictly speaking a letter from his daughter Margaret Roper to her step-sister Alice Alington. Composed as a dialogue between father and daughter, it has been compared by R. W. Chambers to Plato's *Crito*.[69] More's literary imagination is all over it; the editors of the 1557 edition of the *Workes* speculated that he was the true author, as is surely the case.[70] In Plato's dialogue Socrates in prison is offered the chance to escape his fate but chooses in the interests of justice to submit himself to the Athenian state. More in his dialogue in prison is offered the chance to swear and save his life, but also chooses the lonely path of justice and the good.[71] Socrates is told by Crito that all his friends are urging the other path; More by Margaret that his friends and all wise counsellors have already sworn and that he could properly follow them.[72] Socrates replies that it is better to follow the one voice of reason and right than the temptingly pliant voices of the many. More resists the words of others and listens to the one voice of his own conscience.

Alvaro de Silva has observed that More uses the word 'conscience' over a hundred times in the letters of the last year of his life.[73] The word is used forty-three times in this one letter, seven times in the first 100 lines. The repetition is a sign not only of its significance to More but also of a search to understand it. He is reckoning with profound problems of epistemology, of what it means to be certain of what he thinks. This reflects back on what he knows about what goes on in the minds of others, including his daughter in front of him. More acknowledges the good will of the many friends who have tried to dissuade him, even (with some irony) the many

---

[69] 'The Continuity of English Prose from Alfred to More and his School', Introduction to Harpsfield, *Life*, ed. Hitchcock, p. clxii.

[70] *The vvorkes of Sir Thomas More*, 1434.

[71] Plato, *Crito*, 45B–E; *Euthyphro, Apology, Crito, Phaedo, Phaedrus*, ed. and trans. H. N. Fowler, Loeb Classical Library (London: Heinemann, 1977), 156–8.

[72] Plato, *Crito*, 45D.

[73] *The Last Letters of Thomas More*, ed. Alvaro de Silva (Grand Rapids, Mich.: William B. Eerdmans, 2000), 'Introduction', 8.

counsellors of the king, such as Chancellor Audley and Secretary Cromwell. He praises their virtue and wisdom. Yet he also gives voice to a fascinating scepticism: 'And yet all be it that I suppose this to be true, yet beleue I not euen very surely, that euery man thinketh that so saieth' (p. 520). This reflects back on conscience itself; for do they (in all conscience) believe what they say, or even think what they think (for More does *not* say 'saieth' but 'thinketh'). This is a classic problem in the phenomenology of conscience: it sets up a distinction between what I know and what I know that I know, between what I think and what I think that I think, what I 'really' think.

Who knows what another person is thinking? In a brilliant moment, one that is exquisitely painful as well as moving, Margaret is reduced to confronting More's conscience with hers: 'Why should you refuse to swere, Father? for I haue sworne my self.' More can answer this for himself, but he refuses to answer for her. It is a moment of resonant ethical resistance. Repeatedly he says that he will not answer for the consciences of others; that he will not 'pynne my soule at a nother mans backe' (p. 521). These are words which Bolt emphatically noted. They are not quite true, perhaps: More had been pinning his soul at other men's backs for a few years. Even after poor Bilney went to the flames at the stake, More used the powers of the Star Chamber to examine the consciences of bystanders to discover the exact content of Bilney's conscience at the moment of his death.[74] Even in this dialogue More uses his genius for empathy to get inside the minds of others. Yet something has also changed.

In the newly pluralized world of the Henrician court, More is exposed to the fragile comparison between what goes on in his mind and what goes on in another. 'Conscience' is his answer: I know at least what I think. Yet even as he thinks this, he at least imagines what it would be like to think something else. In the privacy of a conversation with his daughter (although also aware that Cromwell would surely also be reading the letter) he imagines what it would be like to swear and to set himself free. Some of these things he has half been 'minded' to do. This is extraordinary existential territory. What does it mean to be 'minded' to do something which he nonetheless refuses to do? More has clearly imagined a number of different scenarios. Which of them has he in all conscience actually 'thought' as such? And which represents what 'in mine owne conscience' he really thinks (as opposed to thinks he thinks, or thinks that he does not think, or hopes that he thinks he does not think, or hopes that he thinks that he hopes he does not think)?

---

[74] Guy, *Public Career*, 167–71; see pp. 133–41, below.

At some point he has to put a stop to this. He has to return to some intuition, some premonition of who he really is when he is not imagining who he might be. Here at last he brings back in the argument of consensus. He thinks what the church has always thought, what the church in the rest of Europe thinks, what perhaps the bishops in England still think when Henry is not near them or at their backs. Yet More's conscience was responding to a world just a little more plural than the world he was born in. In his last letters he travels further than he ever has before, as far as the imagination could go within the limits of his own experience. Does this make him a liberal in the modern sense: hardly. Yet it perhaps makes him a little more modern in his thinking than the reaction among historians and theologians against Bolt's play has wanted him to be. More strove to hold on to the unity of truth he believed in. However, in recognizing this we should also recognize that More's conscience has become something more plural, doubtful, fragile. In a letter just after this to Nicholas Wilson, the king's chaplain and now the king's prisoner, More writes:

> Levyng every other man to there owne consyence my selff will with goode grace folowe myne. For ageynste myn own to swere were perell of my dampnacion and what myne awne shalbe to morowe my selff can not be suer and whether I shall haue fynally the grace to do accordyng to myne owne consyence or not hangythe in Goddys goodnes and not in myne.[75]

He does not know Wilson's mind any more than Wilson does. Wilson changed his mind at least twice, and eventually outlived the king by a year. More had the good grace to do differently. Yet More's conscience is not quite so knowable to others as it seems to be, to historians on both sides of the divide. In More's confrontation with the solipsism of his own decision, and in his earnest attempt to validate it all the same, we can also sense the cost of that decision, perhaps better realize its validity and significance.

---

[75] *Correspondence*, ed. Rogers, 532–3; first printed in *The vvorkes of Sir Thomas More*, 1447.

3

The Writer as Martyr
Cranmer & Foxe

Thomas Cranmer's burning on 21 March 1556 remains the primary martyrdom of the Church of England: the story of his last minute change of mind, and placing of his right hand in the fire to burn first, holds a lasting place in the public imagination. It is a complex gesture, suggestive both of the expression of identity and of his own agency in death as the author of his self. And yet it has very little of the power and resonance of the story of the death of Thomas More twenty years earlier. Diarmaid MacCulloch comments on the 'completely contrasting ways' in which Cranmer is portrayed to us 'as a hero or as a villain'.[1] In 1829, William Cobbett called him this 'cold-blooded, most perfidious man', yet the editors of Cobbett's own collection of *State Trials* said it was impossible not to find him 'sincere and honest'.[2] If anything, the case in recent reception may be worse: to supporters he is not quite a hero, to detractors he is a less than convincing villain. The question of sincerity is raised in stark form because Cranmer's resolution in standing up for a Protestant faith came only after previously recanting this faith; his final resolution perjures itself in a denial of a denial. Never is there a more visceral question of whether two negatives make a positive. If More's end is an emblem of modern conscience, Cranmer's is double-edged: putting his hand to the fire he renounced himself. It is an exemplary fable of lack of steadfastness. While More in the twentieth century achieved the height of his posthumous fame, hailed as a saint in the Catholic church and in the secular imagination as victim of totalitarian political persecution, Cranmer sank into a Gothic obscurity similar to his monument at St Giles in Oxford, a spire without a church, a public sculpture serving (for much of the public) as an over-sized traffic island.

---

[1] *Thomas Cranmer: A Life* (New Haven: Yale University Press, 1996), 1.
[2] William Cobbett, *A History of the Protestant Reformation in England and Ireland* (London: Burnes, Oates and Washbourne, 1925), para. 64; *State Trials* (1809), i. 852.

Doubts about Cranmer set in long before the clergy of the Church of England went irredeemably out of fashion. This is connected to the fluctuating reputation of the popular source of his life, John Foxe's *Actes and Monuments*, commonly known as the 'Book of Martyrs'. From its first appearance in 1563 this became one of the most extraordinary English books: 'far and away the largest work produced up to that time in England by a single printer'.[3] Produced in four substantially different states during the lifetime of Foxe and its printer John Day, *Actes and Monuments* enjoyed special status. Beyond its physical life, the book was endowed with a prophetic status from early times. Sir Francis Drake took it with him on board the *Golden Hind* and showed it to Spanish prisoners to demonstrate 'the imminent end of popery'.[4] In the seventeenth century, when the book was periodically reprinted, it fed the imagination of John Bunyan in creating a fictional identity for the English Protestant nation.[5] Although no new complete edition appeared after 1684, abridgements were produced plentifully, and Lynda Colley argues the book played a leading role in forging British national sentiment and identity in the eighteenth century.[6] John Tillotson, Archbishop of Canterbury from 1691 to 1694, regarded the Marian martyrs as one of the pillars of British history; the constantly renewed interest in Foxe through the nineteenth century reinforced this popular awareness.

However, it can hardly be said even in the heyday of such notions that Cranmer enjoyed untrammelled status as a national hero. In the ninth edition of the *Encyclopaedia Britannica* in 1875, his dying words and actions were dissected (as much as his general reputation) in all their messy detail. Two versions of his death are given, depending on whether Cranmer felt that his recantation would save his life. In either case his final repentance can be read in radically different ways. In one, 'he seems all but entitled to the crown of martyrdom'.[7] The alternative view, expressed by Lord Macaulay, was that he knew he would die anyway, and so 'a lie would therefore serve him as little as the truth': in this case

---

[3] Elizabeth Evenden and Thomas S. Freeman, *Religion and the Book in Early Modern England: The Making of John Foxe's 'Book of Martyrs'* (Cambridge: Cambridge University Press, 2011), 1.

[4] Patrick Collinson, 'Literature and the Church', in David Lowenstein and Janel Mueller (eds.), *The Cambridge History of Early Modern English Literature* (Cambridge: Cambridge University Press, 2002), 383–4.

[5] Thomas S. Freeman, 'A Library in Three Volumes: Foxe's "Book of Martyrs" in the Writings of John Bunyan', *Bunyan Studies*, 5 (1994), 48–57.

[6] *Britons: Forging the Nation, 1707–1837* (New Haven: Yale University Press, 1992), 25–8.

[7] 'Cranmer, Thomas', *Encyclopaedia Britannica*, 9th edn. (1875), <http://www.1902encyclopedia.com/C/CRA/thomas-cranmer.html>, accessed 30 September 2012.

Cranmer was no more a martyr than Dr Dodd, the Anglican clergyman who became the last man to be hanged at Tyburn for forgery. Neither view seems charitable: even Cranmer the martyr is only 'all but entitled' to his crown; whereas Macaulay's interpretation of history makes Cranmer a man scarcely able to tell the difference between truth and forgery, Whiggish without even the cover of politics.[8] Cranmer does not even know what he is standing for, still less whether he is making a stand.

In the later nineteenth century, Cranmer as political model became embroiled with the question of confessional identity. Foxe's book had ambivalent status here: his anti-Catholic bias made him the darling of evangelical opinion but also suspicious to the Tractarians. Cranmer could be appropriated either as a Reformer victim of Catholic tyranny; or as precursor of an Anglican middle way; or, in a Prayer Book sentiment, as the maker of English 'catholic' liturgy and religion; even, by a curious twist (as the author of the Canon of the Mass in the 1549 *Book of Common Prayer*), as a prototype for Anglo-Catholicism. Yet in any form, Cranmer is projected onto a resolutely theological background. Whereas More's agony has been translated from its origin in godly zeal as an icon for a secular age, Cranmer is abandoned in the swamp of the English Reformation. The Oxford Monument bears an inscription of anti-Catholic sentiment aimed as much against the Oxford Movement as it is against Roman Catholicism.[9] MacCulloch comments that to make up our minds about Cranmer is nothing less than to make up our minds about the English Reformation (p. 1).

SECULARIZATION & SINCERITY

There is an irony here. More, as we have seen, explicitly denied the ethic of personal conscience for which he became an icon. He argued for a truth outside himself, transcending his own values. Cranmer's gesture at the stake, on the other hand, speaks to a more modern moral stance both in its ambiguity about how to locate any final truth, and in its reliance, at the final reckoning, on discovering such a truth within. Charles Taylor has identified such a structure in the creation of what he names an 'ethics of authenticity'. This is what he calls 'the massive subjective turn of modern

---

[8] J. W. Burrow warns against seeing Macaulay as in any simple sense following a 'Whig interpretation' and calls it 'a sense of the privileged possession by Englishmen of their history'; *A Liberal Descent: Victorian Historians and the English Past* (Cambridge: Cambridge University Press, 1981), 93.

[9] The monument, designed by Sir George Gilbert Scott and completed in 1843, bears in its inscription the words: *who near this spot yielded their bodies to be burned, bearing witness to the sacred truths which they had affirmed and maintained against the errors of the Church of Rome.*

culture', which 'presents the issue of morality as that of our following a voice of nature within us'.[10] To discover 'authenticity' is a distinctive part of a modern quest for identity: 'Our moral salvation comes from recovering authentic moral contact with ourselves' (p. 27).

Cranmer's action gestures towards a move inwards to find truth, and yet also speaks across it. It is hardly the action of a man appealing to a notion of self-determining freedom, in the tradition of Jean-Jacques Rousseau. Cranmer goes to his death a Christian: his essential claim is not that he determines for himself his moral values, more that he must choose for himself what form of truth Christian value consists in. Outwardly, then—although this is not a claim Cranmer made for himself—Cranmer dies the death of a martyr. A martyr, by definition, dies as witness to something exterior to the self. And yet martyrdom is fundamentally an action that embodies truth claims.[11] These claims are objectively asserted and yet subjectively tested. Martyrdom, then, both in ancient and modern guises, anticipates and contradicts a moral theory of the self.

Martyrdom is crucial to the analysis of early modern selfhood, and challenges many modern assumptions about what selfhood is, especially any claim to autonomy or self-determination.[12] For 'martyrdom is not an assertion of the self through action, but rather a suffering act which refuses that assertion'.[13] The degree to which a history of early modern 'inwardness' is bound up with a history of martyrdom is contested, on similar lines. Susannah Monta writes of how conscience functions as 'a sort of epistemological trump card' in both Catholic and Protestant martyrologies.[14] These accounts suggest the martyrs themselves expected their onlookers to 'infer their inwardly held beliefs from their external performances' (p. 14). Other historical accounts of inwardness dispute the centrality of martyrdom, however. Maus believes the very clarity of confessional statement makes martyrdom narratives atypical of the epistemological uncertainty that surrounds early modern inwardness.[15]

---

[10] *The Ethics of Authenticity* (Cambridge, Mass.: Harvard University Press, 1992), 26–7.

[11] Brad S. Gregory, *Salvation at Stake: Christian Martyrdom in Early Modern Europe* (Cambridge, Mass.: Harvard University Press, 1999), 9.

[12] Among studies which question such a claim are: Kathleen Eisaman Maus, *Inwardness and Theater in the English Renaissance* (Chicago: University of Chicago Press, 1995); Victoria Kahn, *Wayward Contracts: The Crisis of Political Obligation in England, 1640–1674* (Princeton: Princeton University Press, 2004); and Julia Reinhard Lupton, *Citizen-Saints: Shakespeare and Political Theology* (Chicago: University of Chicago Press, 2005).

[13] Michael Jensen, *Martyrdom and Identity: The Self on Trial* (London: Continuum, 2010), 14.

[14] *Martyrdom and Literature in Early Modern England* (Cambridge: Cambridge University Press, 2005), 13.

[15] *Inwardness and Theater*, 18.

Authenticity is 'a child of the Romantic period', Taylor tells us.[16] While it derives from earlier versions of individualism such as in Descartes and Locke, it goes further: 'the inner voice... tells us what is the right thing to do' (p. 26). In that sense it appears to be another facet of the secularization thesis. Lionel Trilling called authenticity 'a more strenuous moral experience than "sincerity"', a concept the formation of which he attributed to the sixteenth century.[17] Both sincerity and authenticity form for Trilling a secular moral grail to replace religious certainty.

The word 'sincere' enters the English language in the reign of Henry VIII, a little later than French, deriving from the Latin, *sincerus*, meaning 'sound' (of materials), 'clear' (of liquids), 'pure' (of genetic race, or else literary style), or in a moral sense, 'lacking... corruption'.[18] Yet the word divides in English almost as soon as it is coined, between something that is 'genuine or pure' and something subtly different, defined by its opposite, what is 'not feigned or pretended'.[19] Purity is only achievable it seems by the avoidance of impurity. With a citational obliquity bordering on wit, the *Oxford English Dictionary* discovers both meanings within three years of each other, each time in Acts of Parliament in the immediate wake of the Act of Supremacy. Of one, we have the example of God's 'sincere' (or pure) doctrine: 'The syncere and pure doctrine of Goddes worde'.[20] For the other, we have the 'sincere' (or unfeigned) self-representation of God: 'Almightie god, the very author and fountaine of al true vnitie and sincer concorde'.[21]

Trilling finds the first motive of this latter 'sincerity' (if you like a show of being not insincere rather than a simple objective truthfulness) in social mobility and visibility:

> Society requires of us that we present ourselves as being sincere, and the most efficacious way of satisfying this demand is to see to it that we really are sincere, that we actually are what we want our community to know we are. (p. 10)

Yet examples from the *OED* suggest rather that the origins of the question of sincerity lie when church meets state. Of a person, 'Characterized by the absence of all dissimulation or pretence; honest, straightforward', the *OED* finds the first citable case to be in the writing of John Frith, arrested on a warrant for heresy by Sir Thomas More in 1533, the year before the

---

[16] *Ethics of Authenticity*, 25.
[17] *Sincerity and Authenticity* (London: Oxford University Press, 1972), 11.
[18] *Oxford Latin Dictionary*, SINCERUS, 1–4.
[19] *OED*, SINCERE, adj., 1a and 3.
[20] Act 27 Henry VIII (1536), c. 42 § 1.
[21] Act 31 Henry VIII (1539), c. 14.

Supremacy. Frith in his *Answer to Mores Letter* wrote that 'Master Wycleve was noted . . . to be a man . . . of a very syncere lyfe'. Thus does one accused of heresy justify the life and action of another. It is as if the Reformation brings the question newly into life, as heresy is redefined as orthodox and vice versa. Once again with wonderful acuity, the *OED* finds the first instance of 'sincerity' as a noun to mean 'Freedom from dissimulation or duplicity; honesty, straightforwardness', in a Pauline affirmation of faith, as translated in the Geneva Bible: 'But as of synceritie . . . speake we in Christ' (here directly quoting the Vulgate, *ex sinceritate*).[22]

This is like a Protestant badge of godliness, a mark of guarantee of truthfulness and faithfulness. The Christian is the person who speaks sincerely in Christ. A little later, in the King James Version, comes the *OED*'s first instance of sincerity as an equivalent to genuineness of feeling or emotion: 'To proove the sinceritie of your love' (2 Cor. 8: 8). Yet already the word contains a seed of doubt. Truth does not come to us unalloyed, but as 'freedom from dissimulation'. The sincere person is the one who does not sound insincere. Trilling articulates acutely the lurking danger:

> In short, we play the role of being ourselves, we sincerely act the part of the sincere person, with the result that a judgement may be passed upon our sincerity that it is not authentic. (p. 11)

Sincerity is, if you like, itself not pure. It quickly comes to mean the absence of pretence. In an extreme version, the Catholic polemicist Miles Huggarde argued that Protestants willingly embraced burning at the stake as a form of display: a perverse desire to draw attention to their own suffering.[23] Sincerity thus becomes a site of cultural concern on a wide scale. Shakespeare uses the word only in this new sense of fabricated authenticity. This echoes the problem of *oratio libera* or *parrhesia*, examined in Chapter 1 in relation to Montaigne. Frankness may be indistinguishable from the appearance or simulation of frankness. Is sincerity the opposite of dissimulation, or only a particularly successful form of it?

Sincerity requires authentification from within. Yet it is also a rhetorical stance that only acquires meaning in a performance seen by others. A fundamental issue here is the status of narrative itself. 'We cannot but strive to give our lives meaning and substance, and this means that we understand ourselves inescapably in narrative', Taylor has written.[24] The idea is disputed.[25] Narrative identity is not the only way of conceiving

---

[22] 2 Cor. 2: 17.
[23] *The displaying of the Protestantes, [and] sondry their practises, with a description of diuers their abuses of late frequented* (London: Robert Caly, 1556), sig. E7ʳ– F1ʳ.
[24] Taylor, *Sources of the Self*, 89.
[25] Galen Strawson, 'Against Narrativity', *Ratio*, 17 (2004), 428–52.

identity; more fundamentally, we could say that narrative is not itself a given. It presupposes a speaker:

> About whom and about what does one construct a narrative? Who is morally responsible for that?[26]

'There is no ethically neutral narrative', Paul Ricoeur concludes.[27] Could the narrative of Cranmer's death be placed within such a context of ambiguity? It is the argument of this chapter that in his distance from the archetypal figure of More, Cranmer's true significance is revealed. At the same time, the representation of his martyrdom reveals something else about narrativity. This is the peculiar symbolic methodology of John Foxe's 'Book of Martyrs'. In Foxe's book—for it is a mistake to see him as in any simple sense its author—there are competing presentations of the Christian martyr.[28] The cult of the venerated body of the saints crosses with the dissident punished for his ideology. In this, the narrative energy of the book plays out against the iconic status of its notoriously graphic and memorable woodcut images.

Central to this, I will argue, is a complex set of meanings surrounding the Greek root of the word 'martyr': this is the idea of 'witness'. The compilatory evidence of Foxe's sources both occludes the 'witness' of the suffering self, and reveals it in sharper relief. This creates a boundary line between inner and outer which complicates the modern understanding of an 'ethics of authenticity' and its origins. The problem of 'sincerity' is brought into sharp relief by Reformation controversies over belief and its self-representation, confusing a distinction between what is inside or outside the self. Indeed Taylor himself insists that it is only a trivial version of moral authenticity which characterizes it as self-created: 'Authenticity is not the enemy of demands that emanate from beyond the self; it supposes such demands' (p. 40).

Martyrdom also complicates a model of moral agency: Cranmer is both the agent of his narrative, and fundamentally not, since his life is brought into focus only by the examination of the trial which brings his death. This is complicated by the formal nature of Foxe's book. Cranmer, by definition, is not the author of his biography. However, throughout *Actes and Monuments*, Foxe self-consciously incorporated textual sources close to his subject in order to verify the authenticity of his account. For

---

[26] Paul Ricoeur, *Oneself as Another* (Chicago: University of Chicago Press, 1995), 19.
[27] *Oneself as Another*, 115.
[28] David Loades, 'Foxe in Theological Context', in *The Unabridged Acts and Monuments Online* or *TAMO* (HRI Online Publications, Sheffield, 2011). <http://www.johnfoxe.org>, accessed: 1 September 2012.

his first Latin history written in exile under Mary, Foxe was largely indebted to material supplied by Edmund Grindal, later Bishop of London and Archbishop of Canterbury. Grindal had collected the writings of Marian martyrs, including Cranmer's and Ridley's disputations at Oxford, and also a narrative of Cranmer's death.[29] For the English editions of his work, compiled under Elizabeth with the cooperation of church authorities, Foxe began to use sources from archives (such as episcopal registers in Norwich, London, and Coventry and Lichfield), as well as a wide variety of printed sources.[30] For the second edition this trawl through sources became obsessively voracious, often compiled by agents and friends. As well as archives, Foxe used personal testimonies and what we would now call life writing, memoirs, and 'autobiographies' of witnesses. Among these were the reminiscences of Ralph Morice, Cranmer's secretary. Morice at first supplied some of Cranmer's writings and a few snippets of anecdote; at Foxe's encouragement, Morice then drafted a full-scale memorial of Cranmer, taken over into Foxe's book.[31]

Foxe's life and death of Cranmer thus has a peculiar literary and generic character, incorporating the records of several legal trials (with verbatim reports of speeches and examinations) but also with various fragmentary kinds of biographical and autobiographical leavening. Cranmer's authorial agency is implied, even when he had no hand in the writing. Beyond this, his agency in a philosophical sense is endowed with enormous significance. For Foxe makes Cranmer's crisis of faith at the end of his life a distinctive kind of Christian story. In the process, Foxe rewrites the rules of medieval martyrdom. Cranmer is anything but steadfast or true to his mother Catholic church; but Foxe's Cranmer also stretches the rules of Calvinist election by being anything but certain of himself or his faith. In relation to this, it will emerge that the test both of authenticity and of agency is applied in its early modern emergence most pressingly in the idea of writing and of the self as writer. For within Foxe's book the figurative status of writing and reading is paradoxical. Protestant martyrology gives new prominence to the idea of the martyr as writer and reader. This is in some ways a very modern symptom of identity. Yet if we look to the Reformation to find the birth of the secular dissident, we see instead a more ambiguous historical figure.

---

[29] Grindal reports this in a letter to Foxe that is in BL Harley MS 417, fo. 113. See Evenden and Freeman, *Religion and the Book*, 90–1.

[30] Evenden and Freeman, *Religion and the Book*, 106–9.

[31] Morice's correspondence with Foxe is in BL Harley MS 416, fos. 183^r–184^r; his biography of Cranmer is Corpus Christi College, Cambridge, MS 128, fos. 405–40. See Evenden and Freeman, *Religion and the Book*, 146.

THE DEATH OF CRANMER: AMBIGUITY
& AUTHENTICITY

The death of Cranmer, like his life, is riddled with ambiguity: indeed, ambiguity is the whole point. The process against the doomed Archbishop drew itself out over nearly three years. At the death of Edward VI on 6 July 1553, Cranmer sided with Council in installing Queen Jane in preference to the late king's sister Mary, debarred from the throne because of Henry VIII's divorce from Katherine of Aragon. This brief flirtation as a Janeite—against his better instincts, Cranmer claimed—was crucial to the progress of his ruin.[32] It enabled the new government to accuse the Archbishop of treason in November 1553. He was thus already legally a dead man when, after the execution of Jane Grey in February 1554, proceedings began in April in Oxford against Cranmer for his religious policies, along with Nicholas Ridley, Bishop of London, and Hugh Latimer, Bishop of Worcester. There was still at this stage some awkwardness about a heresy examination involving Cranmer. Until England returned formally to papal obedience in November 1554, the queen was only able to initiate proceedings against him by virtue of her being (under existing statute) supreme governor of the church—something of a heavy irony.[33] Indeed, Cranmer, since he had been elevated to the Archbishopric by the Pope in 1532, retained his formal title until 1555.

Two years therefore passed, much of it spent either in prison in Oxford in the Bocardo, or under house arrest under the supervision of one of the town's bailiffs, before the formal trial against Cranmer began in the University church in Oxford on 12 September 1555.[34] During this interim the pressure on Cranmer steadily increased. The first burnings took place in February 1555. The three bishops were for the moment spared, in order that they be singled out for the most exemplary treatment. England's descent into heresy was to be pinned on them personally. Cranmer's trial in September lasted two days, at which point an eighty-day period intervened, summoning him formally (but not literally) to answer charges in Rome.[35] The trials of Ridley and Latimer followed in late September and early October. Both were ceremonially degraded from the priesthood, and then, on 16 October 1555, burned at the stake outside the city gates in front of Balliol College. Cranmer was in the middle of being interrogated;

---

[32] MacCulloch, *Cranmer*, 540–2.

[33] MacCulloch, *Cranmer*, 587–8.

[34] Lambeth Palace Library, MS 1136. There is a transcription in *Miscellaneous Writings and Letters of Thomas Cranmer*, ed. John Cox, Parker Society (Cambridge: Cambridge University Press, 1846), 541–62.

[35] Described in detail by MacCulloch, *Cranmer*, 574–8.

at a special moment he was brought to the window of the gatehouse to watch. The motivation was to intimidate him, a contemporary manuscript tract, *Cranmer's Recantatyons*, reports: Cranmer, it says, took off his cap, fell to his knees, and bewailed the fate of his friends.

At this point the policy against Cranmer shifted. He was moved from prison to be housed in Christ Church as the 'guest' of the Dean. While Cranmer initiated an appeal, invoking the idea of a General Council to hear his cause (like Luther a generation before), the authorities had another idea: they hoped to turn him. The story thus changes from examination to recantation, indeed this tortuous final denouement involves no fewer than six recantations, laid out with subdued relish in an official printed text, *All the submyssyons and recantations of Thomas Cranmer.*[36] A seventh, last and most dramatic, text recants all those that preceded it. In this last-minute equivocation—a wavering, a final change of mind in a whole sequence of such changes—Cranmer's great gesture of self-mutilation finds its meaning. In the process, equivocation takes on existential significance. Is recantation of past beliefs a proof of authenticity or its opposite? In one sense, by comparing one state of mind with another, it makes a case for renewed validation. In another, the very fact of undoing one state of the self, puts under question the new state. What status then does a recantation of a recantation possess?

Not surprisingly, Cranmer's opponents and executioners were quick to capitalize on this equivocation. The title of the Catholic tract, *Cranmer's Recantatyons*—in English, while the rest of the text is in Latin—plays with the way Cranmer had apparently turned tergiversation into a branch of dogmatic theology.[37] With a certain want of charity, its probable author, Nicholas Harpsfield, even claimed that the gesture with the hand was not brave at all, since it was about to get burned anyway. To drive the point home, the Spanish theologian Juan de Villagarcia, Cranmer's last confessor, is depicted as eliciting from Cranmer, even on the way to the stake, an admission that he might have changed his mind yet again if offered his life back.[38] Yet perhaps more surprisingly, the other main surviving source, Foxe's *Actes and Monuments*, written from an opposite confessional stance, makes little attempt to gloss over the problem of authenticity. While a vindication of Cranmer, it does not resolve the many ambiguities. Foxe

---

[36] *All the submyssyons and recantations of Thomas Cranmer, late Archbyshop of Canterburye: truely set forth both in Latyn and Englysh, agreable to the originalles, wrytten and subscribed with his owne hande* (London: John Cawood, 1556).

[37] 'Cranmers Recantacyons'; the original is in Paris, BNF, MS Lat. 6056, fo. 1. *Bishop Cranmer's Recantacyons*, ed. Richard Houghton with James Gairdner, Bibliographical and Historical Miscellanies, 15 (London: Philobiblon Society, 1854).

[38] *Cranmer's Recantacyons*, 107.

allows the reader to follow all the indecisions that precede the last decision. Cranmer's death is certainly heroic, unlike in Catholic treatments,
but it is heroic only in the full context of the tensions, uncertainties, du-
bieties, that surround it. It is in its way a thoroughly modern death.

Moreover, Foxe's narrative is not altogether a vindication of Cranmer
in the first place. Cranmer is an ambiguous figure for Foxe, too. Cranmer
is not a clear-cut hero in Foxe's version of the Reformation, and is sometimes even the villain. Foxe upbraids him as a tormentor and persecutor
of the faithful, such as John Lambert, executed as a sacramentarian in
1538, and treated by Foxe as a true martyr.[39] Foxe points out Cranmer
sent Lambert to his death for a position on the eucharist close to that
Cranmer himself was to adopt a few years later.[40] Cranmer here is executioner rather than victim. Pointedly, Foxe also includes the grim prophe-
cies made by Catholic traditionalists that Cranmer would get his
come-uppance in the end, and in the same terrifying manner.[41] Somewhat less expectedly, Foxe also blames Cranmer for his part in the death
of Joan Bocher, Joan of Kent, suspected anabaptist, who was condemned
for denying that Christ was incarnate of the Virgin Mary.[42]

Foxe's narrative redeems Cranmer at the end, whatever his views of
Cranmer's long and winding road through Henrician and Edwardian religion. Put most simply, Cranmer is on the right side. Brad Gregory has
shown that Foxe is not at all doctrinally fastidious about those he identifies as Protestant martyrs.[43] Unlike the earliest Protestant martyrdom narratives, which, in order to prove the truth of an alternative theology, stress
the connection between death and doctrine, Foxe is more eclectic. It is
enough to see who killed Cranmer: Augustine's epigram *causa non poena
martyrem facit* translates, not for the first time, as my enemy's enemy is
my friend. Like Crespin, the French Calvinist martyrologist, Foxe is prepared to overlook or sometimes suppress differences in the precise beliefs
of his martyrs. What matters is the example Cranmer provides of the
practice of faith even in the most harrowing circumstances. This may
seem an odd observation to make in view of the way his final recantation
comes close to demonstrating not steadfastness but vacillation, an image
of Cranmer as doubting or even dithering Thomas. Yet in this image of
recantation, Foxe constructs a provocative revision of the categories of

[39] The proceedings against Lambert are described in MacCulloch, *Cranmer*, 232–4.
[40] *Actes and Monuments of these latter and perrilous dayes* (London: Iohn Day, 1570); *The
Unabridged Acts and Monuments Online* (1570 edition), <http://www.johnfoxe.org>,
accessed 1 May 2012, p. 1322.
[41] *The Unabridged Acts and Monuments Online* (1570 edition), 1398.
[42] MacCulloch, *Cranmer*, 475.
[43] Gregory, *Salvation at Stake*, 186.

conscience and of consciousness, and their place in the ideology of martyrdom. This amounts to an ethics of authenticity, and a reformation of
the category of identity in relation to Christian faith and witness.

'Sincerity' is a structuring concept for Foxe and his book. The word
'sincere' is used increasingly through all the different editions of *Actes and
Monuments*, from 66 times in the 1563 edition to 144 in the 1583; a
striking number for such a new word.[44] In the last of the 1563 Prefaces,
on the 'utility' of his history, Foxe comments on how 'the sincere religion'
of the early church later gave way to 'superstition'.[45] In the 1570 Preface,
'the condition of the true Church of Christ' is contrasted with the domi-
nation of the rule of the Bishop of Rome, beginning with the reign of
Innocent III in 1215. It was then that 'the sincere faith of this English
Church, which held out so long, [began] to quayle'. Nevertheless, Foxe
declares on the same page, a remnant always 'shewed secret good affection
to sincere doctrine'.[46] 'Sincere' here means 'pure' and 'sound', as in the
doctrine of the true church; but elsewhere in the work, such faith is
equated with the interior condition of the person who holds this faith: 'a
marueilous and sincere zeale' (1570, p. 90). Truth claims are thus elided
between a set of assertions and the authenticity of the person feeling
them, who is described (typically) as 'a sincere worshipper of the Christian Religion' (1570, p. 128). Under Queen Mary, when the papacy tri-
umphs once again, the true church is therefore defined by 'the sincere
preachyng of Gods holy word' (1570, p. 1703). This is the church of the
'sincere' as opposed to the 'insincere'.

There is a slippage between adjective and noun such that it is not clear
whether doctrine is 'sincere' on the basis of its content or by means of the
identity of its holder. This is especially true because orthodoxy is now
contingent. One year a doctrine is heresy, the next, it is orthodoxy, and
then heresy again. Testimony comes in the fact that *nova doctrina* was
often a synonym for heresy.[47] Foxe's lexicon uses 'sincerity' as a test against
which mere orthodoxy is a passing phase. Yet at the same time it makes
'sincerity' dependent on the creditworthiness of the bearer. Thus John
Hooper, Bishop of Gloucester, burned in February 1555 in the first group

---

[44] Figures derived from searching *The Unabridged Acts and Monuments Online*.

[45] *Actes and Monuments of these latter and perrilous dayes* (London: Iohn Day, 1563); *The Unabridged Acts and Monuments Online* (1563 edition), <http://www.johnfoxe.org>, accessed 1 May 2012, p. 15.

[46] *The Ecclesiasticall history contaynyng the Actes and Monumentes of thynges passed in euery kynges tyme in this Realme, especially in the Church of England* (London: John Daye, 1570); *The Unabridged Acts and Monuments Online* (1570 edition), 4. Further references to this edition in text, citing year of edition and page number.

[47] Richard Rex, 'The New Learning', *The Journal of Ecclesiastical History*, 44 (1993), 26–44.

of Marian martyrs a month after the revival of the heresy laws, is quoted
in January at his examination as justifying himself 'For the which most
true and sincere doctrine, because I wyll not now accompt it falshood and
heresie, as many other men do' (1570, p. 1721). There is a subtle reworking here both in the meaning of martyrdom, and in the truth claims of
doctrine. By giving his life for doctrine, he comes 'to confirme it with my
bloud'. Rather than a mystical transformation of the body of the saint in
communion with his church, this is a guarantee of sincerity in belief.
Doctrine and sincerity are somehow coterminous. From this point in
Foxe's book, the adjective 'sincere' is increasingly applied to the Protestant
cause: 'sincere doctrine', 'sincere belief', 'sincere truth', 'sincere religion'
are virtually synonyms.

Significantly, Cranmer's 'sincerity' is never directly asserted in Foxe. Yet
the underlying signature of the narrative of his trial is 'what does he really
believe?' The word is once used in relation to Cranmer, but not of him
personally, rather of evidence used for and against him. Of one of his
Catholic witnesses, Foxe declares that he does not 'discharge the part of a
sincere and faythfull reporter' (1570, p. 2091); but Foxe nonetheless
chooses to report him. In this way the compilatory nature of *Actes and
Monuments*, which historians have treated as purely of documentary interest, becomes part of the forensic taxonomy of the work. Foxe's book
sifts between its witnesses in a visible weighing of the sincerity of one view
against another. It is part of his own sincerity as an author that he lends
voice to both sides, if not equally, then at least with some visible claim of
balance. The other side represses, but he honestly bares all. Simultaneously, he makes the status of one piece of writing against another part of
the truth claim of doctrine itself.

Cranmer's 'sincerity' comes to a head in the final, contradictory episodes of his life, the collective climax of his history of recantation: his
speech in the University church at the service preceding his execution,
and his appearance at the stake. For this, there are several surviving textual sources. It was printed in an official narrative published by John
Cawood as well as several years later in Foxe. There was thus a public
debate of authenticity. Nowadays, that test of authenticity has been
played out all over again, as the printed narratives are compared with a
variety of manuscript witnesses: *Cranmers Recantacyons*, in the Bibliothèque Nationale, two manuscripts in the British Library, and another in
Lambeth Palace Library. Historians, such as in MacCulloch's magisterial biography, use the sources to compare the veracity of the accounts.
MacCulloch comments on the remarkable degree to which the accounts
corroborate each other, considering how politically crucial the trial was.
Yet the issue of veracity also redoubles on the question of the textual

evidence, since the trial shows Christian truth to hang on the status of writing itself—in the sincerity of the witness called to martyrdom, and the integrity of the documents brought forward in evidence for and against his word.

In what follows, I will quote from Foxe and from other printed and manuscript sources, not in order to confirm the facts, but in order to lay out the pressure that is placed on writing as a medium of authenticity. All are dramatic in framework, using the process of a heresy trial to create a characteristic peripeteia, in which a theatre of humiliation makes battle with a theatre of triumph. Who is victor and who is victim is presented differently according to whether the source is Catholic or Protestant; but in all the accounts, one theatre plays against another, with 'sincerity' the question at issue.

The stage is set. At his last arraignment, Cranmer is made to listen to a sermon by the Provost of Eton, Henry Cole, outlining his crimes and justifying his punishment; he is then given the opportunity to speak some last words himself.[48] He takes out a piece of paper. The script has apparently been given prior approval: it is supposed to contain Cranmer's penitent confession of his heresy. At the last moment, it seems Cranmer substituted a second text for the text that had been agreed.[49] After Cole's arraignment, Cranmer begins with a prayer and confession in front of the people, almost word for word the same in different sources. Here it is in the Lambeth MS:

> Good chrystyan people my deare brethren and systern in Chryste | I beseache you most hartely to praye for me vnto all myghtye god, that he will forgeve all my synnes & offences, whiche be mayny wthoute nombre and greate aboue measure.[50]

This is a conventional act of penance in a heresy trial. Thus far Cranmer gives only one clue that the penance may yet be turned on its head: 'But yet one thinge grevethe my consyence | more then all the reste whereof godwyllynge I doo entende to speake more of heareafter.' Here was contained Cranmer's final ambiguity. It is a verbal play, which Cranmer now strings out for as long as possible. The trouble to his conscience on the surface is his obstinate fall into heresy. It turns out that below this surface he is concealing a deeper problem of conscience, in a final turn on the self. But this is kept for the moment in reserve.

[48] MacCulloch, *Cranmer*, 600–1.
[49] *Cranmer's Recantacyons*, 105.
[50] London, Lambeth Palace Library MS 3152, fo. 114^r. See Foxe, 1570, pp. 2103–4. Bonner's official version is in Cox, *Miscellaneous Writings and Letters of Thomas Cranmer*, 565–6.

It is not clear where Cranmer is going, but it suddenly becomes clear at least that he is facing an ultimate crisis of conscience:

> And nowe forasmoche as I am com to the last ende of my lyfe wherevppon hangethe all my lyfe passed & all my lyfe to come, eyther to lyve wth our savyor chryste forever in joye or ells to be in payne eyther wth wycked devylls in hell and I see before myne eyes presently heaven reddye to receyve me orelles hell reddye to swallowe me vppe.[51]

It is difficult to think of a parallel to this anywhere in the literature of martyrdom. He is poised at the end of his life, and tomorrow he may either be in heaven or in hell, he does not know which. A martyr conventionally strides to heaven with confidence. A controversialist threatens his opponents with hell. Hell is for other people. Instead, Cranmer stands on the fulcrum, his next step, his next fall, decisive.

It is an extraordinarily existential moment. The theological battleground of the Reformation suddenly narrows to the space of a single person's identity. Truth divides between two equal choices made by one man. The mediation of the church is here irrelevant. Cranmer has in fact at this stage been reconciled to the church and taken part in mass. But now he is alone, at the true moment of sincerity. This is expressed even more acutely in the Latin of Harpsfield: he stands before his peers, he says, *sine omni fuco et dissimulatione.*[52]

In dramatic terms, this is the peripeteia, the scene of recognition, which brings with it Cranmer's leap towards authenticity:

> And nowe I come to the greate thinge that somoche troblethe my consyence then any other thinge that ever I did or sayde in my lyfe and that ys the settynge abrode of wrytynge contrary to the truethe wch I did not thinke in my harte & wrytten for feare of deathe and to save my life yf y^t might be and that ys all suche thinges or papers wch I have wrytten or signed wth my honde signed synce my degradation wherein I have wrytten mayny thinges vntrue | And for asmoche | as my hande offended wrytynge contrarye to my harte therefore my hande shalbe fyrste burned. (Lambeth MS 3152, 115^r)

The reportage style of the narrative is quite rough, but it contains two motifs which are repeated so much as to become an obsessive pulse of self-declaration. One is the bodily assertion of sincerity in the form of an emotional guarantee, presented as a kind of recoil from dissimulation. His

---

[51] Lambeth Palace Library MS 3152, fo. 115^r. Compare the Latin text in *Cranmer's Recantacyons*, 103 ('cumque ob oculos hoc tempore videam vel coelum quod in promptu sit ad me excipiendum, vel infernum qui me absorbeat').

[52] 'ea de causa planum vobis faciam quae mea vere fides sit, sine omni fuco et dissimulatione' (*Cranmer's Recantacyons*, 103).

recantation, summed up in a series of formal performances of selfhood (a set of prayers, an avowal of obedience to the queen, a recitation of the creed, all in the context of the celebration of the mass in jail the night before), are now wilfully set aside as fabricated actions. It is this denial of insincerity that is made the avowal of renewed sincerity in the opposite direction. These are things which he has done, but 'wch I did not thinke in my harte' or are 'contrarye to my harte'. Who knows where this impulse from inside him comes from? Yet it is figured precisely as a boundary between inside and outside, in which what is inside is revealed as truly 'himself'. He takes internal possession of this recognition, and avows it as his sincere belief, for which he is prepared to risk heaven or hell.

The second repeated word which weighs like a burden on this passage is 'writing' or the 'written', cognates of which appear five times in as many lines of text ('signed' also appears twice). Why is it writing, rather than speaking, or kneeling or praying, or hearing the mass, which preys so decisively on his conscience? Partly it may be because recantation in a heresy trial is bound up with formal acts of writing in the form of self-repudiation. But it also seems to be that writing as an action is used by Cranmer to externalize the internal action of conscience. Writing is a boundary experience of the body, the place where the inside of the self leaves its visible mark. Under the pressure of the Reformation, writing is a dividing line between different confessional positions: it is the place where sincere devotion to the new faith declares itself, and where the authorities determining orthodoxy look to find evidence of heresy or sedition. It is in the act of writing that Cranmer defines the doctrine of the evangelical party in England. His religion of the new *Book of Common Prayer* is a religion of literate dissemination of doctrine, as against the bodily performance of ritual. And now, in his degradation, in his defrocking from the priesthood, and participation in his own denunciation (a denunciation of the faith he has spent twenty years painfully constructing) he has once again resorted to writing. Writing is revealed as the liminal act of the self.

In Foxe's book, while clearly based on the same verbal report, there is an attempt to create greater syntactical fluidity and literary felicity, which at the same time brings a further clarification of the figure of writing:

> which now here I renounce and refuse as thynges written with my hand contrary to the truth which I thought in my hart, and written for feare of death, and to saue my lyfe if it might be, and that is, all such billes and papers which I haue written or signed with my hand since my degradation: wherin I haue written many thinges vntrue.[53]

---

[53] *Actes and Monumentes*, 2 vols. (London: John Daye, 1570), ii. 2066. Further refs to the original printed text of the 1570 edition cited using volume and page number.

Foxe further objectifies the action of recantation in the form of physical 'billes and papers'. In the process, he joins the repeated verbal play of heart and writing to create a literary narrative expressing Cranmer's ultimate gamble with literary style, a last display of incandescent irony centred on one further figure, the figure of the 'hand':

> And for as much as my hand offended, writyng contrary to my hart, my hand shall first be punished therfore: for may I come to the fire, it shalbe first burned. (ii.2066)

In the process, Foxe gives new centrality to the symbolic action which is the most memorable aspect of Cranmer's whole life, and also sums up the Lambeth manuscript version:

> The sayde Thomas Cranmer died verye constantlye in Chryste and did firste putt his hande and holde yt still to the fyre and yt was the fyrst membre that was brente. (MS 3152, 115ʳ)

The hand which wrote is now the hand which represents the self at the moment of mortality, and signs his life as authentic.

Cranmer's final speeches, haunting as they are, also contain a subtle and moving analysis of the structure of belief and conviction. He manages to stay true both to his intermittent torment of prevarication and to the singular commitment embodied in his final repudiation. Indeed, doubt, the visible delay between choosing one way and another, the possibility (which remains present throughout) that he might choose the alternative, is part of what gives this story its grain of authenticity. The possibility of insincerity, which is often treated as somehow the whole problem with Cranmer, may even be his ultimate achievement. He confesses the history of his faithfulness as a history which includes failure although it is not circumscribed by that failure. He recognizes the way that the text of his own speech is participating crucially in the formation of his own identity. His speech is not only a retrospective of his career and of his condemnation, it is an intervention in his life, which acts to give that life a narrative meaning. His life has come down to a choice between two texts, two pieces of paper, one compliant and the other defiant, which he carries on his person: a life summed up in a choice between two contrary recantations.

Cranmer's speech is therefore a testimony to the power of narrative, which Foxe, in turn, reapplies to his 'Book of Martyrs'. In the process, he summons up a particular construction of a relationship between writing and subjectivity. Cranmer's life is interwoven with the text which he chooses to give to it. At the heart of his speech is an avowal of one set of writings, which constitute his true identity, and the disavowal of another, which falsifies him. The truth which is in him is therefore contingent upon the textuality which is used to describe him. Cranmer figures this particularly by means of a literary trope in which he refers to his hand as if it is separated from the rest of his body, 'thynges written with my hand contrary to the truth which I thought in my hart'. It is as if his hand writes without the rest of him knowing. This is a trope which reverses the figure of synecdoche, a reversal made the more obvious when he refers later to the commonplace version of such a synecdoche, the 'hand' as signifier of the signature, the everyday mark of personal authenticity. Here it turns out that a signature may be nothing of the kind, that it is even in this case a travesty of authenticity produced by torture and the fear of death: 'all such billes and papers which I haue written or signed with my hand since my degradation' (Foxe, 1570, ii. 2066), he now rejects as counterfeit signatures.

This is all a prelude to Cranmer's signal act, the moment which sums him up for history. This is so famous and at the same time so gruesome an image that it is easy to fail to register some of its many peculiarities. What gives Cranmer's action such force and disturbance, quite apart from the physical courage which made it possible, is its operation within the narrative as a violently graphic irony. Having reversed the everyday synecdoche by which the writing hand is made to stand for the self, having divorced (by a literary trope) one part of his body from another, his hand from his heart, he now brings back synecdoche with a vengeance. His hand, which has so misrepresented him, might as well be someone else's; and as belonging to someone else he now treats it as separate from his body, like an amputated limb. To complete his literary figure, to make it come full circle, he brings his trope to life by treating his physical hand as if literalized as a literary device.

The coincidence of verbal and visual meaning here, and of the physical and literal, is what gives Foxe's final narration a figurative power to match its pathos:

Then was an yron chayne tyed about *Cranmer*, whom when they perceiued to bee more stedfast then that he could be moued from his sentence, they commaunded the fire to bee set vnto hym. And when the wood was kyndled, and the fire began to burne neare him, stretching out his arme, he put hys right hand into the flame: which he held so stedfast & immouable (sauing that once with the same hand he wiped hys face) that all men might see hys hand burned before hys body was touched. Hys body did so abide the burning of the flame, with such constancye and stedfastnes, that standing alwayes in one place without mouing of hys body, he seemed to moue no more then the stake to which he was bound: his eyes were lifted vp vnto heauen, and often tymes he repeated, hys vnworthy right hand, so long as his voice would suffer hym: and vsing often the wordes of *Steuen*, *Lord IESVS receiue my spirite*, in the greatnes of the flame, he gaue vp the ghost. (1570, ii. 2066)

WORD VERSUS IMAGE: WRITING
& REPRESENTATION

Foxe's book represents the fatal denouement of Cranmer's subjectivity not only as verbal icon but in graphic image. In this we can trace a passage between the last rites of Cranmer's struggle at self-representation in his trial and degradation, and a deliberate effort in Foxe to transpose the archive of martyrdom into a fully-fledged articulation of a theory of subjectivity. Subjectivity passes from the first to the third person, and then from text to woodcut. In word and image, Foxe's book reinvents the writer as martyr. In this process, the last gesture of Cranmer's life, the burning hand, becomes transformed into a visual trope for understanding Protestant Christian identity. Three other of Foxe's martyrs, Thomas Bilney, Thomas Tomkins, and Rose Allen, prove their faith by putting the hand to the fire. The hand of the martyr becomes a sign for sincerity, and at the same time shows a transference by which the hand is made the bodily marker of the subjectivity of faith, imagined in the act of writing and reading.

For Cranmer, there survive two woodcuts of martyrdom used in works by Foxe. The earlier of these was produced just three years after Cranmer's death in *Rerum in ecclesia gestarum commentarii* (Basel, 1559), Foxe's Latin martyrology.[54] In it, Cranmer is tied to a central pillar, dividing the picture in two. He stretches his right hand into the flame in a simple gesture, while the index finger of his left points toward it, as if to show what he is doing. The martyr is shown passive and vulnerable, although also upright and unflinching; the long white beard not only proclaims the patriarchal style adopted by Reformed clergy from the 1550s onwards, but emphasizes that Cranmer was an old man, in his late sixties.

This image was replaced (as all four images of 1559 were, since they belonged to a different printer) by John Day in the first English edition of the *Actes and Monuments* in 1563 (Fig. 12).[55] As Elizabeth Ingram and Margaret Aston have commented, the 1563 woodcut has 'more vivid and poignant immediacy' than its 1559 predecessor.[56] Oxford's town walls are visible to lend local authenticity. Cranmer's accusers sit in judgement before him,

---

[54] John Foxe, *Rerum in ecclesia gestarum commentarii*, 2 vols. (Basel: N. Brylinger and J. Oporinus, 1559–63), i. 726.

[55] *Actes and Monuments* (1570), ii. 2067; R. S. Luborsky and E. M. Ingram, *A Guide to English Illustrated Books 1536–1603*, 3 vols. (Tempe, Ariz.: Medieval and Renaissance Texts and Studies, 1998), ref. 11222/44.

[56] Margaret Aston and Elizabeth Ingram, 'The Iconography of the Acts and Monuments', in David Loades (ed.), *John Foxe and the English Reformation* (Aldershot: Ashgate, 1997), 66–142.

Of the Church   1563

This fortitude of mynd, which perchaunce is rare and not vsed among the Spaniardes, whē fryer Iohn sawe, thinking it came not of fortitude but of desperation (although suche maner exāples which ar of the like cōstancie haue ben much common here in England) rātne to the Lord Williās of Tame, crying that the Arch bishop was verid in mynde, and died in great desperation. But he whiche was not ignorant of his countenāces constancie, being vnknowē to the Spaniardes, simpled only, and as it wer by silence rebuked the fryers folie. And this was the ende of this learned Archebyshoy, whome left by euill saying he should haue perished by well recanting, God preserued, and left he should haue liued to shame, he died happely to the glorie of Gods name.

¶ The burning of Tharchbishop of Cant. D. Tho. Cranmer in the town dich at Oxford, with his hand first thrust into the fyre, wherwith he subscribed before.

[In woodcut: "L. Receiue my spirit." — "Priest folke."]

Thus haue you the full storye concerninge the lyfe and death of this reuerend Archebyshop and Martyr of God, Thomas Cranmer, and also of all other the best learned sorte of Christes Martyrs burned in Quene Maries tyme, of whome this Archebyshop was the last, being burnt about the very myddle tyme of the reigne of that Quene, and almoste the very middle man of all the Martyrs, whiche were burned in al her reigne besydes. Diuers bookes and treatises he wrote both in prison & out of prison. Among the whiche especially he had a mynd to the aunswere which he made to S. Antonius Constantius. Which boke was the chiefest cause why he made his appeale, (as he wryting to a lawyer cōfesseth him self, pag.) and peraduenture was some cause also why he recanted, to haue leasure and time to finishe that booke. Of the whiche boke two

partes yet be extant, and peraduenture (if God geue time and life) may hereafter be published: the third part, some same also was wrytten & afterward lost at Oxford, which if it be so, it is great pitie. Maister Ridley also, as it is testified, made an answer to the said M. Antonius Constant. with a cole in the margent of the booke, for lack of inke & paper, and I trust also that the same will come to our handes.

About the time that this good Archbyshop was thus cruely dispatched and burned at Oxforde, there were thwo honest Matrones, Agnes Potten, the wyfe of Robert Potten of Ipswich in Suffolk, & the wyfe of one Mychel Trochfield a thomaker in ysame town, burnt burnt at the said Ipswich the 19. day of Feb. An. 1556. Their opinion or rather certaine persuasion was, that in the Sacrament there was the memoriall of Christes death and passion.

[marginal notes: "The aunswere of Cranmer to M. An. tonius Cō stantius." — "1556." — "February 19." — "Two matrones burnt at Ipswich."]

FINIS.   For

Fig. 12. John Foxe, *Actes and Monuments of these latter and perrilous dayes* (London: Iohn Day, 1563), 'The burning of the Archbishop of Cant[erbury] D[octor] Tho[mas] Cranmer in the town dich at Oxford, with his hand first thrust into the fyre, wher with he subscribed before'. Oxford, Bodleian Library, Douce F subt.3. fo. 1503

transformed by the scene into voyeurs and armchair sadists. Fray Juan de Villagarcia, the Spanish jurist, is presented on the left as a mocking monk. Cranmer's portrait is much more expressive: he thrusts his right hand into the fire in conscious defiance, holding up his left to draw attention to the gesture. A banderole (above left) gives him a voice, repeating the words of the founding martyr Stephen. Day paid special attention to the creation of these banderoles, to the extent, Evenden and Freeman comment, of getting them 'aesthetically correct'.[57] What they do not comment on is how the banderole gives the suffering body agency in its final moment. In Cranmer's final agony, he confirms his final recantation with a disturbing bodily gesture of defiance and assertion of his identity, by choosing which part of his body will burn first. Here Foxe's verbal and visual languages coincide and confront each other in a fascinating formation. His hand burns alone, while the rest of his body is as yet untouched. The right hand is curled in a distinctive manner, as if to suggest that it is after all his writing hand that is being punished, for making his recantation; the striking pose is enhanced by its mirroring in the gesture of Villagarcia's hand below.

The full complexity of Cranmer's excruciating bodily irony is transformed by Foxe and Day into a complex double form, revealed in an interplay with the text alongside, where Cranmer during his last examination makes repeated verbal play with the literary figure of his hand as a signifier of his self, as the literal maker of his signature: 'now here I renounce and refuse as thynges written with my hand contrary to the truth which I thought in my hart, and written for feare of death'. In this way, the visual gesture in the woodcut completes a kind of reverse metonymy: his physical hand stands in place of the figurative hand that misrepresented him, a hand that behaves now as if it belongs to another body entirely:

> he put hys right hand into the flame: which he held so stedfast & immouable (sauing that once with the same hand he wiped hys face) that all men might see hys hand burned before hys body was touched.

As his right hand signed his recantation, and thus betrayed himself, so this hand now perishes before he does, in front of his own eyes. The visual grammar of the scene is bound up with Cranmer's excruciating literary metonymy.

The use of images in Foxe's book, as Elizabeth Evenden and Thomas S. Freeman comment, was at the least 'paradoxical'. Calvinist book production shuddered in the face of the implications of idolatry embodied in illustrated books.[58] The Protestant martyrologies produced by Adriaan

---

[57] Evenden and Freeman, *Religion and the Book*, 220.
[58] Andrew Petegree, 'Illustrating the Book: A Protestant Dilemma', in Christopher Highley and John N. King (eds.), *John Foxe and his World* (Aldershot: Ashgate, 2002), 133–44.

van der Haemstede in the Netherlands and by Jean Crespin in Geneva contained no images.[59] Foxe himself not only argued in favour of iconoclasm but also participated in at least one act of destruction. During the reign of Edward, Foxe found employment as a tutor in the household of the evangelical patron the Duchess of Richmond. At her manor at Reigate in Surrey sometime after 1550, Foxe organized the suppression of a cult attached to the shrine of the Virgin Mary at Ouldsworth, which had been credited with miraculous healing powers.[60] What business did he have, Evenden and Freeman ask sharply, in making his book 'the most lavishly illustrated book hitherto produced in England?' Their answer lies partly in that it was probably Day the printer rather than Foxe the writer who was responsible for the commissioning of the images, and that the design was perhaps often down to the individual artists hired. Day's motive was most likely to attract patrons to his business.[61] Day took enormous trouble and expense to illustrate his first edition. The second edition of 1570 contained double the number of woodcuts found in the edition of 1563.[62] The primary figure here is Archbishop Matthew Parker. There is evidence that the production of the Book of Martyrs was connected with Parker, whose workshop at Lambeth Palace was the location for the hand painting of two surviving copies now in Cambridge.[63] Parker's interest in book production and especially illustrated books provided an opportunity which was shortlived: after 1580, Protestant England largely shunned images of any kind in religious books.[64]

However, the images in the book themselves at some points engage directly with the deep anxiety between word and image in Protestant religion. Among the new woodcuts of 1570 is a fresh opening page to Book IX, the book devoted to the reign of the boy-king Edward VI, a complex

[59] Adriaan van Haemstede, *De geschiedenisse ende den doodt der vromer Martelaren, die om het ghetuyghenisse des Evangeliums haer bloedt ghestort hebben* (Emden, 1559); Jean Crespin, *Histoire des vrays tesmoins de la verité* (Geneva, 1570).

[60] *Christ Iesus triumphant A fruitefull treatise, wherin is described the most glorious triumph, and conquest of Christ Iesus our sauiour, ouer sinne, death, the law, the strength and pride of Sathan, and the world* (London: Iohn Daye, 1579), sig. A4ʳ. See Thomas S. Freeman, 'Foxe, John (1516/17–1587)', *Oxford Dictionary of National Biography* (Oxford: Oxford University Press, 2004), <http://www.oxforddnb.com/view/article/10050>, accessed 3 July 2006.

[61] Evenden and Freeman, *Religion and the Book*, 190–4.

[62] Precise figures may be calculated in different ways. There are 53 cuts in 57 occurrences in the 1563 edition, and 105 cuts in 149 occurrences in the 1570 edition; for a catalogue of all the cuts as they appear in the four editions in Foxe's lifetime, see Luborsky and Ingram, *English Illustrated Books*, i. 367–82.

[63] Evenden and Freeman, *Religion and the Book*, 222–4.

[64] Patrick Collinson, *The Birthpangs of Protestant England: Religious and Cultural Change in the Sixteenth and Seventeenth Centuries* (London: Macmillan, 1988), 116–17.

interlocking set of three different images which occupy in total about two-thirds of the whole page.[65] Taken together, these three images provide a brief but dramatic symbolic history of the six short years of cultural revolution which encompassed the boy-king's career as the last great hope of the zealous godly. At the bottom left, the king himself sits in state, delivering the Bible to his prelates. This image, as Margaret Aston has shown in detail in *The King's Bedpost*, had by now done the rounds, being based originally on a detail taken from Holbein's title-page for Coverdale's Bible of 1535 (the first complete printed Bible in English).[66] In the meantime the figure of Henry VIII has been replaced neatly with his son Edward, and more significantly, the bishops have lost their mitres and kneel bareheaded and bearded.[67]

The choice of head-dress and hairstyle, like everything else in the 1570 woodcut, is iconographically and ideologically loaded with significance. The king's enthronement takes place in a cut-away within the massive body of the Edwardian church. The seven sacraments have been carefully peeled away to leave just two, presented in stark triumph as the centrepiece of the whole image, the baptismal font on the right and the Communion Table in the middle, a simple cup on a simple table. In case we had not noticed, it is provided with a huge inscription behind it, 'The Communion Table': a highly charged description, since it is a wooden table rather than a stone altar, and has been placed in the midst of the church rather than the East End. To complete an image of a Protestant church following Edwardian religious rule, the godly are crammed in to every available space beneath the table, listening intently to a bearded preacher who gives a homily from a pulpit. The godly, who number women as well as men, are dramatically presented as literate; several carry books and one of them, a woman on the left, has a book open on her lap, perhaps to help her follow the scriptural text of the sermon.

Meanwhile, above this scene of serene evangelical steadfastness, a different narrative is acted out. In this scene, everything is full of violence, of distraction, of disorderly energy. The 'ship of the Romish Church' is set ready to depart from harbour at the far right. On to this ship of fools the rump of the papist crew, mostly monks and priests, is scurrying with unseemly and greedy haste. They are carrying as many goods as they can take

---

[65] Foxe, *Actes and Monuments* (1570), ii. 1483.

[66] Margaret Aston, *The King's Bedpost: Reformation and Iconography in a Tudor Group Portrait* (Cambridge: Cambridge University Press, 1993), 155.

[67] Edward first replaced his father in a woodcut in Cranmer's *Catechismus, that is to say, a shorte instruction into Christian religion for the synguler commoditie and profyte of childre[n] and yong people* (London: Nicholas Hyll, 1548). In the *Catechism*, unlike here, the bishops are mitred and clean-shaven (Aston, *The King's Bedpost*, 158).

with them and the ship is groaning under the weight of their baubles and vanities. Yet more is going on than an eviction. The salvage operation of the Catholic remnant discloses on more careful inspection a process of cultural cleansing. Another caption, placed on the roof of the new church, confirms this: 'The Temple well purged'. Just behind, at the top centre of the woodcut, lies the iconographic centrepiece, a scene of conflagration and summary violence. This, too, is given a heading in case the message is missed by the reader: 'Burning of Images'.

In this way the woodcut at the new opening of Book IX in the 1570 edition of Foxe encapsulates the paradox within the very idea of an 'art of the Reformation'. It is an image of iconoclasm, of the destruction of art.[68] In a larger cultural sense, too, Foxe and Day's book participates in the same process of iconoclasm. The new church is a church of readers, their books at the ready on their laps or in their hands. In this new order of things the world of reification or of visualization is seemingly stripped away to leave a purer epistemology of verbal statement. Foxe's book, 2,300 folio pages bound in two giant volumes, several million words of doctrine, exegesis, and textual archive, is a signal part of the triumph of the literate. Cathedral churches were ordered to replace their images of virgins and saints with giant books, the Bible, Erasmus' *Paraphrases* explicating inordinately the literal sense of the Bible, and (in an order of Convocation in April 1571) Foxe's Book of Martyrs itself.[69]

Yet it does not take much imagination to see that this particular page in Foxe is an odd place to assert a rigid line of demarcation between verbal and visual worlds. The burning of images is represented here in an image. Indeed it is the most brazen example of iconoclasm in Foxe's book: in the text, the breaking of images is barely mentioned. This is only one of a number of ways in which the *Actes and Monuments* is a profoundly visual book, and not only at the literal level. First of all, of course, the 1570 edition contained 149 illustrations.[70] The illustrations vary in size from boxes within the text about ten centimetres by seven, all new for the 1570 edition, to vast pop-out inserts which spread wider than the folio width of

---

[68] The fullest accounts of iconoclasm in the English Reformations are Patrick Collinson, *From Iconoclasm to Iconophobia: The Cultural Impact of the Second English Reformation* (Reading: University of Reading Press, 1986); and Margaret Aston, *England's Iconoclasts: Laws against Images* (Oxford: Clarendon Press, 1988).

[69] David Loades, 'The Early Reception', in *The Unabridged Acts and Monuments Online*, <http://www.johnfoxe.org>, accessed 1 September 2012. There is no basis for the idea that it was placed in every parish church; see Patrick Collinson, Alexandra Walsham, and Arnold Hunt, 'Religious Publishing in England 1557–1640', *The Cambridge History of the Book in Britain*, vol. iv (1557–1695), ed. John Barnard and D. F. Mackenzie (Cambridge: Cambridge University Press, 2002), 37.

[70] Luborsky and Ingram, *English Illustrated Books*, i. 375.

the page (and in one case wider than a two-page opening).[71] The labours involved in this production were both enormous and expensive. The layout for every page on which a woodcut appeared was a fresh techno-logical problem, compelling Day and his compositors into tortuous im-provisations in the setting of text against image.

We do not know Foxe's precise part in the choice and design of images. Sometimes Foxe stayed in Day's house, as in January 1567, at others he was nearby in the home of the Duke of Norfolk in Aldgate.[72] Day probably had the primary role in the visual dimension of the book. Freeman and Evenden have challenged the conventional view of the social purpose of the woodcuts. In the past, the woodcuts were seen in terms of instruction of the unlearned.[73] The pictures enabled, it was argued, a graphic inculcation of the message of the text. Freeman and Evenden cut through some of the Protestant sentimentalism involved here and state instead that the images are 'a by-product of the attempt to impress influential élites'. The hand-coloured copies, they propose, were presentation copies for important patrons.[74] Day's volume was no ordinary book, they point out, and nor was it a popular book. It was costly to produce and costly to buy: Cecil enlisted the support of the Privy Council. Letters were dispatched to the Archbishops of Canter-bury and York and the Bishop of London to ensure that Day would not be out of pocket.[75] As often, no one gave a thought to the pocket of the reader. William Turner in November 1563 had already written to Foxe saying that everyone he met praised the book but that some 'of the poorer sort' were complaining that the price was beyond them. This was surely an understatement. John Knox in 1566 repeated the view that the book 'for the great price therof is rare to be had'.[76] 1570, it is safe to assume, was double the money again.

---

[71] A three-page foldout of the trials of the 'Primitiue Church', with thirty-seven sadistic scenes: Luborsky and Ingram, *English Illustrated Books*, i. 374.

[72] Aston, *The King's Bedpost*, 161.

[73] The fullest account of the contribution of Foxe's book to popular culture is in Tessa Watt, *Cheap Print and Popular Piety, 1550–1640* (Cambridge: Cambridge University Press, 1991).

[74] In an unpublished paper accompanying an exhibition of the Trinity copy at the Wren Library, given at the History of the Book Seminar, Trinity College, Cambridge, 26 January 2006.

[75] Julian Roberts and Elizabeth Evenden, 'Bibliographical Aspects of the Acts and Monu-ments' in *The Unabridged Acts and Monuments Online*, <http://www.johnfoxe.org>, accessed 1 May 2012.

[76] Elizabeth Evenden and Thomas Freeman, 'John Foxe, John Day, and the Printing of the Book of Martyrs', in Robin Myers, Michael Harris, and Giles Mandelbrote (eds.), *Lives in Print* (London: British Library, 2002), n. 51.

THE BURNING HAND

If the *Actes and Monuments* is part of Day's attempt to create a luxury market for the production of an important part of his list, this still leaves open the visual meanings of the images themselves and how they relate to the text. Interpretations in the past have turned on strong dichotomies. Yet the same book may appeal to both luxury and popular taste; and a humanist intellectual framework does not exclude strong visual appeal. Nor does Day's economic motive have to be seen in contradistinction to a religious significance. Yet of all the dichotomies in interpretation of Foxe's book, none has been more powerful than the conflict over medieval arguments about the use of images in popular religion. For a scholastic argument about 'laymen's books' has always provided an unspoken backdrop for our appreciation of Foxe's Book of Martyrs, in ways that relate in a complex or even contradictory fashion to Foxe's associations with iconoclasm.[77]

Indeed, however hard we try, it seems difficult, when assessing the visual impact of the Reformation, to avoid the brutal epistemological distinctions promoted by Foxe and Day themselves in the image of the two churches. They have recently reappeared, in an elegant and sophisticated form, in Joseph Leo Koerner's *The Reformation of the Image*, and, by a subtle reverse psychology, in Eamon Duffy's careful deconstruction of Koerner's argument in the *London Review of Books*. Koerner has reformulated and revived Hegel's narrative (in his lectures on aesthetics in the 1820s) of the place of the Reformation in the history of western art as a process of inevitable secularization.[78] Art loses its sense of the numinous and its participation in the world of the sacred and becomes (in Duffy's phrase) 'an alternative form of textuality, mere food for thought'.[79] Koerner identifies within Luther's Wittenberg the development of a new aesthetic. The great altarpiece by Lucas Cranach in the Stadtkirche is a restatement in pictorial terms of the literal sense of Luther's text: visually dominating, it is nonetheless strictly redundant.[80] Again, using Duffy's uncharacteristically Derridean language at this point, it is 'a mere system of useful signs, not so much an alternative as a supplement to text, a vehicle for information and affirmation of the new gospel'.

Duffy plays along so far and then starts to demur. His main line of attack is the model of medieval religion and Catholic art which Koerner

---

[77] The classic discussions of 'laymen's books' in this context are in two articles by Margaret Aston, 'Devotional Literacy' and 'Lollards and Images', both collected in *Lollards and Reformers* (London: Hambledon Press, 1984), 101–92.

[78] *The Reformation of the Image* (London: Reaktion Books, 2004), 33–7.

[79] 'Brush for Hire', *London Review of Books*, 26.16 (19 August 2004).

[80] *Reformation of the Image*, 171–5.

is forced to construct in order to assert his 'new aesthetic'. Duffy dismisses
this as a rehash of the old Reformation propaganda that Catholic ritual
required no understanding in its observers, that it was a superstitious
ritual, an empty fetish. Duffy reminds us both that medieval sacramental
theology demanded interiority as much as Luther did, and also that medieval altarpieces involved complex intellectual structures and required intricate acts of reading in observers. And yet Duffy makes no similar
recuperation of the argument in relation to the art of the reformers.
Indeed, apart from the odd snipe at Cranach's cupidity and his inclination
to peddle his mass-produced work among Catholic as well as Protestant
clients, Duffy rather approves Koerner's picture of Protestant art as a
didactic and propagandist tool.

It is easy enough at first sight to fit Foxe into the same pattern; indeed
the woodcuts seem ready made for Duffy's formula of an art that is 'relentlessly didactic rather than devotional, often heavily encrusted with
explanatory text and biblical quotations'.[81] Yet what is Duffy doing here
but applying in reverse his own rejected model of a rigid distinction between image and text, devotion and doctrine, object and meaning? For of
course even the assertion that the Edwardian reformers by breaking images
rejected *in toto* 'the image' relies either on a simplistic category mistake or
else indulges in propagandist rhetoric. The iconoclasts did not break up
images indiscriminately in an aesthetic panic or Nietzschean will to oblivion; they rejected not the sense of sight itself but a particular way of
seeing.[82] They pursued not images of saints even, but images in particular
places used for particular religious practices: getting rid of the object elim-
inated the offending practice. At the same time those who were outraged
by these acts of destruction were not Victorian aesthetes mourning the
loss of vernacular and insular art, but devotees of this same religious practice, who lamented the suppression of the desire to venerate, to make of-
ferings, to place candles or gifts of wool or cheese or cake in front of the
sacred objects.[83]

The relation between image and text is much more complex than this
in *Actes and Monuments*. Some of the most famous episodes are remembered

[81] On Foxe's book in the traditions of Protestant illustration and iconoclasm see Pette-
gree, 'Illustrating the Book: A Protestant Dilemma', 133–44.

[82] Brian Cummings, 'Iconoclasm and Bibliophobia in the English Reformations,
1521–1558', in Jeremy Dimmick, James Simpson, and Nicolette Zeeman (eds.), *Images, Idolatry and Iconoclasm in Late Medieval England* (Oxford: Oxford University Press, 2002), 194.

[83] On late medieval practices before images, see Eamon Duffy, *The Stripping of the Altars:
Traditional Religion in England, 1400–1580* (New Haven: Yale University Press, 1992),
183–6; for specific injunctions against such practices, see Aston, *England's Iconoclasts*,
255–7.

most of all for visual details in the images, or equally for texts placed within the image as banderoles, particularly the *obiter dicta* of the martyrs themselves (such as William Tyndale, 'Lord open the kyng of Englands eyes').[84] Yet this is not the only way in which the image-breaking spirit of the book fights with its image-making power. Foxe's book, as well as containing images, is itself an artefact with enormous visual impact. It was designed as a book to be put on show, to impress, even overpower its readers, from a distance or within a group as well as a reader sitting on his or her own. The images are part of the startling vernacular idiom. By the 1570 edition, the visual economy of the page is elaborate, complex, and full of visual layering, which demands the full attention of readers to decipher it in detail but which also has a compelling effect on the onlooker. Its multiple columns, division into books and sections, different typographies (Gothic, Italic, and Roman, in one case even Anglo-Saxon) and font-sizes, use of captions and marginalia, extravagant tables of events and dates, inclusion (again in distinctive fonts or sizes) of documents, trial records, formal speeches, letters, or set-piece dialogues, all leave a visual trace as well as a verbal one.

Finally, and powerfully, the book is visual in the figurative sense, too. For the purposes of his martyrology, Foxe invents a peculiar narrative style. It is different in literary character from the accounts in Crespin's French or van Haemstede's Dutch, or from Foxe's Latin work of 1559. It is different also from the considerable vernacular chronicle tradition which would have been very familiar both to Foxe and his printer. A work of astonishing stylistic diversity, Foxe's book nonetheless has as its central mode a relentless series of short narrative episodes of violent death.[85] These are repetitive and to some degree formulaic, establishing what becomes a familiar pattern of steadfastness and faithfulness in response to persecution and cruelty. Yet they also contain a lavish eye for visual detail, for touches of pathos, grandeur, horror, mutilation, or visceral human cruelty, but also sometimes of comedy and the grotesque. In his text, then, as well as his woodcuts, Foxe is a visual master, with an operatic range of favourite forms of visual idiom, from high tragedy to high camp, from biblical simplicity to tawdry tabloid sensationalism.

The images, in turn, do not flinch from depicting physical pain in intricate detail, flesh burning or melting, body parts split asunder. John Hooper's hand, in one particularly famous example, can be seen broken

---

[84] Tyndale's martyrdom is portrayed in *Actes and Monuments* (1570), ii. 1229.

[85] See John R. Knott, 'John Foxe and the Joy of Suffering', *Sixteenth Century Journal*, 27.3 (Autumn 1996), 721–34.

away from his torso by the sheer force of heat, a mutilated fragment in the middle of the flames.[86] In other scenes there is humiliation, scourging, flogging, torture, and the rack. In the example of the woodcut of Bishop Bonner flogging his victims in his garden at Fulham Palace, the image gets away with something that the text cannot, perhaps, risk.[87] Within the margins of the woodcut a direct accusation of physical cruelty is made. At the same time the tone takes the form of bodily lampoon. Bonner is not just exposed as a torturer, he is a dominatrix, a sadist, a sodomite.[88] In this way, the narrative effect is achieved by a process in which text and image feed off each other and mutually influence each other. Although it is customary to see the woodcuts as the servants of the text, the process is two-way and fluid in its dynamic. We learn to read and see in different ways through each of Foxe's printed media, but they work in intricate tandem.

Nowhere is this more innovative and original than in Foxe's iconography and theological theory of sainthood. Medieval image-making was of course inextricably linked to the cult of the saints. Yet this embodied a complex form of substitutive metaphor. Where the body of the saint was not preserved, an image stood in its place. Yet it was not image alone: it embodied within it the presence of the person. Something like a reverse process happens in the iconoclastic lens of the arch-Protestant Foxe. For the book of martyrs is quite obviously, among other things, itself a form of cult of the saints. Foxe applies his own iconology of sainthood, and mediates his own ideal of a proper understanding of his imagery, a proper form of worship among his readership.

Foxe's verbal and (via Day's busy printshop) visual language for sainthood is complex, layered, not completely articulated and at some level confused. Despite counter-propaganda, he is not at all afraid of the word 'saint' or unselfconscious of the fact that his opponents will affect surprise at this. He includes quaint stories to satisfy the tastes of his more gullible or simpler readers.[89] The body parts of some of his martyrs are miraculously preserved against decomposition or putrefaction. The body of a German Lutheran beheaded at the stake continues to writhe after the head is removed. Foxe also mentions the heart of Cranmer, which was reported to have survived his burning intact, and compares it with the

---

[86] Luborsky and Ingram, *English Illustrated Books*, ref. 11222/25.
[87] Luborsky and Ingram, *English Illustrated Books*, ref. 11222/51.
[88] Discussed by Tom Betteridge, 'The Place of Sodomy in the Historical Writings of John Bale and John Foxe', in Tom Betteridge (ed.), *Sodomy in Early Modern Europe* (Manchester: Manchester University Press, 2002), 17–20.
[89] See Thomas S. Freeman, 'Through a Venice Glass Darkly: John Foxe's Most Famous Miracle', *Studies in Church History*, 41 (2005), 307–20.

incombustible heart of Zwingli.[90] There is an element of wilful pastiche here, as Foxe turns the tropes of his enemies back on them. The heart of Cranmer was controversial: Harpsfield in *Cranmer's Recantatyons* said that maybe Cranmer's hard heart was proof that like Pharaoh he was beyond conversion. In fact, he sneered, it more likely showed that Cranmer was suffering from heart disease.[91]

It is not as if, then, as in the dichotomy presented in Koerner or Duffy, Foxe's image of sainthood is shorn completely of a mysterious or miraculous somatics. The body of the saint is still capable of being seen as sacred, just as his or her life and death is reserved for a special purpose by divine providence. In other ways, Foxe preserves elements of traditional hagiographic iconography but subtly reinterprets them for evangelical ends. The portrait of Hooper at the stake, like a number of others, seems to be modelled consciously on the crucifixion. His body is stretched on the stake as if on the cross, facing the viewer head on. He is surrounded by soldiers, one of whom thrusts a spear into the fire. The bystanders include some who clearly oppose the death; one of them is a lamenting woman. Hooper himself utters his last words in a simple banderole, in an echo of Jesus's last words in St Luke, 'Lord Iesu receaue my soule'. Hooper in life was an iconoclast who opposed even what seemed to other evangelicals the acceptable face of imagery, the figure of the dead Christ on the rood.[92] Here his own dead figure is redeemed in a Christocentric pose that is mimetic rather than substitutional.[93] It is perhaps a dangerous move for Foxe to make, yet it shows his theology is experimental rather than an *idée fixe*.

In the light of Koerner's book it is interesting that Margaret Aston has identified what she calls a Lutheran aesthetic in Day's version of Foxe's text, perhaps even a conscious rejection of Calvinist thinking. She notes that the word 'Description' is applied as a heading to many of the images, and in a characteristically subtle piece of argument comments on how the word 'description' is polysemous between visual and literary representation.[94] She is especially interested in the interplay between the two standard sizes of image, the full stage tableaux and the smaller, iconic cut-ins.[95]

---

[90] *Actes and Monuments* (1570), ii. 2066–7.

[91] *Cranmer's Recantacyons*, 108–10.

[92] John Hooper, *A Declaration of Christe and of his offyce* (Zürich: A. Fries, 1547), sig. E6ʳ; see also Cummings, 'Iconoclasm and Bibliophobia', 195–7.

[93] On the figure of the cross in Protestant art, see Koerner, *Reformation of the Image*, 171–90.

[94] Aston, 'The Illustrations', in *The Unabridged Acts and Monuments Online*, <http://www.johnfoxe.org>, accessed 1 May 2012.

[95] Thirty-four woodcuts of this type were introduced in the 1570 edition for the first time; they are analysed by Ruth Luborsky, 'The Illustrations: Their Pattern and Plan', in David Loades (ed.), *John Foxe: An Historical Perspective* (Aldershot: Ashgate, 1999), 74–6. Luborsky and Ingram argue that four different designers or cutters were employed on these images (*English Illustrated Books*, i. 375).

If it is right to use the word 'Lutheran' of this method it is wrong to apply too easily Koerner's rigid concept of the didactic to explain it. Aston's phrase, 'the double act of reading and seeing', is preferable as a way of appreciating the many different negotiations that take place between text and woodcut.

It is in this regard, in order to give flesh to Aston's abstract phrase, that I return to the image of Cranmer putting his hand in the fire. Although such a group has not previously been identified, the image of a burning hand is repeated on four occasions in Foxe's *Actes and Monuments*, all in images first used in 1563, enough for it to become a significant figure. This seems to constitute a distinctive iconographic subgroup of woodcuts. Through this, I believe, Foxe and Day attempt a reconstruction of Protestant sainthood. Perhaps more significantly, it is achieved by neither word nor picture alone. Rather there is a cross-referencing of the two media, in which each is reinterpreted by the other. Nor is it the case that the images are simply didactic or simply illustrative. Indeed some of the most important messages of these images are not stated at all: they work instead obliquely, through counterpoint, suggesting both an alternative tradition of artistic iconography from the Catholic cult of the saints and a distinctive form of visual grammar. As the argument develops, it appears that although the images are deliberately vernacular and homely in style, referring to recognizable domestic events, the visual language is complexly humanist in origin, and refers to a particular humanist topos.

The first of these images (Fig. 13), preceding that of Cranmer, is one of Thomas Bilney, on the night before his execution in Norwich in 1531.[96] It shows Bilney at his desk, a friend keeping vigil with him in bed on the right. Bilney is rapt in his book, and with his left hand he traces the Bible verses that he is reading. Meanwhile he holds a finger of his right hand, as if impassively, stock still in the flame of a candle. The light from the candle fans out, filling the bedchamber. Foxe's text below explains the meaning of the scene. Bilney's Vulgate is open at Isaiah 43; Foxe supplies a translation from the Geneva version: 'When thou walkest in the fire, it shall not burne thee, and the flame shall not kindle vpon thee'. A further philosophical statement of the meaninglessness of pain accompanies the verse. The anecdote is presented as a proof of Bilney's serenity in advance of his execution. Bilney has just been cheerfully supping a beer. The symbolic parallel of fire and fire is abundantly evident.

If the ethereal glow from the candle suggests a sacred presence, it is nonetheless displaced from the figure of the martyr himself. If it is like a

---

[96] *Actes and Monuments* (1570), ii. 1151; Luborsky and Ingram, *English Illustrated Books*, ref. 11222/15.

Ex relatione cuiusdi ipsius disci- puli.

Stackerd, whan he aunswered for his former in diuinitie. Therfore this doctor Barnes boldened in Christ preached his sermon and was accused by two of the kings hall to be an heretick as here after shall more appere. After that he (This malster Latisaide Bilney had conuerted M. Latimer, he pro-mer bpon cedding forward in his iurney towarde London ght Bilney preached, emonge many sermons, one especial-fromhis ly at S. Magnus, against the new idolatrous desperation roode newly erected, before it was gilded: and And than there was apprehended & caried with Arthur, & she sayde as is aforesaide, to Constall, and so to the cole Bilney won house: And from thens to to the towre, till they him to gos-abiured, and bare faggots at Paules crosse, as pell. we haue before specified. Concerning his diet which we spake of, it was so straight, y for the space of a yere and halfe comenly he toke but one meale a day. So that if he were disposed to sup, he would kepe his commons: And like wise his supper, if he were disposed to dine, & would beare it to some prison: Where he vsed commonly to frequent and to exhorte such as were infamed or prisoned for euil life. Emong whome there was a certeine woman, one of y officers wifes, there cast in prison for adultry: whome he there conuerted with his dayly exhortation, and brought to such repentance and also syncerity of faith, that afterward she offered her self redy to dye for the same in detesting of her former life. His scholler which had daily conuersation with him, told vs that to his thinking, no night he slept aboue iiii. hours, & yet he spake of more then he reposed to vs.

He could abide no swearing, nor singing. Comming from the church where singing was, he would lament to his schollers, y curiositie of their deinty singing, which he called rather a mockery with god, then otherwise. And when Doct. Thurlby Bishop after, then scholler lieng in the chamber vnderneth him, would play vpon his recorder (as he would often do) he would resort straight to hys prayer.

At last M. Bilney taking his leaue in trinitie hall at ten of the clock at night of some of his frendes: Saide, he would go to Ierusalem and so to see them no more. And imediatly departed to Norfolk, and there preached first pri uatly in houseldes, to confirme the bretherne & sistern, & also to confirm thankris, whom he conuerted to Christ. Then preached openly in the fieldes, confessing his fact and preaching open ly that thing, which before he had abiured, to be a very truth, and had al men beware by him and neuer to truste to their fleshly frendes in causes of religion.

And so setting forward in his iurney towar des the celestiall Hierusalem, he departed from (Bilney in-thens to the Anchrise in Norwich, & there gaue tendeth to her a new testament of Tindalls translation, go to Ieru and thobedience of a christian man. And forth salem. with was apprehended and caried to prisone, (In Norwich ther to remain til the blind bishop Sir set for a conuerted wryt to burn hym. In the meane season the fri-by Bilney. ers & religious men with the residue of their do ctors Ciuil & cannon resorted to him & labored to perswade him not to dye therein, saying: he shuld be damned body & soul, but he buildig him self fast on the rock bad the al aboid, & bad the send two of their best doctors they had, to con found hym if they could, and to shew abetter (Bilney the truth then he had to shew for him by the word second time of God. And then did the blind bishop of Nor-apprehended wich send to him Doct. Call a gray frier: And and impresio Docter Stokes and Aukt frier, who lay with ned. him in prison in disputation till the white came (Docter that he should be burned. Doct. Cal by y word Cal and of God through holy ghost, and by Master Docter Bilneyes doctrine and godly life, whereof he Stokes sit had experience, was conuerted to Christ. The to dispute other Doct. Stokes remained obdurate and with Bil doth vnto this day, whose hart also the lord, if ney. it be his wil, conuert, & open y eies of his age, & Docter he may forsake y former blindnes of his youth Call conuer Emong thother, that were doers against him ted by Bil was one Fryer B ney. ird with one eye. A Docter nother was a black Stokes Frier called Hodg. now placed kins, who after be and benefic ing vnder y bishop ced at Lin. of Canterb. maried This Bird & in Paris time put was a suf-alway his wife. fagame in As it is reported by Couentry him y it was hys scho and was he ler he would manye that brou times attempte to ght epples proue the fier with hol to Poner ding his finger nye mentioned to the candle, but es in the story pecially the night be of Haukis. fore he suffered mar tirdo, at what time he did hold his figer (in y pistle at peth hall) after twise pruning so log in the flame, y he burnt of the first iognt.

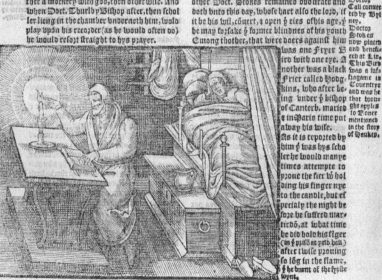

Fig. 13. John Foxe, *Actes and Monuments of these latter and perrilous dayes* (London: Iohn Day, 1563), 'Tho. Bilney being in prison, diuers tymes proueth the fire with hys finger'. Oxford, Bodleian Library, Douce F subt.3. fo. 466

halo, it clearly also is not; indeed it seems more like the presence of a light beyond the martyr, a grace that guides or awaits him. Once again, the bodily configuration of sainthood, and also its theology, is shifting. Indeed, the image has a further local significance which can help explain this shift. Evenden and Freeman have commented on the controversial significance of this woodcut.[97] Taking his cue from Sir Thomas More, Harpsfield had claimed that Bilney had recanted prior to his execution at the stake. The political status of recantation, as in the case of Cranmer, is acute: More's involvement in the posthumous investigation of Bilney's conscience will be examined in the next chapter. However, the controversial meaning of the image is not only local. Bilney's body is put to the test. This is the meaning of martyrdom throughout the Middle Ages. Faith is proved by the body, and the body takes on the miracle of faith to become part of its physical make-up. Saintliness lies within the body. The image of Bilney at his desk partakes of such meanings but also transforms them. The proof of sanctification occurs at the very borderline between the interior and the exterior of the body, at its nerve-ends. Pain is not only an interior proof, it has an outward meaning easily comprehended by the reader. Putting his finger to the candle is a guarantee, above all, of sincerity. Bilney's sincerity is vindicated against the calumnies of More and Harpsfield, but is also a witness to interior faith as understood by the Protestant writer Foxe and his literate following. The figure on the bed acquires his significance silently in this transaction of meaning: he is a guarantor of the verbal statements made by Bilney, as of the physical proof which puts them to the test.

Yet in all this we may also miss a key element in the scene. The member of the body that is put to the test is the digit of his right, the writing hand. Like Cranmer who punishes his hand as the locus of his self-betrayal, Bilney affirms his truth through the instrument of interior assertion. In the visual trajectory from the eye that reads to the hand that writes, Bilney's bodily posture is a somatic symbol of Protestant faith. Scripture and doctrine are corroborated by the hand that signs, in a signature of the whole body. The pain of martyrdom transfers itself from the sacred body of the saint to the sacred imprint of biblical faith. At the same moment, and in the same physical grammar of gesture, reading and writing are confirmed as the counter-indicators of human identity. This is a religion of the literate, of those who subscribe to articles of faith. Sincerity is an ambiguous test open to public reinterpretation, but authenticity is recovered in belief in the written word.

---

[97] Evenden and Freeman, *Religion and the Book*, 214.

A similar structure of meaning is continued in the next example, but it also widens the social implications of a religion of literacy. Whereas Bilney was a key heretic of the 1520s, a theologian and priest, this image represents the other end of the social fabric of Foxe's godly nation, a lowly weaver from Shoreditch, Thomas Tomkins (Fig. 14).[98] Tomkins was arrested for denying the mass late in 1554 and examined by Bishop Bonner. Foxe tells the story of Tomkins's examination in Fulham Palace with lurid detail, for which he claims (claims denied forcibly on the other side) several reliable witnesses. He accuses Bonner of torture, of keeping Tomkins locked up for several months, and of beating the prisoner, sometimes savagely. At the climax of the story, shown here, Bonner (on the far right) forcibly grips the fingers of Tomkins, who is shown standing bare headed and bearded. Bonner presses the victim's hand against a three-week-old candle until the flesh spurts in the face of Harpsfield, another of the examiners, who stands over them (second from right). This is the pain Tomkins will feel, he says, if he does not recant. However, Tomkins defies both the pain and its perpetrator, and is sent to the stake; a second woodcut of the smaller size was added in 1570 showing the moment of martyrdom in generic form.[99]

One question we could ask of this image is why Day includes it at all. Tomkins, unlike Bilney or Cranmer, is neither a theologian nor a public figure. If the images are (in Evenden and Freeman's view) aimed at élite patrons, Tomkins's is an ordinary and unexceptional martyrdom. Yet the point of Tomkins's portrayal may lie exactly here. A religion of the literate does not have to be seen as one requiring special education or social elevation. With his beard reminiscent of the style of the patriarchal Edwardian bishops, he also figures as part of Luther's 'priesthood of all believers'. Tomkins is an exemplary Protestant, resolute in his scriptural steadfastness and his religion of sincerity. Yet if Tomkins is a lowly weaver and a saint of the people, his image is enhanced and socially ameliorated by its assimilation with humanist learning. Foxe's text supports and enlarges the image by using a literary figure, in the form of a classical *ekphrasis*.

Just as Bilney's putting his finger to the flame was an example of stoic *apatheia*, so Tomkins's perseverance is compared by Foxe to the old Roman virtue of the early republican hero Gaius Mucius Scaevola:[100]

hee called for *Thomas Tomkins*, who commyng before the Bishop, and standing as he was wont in defence of his faith, the bishop fell from beating to burning. Who hauing there a taper or waxe candell of iii. or iiii. weekes

---

[98] Luborsky and Ingram, *English Illustrated Books*, ref. 11222/28.
[99] *Actes and Monuments* (1570), ii. 1712.
[100] *Actes and Monuments* (1570), ii. 1710–11.

Marche.
5.

The next moneth of Marche, the .v. daye of the same moneth, a godly man, one named Rowland Whyte, was burned at Cardyffe in Wales.

※ The hystorye of Thomas

Tomkyns, fyrſt hauyng hys hande burned, after burned hymſelfe by Byſhoppe Bonner, for the conſtant teſtimony of Chriſtes true profeſſion.

March.
15.

Like as the former moneth of February, as it hath bene told before was notable, by the martirdome of fyue moſt worthye preachers and true Byſhops: ſo no leſſe memorable was the next moneth of Marche, by the death & murther of eyghte moſte conſtant wytneſſes of the Chriſtian doctrine. Amonge whom Thomas Tomkins, citizen of London and Weauer by his occupation, bath the firſt place. Now thoſe former perſons that hyther to haue bene ſpoken of, were all condemned by Stephan Gardiner, byſhop of Wincheſter which then was hygh Chauncellour: but he beyng now weary, as it ſeemeth, of the payne and trouble, put of al the reſt to Edmund Boner, ner byſhoppe of London, to be condemned by hym, as hereafter God wyllyng ye ſhal heare. And touching Wyncheſter, we haue ſpoken ſomewhat before in the hiſtories aboue. Now

concernyng Boner, becauſe wee ſhall often make mencion of hym hereafter, the occaſion of this place woulde require, that we ſhoulde wryte ſomewhat of hym likewiſe, who was almoſt nothing els (in one word to ſpeake al his qualities) but a belly. And as for hys prodigious crueltye, in ſheddyng of bloude, to whych thing onelye he ſeemed to haue bene brought forth of nature, here might we haue a great field to walke in: but becauſe we wryte an hyſtory, and not inuectiues, we wyll leaue hym to hys Iudge, eſpecially ſeyng the very Martirs them ſelues, whom he hath condemned, haue ſufficiently performed thys part, as here after we ſhall heare. Now reſuming our hiſtory of Tomkyns, let vs procede in the matter which we haue begonne. Thys Weauer therfore who I ſpeake of, being brought forth vn to Boner, among al the other parties, which after folowed in great nomber, had this thing as a peculiar deſtiny, that he was the fyrſt of them al whych ſhould try the violence & rage of this byſhop of London. Who alſo begyn nynge hys perſecution, gaue ſoorth in this man a notable example or declaration of hys cruelty to be conſidered. For Tomkyns, although he was vnlearned, yet was he better learned then that he coulde bee ouercome by hym, and more louyng the truthe, and better ſtyckyng to it, then that he woulde geue place to anye falſe diſallowed erroures. Therefore

Tomkyns with his ſermon tymes the came before Boner in Maries tyme.

The ſharpe burnyng of Thomas Tomkyns hand, by cruel Boner hym ſelfe, who not long after burnt alſo hys body.

standing vpon the table, thought there to represent vnto vs, as it were, the old image of king *Porsena*. For as he burned the hand of old *Scæuola*: so this catholicke bishop tooke Tomkins by the fingers, & held his hand directly ouer the flame, supposing that by the smart and payne of the fire being terrified, he would leaue of his defence of his doctrine, which he had receaued.

Mucius, captured in an attempted assassination of King Porsenna, was threatened with being burned alive if he does not reveal the other conspirators. Instead Mucius thrust his hand into a brazier nearby, letting it burn there as if unconscious of the pain (*Quam cum velut alienato ab sensu torreret animo*).[101] Three hundred young Romans, he says, are standing ready to do the same if Porsenna carries out his threat. Without having to spell it out, Foxe brings in the same message, that 300 Protestant martyrs were willing to make the sacrifice in the face of the tyrant Mary, and all of them held physical fear in the same spirit as Mucius. Yet he also transfers the meaning towards his understanding of Christian Stoicism. If Scaevola represents republican virtue, the ability to ignore pain and desire in order to follow a philosopher's path to wisdom, Tomkins's purpose is the 'defence of his doctrine'. His faith, like Bilney's, is also figuratively represented by his writing hand, oblivious to 'the smart and payne of the fire'. The metonymy of 'hand' standing for 'faith' is confirmed by a small detail in the story where Foxe is mistaken. Foxe thinks Scaevola ('left-handed') acquired his nickname because he put his left hand in the fire; whereas in fact the story went that after mutilating his right, he became left-handed thereafter. The significance here is that Foxe thinks Scaevola loses the use of his left, but writing hand—and represents Tomkins doing the same with his right. Indeed, Tomkins, and Bonner his tormentor, surpass their Roman examples:

> I would to God the other had as wel folowed yᵉ example of that *Hetruscan* Tyrant. For hee after the left hand of *Scæuola* was halfe burned, eyther satisfied with his punishment, or ouercome by his manhood, or driuen away by feare, sent him home safe vnto his people: where as Boner hetherto not contented with yᵉ burning of his hand, rested not vntill he had consumed his whole body into ashes at London in Smithfield.

The body of the Protestant saint is consumed in the act of sincerity.

The woodcut lends supports to the argument in subtle ways. It presents a legal arraignment, with five capped examiners in attendance, in the course of being perverted by a wicked magistrate, Bonner. The other magistrates are appalled but do nothing to interrupt the improvisatory act of

---

[101] Livy, *Ab urbe condita*, II.xii.12–13; ed. and trans. B. O. Foster, Loeb Classical Library, 14 vols. (Cambridge, Mass.: Harvard University Press, 1961), i. 258.

torture. The image is full of expressive hands. The guard on the left puts a finger to his eye as he turns away in recoil, indicating his sympathetic horror, while at the same time showing his dissent by clutching his hat tightly to his chest with his left. Two of the officials on the left murmur in dissent, but their hands dangle indecisively at the table. A third, facing Bonner, half raises his hand to stop the violence; Harpsfield holds his to his chest but, with his eyes averted, distances himself from the victim, whom he leaves well alone. Bonner himself, who is labelled, carefully grips two of Tomkins's fingers to hold the right hand steady, while with his own left hand he grasps the candle firmly in position. Tomkins himself answers the gaze of the Bishop head-on. His stance is balanced and upright, one foot lifted slightly from the floor giving him forward momentum towards the flame. With his left hand he dangles his hat at the edge of the table, in an attitude of impassive disdain.

The use of a classical exemplum from Livy in Foxe's book of English martyrs is instructive and significant. It is a surprise only to those who have reduced Foxe to a stereotype. Foxe started out in Oxford as a humanist, and wrote two Latin comedies, one notably Terentian. Indeed, despite the vast size of *Actes and Monuments*, the larger part of Foxe's writing is in Latin, and not theological but humanist in style and frame of reference. The example of Mucius, nicknamed *Scaevola*, was well-known among humanists in the sixteenth century. In addition to its source in the second book of Livy's *History of the Foundation of the City* it is mentioned in Plutarch, Cicero, and Seneca. There are references in Machiavelli, and in England in Spenser's *Complaints* and William Painter's *Palace of Pleasure*, a commonly read book.[102] Chronicle histories of England use it to prove English virtues; one anti-Catholic work contrasts the lack of patriotism among English recusants.[103] The Jesuit Robert Southwell, by contrast, uses the case of the heathen Scaevola to vindicate the new Catholic martyrs.[104] In one case, later than Foxe, a comparison is made between the bravery of Scaevola and of Cranmer.[105]

There is also a considerable humanist pictorial literature around Scaevola. Mucius is the subject of one of Mantegna's wonderful classical topoi in

[102] Edmund Spenser, *Complaints Containing sundrie small poemes of the worlds vanitie* (London: William Ponsonbie, 1591), sig. K3ᵛ; William Painter, *The palace of pleasure beautified, adorned and well furnished, with pleasaunt histories and excellent nouelles* (London: John Kingston, 1566), sig. B4ᵛ.

[103] Thomas Lupton, *A persuasion from papistrie vvrytten chiefely to the obstinate, determined, and dysobedient English papists* (London: Henry Bynneman, 1581), sig. G3ʳ.

[104] *An epistle of comfort to the reuerend priestes* [London: John Charlewood?, 1587?], 185ʳ.

[105] Thomas Bastard, *Chrestoleros Seuen bookes of epigrames* (London: Richard Bradocke, 1598), sig. G2ʳ.

grisaille. This dates from 1490 and is now in the Alte Pinakothek in Munich. The topos passed into the visual register of both southern and northern European humanism, and is found in a variety of media, in oil and fresco, on vases, in engravings, on glazed plates. There is a sixteenth-century fresco by Tomasso Laureti in Michelangelo's remodelled palazzo on the Capitol in Rome; there is a painting on limewood by Hans Baldung Grien dated 1531 now in the Gemäldegalerie, Dresden. In the Walker Gallery in Liverpool there is a large tapestry (about five metres by four), high quality, Flemish, probably from a Brussels workshop, dating from about 1525. It represents *The Triumph of Fortitude*, containing a range of exemplary characters whose names can be seen or whose famous deeds can be read from the image. The Latin motto at the top of the tapestry reads, 'Valour matches intrepid hearts against adverse perils. Likewise, salvation accepted from death pleases'. The stories are an eclectic mix: historical Romans from Livy and Pliny, mythical Greeks, plenty of women, Penthesilea, queen of the Amazons, and a number from the Old Testament or the Apocrypha, including a splendid depiction of Jael the Hebrew woman driving a tent-peg into the head of the Philistine general. Scaevola is prominent with a magnificent plumed hat, an utterly cool face and demeanour, just the slightest hint of cockiness in his hips and his dandily placed left leg.

The Triumph of Fortitude would have been part of a series of seven tapestries showing the virtues, a common topos for display in wealthy European households. Scaevola also figures in emblem books. Geoffrey Whitney's *Choice of Emblemes*, published in Leiden by Christopher Plantijn in 1586, one of the earliest copies of Alciato's *Emblemata* into English, has a woodcut emblem of Scaevola's arm, holding a sword, thrust steadfast in the fire. The short poetic tag attached to the image emphasizes bodily courage and strength of purpose, but the title for the emblem is also interesting in relation to Foxe: *Pietas in patriam*, love of country.[106] Foxe's reference to Scaevola also contains a savour of English valour and honour to the motherland in the face of Spanish persecution.

At the same time the frame of reference introduced by Scaevola into Foxe's histories of martyrdom suggests a different kind of moral language. It places Christian martyrdom within the realm of civic humanism, consonant with secular virtues of fortitude and courage. The emblematic verse in Whitney addresses Scaevola in such terms:

> Oh noble minde, althoughe thy daies bee paste;
> Thy fame doth live, and eeke, for aye shall laste.

In 1594, in a painting by Marcus Gheeraerts the Younger of Sir Thomas Lee (now in the Tate), Lee appears as a wild Irishman, semi-naked in a rugged landscape. The painting dates from a time when Lee was suspected of treason. A verse painted under an English oak refers once again to the ancient Roman, Scaevola, image of courage and patriotism. Tomkins, it seems, is also being praised for his virtue and for the fame of his fortitude as well as his bodily sacrifice at the stake.

Scaevola's example is quoted again by Foxe when he comes to describe the last example of an image of the burning hand. Cranmer comes in between. This shows Rose Allin (Fig. 15), one of the Colchester martyrs of August 1557, seized by Edmund Tyrrell on her way with a pitcher to give her mother a drink of water.[107] Her sick mother is about to be arrested for heresy; Tyrrell interrupts the daughter in order to conduct an impromptu interrogation, using the candle to test her. Rose stays steadfast until her sinews crack, whereat Tyrrell gives up and carries her off to Colchester castle. There are subtle differences between this case involving a woman, and the others we have seen. Foxe intimates the sexual violence of the scene. Tyrrell calls her a whore for her intransigence, for not crying out and giving up. The sexuality of the woodcut, with the joining of the hands just above Tyrrell's codpiece, and the symbolism of candle and pitcher, is evident. Nonetheless, the iconographic composition of the scene is very striking. Rose is like a flagellated Christ surrounded by guards with spears; the scene of her own martyrdom is represented in a small frame above her head. At the same time, in the text, Foxe draws the parallel with Scaevola in Livy once again, and perhaps compares Rose implicitly with figures of Roman female virtue such as Lucretia.[108] Interestingly, while in the Tomkins story Foxe mistakenly writes that it is Scaevola's left hand that is burned, here he corrects his error in an insertion stuck over the original text.[109] But whereas the heathen Romans burned only the hand, these Christians 'consume their whole bodies without any iust cause' (ii. 2200).

In this realignment of the iconography of martyrdom there is then, finally, a subtle readjustment of the bodily meaning of sainthood. Foxe continues to draw attention to the bodily suffering of the martyr, but with a difference. Rose is like a medieval martyr but she is also, the text suggests, like a Roman matron. In this process, the meaning of bodily pain is itself transformed. These are not the bodily marks of sacrifice, of a sacramental incorporation of the blood of martyrs with the blood of Christ

---

[107] Luborsky and Ingram, *English Illustrated Books*, ref. 11222/52.
[108] *Actes and Monuments* (1570), ii. 2200.
[109] Compare *Actes and Monuments* (1570), ii. 1710 and ii. 2200.

What a ſtroke of Gods hande was alſo wrought vpon the cruell condemner and perſecutour of the holy and harmles Sayntes of the Lord, biſhop Thornton, Suffragan of Doner, who after he had exerciſed his cruell tyranny vpon ſo many ſimple and good men at Canterburye, at length cōming vpon a ſaterday from the chapter houſe at Canterburye to Borne, and there vpon ſonday following being vertuously occupied, loking vpon his men playing at the bowles, fel ſodainly in a palſy, and ſo being had to bed, was moued to remēber God, yea, ſo I do, ſaide he, and my Lorde Cardinal to. &c.

After bym ſucceded an other byſhop or Suffragane, ordained by the late Cardinal. It is reported that he had bene ſuffragan before to Boner, who not long after he was made Byſhop or Suffragan of Doner, brake his necke falling downe a payre of ſtayres in the Cardinals houſe at Lambeth, as he had receiued the Cardinals bleſſing.

To theſe examples alſo might be added the vnprepared death of M. Geffrey, Chauncellor of Saylſburye, who in the middeſt of his buildings, ſoddainly being taken by the mighty hand of God, yelded his lyfe, which had ſo litle pity of other mens lyues before. Concerning whoſe cruelty partly mention is made before pag.1702. As touching moreouer this foreſaid Chauncellor, this is to be noted, that he depar-

tinge vpon a ſaterdaye, the daye before that, had appointed to cal before him.90.perſons,& not ſo fewe, to examine them by inquiſition, had not the goodnes of the Lord, and his tender prouidence, thus preuēted him with death, prouiding for his poore ſeruantes in tyme.

The lyke alſo is to be ſaid of D. Donning, the bloudy and wretched Chauncellor, or rather tormentor, of Norwiche, who after hee had moſt rigorouſly condemned and murdered ſo many ſimple & faithful ſaintes of the lord, continued not long himſelfe, but in the mpoſt of his rage in queue Maries time, was cut of & taken away to an other Danding. Such is the merciful dealing of the almighty with his people, whom after her ſcourged a litle in his diſpleaſure, at length he burned the rod.

After the like worhing of Gods holy mercy, diuers other ſharpe & bytter rodde alſo were cut of in this tyme of queue Maries perſecutiō. Although ſome ther be which eſcaped, and are aliue, for what purpoſe ſuffred of the lord, whether for a further trial of gods people, or for ſpace to repent, the lord knoweth. As Boner, Nicholas Harpesfeld, D. Story, D. Draicot, and the Juſtice which burnt the hand of a maide in Suffolk, mentioned before, pag.1608 The ſhew of which her burning here followeth in this table expreſſed, to thentent that he which was the doer therof, beholding the crueltye of the bede, may come the ſoner to repentãce.

Certeyne perſecutors alyue.

The burning of Roſe Allins hand, by ſyr Edmond Tiryll, as ſhe was going to fetche drynke for her Mother, lyeng ſycke in her bed,

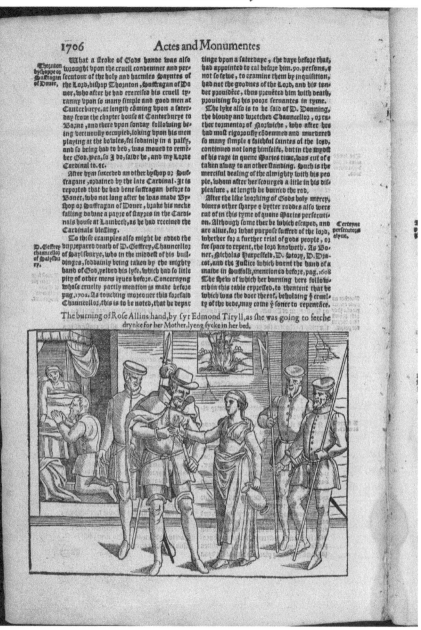

Fig. 15. John Foxe, *Actes and Monuments of these latter and perrilous dayes* (London: Iohn Day, 1563), 'The burning of Rose Allins hands by Syr Edmond Tirryll, as she was goyng to fetche drynke for her Mother, lyeng sycke in her bed'. Oxford, Bodleian Library, Douce F subt.3. fo. 1706

and his church. The burning hand signifies instead, as in the death of Cranmer, metonymically. The hand signifies the hand of the writer and the hand of the reader. Cranmer burns his right hand because of its act of false witness in signing his bill of recantation. Bilney, as he places his right index finger in the candle, traces with his left the lines of the Bible on the page in front of him. This relates to another brilliant remark made by Aston, that in his creation of a modern pantheon of martyrdom, 'the choice of emphasis in portraying the leading martyrs bears some relationship to their literary record'.[110] If the early church drew attention to the acts of the martyrs, Foxe is interested in their testimony, the words they wrote or said, the written record of their faith. Foxe's church is indeed a church of readers and writers, a kingdom of the literate, united in their faith by their attention to the word. His book celebrates above all the deaths of heroic readers and writers in the evangelical cause.

This is a second respect in which his book might be thought to show a modernist tendency. By making his martyrs into suffering humanists he seems in some way to secularize, certainly to demystify, the idea of sainthood. And in making the writer the principal bearer of the idea of Christian witness he offers a premonition of the twentieth- and twenty-first-century cult of the dissident idealist, the prisoner of conscience. Perhaps in this sense he concurs to some degree with Koerner's model of reformed art. But this is not a world of the ear divorced from the world of the eye. The eye too is involved in reading, and in visualizing through reading. Nor is the act of seeing an image divorced from the act of reading. Foxe's readers read the images, too, and form a narrative from them in tandem with the narrative of the text. This in turn has its effect on the visual grammar of the woodcuts themselves. They are not, in Duffy's words, 'relentlessly didactic' in any simple sense. They signify at many levels. Literary figuration and visual language come together in Foxe's woodcuts, never more so than in the metonymy of the burning hand.

---

[110] Aston, 'The Illustrations', *The Unabridged Acts and Monuments Online* (1570 edition), <http://www.johnfoxe.org>, accessed 1 May 2012.

4

Public Oaths & Private Selves

More, Foxe, & Shakespeare

On 16 August 1531, Thomas Bilney, one-time fellow of Trinity Hall in Cambridge, was taken to the place of public execution just outside the city gates in Norwich, commonly known as Lollard's Pit, and burned to death as a heretic. At the stake, he took a piece of paper and read out loud a recantation of all his heresies, swearing in public the error of his ways. Kneeling in front of the Bishop's chancellor, in the presence of all the people of Norwich, he sought absolution from his excommunication and held himself content with his punishment. He recited the collect *Domine Iesu Christe*, emphasizing the words *ecclesiae tuae pacem & concordiam*, made some ritual gestures of penance, 'tunsyons & knokkynges vppon hys breste', before receiving the sacrament and a final blessing from the priest in attendance, and submitting himself willingly to the torment of the fire as a newly reconverted Catholic Christian.[1]

Or did he? According to a second version of the story, on the way to Lollard's Pit on 16 August, Bilney distributed gifts of alms to passers-by and extended words of comfort to some friends who accompanied him. At the stake, he made no speech of recantation, but instead rehearsed the articles of his faith in order, justifying the sermons that had been deemed heretical. Kneeling down, but in full public view, he immersed himself for a few moments in earnest private prayer and silent contemplative devotion. At length he ended, calling out in a clear voice the first words of Psalm 143, 'Heare my prayer O Lord, consider my desire. And enter not into Iudgement with thy seruaunt: for in thy sight shall no man liuyng be iustified'. Removing his jacket and doublet, he made his peace with the executioners and submitted himself to the fire. The flames encircled him immediately, deforming the visage of his face, but holding his hands in

---

[1] Thomas More, *The Confutation of Tyndale's Answer, Complete Works of Thomas More*, viii/1. 22–5. More does not tell a linear narrative; this is a reconstruction of those details that he emphasizes.

front of him, and knocking his breast, he cried out sometimes 'Jesus', and sometimes 'Credo', the flame being blown away from him for a moment by the unusual violence of the wind that day:

> so for a little pause, hee stoode without fire, the flame departyng and recoursing thrise ere the woode tooke strength to be the sharper to consume hym; and then he gaue vp the Ghost, and his body beyng withered bowed downeward upon the chaine.[2]

READING IN PUBLIC

It is a moving story in either version, yet the trial and execution of Thomas Bilney was also one of the most controversial narratives of the English Reformation, argument still raging about minute details of reportage forty years later.[3] The first version was written a year after the events by Thomas More in one of his vindications of the Catholic church against William Tyndale, author of the first printed English Bible. The second comes from John Foxe's famous vindication of English Protestantism, the *Actes and Monuments* first published in 1563. At first sight More's story has an obvious priority in date, especially since the full version of Foxe's account does not even appear in the first edition but was added later. However, the official story, later recounted by More, was disputed within days of the burning taking place. More himself took no part in the proceedings against Bilney, but as Lord Chancellor became concerned by the spate of rumours surrounding the death of a man who was locally regarded around Norwich as a saint. The noise abroad was of mistrial, miscarriage of justice, and particularly of the total fabrication of the recantation which had played a central part in the Bishop's public report of the execution.[4] More's reaction to these rumours was extraordinary: without waiting for a bill of complaint, and in a quite irregular manner,

---

[2] John Foxe, *Actes and Monuments* (1570), ii. 1152. This is a greatly expanded version of the brief record in the first edition (1563), 477–8.

[3] Foxe's expanded account is an explicit refutation of More, using the testimony of Archbishop Matthew Parker, who in his youth had been a witness at the burning ('M. More proved a lyer, by witnes present at *Bilneys* death', marginal note, ii. 1151; see also Foxe's attack on More which precedes the death of Bilney, ii. 1150).

[4] The history of this contention is described in detail by Guy, *Public Career*, 167–71. Modern bibliography of the episode is extensive and also contentious: see especially A. G. Dickens, *The English Reformation*, rev. edn. (London: Fontana, 1967), 119; John F. Davis, *Heresy and Reformation in the South-East of England, 1520–1559* (London: Royal Historical Society, 1983), 66; Christopher Haigh, *English Reformations: Religion, Politics and Society under the Tudors* (Oxford: Clarendon Press, 1993), 67–8.

he took it upon himself to summon witnesses from Norwich to London, and conducted a virtually private investigation in Star Chamber, taking evidence under oath in person, and soliciting signed depositions of eye-witness accounts of the burning.[5]

More interviewed three witnesses: Thomas Pelles, the chancellor of the Bishop of Norwich; Edward Rede, the Mayor of Norwich; and John Curatt, an alderman. There are crucial inconsistencies between the three depositions, and the evidence changed under pressure of investigation. Without enquiring too closely into More's methods, the sense of intimidation among the surviving state papers is palpable. Pelles declared that he had presented a bill of recantation to Bilney in advance, which was then given to the accused once more at the stake. This bill Bilney had read out clearly to the assembled people. After the execution, Pelles presented the bill to Mayor Rede in order to have it scrutinized by the city aldermen and authenticated under the civic seal. Alderman Curatt in turn presented two widely differing sets of evidence. At first he expressed doubt that the bill produced after the event by Pelles was really the same as the original bill of recantation. Later, however, he swore in front of More that Bilney had made a revocation of his opinions, that Bilney had read it from a bill which he clearly recognized, and that he, Curatt, had stood close by and heard every word. Even so, and even in front of such an importunate inquisitor as More, Curatt equivocated, claiming that he had not heard the last part, as he had been forced to stoop in order to amend his shoelace.[6]

However, it is Rede's deposition that is the most remarkable. He had seen, he said, Pelles's bill of Bilney's heresies, but he could not tell whether these were actually Bilney's own opinions. At his burning, Bilney had made a 'good and godly exhortation to the people'; Pelles had handed him a bill, and Bilney read it, but not aloud or in public, only 'softly and to himself'; in any case Rede could not hear it although standing very near. Later, Pelles had shown him a copy of his bill for exemplification, but neither Rede nor others could verify that it was the same one and indeed suspected it to be different.[7] Examined again a week later, Rede now said that the bill originally shown to Bilney some days before the execution was the same as that used at the stake, but still 'could not say' that it was the same as subsequently produced.[8]

---

[5] The signed depositions taken under oath are preserved in The National Archives, SP 1/68, fos. 45–52, 80–5, 86–9; they are summarized in *Letters and Papers, Foreign and Domestic, of the Reign of Henry VIII* [hereafter *LP*], ed. J. S. Brewer, J. Gairdner, R. H. Brodie, 36 vols. (1862–1932), v. 522, 560, 569; and analysed by Guy, *Public Career*, 167–8.

[6] *LP*, v. 522.   [7] *LP*, v. 560.   [8] *LP*, v. 560.

Questioned a third time, Rede's responses acquired an urgent economy which show more than a hint of the menacing pressures ranged against him: he confessed that he had seen the advance bill of recantation. Pelles did give Bilney a bill, but Rede does not know whether it was the same. He did not hear Bilney read the bill, but saw him look upon it. If he did read it, he read it softly. He does not remember precisely whether Bilney then revoked his errors. Bilney did kneel down and desired absolution. He does not know whether Bilney submitted to the determination of the church, but thinks he did. He does not remember that Bilney exhorted the people to obey God and the ministers of the church. He thinks Bilney desired to be houselled, but does not remember perfectly.[9]

Bilney's recantation turns on some finely balanced questions of interpretation both of public gesture and of public speech. Did he read out the paper aloud as a declamation to the people, or did he read it over to himself, muttering the words 'softly' as he went along? The question of what constitutes private reading is a problematic issue in this period.[10] There was a distinction between *legere sibi* and *clare legere* (or *viva voce*) already in the early Middle Ages, one style of reading being for private *meditatio* and the other a public *lectio* with an audience of other participants.[11] To some degree *legere sibi* meant also *legere tacite*, but this may have meant a low mumble rather than total silence: even in libraries one would have heard a constant murmur as the monks burbled through the manuscripts. Such reading habits correspond to some recognition of different rules for private and public reading, attested to by Augustine's classic account, describing with awe how Ambrose read silently to himself even in the presence of others.[12]

By the later Middle Ages the signs of what constituted private reading were subtly changing. During the fifteenth century, silent reading was a common practice among the learned, although not yet among the poorer classes.[13] Print changed the rules once again, greatly increasing the number of private copies of books and altering habits of digesting them. It is probable that in the early sixteenth century the social meaning of reading a

[9] *LP*, v. 569.

[10] Private reading is discussed by Roger Chartier, 'The Practical Impact of Writing', in *A History of Private Life*, iii: *Passions of the Renaissance* (Cambridge, Mass.: Harvard University Press, 1989), especially 124–7.

[11] Mary J. Carruthers, *The Book of Memory: A Study of Memory in Medieval Culture* (Cambridge: Cambridge University Press, 1990), 170, using terms from the Rule of St Benedict.

[12] *Confessiones*, VI.3; discussed by Carruthers, *The Book of Memory*, 170–3.

[13] Paul Saenger, 'Silent Reading: Its Impact on Late Medieval Script and Society', *Viator*, 13 (1982), 367–414.

page was not at all clear, and may have meant different things to the scholar Bilney, the middle-class observers interviewed by More, and the mass of people who comprised the crowd at a public execution. Was Bilney reading in public, or only reading, in public? Perhaps Bilney's habit of private reading was to pronounce the words of a book as he went along; certainly others might have interpreted it that way. Bilney was used to such ambiguities of perception, and capable of exploiting them in his own trial.[14] More later accused him of mendaciousness in his uses of silence or misconstruction.[15]

The problem at the scene of his execution is all the more entangled, however. What does reading something through imply about the contents of that person's head? Does reading out imply assent, even a conscious desire to mean the words that are written on a page? The act of reading aloud equivocates between the private and the public sphere. At some point the private consideration of words on a page is interpretable as a public statement of the words on the page as one's own. However, the words Bilney was asked to read were not his own, but written (so we are told) by another.

This brings us to the crux of the Bilney case. He was asked to perform a series of exterior acts: recantation, penance, submission to the church and its officers. On the other hand, his supporters hoped he would perform another set of public acts: faithfulness to his beliefs, steadfastness in the face of ecclesiastical oppression, absolute trust in God *in extremis*. But these acts were only considered to have meaning if they were instantiated by Bilney's interior state of mind. This interior state was in constant doubt, and open to different interpretations. The two stories of Bilney's execution are thus each a complex mixture of private and public acts, in such a way that it becomes alarmingly arbitrary as to which is which.

LOCATING THE PRIVATE

The depositions presented to More during his investigations are characterized by an opposition between the terms 'privily' and 'apertly'. State proclamations in the reign of Henry VIII routinely use these words to

---

[14] Davis, *Heresy and Reformation*, 46–7. Bilney refers to the theory of equivocation in a marginal note to his copy of the Vulgate, which still survives.

[15] More, *Dialogue Concerning Heresies*, III.2; *Complete Works of Thomas More*, vi/1. 256–7. More compares what Bilney used to say among his 'secte' with what he would aver in 'open audyence'. During his trial Bilney had in fact claimed that he could not remember what he had preached, and asked for the trial to be suspended accordingly.

denote the boundaries of political space.[16] Yet there is also a difficulty in locating the frontiers between the two. Repeatedly, More asked his three witnesses whether Bilney had read the recantation 'openly' or 'secretly'. This excruciating question then turned on whether he had made his reading 'loudly' or 'softly'. More wished to assure himself that the public is 'openly' knowable, but he could not persuade his witnesses of the transparency of the distinction.

More's difficulty is reflected in a struggle over emerging vocabulary to describe these areas. The everyday medieval opposition of 'privy' and 'apert' was in the process of giving way to the more familiar modern opposition of 'private' and 'public'.[17] 'Apert' has a much narrower range of signification than 'public'. It means 'open, unconcealed', and hence 'plain, evident, manifest to the understanding'. In more colloquial usage it could mean 'straightforward, direct' and even 'outspoken or insolent', in which form it survives in the modern English 'pert'.[18] 'Privy' in contradistinction to 'apert' meant, then, something like 'concealed from open view'.

'Private' in contradistinction to 'public' means something rather different, more diffuse perhaps, and more disturbing politically and ethically. This could be understood in a number of different ways. One would be to ascribe to the sixteenth century the emergence, or the invention, of a more modern understanding of the 'private'. However, the word 'privy' already covered such meanings as 'things that are intimate or familiar', 'things that pertain to a particular individual', 'a person not in an official capacity', 'knowledge that is held in secret', or 'something that is concealed or hidden'.[19] In the fourteenth and fifteenth centuries the word 'private' began to cover some of the same senses: in connection with 'an ordinary person', 'a concealed affair', 'something of restricted use, for privileged enjoyment'.[20] What is peculiar to sixteenth-century usage is not the emergence of a category of the 'private', but the way in which this category comes to be formulated as part of a precise opposition between the terms 'private' and 'public', so that the one word virtually implies the other in order to demarcate its own usage.

In that sense, paradoxically perhaps, the sixteenth century sees not so much the invention of the private as the invention of the public. I say

---

[16] For instance, *Tudor Royal Proclamations*, ed. P. Hughes and J. Larkin, 3 vols. (New Haven: Yale University Press, 1964–9), i, No. 122, 'Enforcing Statutes against Heresy' (1530), probably drafted by More himself; and the proclamation endorsing the *King's Primer* (1545), fo. cii.

[17] I here use various citations for 'private' and 'public' (and related words) in the *OED*.

[18] *OED* APERT, *adj.*, 1a, 2, 3, and 5.

[19] *OED* PRIVY *adj.*, 2b, 3, and 4.

[20] *OED* PRIVATE, *adj.*, 2, 3, 4, and 6.

'paradoxically' because so much of medieval life was conducted in what we might term 'public'. Indeed, it is possible that there was little need for the word in a medieval context because there was so little sense of the private that everything, practically, came into the domain of the public. The public was so pervasive that it did not need identifying. It seems, on the contrary, that in the sixteenth century this became necessary.

The word 'public' was used before the sixteenth century almost exclusively in order to translate the Latin phrase *res publica*. The period 1509 to 1547, however, sees four identifiable new meanings attaching to the word: 1. 'Belonging to the community or nation as a whole'; 2. 'Something that is open to, or may be used or shared by, the whole community, rather than restricted to the private use of some person or persons' (appropriately, the first reference in the *OED* to this sense is 'readynge a publique lecture'); 3. 'Open to general observation or sight, existing, done or made in public, manifest, not concealed'; and 4. 'Of or pertaining to a person in the capacity in which he comes in contact with the community, as opposed to his private capacity'. The 1530s also sees the emergence of a new and characteristic oppositional collocation, 'the private and the public'. Potentially the two terms cover different areas of life, separable from each other, and perhaps needing to be separated. Early sixteenth-century English usage manifests in fact an urgent need to denote this separation, and particularly to clarify the limits of the public in order to find some room for a distinguishable private sphere. It is a newly apprehended conflict of interest between the two areas that requires some new linguistic regulation to negotiate the boundaries between them.

The burning of Bilney manifests just such a conflict. It was, of course, a public execution, but Foxe's narrative also makes it sound strangely like a private leave-taking between Bilney and his God. The manner of its proceeding also raised a highly charged question of what is referred to by the *OED* as 'open to general view, what is done in public, and not concealed'. However, its peculiar complexity seems to revolve round the linguistic distinction which is first recorded in the work of Thomas Starkey in the 1530s, between 'the pryuate and publyke state of euery man'.[21] This use of 'pryuate' is in line with a general reinterpretation of the word visible at the beginning of the sixteenth century. 1502 sees the first reference to 'private' property; 1542 to a 'private' house. 1526 sees the use of the word to denote 'something that pertains to a small group rather than the general community', and also 'something that is special to an individual'.

---

[21] Thomas Starkey, A *Dialogue between Pole and Lupset*, ed. T. F. Mayer, Camden Society, Fourth Series, 37 (London: Royal Historical Society, 1989), 41; cited in *OED*, PUBLIC, *adj.*, 5.

1549, crucially, sees the first reference to the word in terms of 'a private or personal matter', as in 'a person's private affairs'. In this connection, we may note also the following new phrases, reverberating with potential significance: 'priuate interpretation' (1526), 'priuat judgement' (1565), 'private opinion' (1586).

I wish to suggest that the Bilney case has an exemplary historical significance in the relationship of public and private, within an English social register, for two reasons. One concerns the individual in relation to the state, and the other concerns the construction of religious belief as public or private realm. In both these respects the reign of Henry VIII is critical. What is interesting in the Bilney case is that we see the eruption of argument over fraught areas of new definition and differentiation, without a vocabulary yet trained for its denotation. Bilney's case attests to a tension in judging the private in the context of, or perhaps in contradistinction to, the public; of how far or in what way a private utterance can be construed as having a public meaning, and just as importantly, whether a public utterance can properly manifest to its listeners a private meaning.

Here we come to quite radically different religious interpretations which are possible of Bilney's recantation. In More's version it consists in a series of exterior actions. The degradation of the heretic, the confessing of sins, the conferring of absolution, the taking of the sacrament, the burning of the body, are all public performances of ritual with a clear symbolic meaning and function. In More's terms they are self-reflexive actions which demonstrate irrefutably that Bilney is a sinner, recognizes himself as such, and thus subsumes himself within the visible performance of the church as a material representative of God in institutional form.[22] For Foxe, on the other hand, the crucial moral and narrative question is whether Bilney maintained during the final moments of his life the full integrity of his belief. This belief is constructed not as an exterior performance of ritual but a private state of mind. The key events in Foxe consist in Bilney's declaration of his 'right belief towards Almighty God', his rehearsal of his 'fast faith' in the form of articles of a personal creed, and his final 'priuate prayer' (that is Foxe's exact phrase) performed 'in so good and quiet behauiour, that he seemed not much to consider the terrour of his death'.[23]

So far we have the conventional historical distinction long established between the 'outward' form of Catholicism and the 'inward' form of

---

[22] Bilney is said by More to give special emphasis to the word *ecclesia* (and just as importantly, says it in Latin).

[23] Foxe (1570), ii. 1152. Significantly, the collect is replaced by a Psalm, in English.

emergent Protestantism. But my argument is that the distinction is nowhere near so clear-cut as that. More's public drama requires verification in an examination of Bilney's private state of mind, or otherwise the recantation will be considered worthless. This is why he spent so much time interviewing witnesses who were close to Bilney in his last days, not just eyewitnesses to the execution. Foxe, equally, looks for proof of Bilney's inward faith in exterior signs. The common problem for each writer is finding some precise enough medium for correlation between the private and public spheres. Yet no one should think that the difference between the two writers is therefore small or trivial. The taut complexity of both narratives arises from the attempt to acquire determination over this area of conceptual indecisiveness. More attempts to demonstrate that even Bilney, one of the most highly regarded of the new religious movement, fails in his reliance on individual religion, and submits himself in death to the visible assurances of the embodied church. The life of faith claimed for Protestant evangelicals is a meaningless charade, invisible and therefore non-existent. His readers should trust to what they can see: the visible testimony of miracles, sacraments, martyrs, and saints. Foxe attempts to make an equally public proof of the triumph of the invisible world of the spirit over the visible tyranny of the Catholic church, as a paradigm act and monument in his rewriting of history. The key to his meaning lies in the popular subtitle of his work, the Book of Martyrs, which of course means in Greek, 'witnesses'. Bilney is a martyr to the truth; a public witness to the transcendent world of private faith. Even, or especially, in death, the phenomenological interpretation of minute gestures reverberates with meaning.

HERESY TRIALS

Historians still argue over which picture of Bilney is the more accurate, and over which of More's three witnesses is to be believed, but these are false questions.[24] The issue is not 'what happened to Bilney', but 'what people saw', and what they saw was conditioned by what they believed. Like any public event, the execution of Bilney was subject to a thousand tellings, each a report of a perception, not a record of reality. It is quite possible that Pelles saw what he says he saw, and Rede saw what he says he saw. No doubt Bilney's actions were ambiguous, and in any case, as we are told, it was a very windy day. Yet even so, and here we find ourselves at a

---

[24] For instance, G. Walker, 'Saint or Schemer? The 1527 Heresy Trial of Thomas Bilney Reconsidered', *Journal of Ecclesiastical History*, 40 (1989), 219–38.

further remove from the 'reality' of the case, the fragile handwriting preserved in the National Archives does not tell us what Pelles, Rede, or Curatt saw, but rather, what they were prepared to swear to.

Or rather, what Rede and Curatt swore to, for More, crucially, did not require Pelles to swear. This intricate legal decision by England's cleverest lawyer is worth paying attention to, for within it lies compacted a set of meanings of great complexity. Pelles was not required to swear because, as the Bishop of Norwich's chancellor, he was considered to be a safe witness, who could be trusted to say what he wished. Under oath, by contrast, he would feel constrained by the risk of perjury, and might be less ready with his testimony. Rede and Curatt, on the other hand, gave their evidence under oath, and the signs of this are all too evident in the statements they very carefully made. Notice how Curatt at a crucial point in his story claims that he had to stoop to tie a shoelace, and so could not precisely hear what Bilney said; how Rede repeatedly answered that 'he could not remember', or 'he could not tell'. Bilney, too, during his trial claimed not to remember his past words and so refused to swear to what he meant by them. These are remarks made under pressure, an intense instinct of self-preservation in the shadow of a public oath, in front of a judge who is all too knowingly capable of exploiting any inconsistency as blatant perjury.

Some of the procedural intricateness of this is visible to a modern readership familiar with the proceedings in a court of law. Evidence that is sworn is still given greater legal credence than a written 'statement', however explicit. Nevertheless, it is extremely difficult now to reconstruct the gravity and immediate physical intimidation of the oaths made in More's Star Chamber inquiries of 1531. For More made his key witnesses swear oaths *ex officio*, in other words following the standard procedure not of a secular court but of a heresy trial. This was a quite extraordinary extension of Star Chamber procedure, and it gave More overwhelming powers of examination.[25] Indeed it turned the enquiry arguably into an Inquisition.

It is necessary to describe briefly what an *ex officio* oath meant. It was a procedure whereby a charge of heresy could be pursued even where there were no independent witnesses, when the defendant was accused instead by *clamosa insinuatio*, that is by 'public scandal'. In such a case the judge or ordinary was empowered to act *ex officio* (on the authority of his office), and to ask the accused to take an oath to answer truthfully absolutely any question that was asked of him. There was thus no specific bill of charges,

---

[25] Guy, *Public Career*, 171; see also Guy, *The Cardinal's Court: The Impact of Thomas Wolsey in Star Chamber* (Hassocks: Harvester, 1977), ch. 4.

no indictment providing the limits of allowable questioning. There was also no legal counsel for the accused. The judge effectively took the part also of prosecution and even (more or less disingenuously) of defence. The odds against the accused in such circumstances were catastrophic. Unless he was himself expert in theology, he was virtually certain to convict himself of some heresy or other under such open rules of examination.

The whole process was constructed around rules of swearing.[26] A refusal to swear the oath in the first place was taken as an acknowledgement of guilt, and subject to an immediate penalty of imprisonment. Once under oath, a refusal to answer any particular question was also tantamount to confession, and was read in the worst possible light. On the other hand, agreeing to swear to an answer invited the charge of perjury later in the proceedings if a contrary argument could be proven. Once convicted through some act of inevitable self-incrimination, the accused had to abjure the heresy or face the consequences. Such recantation included a solemn oath not to reoffend, and in case of a second offence the resulting trial always, even when the accused confessed and repented, terminated in death by burning. If the accused was unrepentant, he or she died excommunicate and was therefore presumed damned for eternity. If the accused repented, he or she was allowed the comfort of final expiatory sacraments and died in torment with the prospect (officially at any rate) of comparatively untormenting purgatory.

Unknown to Roman law, the procedure *ex officio* was implemented under Pope Innocent III in 1215 and promulgated in England by statute under Henry IV in 1410 in the campaign against Lollards.[27] In the sixteenth century it was the object of enormous controversy. In 1533, shortly after the Bilney case, as part of the new religious polity of Henry VIII in which he declared himself supreme head of the church, the use of the *ex officio* procedure against heretics was severely limited.[28] Since Henry was hardly renowned for voluntarily relinquishing powers of suppression or intimidation, at first sight this appears a piece of ecclesiastical law he would have been happy to take over. However, *ex officio* proceedings had become a primary source of the kind of anti-clerical feeling which Henry was keen on promoting. It is the grounds of this feeling which I will now investigate.

---

[26] Something of the flavour of these rules of swearing in the fourteenth century can be gleaned from the specimen examination described with sadistic relish by Bernard Gui in his *Practica*; translated in H. C. Lea, *The Inquisition of the Middle Ages*, ed. Walter Ullmann (London: Eyre & Spottiswoode, 1963), 164–7.

[27] The procedure was outlined in *Licet Heli* in 1213 and ratified at the Fourth Lateran Council of 1215, canon 3; G. D. Mansi, *Sacrorum Conciliorum Collectio* (Venice, 1778), xxii, col. 986–90.

[28] 25 Henry VIII, c. 14; Davis, *Heresy and Reformation*, 12–13.

The official medieval view was that only a rebel or a heretic would ever refuse to swear an oath. It was like admitting dishonesty: if you didn't swear you obviously didn't want to tell the truth. Taking an oath served several functions at once: it was a public witness, an act of obedience, and virtually a truth condition. Among fifteenth- and early sixteenth-century Lollards, however, there was an argument that there were areas of conscience which were secret, that it was unlawful to expose into public view by the artificial process of swearing, an argument which was taken up by early English Protestants.[29] Thus William Tyndale asserted that judges should condemn an accused only through exterior witnesses. Trying a case by examining the accused himself under oath was effectively to 'break up the consciences of men', and to compel a man either to forswear himself before the divine judge or condemn himself before the human judge. He concluded: 'Let that which is secret to God only, whereof no proof can be made, nor lawful witness brought, abide unto the coming of the Lord, which shall open all secrets'.[30]

Tyndale brings together several complaints against swearing that became a staple of sixteenth-century criticism. One is a legal objection to self-incrimination; another is a sense that truth should be established by other means than a test of asseveration; but the third is a principle that there is a sphere of life, which he calls 'conscience', which should be allowed to remain legally sacrosanct as a private matter, to be determined between the individual and God in the final judgement, but which is not the business of human law or the state. Protestant reinterpretation of heresy laws, later taken up by puritans and other dissenting traditions such as the Quakers, was that religious belief constituted a matter of private conscience, of no public interest beyond obedience to the secular laws.[31] To force a person to swear to his religious faith was therefore an act of illegitimate violence. As a 1586 puritan petition to parliament puts it: 'to a conscience that feareth God, [an oath] is more violent than any [torture or] rack to constrain him to utter that he knoweth'.[32]

The limits of swearing, then, were proposed as a boundary that could be located between public citizenship and private opinion. In 1533 such a

---

[29] Margaret Aston, *Lollards and Reformers: Images and Literacy in Late Medieval Religion* (London: Hambledon Press, 1984), 110–11; Susan Brigden, *London and the Reformation* (Oxford: Clarendon Press, 1989), 96.

[30] William Tyndale, *Obedience of a Christen Man*, in *Doctrinal Treatises*, ed. Henry Walter, Parker Society (Cambridge: Cambridge University Press, 1848), 203; see also *An Answer to Sir Thomas More's Dialogue*, ed. Henry Walter, Parker Society (Cambridge: Cambridge University Press, 1848), 147.

[31] See Ch. 1; and Christopher Hill, 'From Oaths to Interest', *Society and Puritanism in Pre-Revolutionary England* (London: Secker & Warburg, 1964), 382–419.

[32] Quoted in Hill, 'From Oaths to Interest', 384.

distinction was given some legal credence by the abolition of the use of *ex officio* oaths in heresy cases. But characteristically, what Henry liberally granted with one hand, with the other he took gruesomely away. 1534 saw the Act of Succession, in which the divorce from Katherine of Aragon and the marriage to Anne Boleyn was confirmed, and the issue of Henry and Anne declared the heirs to the throne. This Act was enforced by an oath of allegiance promulgated by Parliament in the same year.[33] The most famous victim of the Act was of course Thomas More himself, who refused to swear, and was beheaded a year later.[34] More's own trial shows that the state was determined to control whatever space was being redefined for the private in relation to the public. Specifically, the definition of treason was extended to the category of 'misprision', where mere 'words' against the king were construed as treasonable in a second degree.[35] Refusal to swear the oath of succession was even more dubiously construed as misprision on the basis that such a person was secretly sheltering treasonable thoughts. Still, on this ground alone More could only be imprisoned; there was a residual reluctance to execute a man on the basis of silence.

More's death raises a double question of privacy because ultimately he was only tried for treason proper on the basis of an apparently private conversation with Sir Richard Rich. Rich claimed—or rather swore—that More had spoken against the supremacy in a private debate with him. More's defence—so far as it can be reconstructed—was based on three principles, each of which was constructed round a theory of private meaning.[36] First, Rich was swearing evidence in an event of which More himself was

---

[33] The Act (25 Henry VIII, c. 22) stipulated an oath without declaring its wording. A specific oath was first formulated for members of parliament in 1534 (*Lord's Journals*, i. 82); a general form of oath was defined in the amended Act of Succession in the next session of parliament (26 Henry VIII, c. 2). G. R. Elton, *Policy and Police: The Enforcement of the Reformation in the Age of Thomas Cromwell* (Cambridge: Cambridge University Press, 1972), 222–4.

[34] In February 1535 a further Act (26 Henry VIII, c. 13) made the denial of any royal title treasonable; it applied retrospectively to the title of Supreme Head of the Church defined in the Act of Supremacy of December 1534 (26 Henry VIII, c. 1). It was this last manoeuvre which made the refusal of the Oath of Succession equivalent to treason.

[35] The Treason Act (26 Henry VIII, c. 13) was passed in November 1534. Treason was first extended from exterior acts and deeds to include writing, and then eventually to encompass spoken words, although this caused some difficulty in drafting. See Elton, 'The Law of Treason' in *Policy and Police*, and esp. 276–8. On More's trial, see J. D. M. Derrett, 'The Trial of Sir Thomas More', *English Historical Review*, 79 (1964), 450–77; a rebarbative analysis is given by Elton, *Policy and Police*, 400–19. On More's last years in general I have made reference to Marius, *Thomas More*.

[36] Rich's record of the conversation is preserved in London, The National Archives, TNA SP 2/R, fos. 24–5 (see *LP*, viii. 814.2); it was also translated into Latin in the Indictment against More. The only documentary evidence for More's response is in William Roper's *Life of Sir Thomas More*, which translates More's defence into the embellished form of *oratio recta*. On this part of the trial, see Marius, *Thomas More*, 505–8.

the only other witness, that is, his word against More's; legally, More could counter it simply by accusing Rich of perjury, all the more reasonably since Riche was a habitual liar. Second, whatever Rich heard spoken was 'but in familiar secret talk', and therefore uninterpretable as a public action. Third, More recounted his own private meaning during the fatal conversation and stated that everything he had said was stated hypothetically, and therefore could not be construed as a speech act of treason.

More's final defence has traditionally been seen as one of the defining moments of modern individual conscience, preserving his private integrity in the face of the state. But I want to question this liberal interpretation. It assumes too readily, I think, that More's private self can be identified and located. More's case seems rather to show how difficult it was to make this identification, for More himself, for his society, and *a fortiori* for his modern interpreters. If sixteenth-century oaths show a nervousness about the intrusion of the public into the private, they also show a nervousness about where the private really is, what it constitutes. More wrote a short memorandum on perjury while in the Tower, justifying a refusal to swear in certain cases of conscience, or even to lie without perjury having taken such an oath, saying that 'No one has the power to tender an oath to anyone else binding him to reveal such a secret as can and should be kept secret.'[37] Yet only a few years earlier More had accused Bilney of committing perjury at his trial, when he equivocated on an oath he considered contrary to conscience. For Bilney was indeed charged *ex officio*. He employed many ingenious tactics in avoiding the power of the oath. He agreed, for instance, that certain statements were heresies, but refused to abjure them, on the basis that he would not admit to ever having held these heresies as his own opinions. If he abjured them he would have convicted himself of heresy; by not abjuring he placed the onus on his accusers to prove the linguistic presence of these heresies within his sermons, for which no texts survived, and memorial reports of which he dismissed as inaccurate. More condemned Bilney's replies as monstrous cavillations, but they are not unlike the brilliant deconstructive devices of his own defence, playing on the very idea of extrapolating private meanings from speech.

Thomas Cromwell challenged More shortly before his death over the discrepancy between his attitude to oaths in heresy trials and in treason cases. More's reply, in the circumstances, was scrupulously enigmatic.[38]

---

[37] BL MS Royal 17.D.XIV, reprinted and translated as Appendix B to the *Complete Works of Thomas More*, vi/2. 764–7; cited here from p. 765. Perjury is also discussed by More in the *Dialogue Concerning Heresies*, III.7.

[38] Described in a letter to his daughter Margaret Roper, 3 June 1535, *Correspondence of More*, ed. Rogers, 557–8.

Cromwell, with gruesome and deadly humour, answered that 'thei were as well burned for the denienge of that, as thei be beheaded for denienge of this' (p. 558). The twin cases of Bilney and More together show the extreme volatility of notions of conscience and privacy. Yet this did not discourage government from trying to seek them out, in every nook and cranny in the land.[39] Official commissioners were employed to administer the oath to every single person in England. At least in theory; in practice women in general were considered too insignificant, and in some parts of the country only men over the age of 14 seem to have taken the oath.[40] Yet even in the case of those who were constrained to swear, there is an interesting official ambiguity over how to interpret oaths. For the oath itself was insufficient as a guarantee; in order to confirm the oath had taken place, the commissioners had to certify each oath in writing, and each person had to sign his name in order to subscribe his spoken oath.[41]

Swearing and signatures have a special place in the philosophy of language. For each is understood to locate the place of the individual person in language use, the one in speaking and the other in writing. They are the marks of authenticity. Yet as Derrida showed in a series of arguments, claims for such authenticity are made on very doubtful grounds.[42] The supervision of the oaths under the 1534 Act testify to this dubiety. For how could the government know that an oath had been sworn at all, let alone truly? What does an oath signify? In one sense, nothing at all, except the veracity of the speaking subject; and yet only (perhaps not even) the subject himself knows the truth of this. Just to make sure, signatures were required as well, but there were equal problems here. Archbishop Cranmer in a letter raised the fraught question of illiteracy; was the mark of an illiterate authentic? And if so, what mark? Could a secretary sign in lieu? Would a sheep mark suffice, or the sign of the cross? Could a seal be used?[43] A Norwich commissioner

---

[39] The oath was applied with unprecedented thoroughness; Elton, *Policy and Police*, 224–7.

[40] Stephen Gardiner, Bishop of Winchester, reporting to Thomas Cromwell on the progress of the oath in his diocese (5 May 1534): *The Letters of Stephen Gardiner*, ed. J. A. Muller (Cambridge: Cambridge University Press, 1933), 56–7.

[41] 25 Henry VIII, c. 22; see David Cressy, *Literacy and the Social Order: Reading and Writing in Tudor and Stuart England* (Cambridge: Cambridge University Press, 1980), 62–5.

[42] Most obviously in 'Signature Event Context', in *Margins of Philosophy*, trans. Alan Bass (Chicago: Chicago University Press, 1982), 307–30 ('the most improbable signature'); and *Limited Inc* (Paris: Galiléc, 1990).

[43] *The Remains of Archbishop Cranmer*, ed. Henry Jenkyns, Parker Society (Cambridge: Cambridge University Press, 1833), i. 112.

asked if it was sufficient for an oath-taker to kiss the book in which the statute was written.[44] There is no record of lip-prints being taken to authenticate every kiss.

The 1534 Act raised wild linguistic undecidables, and at the same time wild uncertainties about the locus of private authenticity. But it was only the beginning of a rash of public swearing enforced by government over the next 150 years. Almost every revolution of religion and politics in these revolutionary years was accompanied by a new oath of allegiance to it. As Christopher Hill has succinctly written, this sometimes involved swearing contradictory oaths over the space of a few years. Between 1640 and 1660 ten conflicting oaths were enjoined on the citizenry. In 1685 James II's loyal subjects were asked to swear undying loyalty to him, and in 1688 they were asked to swear that he had never been the legal king in the first place.[45]

How do we interpret the social impact and the social meaning of oaths in this context? On the one hand they were perceived as an act of violence. The imperial ambassador Eustace Chapuys remarked in 1534 that the private talk among the people was that a law that could only be enforced by oaths violently obtained from the people was not a good one.[46] Yet there was a clear methodology behind this: it was a means of publicly identifying even private dissidence. Hill shows plenty of evidence, however, that the frequent use of such a strategy induced at least in some parts of the community a contemptuous disregard for the meaningfulness of oaths. If government required that people swear to anything, then so be it. Swearing to an oath thus became a means of concealing private dissidence under public obedience. In 1648 a royalist song promised to swear two oaths to Parliament, and a third that they would never keep them. In 1658 the joke went that people had 'called God Himself to witness that his name was no longer of any validity'.[47]

FOUL OATHS

The sixteenth century sees a rash not only of oaths of allegiance, but of that other, unmentionable, kind of swearing, of execrations, foul language, and profanities. There was also an acute attentiveness to the meaning of this kind of swearing, and a flurry of attempts to censor its public

[44] *LP*, vii. 610, 702; xi. 29. See Cressy, *Literacy and the Social Order*, 64.
[45] Hill, 'From Oaths to Interest', 409.
[46] *Calendar of State Papers* (Spanish), 5, 45.
[47] Hill, 'From Oaths to Interest', 411.

utterance. Swearing expletives is the location, I am going to argue, of an extreme of nervousness in the regulation of boundaries between public and private in sixteenth-century England. Of course the first part of my proposition, that there was an effusion of swear words, is hard to substantiate. Swearing of its nature is unmentionable and therefore often unrecorded, especially in writing, which is its only form of survival but where special rules of taboo obtain. Swear words in writing are often erased altogether, or else mangled or truncated in a more or less transparent effort of obscurity.[48]

Thus the survival of ancient swearing is a delicate business. The first instance in the *OED* of the ineffable F-word is 1503 in one of Dunbar's flyting poems, but who knows what shameless verbal history precedes that first written exposure.[49] In addition, and even more confusingly, the actual offensive register of words from the past is irremediably lost. Words that in one decade or even in one form of social context are taboo, can quickly become acceptable in another. The history of swearing is of constant readjustment of the rules of offence. This is complicated still further by the pressure of euphemism. Euphemisms—which may start life as self-bowdlerizing efforts of substitution—in time take on the effect of independent swear words. The *OED* gnomically suggests that the word 'piss' was originally a euphemism, but what for was evidently so shocking that it is nowhere even recorded.[50]

Still, allowing for such caveats, it is possible to attempt some social history of swearing. Most early modern swearing was, significantly, not about sex but about God.[51] Although medieval swearing shared this characteristic, evidence exists for an extraordinary set of coinages of new swear words through the sixteenth century, in a series of formulations swearing by attributes of God: By God's Body, By God's Bread, By God's Brother, God's Crown, God's Deed, God's Fish, God's Foot, God's Gown, God's Guts, God's Hat, God's Lady, God's Lid (that is Eyelid), God's Life, God's Light, God's Lord, God's Mother, Pity, Plenty, Precious, Sacrament, Will, Word, Wounds.[52] There are numerous medieval versions of 'By God', but differences are observable. Medieval examples, which include 'By God's Corpus', 'By God's Precious Heart', 'By God's Mercy', 'By God's Passion', tend to refer to the ritual and doctrinal surface of the church. The sixteenth-century examples are like a dismemberment of this corporate

---

[48] On swearing in general, I have made use of Geoffrey Hughes, *Swearing: A Social History of Foul Language, Oaths and Profanity in English* (Oxford: Blackwell, 1991).
[49] Hughes, *Swearing*, 20.
[50] Euphemism is surveyed in general terms by Hughes, *Swearing*, 7–21.
[51] On Reformation swearing, Hughes, *Swearing*, 91–100.
[52] *OED* GOD, 14.

body of God into randomly disposable fragments, a Rabelaisian naming of parts, virtually of private parts. Whereas medieval swearing is concentrated on elements of clearly sacred significance, the effect of referring to God's Eyelids, Guts, or Foot is to deconsecrate him, socializing him and even dressing him up in a coat and hat. The body of Christ is reconstituted as any old body. God is turned into a private and yet unidentifiable individual.

At the same time, this proliferation of oaths by the attributes of God has a parallel and seemingly parasitic relation to oaths of allegiance. They embody a formulary of unofficial swearing to go alongside official swearing, like an alternative etiquette of improper terms. Some testify to a sacred register of metaphorical violence corresponding to the bodily violence of the state in enforcing political oaths; others are motivated more by flippancy, gallows humour or plain farce. At an extreme there are joke diminutives, such as 'lidikins' for God's eyelids and 'bodykins' for his body. The violence and comedy each has a very precise logic in relation to the social demands of swearing. Turning oaths into profanities is a way of rendering their bloody implications meaningless and fruitless, displacing verbal violence into violent verbiage. If oaths represent an extreme of linguistic meaningfulness, suggesting the saturation of language with the full personating presence of the individual consciousness, swear words represent an extreme of linguistic meaninglessness, suggesting an emptying from language of any such presence, in which a person simply impersonates himself for the purposes of official obfuscation. Swearing profanities seems to be a way of cutting the swearing of oaths from its context, and so rendering it inert. The absolutely public gesture of taking an oath finds its obverse in vulgar swearing, effectively turning oaths into private obscenity. The public meaning of language is deflected in a turning in of language on itself.

Not surprisingly, officialdom attempted to control such unofficial eructations. The 1547 Book of Homilies includes one against swearing, which attempts some regulation both of swearing and its meaning.[53] The homily specifically compares official and blasphemous oaths, using the latter as a means of defining the former. It attempts to demarcate rigidly a threefold division: between public and private swearing, between true and false swearing, and between necessary and gratuitous or 'vain' swearing. The suggestion here is that we might be able to use the contrast between oaths and profanities as an index of public versus private meaning.

---

[53] 'Agaynst Swearyng and Perjurie', *Certain Sermons or Homilies (1547)*, ed. Ronald B. Bond (Toronto: University of Toronto Press, 1987), 128–36.

But once again the barrier between the two seems to break down. The Homily finds its own distinctions impossible to maintain. First, it found hardly any way of telling the difference between true swearing and false swearing. When Tyndale produced examples of solemn promises as lawful types of swearing, he could hardly find a formula distinguishable from the unacceptable 'By God I will do it'. St Paul, after all, swears his truthfulness by the habitual phrase, 'I call God to witnesse'.[54]

Second, there is a strong connection between unofficial swearing and official cursing. The Homilies demonstrated the infamy of vain swearing by recalling the penalty for it prescribed by the prophet Zechariah in the Bible. But the punishment for cursing in Zechariah is a curse, a spectacular one at that. It takes the form of perhaps the longest expletive in history, described as a flying book twenty cubits long by ten wide (about thirty feet by twenty), so unmentionable that of course the prophet is unable to repeat it. Even when swearing, God has the best lines.[55]

Third, the distinction between public and private swearing broke down. For profanities, too, work on a principle of public meaning. Just as oaths eradicate content from meaning so as to signify only the assent of the speaker, so profanities, too, eliminate content in order to signify the desire of the speaker to give offence. Once again, profanities feed parasitically off official oaths, in rendering language as pure public context. This most anti-social form of language is therefore also the most radically social in formation.

Swear words, then, are signs of the nervous energy attaching to both the construction and the enunciation of oaths in early modern England. They are a volatile linguistic feature, and their volatility attests to the sense of the violent risk at stake in making statements of public allegiance. The friction between private and public sense manifests itself both in new forms of offensiveness, and new forms of obscuring that offence. Disguising oaths in the form of apparently innocuous nonce words has a long history: 'geewiz', 'drat', 'cobblers', 'git', and 'sod', are just a few modern examples where the disguise is so long-standing that people often do not know what they are uttering or how rude it is. Sixteenth-century usage abounds with such disguises, and at the end of the century invented even a new linguistic form, now known as the minced oath.[56] Thus 'God's

---

[54] Tyndale glossing Matthew 5: 33–7, in *Expositions of Scripture*, ed. Henry Walter, Parker Society (Cambridge: Cambridge University Press, 1849), 55–7; 2 Cor. 1: 23, cited in *Homilies*, 129.

[55] Zech. 5: 1–4; cited in *Homilies*, 134.

[56] On minced oaths, Hughes, *Swearing*, 104–5.

Blood' was shortened or minced to 'Sblood, God's wounds to Zounds, Light to 'Slight, Eyelid to 'Slid, Nails to 'Snails, Death to 'Sdeath', Foot to 'Sfoot.

The first *OED* references for all these forms occur between 1598 and 1602. The usual explanation given is reaction to censorship, but this is perhaps too facile. Older forms of disguise, such as 'By Gog' or 'By Cock', were a more effective protection against censorship since they concealed their referent in nonsense. The new forms, however, sail with deliberate exactness close to the edge; they invite a simple decoding back into the offensive term apparently avoided, and the elision scarcely conceals anything at all. Besides, the censors took exception as much to minced oaths as to oaths proper. The evidence is that saying ''sblood' was as socially unacceptable as saying 'God's blood', and was capable of giving as much offence.

The mincing of oaths involves a complex register of exposure and concealment. If it is a reaction to censorship it is double-edged. In this respect, it is a further sign of the tension between public and private codes of speech. Another sign of this tension lies in the forms of actual censorship themselves. There were in fact two Acts of Parliament against swearing in the period, both in the reign of King James, in 1606 and 1622. The first was aimed specifically against the theatre. Its provisions aimed to prevent 'the great abuse of the holy Name of God', and specified a fine of ten pounds against any person who uttered the name of God, or Christ, or the Holy Ghost, in a jesting or profane manner, or without proper fear or reverence, in any 'Stage-Play, Interlude, Shew, May-Game or Pageant'.[57] The second act was more general in application. Any person heard anywhere profanely swearing or cursing was subject to a twelve pence fine; those who could not afford it would spend three hours in the stocks; a person under 12 years old would be whipped by the constable, or else a parent or schoolmaster in presence of the constable.[58]

The origin of these Acts against profanities has always been blamed on the puritans, and the motivation has been assumed to be a general hatred amongst puritans of any type of enjoyable behaviour. But there is a much more specific reason for puritan edginess about swearing, related directly to the social and political meaning of oaths of allegiance. For puritans were among the groups most at risk from the promulgation of oaths. If much of the population was prepared to swear with indifferent obedience, and some with flippant disingenuousness, men and women of conscience who respected the sanctity of God's name

[57] 3 James I, c. 21.   [58] 21 James I, c. 20.

were peculiarly endangered by the compulsion to swear. The government deliberately exploited this, both with puritans and with Roman
Catholics. In 1583, with savage cynicism, Archbishop Whitgift revived
the practice of *ex officio* swearing in order to inveigle presbyterian sectar-
ies into giving themselves away.[59] Puritan writers and common lawyers
reacted with a vociferous campaign of opposition, in which Foxe's Book
of Martyrs played a prominent part.[60] Foxe argued that respect for faith
as private conscience was one of the primary victories of the Reformation, and that the bishops were turning themselves back into papistical
oppressors. But Whitgift was adamant about the necessity of swearing
and answering, and ruthlessly revived also the interpretation of a refusal
to swear as confession of guilt.

Some puritans obeyed, others made a refusal to swear a point of conscience. Oaths became a shibboleth between conforming puritans who
tacitly remained within the Church of England, and dissidents who splin-
tered into sectarian groups, including those who departed to America. In
this context it is hardly surprising that the uncontrolled linguistic and
social force of common swearing should become such a fetish for puritans of all colours, including those within parliament and court. The
same group in parliament was responsible for the unsuccessful move
against *ex officio* oaths in 1593 and the successful one against profane
oaths in 1606.[61] If oaths of allegiance or in *ex officio* trials brought a sup-
posedly private conscience into direct conflict with public performance
and interpretation, oaths of cussing seemed to disregard all such niceties
altogether.

Hence the peculiar sensitivity of the Acts of censorship against swearing to questions of public space. The 1622 general Act drew attention to
the problem of interpretation by declaring a need for witnesses and applying a twenty-day statute of limitation on proof. Swearing, then, needed

---

[59] Patrick Collinson, *The Elizabethan Puritan Movement* (London: Jonathan Cape, 1967), 266–71.

[60] Foxe's attack on the *ex officio* statute of Henry IV and Arundel's Oxford Constitutions immediately follows the account of John Badby's burning. See also James Morice, *A briefe treatise of oathes exacted by ordinaries and ecclesiasticall iudges, to answere generallie to all such articles or interrogatories, as pleaseth them to propound And of their forced and constrained oathes ex officio, wherein is proued that the same are vnlawfull* (Middelburg: Richard Schilders, 1590).

[61] On the aims of the puritans in the 1593 parliament, see Collinson, *The Elizabethan Puritan Movement*, 431. Morice's speech in the Commons against unlawful oaths is re-ported in J. E. Neale, *Elizabeth I and her Parliaments 1584–1601* (London: Jonathan Cape, 1957), 268–9, and the proceedings of the bill on 269–75. As a result, Morice was placed under arrest for several weeks. Continuities between the puritan movements of the latter years of Elizabeth and the first years of James are discussed by Collinson, *The Elizabethan Puritan Movement*, 448–67.

an identifiable public context. The Act against the theatre is all the more convoluted in its attitude to public location. The theatre was a public place but of a very specialized kind, involving peculiar rules of behaviour governing the relation between spectators and actors, and representing on the stage scenes of private location watched by an attendant public which is both inside and outside the action. Swearing here is mimetic.

SWEARING IN *OTHELLO*

I conclude with an illustration of the interpretation of swearing in public, and of problems in relating the public to the private, taken from the theatre. *Othello* was first performed perhaps in 1602–3, but remained unpublished until a Quarto version finally appeared, after Shakespeare's death, in 1622, quickly followed by the First Folio in 1623.[62] Among the numerous differences between the two texts is the systematic expurgation from the First Folio of fifty-three swear words in the Quarto.[63] This censorship is conducted with great care: sometimes words of less offence but identical rhythm are substituted; sometimes words are excised altogether, with some rewriting to complete both sense and metre.

The pretext for the censorship has been assumed to be the 1606 Act, but why a 1606 Act should explain a difference between texts dated 1622 and 1623 has not been sufficiently argued. The occasion for this expurgation was probably more complicated than the application of a particular statute, just as its motivation was more than a matter of mere delicacy or good taste. Swearing involved a complex social and political register. In the 1630s, Sir Henry Herbert, Master of the Revels, had a debate with King Charles about the force of various swear words. The king went over Herbert's expurgations of a play by William Davenant, and requested certain words should be restored, since they were 'asseverations', not 'oaths'. Herbert dutifully complied, but not without private reservation: 'The kinge is pleased to take *faith, death, slight*, for asseverations, and no oaths, to which I doe humbly submit as my masters judgement; but under

[62] All quotations from *Othello* are from the First Quarto (Q1) or the First Folio (F), as indicated. The text of the Second Quarto (1630) is taken from Q1 but incorporates the expurgations of F. This chapter makes no argument about the authority of either Q1 or F, but treats both texts as independent witnesses to the play.

[63] On expurgation in Shakespeare's text between 1606 and 1623, see W. W. Greg, *The Shakespeare First Folio: Its Bibliographical and Textual History* (Oxford: Clarendon Press, 1955), 149–52, and on *Othello* in particular, *The Editorial Problem in Shakespeare*, 2nd edn. (Oxford: Clarendon Press, 1951), 108–11. The whole matter has been extensively reviewed by Gary Taylor, ''Swounds Revisited', in Taylor and J. Jowett, *Shakespeare Reshaped* (Oxford: Clarendon Press, 1993).

favour, conceive them to be oaths, and enter them here, to declare my opinion.'[64]

Herbert, who carefully removed 'oathes, prophaness, and publique ribaldry' both on stage and in books, was in fact appointed in 1623, but probably too late to have influenced the textual supervision of the First Folio.[65] Both his sensitivities, and the king's largesse, have wider significance, however. Ten years later, during the civil war, the royalists were dubbed the 'dammees', because of their propensity for swearing.[66] A liberal use of profanities was associated with the highest and lowest classes, with middle-class puritans marked out in between by their rigorous self-censorship. Swearing was a class issue, something recognized in the Quarto text of *Othello*. The very first word, uttered by Roderigo, is a swear word, 'Tush!' Folio erased both this and the much stronger oath which is Iago's first word in the play:

IAGO 'Sblood, but you will not heare me,
If euer I did dreame of such a matter, abhorre me.

The easy familiarity of swearing between the two men establishes a sense of a shared language and a shared interest. It also demonstrates their attitude to oaths: it is part of Iago's bluff honesty that he should show such confidence, as if he is a man whose oaths are easily believed.[67] Cassio, on the other hand, does not swear, just as he does not drink. When this high-minded puritan is induced to do both, in Act 2 scene 3, Iago is able to remark on '*Cassio* high in oath: Which till to night | I nere might say before', and Cassio, too, rebukes himself for swearing.[68]

In this way, swearing acts as an acute social index of register. Iago is a careful swearer. He uses it with control, as a public gesture of rapport with individuals. He does not swear to himself, nor, crucially, to the audience. Nor, contrary to expectation, perhaps, does he swear in his roughest manner in the presence of Othello. Othello, after all, is his superior, and for all the false and over familiar intimacy Iago establishes with Othello he makes sure he does not risk alerting him by breaking the rule of patronage

[64] Joseph Quincy Adams, *The Dramatic Records of Sir Henry Herbert, Master of the Revels, 1623–73* (New Haven: Yale University Press, 1917), 22; also E. K. Chambers, *William Shakespeare: A Study of Facts and Problems*, 2 vols. (Oxford: Clarendon Press, 1930), i. 239.

[65] 'By the time he took office, the First Folio was nearing completion' (Greg, *First Folio*, 150).

[66] Hill, 'From Oaths to Interest', 419. Trotsky made a similar point about the Tsarists.

[67] Compare here William Empson's essay '*Honest* in *Othello*', in *The Structure of Complex Words* (London: Chatto & Windus, 1951).

[68] 2.3.216 and 257. F, somewhat ludicrously, includes both comments but excises the point of comment, Cassio's 'Zouns' at 128.

that a superior swears with an inferior but not vice versa. Sometimes it is said that Othello learns swearing from Iago as part of his linguistic contamination and degradation.[69] But Othello is not contaminated by Iago's profanities, he swears of his own accord.

Othello's swearing is an index of an altogether deeper religious and political turmoil over language and belief within Elizabethan and Jacobean culture. In 1591, when the recusant priest Edmund Gennings cried out at the scaffold to St Gregory for assistance, the executioner swore without apparent irony, 'God's wounds! His heart is in my hand and yet Gregory is in his mouth.'[70] It is a moment of terrifying linguistic uncertainty. For an instant, the full power of religious oath (St Gregory was the priest's patron) comes face to face with bewildered execration, so that the executioner can no longer distinguish one from the other. In the midst of carrying out an act of disembowelment, what is it that possesses him to call to witness 'God's wounds'? For once, 'his heart is in my hand' is no metaphor, and 'God's wounds' is not uttered in vain.

In this scene of public execution, acts of speech are exposed to a tormented scrutiny of meaning. In the process, private conscience is exposed with equal violence to public interpretation. Foxe tells the hideous story of the Lollard John Badby who, when he cried out 'Mercy!' while burning in the fire, was extracted by Prince Harry for a renewed theological inquisition, in case he were making an abjuration; when it became apparent that Badby had only been shouting out in agony, he was thrown back in to finish the job.[71] Who is to know what Bilney meant as he cried out 'Jesus' in the flames?

Othello is a play about the savage examination of private actions in a trial of public meaning. It is strewn with tortured, stuttered execrations, and it ends in violent death. It is also a play contorted by the definition of public and private space. Although conventionally described as the most domestic of the tragedies, the play works on a constant knife-edge between

---

[69] S. L. Bethell, 'The Diabolic Images in Othello', *Shakespeare Survey*, 5 (1952), 62–80; also 'the stylistic corruption of Othello's speech by Iago', Norman Sanders (ed.), *Othello* (Cambridge: Cambridge University Press, 1984), 202.

[70] *Unpublished Documents Relating to the English Martyrs*, ed. J. H. Pollen, Publications of the Catholic Record Society, 5 (London: J. Whitehead, 1908), 207; quoted in Geoffrey Hill, *Collected Critical Writings*, ed. Kenneth Haynes (Oxford: Oxford University Press, 2008), 30.

[71] 'And when he felt the fire, he cryed mercy (calling belike vpon the Lorde)', Foxe (1570), i. 623. The story is authenticated by fifteenth-century chronicles such as the *Great Chronicle of London*, ed. A. H. Thomas and I. D. Thornley (London: Corporation of the City, 1938), 87 ('and when he felte the fire he cryed mercy'); the incident is reviewed by Peter McNiven, *Heresy and Politics in the Reign of Henry IV: The Burning of John Badby* (Woodbridge: Boydell Press, 1987), 214–19.

private and public. Act 1 begins in the middle of a private conversation between Iago and Roderigo about jilted love; it then moves to another domestic context, the house of Brabantio. But this private scene is suddenly convulsed by an occasion of public slander, with Roderigo and Iago making open accusations of rape and elopement. From here we are swung into the sharply public arena of a council of state, only for this to be interrupted in bewildering fashion by the domestic quarrel of Brabantio with Othello, a public servant suddenly having to fight a private suit of law. With awkward shifts from affairs of state into affairs of the heart, the Duke conducts a council of war in tandem with a family trial, in which the main evidence takes the form of public testimonies by Othello and Desdemona of moments of extreme privacy.

These discomforting lurches between public and private continue throughout the play. Whereas Act 2 is mostly conducted in public, Act 3 is a series of private interchanges, vignettes of often leering intimacy, fragments of tête-à-tête conversation between Iago and Cassio, Cassio and Desdemona, Desdemona and Emilia, Emilia and Othello, Othello and Desdemona, and most of all, of course, Othello and Iago. In Act 4 such private exchanges are increasingly interrupted by public scenes where intimacies are transformed into violent embarrassments and savage confrontations. In the last Act we have the most vicious contrast of all. The central action of Desdemona's murder, a scene of terrifying domestic violence, takes place not only in the marital chamber but inside the bed. Othello conducts it as if it were a public trial of law, and Desdemona a judicial victim, but there are no witnesses, and he is careful to draw the curtains once the deed is done. From here we are thrown finally into the public scenes of accusation, humiliation, suicide, and rough justice, all conducted against the bizarre backdrop of the wedding bed, still occupied by the fresh corpse of the bride.

In all of this, the theatre creates conditions of special tension and confusion. For privacy here is only a construction; nobody is ever truly alone, but watched with increasingly complicit involvement by the audience. *Othello* exploits the uneasy social relationship of stage to spectator with remorseless aptness. Within this theatre of terror, nothing is confidential, nothing sacred. The incipient voyeurism culminates with the intrusion into the bed-chamber, a social embarrassment which has its visual counterpart in the obtrusiveness of the bed itself, requiring a cumbersome novelty of stage-management in probably the first physical representation of a bed in the English theatre.[72] The bed subsequently becomes a scaffold,

---

[72] On the many theories proposed for the appearance, and location, of this most awkward of props, see Sanders, *Othello*, 192.

and the theatre a place of public execution. Yet its public meaning is extremely unstable. In this peculiar space of mingled public spectacle and private commerce, the mock execution of Desdemona reveals itself as a tawdry entertainment, a grisly show-game cheaply exchanged for the price of a seat, and enjoyed in semi-private comfort. Imprisoned in their places, the spectators enter into a sadistic contract with the stage, witnessing and seemingly abetting a marital murder, while listening intently to Othello's fully eroticized participation in his wife's sexual *quietus*.

This conflict of public and private interpretation is at its most acute in the central action of the play, which takes the form effectively of a criminal trial. Desdemona is not casually slaughtered but arraigned, through an indictment, interviews with witnesses, presentation of visible evidence, conviction, and punishment. Lorna Hutson calls this part of Shakespeare's 'increasing interest in dramatizing the abuse of evidentia', and attributes this to the role of forensic rhetoric.[73] The rules of evidence and the conduct of justice are, of course, a vicious travesty. However, they are not unlike a specific legal procedure familiar to a sixteenth-century audience, the *ex officio* trial of heretics and traitors. Although transferred to a sexual context in *Othello*, this is not, as might be thought, a process of secularization. Adultery trials, after all, took place in ecclesiastical, not in secular courts. Blasphemous swearing was a familiar noise in such circumstances; Elizabeth Wheeler, brought before the 'bawdy court' of Stratford in 1595, shouted out 'Goodes woondes, a plague of God on you all, a fart of ons ars for you', and was promptly excommunicated.[74] Marriage involved taking sacred vows, and breaking them was a matter of blasphemy. In both forms of oath-taking, sacred and profane, *Othello* is entirely in tune with the religious culture of the day.

Heresy trials, treason trials, and adultery trials, shared in common a polarization in the analysis of evidence between outward behaviour and inner belief. Within each process, the issue was not physical actions alone, but the state of mind of the accused. Each crime was construed as a breach of faith, so that the examination of guilt involved the instantiation of inner beliefs. All three forms of trial therefore shared an obsession with bringing beliefs to the surface. However, the exteriorization of belief is no simple matter. It is of the nature of a belief to lie beneath the surface; once brought into the open it no longer has the character of a belief but of a public performance. Statements of belief are not the same

---

[73] *The Invention of Suspicion: Law and Mimesis in Shakespeare and Renaissance Drama* (Oxford: Oxford University Press, 2007), 310.

[74] Stratford Church Court Act Books, 1 October 1595; printed in E. R. C. Brinkworth, *Shakespeare and the Bawdy Court of Stratford* (London: Phillimore, 1972), 128.

as the holding of belief, and involve a set of speech acts all of their own. It was at this level of performance and rules of statement that all three forms of trial operated. The conduct of the trial demanded standard routines of performance to identify and make visible both the transgression and the remedy in the mind of the accused. Hence the enormous burden of proof placed in swearing oaths. By compelling the accused to replace locutionary statement with illocutionary performance, oaths appeared to turn utterance into an act of self. Yet there was no guarantee that even these performances were real. The law worked itself out in a linguistic lacuna, and satisfied its will to closure only in ritual forms of penance and punishment.

These legal procedures together indicate a preoccupation with examining individual conscience by the conduct of public behaviour, in which swearing becomes a proof-test. The text of *Othello* is a witness to this cultural crisis of swearing, both in its enforcement of legal oaths and in its compulsive swearing of obscenities, and even in the desperate remedy of the Folio edition in systematically erasing the evidence. The cultural meaning of oaths is so powerful that its appearance in a physical text is as controversial as its utterance on a public stage. It is this drama of performative utterance which gives the exposure of transgression such excruciating tension.

Applying the performance of oaths to an adultery trial is in some sense the play's novelty, yet there was in fact an Old Testament precedent for trying adultery by a test of sacrally binding oaths. In the most important of the puritan treatises attacking *ex officio* oaths, the common lawyer James Morice discussed in 1590 the so-called 'law of jealousy' found in the book of Numbers. A husband who suspects his wife of adultery, but who has no witness against her, takes her to a priest, who tests her by a series of ritual adjurations:

> For as concerning the lawe of jelousie, although the wife were to be tried by oath and adjuration in that manner and with those circumstances as is there prescribed, either to satisfie the restlesse head of her jelous husbande, if shee were guyltlesse, or to receyue by the wonderfull working of that accursed water, if shee were faultie condigne punishment for her heynous offence, both of perjurie and adulterie, yet is it verie manifest in this case that the wife is not sommoned or cited by the Priest or Magistrate *ex officio,* but brought vnto him by her accusing husband, who vpon offence conceyued offring vp his complaint, and thervpon the woman is called for, and put to her purgation, well knowing her accusor, and hauing perfect notice before shee sweare of the crime objected.[75]

---

[75] Morice, *A brief treatise of oathes*, sig. B3ʳ; citing Num. 5: 14–30.

The basis of the trial is simply 'the spirit of jealousy' felt by the husband; the substance of either conviction or acquittal is in a physical proof-test conjured up by the priest's liturgical swearing. If the 'cursing water' ministered to the wife by the priest causes her bodily injury, she is visibly guilty.

Desdemona's trial follows a comparable structure of visual proof-tests and rules of swearing. When Iago first insinuates some hint of misconduct between Desdemona and Cassio, he does so by dropping loaded questions and apparently casual oaths:

> IAGO   For *Michael Cassio*,
> I dare be sworne, I thinke that he is honest. (3.3.125, F)[76]

When Othello challenges him to substantiate his case, Iago replies like a witness, struggling to protect his opinion until he is sworn to reveal all:

> IAGO   Good my Lord pardon me,
> Though I am bound to euery Acte of dutie,
> I am not bound to that all slaues are free to (3.3.134, Q1)

'Thought is free', the saying goes, except (that is) in a heresy trial.[77] For in a heresy trial, silence and a refusal to swear is an indication of guilt, an interpretation Othello proves willing to subscribe to.

When Othello presses for a full statement of Iago's inner suspicions, Iago reels like a witness under intimidation:

> OTHELLO   By Heauen, Ile know thy Thoughts.
> IAGO   You cannot, if my heart were in your hand,
> Nor shall not, whil'st 'tis in my custodie (3.3.163, Q1)

The intimidation is not idle. Othello's sudden oath, 'By Heauen' (cut from Folio), carries an implication Iago is not slow to recognize. The example of Father Gennings's executioner shows us that Iago's words, 'if my heart were in your hand', are no casual metaphor. Swearing 'thoughts' under oath involved appalling physical risk.

For the moment, Othello still demands 'Occular proofe', and conjures Iago on the safety of his own soul, with the direst of religious threats, to provide 'probation' free of any 'Hindge, nor Loope' to hang a doubt on. However, the impulse to physical observation is unsatisfiable. What 'probation' could ever be secure enough? With savagely knowing sarcasm, Iago asks Othello how insatiable his appetite is for 'Occular proofe':

---

[76] Only in F; Q1 reads 'presume' for 'be sworne'. F, while expurgating swear words, is not inattentive to rules of swearing.

[77] Morris Palmer Tilley, *Dictionary of Proverbs in England* (Ann Arbor: University of Michigan Press, 1968; hereafter 'Tilley'), T244.

IAGO Would you, the superuisor grossely gape on?
Behold her top'd? (3.3.396, Q1)

For the purposes of his joke, Iago entertains the possibility of arranging such a voyeuristic charade, only to dismiss the mechanics as overcomplicated. Indeed, he makes this seem what Maus calls 'an impossible aspiration to the absolute knowledge of another person'.[78] In lieu of such a vivid demonstration of guilt, he contents himself with providing aural rather than visual forms of 'satisfaction'. For the evidence of the eyes he substitutes gossip and hearsay. Othello is spell-bound by this judicial fix-up; after a few seconds consideration, he declares the case a 'foregone conclusion'. His 'Occular proofe', we may note, takes the form of a second-hand report of Iago eavesdropping on something Cassio let slip while dreaming, as he purportedly acted out his desire for Desdemona on Iago in his sleep.

On the grounds of this novel form of justice, Othello and Iago proceed to kneel in making each a 'Sacred vow' to perform the necessary rites of legal retribution. The legal travesty takes its course, centring on the brilliant device of that forensic fetish, the missing handkerchief spotted with strawberries. Private conscience is entangled in the ambiguous testimony of public witnesses, as the absent sign of the handkerchief takes on any number of meanings depending on who is watching. Just as the bystanders at Bilney's burning are required to read his mind by reference to minute details of reportage, so the dropping or the picking up of a napkin is exposed to contrary readings, which the bystanders in the theatre must sift as they can. Desdemona's arraignment, like Bilney's recantation, turns on report and misreport, on statements or hearsay direct and indirect, on what people say that they think they saw, or say what they hope other people will think they saw. Most significantly of all, the play's action depends on what people will swear to. For this, it turns out, is the evidence Othello is most likely to believe.

The full significance of the handkerchief lies in that Desdemona swore to keep it. The handkerchief becomes a totem because it appears to give physical form to Desdemona's promise in marrying Othello. It is therefore far more than a material exhibit in the case for prosecution. It is a witness of faith. Bilney's recantation revolved around the fetishing of a piece of paper, a text or set of texts which circulated before and after the execution. Pelles claimed to have seen one text and Rede another, but neither could verify reliably whether either text corresponded to what Bilney read, still less whether he believed it. In any case, the vital docu-

---

[78] Maus, *Inwardness and Theatre*, 120.

ment was now lost. More's Star Chamber inquiries attempted to establish a comprehensive *apparatus criticus* of its variants, but were constantly prone to the vagaries of memorial reconstruction and editorial corruption.

The spotted handkerchief is read by Othello as the text of Desdemona's betrayal, but it is an even more unreliable witness than a piece of paper. The giving and taking of presents means both everything and nothing. Meaning resides entirely in the minds of the giver and the receiver. Although Othello comes to have an irresistible belief that Cassio comes to acquire the handkerchief, he cannot be sure it is significant unless he knows that it is his wife's gift to her lover; and this he cannot prove without access to their thoughts. He can only test this evidence ultimately by Cassio's sworn confession. Iago tantalizes him with the prospect of this testimony at the beginning of 4.1, only further to tantalize him with the notion that Cassio will never swear to it:

> OTHELLO Hath he said any thing?
> IAGO He hath, my Lord, but be you well assur'd
> No more than hee'l unsweare.
> OTHELLO What hath he said?
> IAGO Faith that he did—I know not what he did. (4.1.29, Q1)

This is typical of Iago's method, appearing to swear to the truth, then withdrawing at the moment of admission, leaving Othello to draw his own conclusions. It is the practised method of the sworn witness, scrupling at his memory or conveniently tying his shoelace, only here it is turned to calculatedly vicious use. Iago lets slip the word 'lye', which Othello seizes on as meaning 'lye with her'; Iago plays with words, 'Lie with her, lie on her, what you will', reducing Othello to a manically confused utterance of mixed puns and execrations, powerfully spiced with a swear word and punctuated by his two totems, 'handkerchiefs', and crucially, 'confession'. Sexual and verbal lying have for him become the same thing:

> OTHELLO Lie with her, lie on her? We say lie on her, when they bely her; lye with her, Zouns, that's fulsome, handkerchers, Confession, hankerchers.
> [*He fals downe*]. (4.1.35, Q1)

It is precisely in the context of this system of confession and proof that swearing execrations reveals itself as the characteristic idiom of Othello's jealousy. He begins to swear habitually in Act 3, scene 3, as Iago begins on his insinuating process of indictment. Iago's refusal to reveal his private thoughts provokes Othello into the execration, 'Zouns, what does thou meane?' (3.3.154, Q1), the swear word threatening to force Iago's meaning into the open. The sign of Othello's utter social disintegration is when

he can no longer confine his profanities to the private sphere, and suddenly swears straight at Desdemona, in public, as he turns public accuser
in Act 4, scene 1.

The last two acts of *Othello* are marked by a compulsion to utterance, of which swearing is the most pointed and the most violent evidence, a spilling out of this violence of exposure into acts of verbal
aggression. The emptying out of belief into outward signs, and the ab-
sorption of outward signs in inner belief, places such pressure on speech
that the only alternatives are seemingly uncontrollable outspokenness
and unspeakable silence. The difference between 'interior and exterior'
breaks down.[79] As a consequence, the play veers with virtuoso command of theatrical register between extremes of shouted cussing and
secretive whispering. Yet even whispering is dangerous. When Emilia is
questioned by Othello on the intercourse that has passed between her
mistress and his lieutenant, she replies that she has not only seen nothing pass between them, but heard or suspected nothing either. Othello
is not satisfied by 'nothing':

> OTHELLO Yes, you haue seene *Cassio*, and she together.
> EMILIA But then I saw no harme: and then I heard,
> Each syllable that breath made vp betweene them.
> OTHELLO What? Did they neuer whisper?
> EMILIA Neuer my Lord. (4.2.3, F)

Emilia's description haunts Othello because it apprehends speech in a
physical form ('Each syllable that breath made vp'), and thus appears to
render interior meaning in an exterior action. It is precisely such verifiable
forms of public behaviour that he seeks in order to prove mental transgression. But he can never acquire a sufficient version of exterior description. He cannot get close enough to hear the 'whisper'.

Public and private codes of behaviour are marked by an acute awareness of aural volume, but it is not a reliable measure. The rules of speech
can be distorted and the niceties of registral propriety wilfully denied.
Silence can have meaning, too. A witness who does not confess is simply
hiding the truth:

> OTHELLO This is a subtile Whore:
> A Closset Locke and Key of Villainous Secrets,
> And yet she'le kneele, and pray: I haue seene her do't. (4.2.20, F)

Othello wrenches meaning even from Emilia's ignorance. Under the pressure to identify transgression, behaviour is read according to a rigid rule

---

[79] Maus, *Inwardness and Theatre*, 123.

of perversion: silence equals unconfessed criminal knowledge, and prayer is a heretical masquerade. Whole scenes are constructed around such behavioural misconstruction, as Cassio or Desdemona appears to say or do one thing, Iago reports another, and Othello overhears something else again. Misgiving and mistaking follow on each other's heels.

Above all, this is true of the confession which Othello requires from Desdemona. He asks not so much for a signed confession as a sworn statement of guilt. His final two scenes with her are contorted by a will towards affidavits. In Act 4, scene 2, he asks her vituperatively what she is, and she replies with absolute simplicity,

> DESDEMONA Your wife, my Lord, your true and loyall wife.
> OTHELLO Come, sweare it, dam thy selfe,
> Least being like one of heaven, the divells themselves
> Should feare to [seize] thee, therefore be double-dambd.
> Sweare thou art honest. (4.2.34, Q1)

When Desdemona duly swears,

> DESDEMONA Heaven doth truely know it.

He replies,

> OTHELLO Heaven truely knowes, that thou art false as hell.

This scene sets up a characteristic pattern. Othello demands confession, and forces abjuration; Desdemona swears, following the full solemn form; Othello disbelieves her, and accuses her of perjury, damning her in the process. This pattern is littered with another characteristic pattern of imprecations. Othello's 'damns' and 'devils' are matched by Desdemona's repeated refrain, 'I'faith', and 'By Heaven'. Crucially, almost inexplicably, the Folio expurgates these subtlest of swearings, omitting the very register which most testifies to Desdemona's truthfulness even under the threat of arbitrary violence.

The culmination of this is the murder scene in Act 5. This too takes the form of a forced confession. Othello asks whether Desdemona has prayed, and attempts to play the part of her private confessor, shriving her before her ritual execution. For any crime she has committed she must seek reconcilement now with God before it is too late. When Desdemona swears her innocence, Othello replies 'amen', but it is clear he will not take amen for an answer. He asks her about the handkerchief she gave to Cassio, she swears she did not, he accuses her once again of perjury.

Othello's judicial procedure follows a structure with which the sixteenth-century listener was well familiar. He acts as an *ex officio* judge. Throughout the period surrounding the performance and the printing of the play, *ex officio* oaths continued to be a prime source of political disaffection. In

1604, oaths were one of the abuses singled out by puritan campaigners at the Hampton Court conference.[80] A further bill of opposition to the oaths was mounted in 1626.[81] In 1641, one of the first acts of Parliament in the revolt against the bishops and the crown was the repeal of the method of inquisition implicit in the *ex officio* oath. Othello's arraignment of Desdemona carries a cultural charge way beyond a miscarriage of justice. He puts her to death on a point of swearing, in the same way as Badby, Bilney, and Father Gennings. James Morice argued in 1590 that the 'law of jealousy', however strange, was lawful because the husband, as plaintiff, had a separate judicial function from the priest, as judge. Whitgift's procedure *ex officio* conversely made the judge also the accuser.[82] Othello, too, is judge and accuser, and Desdemona's executioner as well. He forces Desdemona to swear a general oath; he then requires her to answer any question which he chooses to ask. A refusal to swear is a confession of guilt; a refusal to answer a question is equally self-incriminating.

Only in this case, Othello adds the refinement that oaths correctly sworn, and answers comprehensively given, also constitute conviction because confession by definition should be disbelieved. When Desdemona swears she never loved Cassio, Othello replies 'By Heaven' he saw Cassio with her handkerchief, and calls her 'O periured woman'. Desdemona swears she never gave it to him, and asks for Cassio to be brought as a witness, and sworn to tell the truth. But Othello as judge, prosecutor, and chief witness, has a final trump card:

> DESDEMONA He found it then,
> I never gave it him, send for him hither,
> And let him confesse a truth.
> OTHELLO He has confest.
> DESDEMONA What, my Lord?
> OTHELLO That he hath—uds death. (5.2.66, Q1)

So at any rate, in Quarto. But in Folio, and in all modern editions, the minced oath is removed, and replaced with 'us'd thee'.[83] I find this a diminution as

---

[80] Collinson, *Puritan Movement*, 457.

[81] Conrad Russell, *Parliaments and English Politics 1621–1629* (Oxford: Clarendon Press, 1979), 277.

[82] Morice, *A brief treatise of oathes*, sig. B3ʳ.

[83] There is a long discussion of these variants in the note to this line in M. R. Ridley's Arden 2 edition (London: Methuen, 1958). Ridley, in using Q1 as his base text, restores most of the expurgations, but makes an exception here, evidently concurring with Alice Walker's opinion ('The 1622 Quarto and the First Folio Text of *Othello*', *Shakespeare Survey*, 5 (1952), 16–24) that this is among the grosser 'vulgarisations' of Q1. Ridley adds the argument that 'vds dethe' could be a simple mistranscription of the likely reading in the manuscript 'vsde the'. Like many textual arguments, however, this is entirely reversible, and

well as a bowdlerization. At the beginning of the scene, Othello professes himself unable to name the crime aloud, even to himself or to the 'chaste Starres' (5.2.2, F). In Quarto, Othello indeed refuses to name the sexual act itself, makes a fetish of it, and replaces it with an imprecation. The imprecation takes the form of a blasphemous linguistic corruption of the ultimate testimony of the Christian faith—God's death in the passion. Othello, even as judge and accuser, will not name his accusation. Desdemona is prepared to answer any question on oath, even though she does not know (although she can clearly guess) what she is answering to. On this basis, remorselessly illegal, Othello kills her, smothering her with her pillow, Desdemona's breath caught in the middle of a last prayer, poised with graceful equivocation between Christ and her husband, and between propitiation and an oath: 'O Lord, Lord, Lord'.

Othello is a play that works on the boundaries between person and person, between self and other, between private thought and public performance. In the tragedy of misplaced confidence and mistaken words and actions, language is exposed as founded on a fragile process of belief. The most radical dubiety lies not in how wild an injustice Othello is capable of, but in how easy it is for him to misread Desdemona so wildly, and with such terrifying conviction. Exterior and interior explanation, and public and private valuation, fold in on each other: interior virtue requires exterior verification, while external crimes are revealed only by internal interpretation. *Othello* is therefore a play of utterances *in extremis*, of language and desire on the edge of death and of hell. Swearing is its natural register, since it calls into the open the self that otherwise can remain hidden. Indeed conscience, and even consciousness, in some sense only comes into existence when made visible in the exterior performance of the oath. Oaths torment the conscience to a point beyond the grave. Replying to Cromwell's deadpan joke about the difference between swearing for a hanging and a beheading, More rebuked him with the most composed of answers, that rather 'the difference standeth betwene headinge [beheading] and hell'.[84] The extreme seriousness of swearing in the sixteenth century shows us why oaths were sought so ferociously, and why profanities were scrutinized so carefully, in speech and in text. It is therefore

to say that the one is a vulgar error is no more natural than to say that the other is a sentimentalizing euphemism. Stanley Wells and Gary Taylor, in *William Shakespeare: A Textual Companion* (Oxford: Clarendon Press, 1987), while similarly sympathetic to swear words in general, also find 'vds death', at this point in the play, too much to bear. But this may be the point; and the capacity of the line to shock even the most hardened of textual critics may be one reason for accepting it as a genuine reading.

[84] *Correspondence of More*, 558.

no surprise that *Othello* marks the first identified textual occurrence of 'damnation' as a swear word.[85]

The *ex officio* process in law is the ultimate travesty of an act of trust. The accused lays bare the private conscience in a perverted intimacy of false trust, forcing the self into betraying itself in public. It is a relationship of complete imbalance, in which the judge risks nothing and the accused stakes and usually loses life. The violent irony played out by Othello is that he substitutes for the relationship that is most clearly structured on trust based on public swearing of vows of mutual private consent—namely marriage—a relationship structured on the opposite of such trust, based on the private swearing of vows of mutual public dissent. At the beginning of the play, he swears 'My life upon her faith', but at the end of the play, he demands her life upon his faith. In perhaps the most tortuously private scene in Elizabethan and Jacobean literature, he murders his wife in a gruesome ritual of public swearing.

[85] *OED*, DAMNATION, 3.

5

Soliloquy & Secularization
Shakespeare

'Enter Richard Duke of Gloucester, *solus*'.[1] This stage direction, common to all the early Quartos of *Richard III*, beginning with the first of 1597, and repeated in the First Folio, is the first occasion in any of the early editions of Shakespeare in which a person is characterized specifically as entering the stage alone, *solus*.[2] It is in this play, too, that we encounter the peculiar stage direction (this time unique to the Folio text), '*Speakes to himselfe*', as Richard breaks off to make an aside in mid-speech.[3]

What is the significance of being alone? It is not that the stage direction 'solus' is an oddity: it is found frequently in other play texts of the period, such as Jonson's *Every Man Out of His Humour*, Chapman's *Bussy d'Ambois*, Beaumont's *The Knight of the Burning Pestle*, and also *Eastward Ho*, *Mucedorus*, and the chronicle *King Leir*.[4] The term was familiar enough to an audience to provide a joke in *Henry V*. Here, Nym cries out to Pistol:

> Will you shog off? I would have you *solus*. (2.1.45)

Pistol is ignorant enough not to recognize the Latinism and assumes Nym is insulting him:

> *Solus*, egregious dog? O viper vile!
> The *solus* in thy most marvailous face,
> The *solus* in thy teeth, and in thy throat. (2.1.46–8)

However, the audience is in on the joke, and has no difficulty in making the connection between Nym's desire to get Pistol to shove off on his

---

[1] *The Tragedy of Richard the Third* Q1 (1597), sig. A2ʳ; F (1623), sig. q5ʳ.
[2] W. W. Greg, *The Shakespeare First Folio*, 193.   [3] F TLN 792, sig. r2ʳ.
[4] *The comicall satyre of euery man out of his humor. As it was first composed by the author B.I.* (London: Adam Islip, 1600), sig. C2ʳ; *Bussy d'Ambois a tragedie: as it hath been often presented at Paules* (London: William Aspley, 1607), sig. A2ʳ; *The knight of the burning pestle* (London: Nicholas Okes, 1613), sig. I3ʳ; *Eastward hoe As it was playd in the Black-friers. By the Children of her Maiesties Reuels. Made by George Chapman. Ben: Ionson. Ioh: Marston* (London: George Eld, 1605), sig. B4ᵛ; *A most pleasant comedie of Mucedorus* (London: William Jones, 1598), sig. A4ᵛ; *The true chronicle history of King Leir* (London: John Wright, 1605), sig. C2ᵛ.

lonesome, and the stage convention which allows an actor to speak to the blank and empty theatre, as if addressing only himself, in true privacy.

The idea of the soliloquy is central to Shakespeare's dramatic poetry, especially as a dramatist of personhood. Indeed, it is the argument of Catherine Belsey in *The Subject of Tragedy* (1985) that the modern liberal ideology of individualism is epitomized by Hamlet, and that this individualism is epitomized by the soliloquy:

> How is the impression of interiority produced? Above all by means of the formal development of the soliloquy.[5]

Raymond Williams, in his classic *Culture* (1981), argued that the stage presentation of the soliloquy brought with it a new visibility to the condition of the individual.[6] Within the framework of Williams's Marxist theory the soliloquy is an agent of capitalism. In Belsey's turn it is also a function of secularization. The soliloquy is one of the markers of the emergence of modernity (p. 48). This chapter will take issue with both of these tenets: that the soliloquy in any simple sense either represents or sublimates interiority; and that the impulse for this is a secularizing one.

Accounts of the peculiarity of Shakespeare's sensitivity to selfhood from Coleridge onwards are littered with references to soliloquy. Of Hamlet's most famous soliloquy, Coleridge wrote: 'This speech is of absolutely universal interest,—and yet to which of all Shakespeare's characters could it have been appropriately given but to Hamlet?'[7] The generality of the speech should belong 'to all mankind', he says; and yet instead it appears as a personal idiolect. Nobody else speaks like me; my way of speaking *is* me; and I am most myself when I speak to myself. 'Now I am alone'. Matthew Arnold, in a highly influential phrase, called this 'the dialogue of the mind with itself'.[8] Stephen Greenblatt calls this feature of Hamlet's soliloquies a kind of 'involuntary grappling'.[9] A. C. Bradley in his classic account traced Hamlet's personal development from soliloquy to soliloquy, until, in Act 5, Hamlet stops talking to himself *solus*, and prepares for death.[10] Modern commentaries readily reprise.[11]

---

[5] *The Subject of Tragedy: Identity and Difference in Renaissance Drama* (London: Methuen, 1985), 42.

[6] *Culture* (London: Fontana, 1981), 142.

[7] Coleridge, 'Notes on Hamlet', *Lectures upon Shakespeare and Other Dramatists*, in *Collected Works*, 7 vols., ed. W. G. T. Shedd (New York: Harper, 1853), iv. 159.

[8] 'Preface to the First Edition of *Poems*', in *The Poems of Matthew Arnold*, ed. Kenneth Allot (London: Longman, 1965), 591.

[9] Stephen Greenblatt, *Hamlet in Purgatory* (Princeton: Princeton University Press, 2001), 213.

[10] *Shakespearean Tragedy* (London: Macmillan, 1904), 117–28 and 143–4.

[11] Alex Newell, *The Soliloquies in* Hamlet: *The Structural Design* (London: Associated University Presses, 1991), 26.

Frank Kermode, a century later, in another summation of Shakespearian art, took the central feature of Shakespeare's uniqueness to be his development of a language characteristic of an individual's train of thought. These ways of speaking constitute Shakespeare's uniqueness: 'different ways of doing things...developed, ways that involved breaking down the endlessly varied and repeated set forms in favour of less settled representation of the movement of thought and emotion'.[12] The formal technique of the soliloquy, while not the exclusive domain of such thought patterns, is like a ground note through Kermode's analysis. There is a way of feeling, it is suggested, which is peculiar to me, and which only I can fully express.

Yet the soliloquy is also felt to be an ambiguous mode of address. Bradley expressed considerable discomfort with the device, even as he expended so much effort in commentary on individual examples. He was worried by its artificiality as a signifier of selfhood: can it ever be natural, he wondered, to be witnessed talking to oneself on stage? To this concern he added a defence in a vexed footnote: '*No* dramatic language is "natural"; *all* dramatic language is idealised.'[13] Yet to counter the suspicion that the soliloquy is a clumsy intrusion in dramatic language he felt forced to create a law:

> It will be agreed that in listening to a soliloquy we ought never to feel that we are being addressed. (p. 72)

Bradley is caught between the feeling that the soliloquy is the acme of self-representation and the doubt that it is an infuriating defect of the theatre. He cannot decide whether we are listening to the inner record of Hamlet's soul or else a stagy rhetorical pumping up of egoism. De Grazia is more forthright: 'To be life-like, the illusion of Hamlet thinking requires privacy and silence, but the presence of an audience precludes both.'[14] The soliloquy is thus we might say the *locus classicus* of the problem of the self.

SPEAKING TO HIMSELF

Who is Richard of Gloucester speaking to, *solus*?

> RICHARD Now is the winter of our discontent
> Made glorious summer by this son of York;
> And all the clouds that lour'd upon our House
> In the deep bosom of the ocean buried. (1.1.1–4)

---

[12] Frank Kermode, *Shakespeare's Language* (London: Penguin, 2000), 41.
[13] *Shakespearean Tragedy*, 72.
[14] Hamlet *without* Hamlet (Cambridge: Cambridge University Press, 2007), 185.

A doubt is introduced immediately by the curious possessive pronoun 'our'. Of course, this could be an example of a royal 'we', and Richard could be referring, with mild megalomania, to contemporary political struggles as an extension of his personal state of mind. However, after ten lines there is a marked pronoun shift, and Richard twists sharply into a quite distinct mode of address:

> But I, that am not shap'd for sportive tricks,
> Nor made to court an amorous looking-glass;
> I, that am rudely stamp'd, and want love's majesty
> To strut before a wanton ambling nymph:
> I, that am curtail'd of this fair proportion,
> Cheated of feature by dissembling Nature,
> Deform'd, unfinish'd, sent before my time
> Into this breathing world scarce half made up— (1.1.14–21)

Pronoun shifting has a number of significations, primary among which is social class. Charles Barber commented on the marked preference for the use of 'thou' among lower classes in *Richard III*, and 'you' among upper classes.[15] Yet as well as showing his magnificence and *hauteur*, Richard's shift from 'our' to 'I' marks a sense of the boundaries of his private space, as he descends from the public assurance of a display of power after victory in civil war into the troubled intimacy of interiority.

Whatever else it is, talking to himself is not a comfortable register for Richard. Slippage into the singular pronoun 'I' brings with it an acute moment of self-reflection, realized literally in the mirror of his own visage. The 'looking-glass' reveals his physical deformity; but more than this, self-reflection appears to lead inexorably to a sense of the self as incomplete, 'unfinish'd', only 'half made up'. Philip Schwyzer suggests that this is the source of Shakespeare's interest in the peculiarly fragmented historical memory of Richard.[16] All of this is captured, it seems, in the uncertainty of his mode of address. The interplay between speaker and listener is caught in no-man's land. It is not clear that the representation of self ever reaches its intended place of existence or experience. This is also the inference as Hamlet, Shakespeare's foremost and most fatal soliloquist, first finds himself alone on stage, as all others withdraw from him and leave him in the company of his own self:

[15] ' "You" and "Thou" in Shakespeare's *Richard III*', *Leeds Studies in English*, new series, 12 (1981), 273–89, this ref. p. 287.
[16] Philip Schwyzer, 'Lees and Moonshine: Remembering Richard III, 1485–1635', *Renaissance Quarterly*, 63 (2010), 850–83.

HAM. O that this too too sullied flesh would melt,
Thaw and resolve itself into a dew (1.2.129–30)

Hamlet's self-construction affects even the text. The Second Quarto reads 'sallied' (as does also the possibly memorial text of the unreliable First Quarto), but Folio prefers 'solid'. Does Hamlet feel too material for his own liking, or overly corrupt? Either sense, however, reinforces the feeling in this first soliloquy of a person unhappy in his own skin, an identity ill-formed rather than self-assertive.

Could it be, in fact, that the soliloquy, far from a marker of self-confidence and self-assertion, is a place of self-doubt and even self-cancellation? The awkwardness of the device continues to strike critics without this inference striking home. If it is clear who is speaking, it is not at all clear who is listening. The question of the recipient of the soliloquy has been given renewed attention recently in the work of James Hirsh. Hirsh distinguishes three types of soliloquy in history. One is where the audience is addressed: 'The character (not just the actor) is aware of and speaks to playgoers.' The second is self-address proper: 'The character is unaware of playgoers and speaks only to himself.' The third is a variation of the second: 'The words spoken by the actor do not represent words spoken by the character but words merely passing through the mind of the character.'[17] Hirsh also believes that these different modes of address are historically highly determined. In Greek tragedy and comedy, audience address dominated; in new comedy and especially in the Roman comedy of Plautus and Terence, self-address is strikingly frequent. In medieval drama, audience address is the norm again. In the Elizabethan theatre, however, 'Audience address by characters in the midst of the action, a staple of medieval and early sixteenth century drama, came to seem amateurish, undramatic, outmoded and exhausted as a dramatic convention' (p. 19). It is only in the seventeenth century, Hirsh avers, that anything like interior monologue occurs. This is the point when William Congreve first uses the word 'soliloquy' as a term in dramatic convention:

> when a man in Soliloquy reasons with himself…We ought not to imagine that this Man either talks to us, or to himself; he is only thinking, and thinking such Matter as were inexcusable Folly in him to speak.[18]

Once again, at this point a new tradition quickly eradicates the old, and makes the old seem old-fashioned and derelict as a convention. In the

---

[17] James Hirsh, *Shakespeare and the History of Soliloquies* (Madison: Fairleigh Dickinson University Press, 2003), 13.

[18] 'Epistle Dedicatory' to *The Double Dealer*, *The Complete Plays of William Congreve*, ed. Herbert Davis (Chicago: University of Chicago Press, 1967), 120.

twentieth century the same thing occurs to interior monologue, which drops out of the stage as hopelessly conventional.

What is important about Hirsh's account is that he insists on the soliloquy as an instrument of theatricality rather than a rendition of pure mind. The soliloquy is always *performative* rather than *cognitive*. Yet in the process he becomes aggressively doctrinaire about his own distinctions, which are not perhaps as precise as he claims. It is only because he makes the distinctions so absolutely that he finds the historical divisions so absolute between one fashion and another. Of interest here is the way that he defines *Doctor Faustus* as a transitional play. The Chorus, he says, begins as part of a morality play, speaking to the playgoers and then making his exit:

> CHORUS Not marching now in fields of Trasimene
> Where Mars did mate the Carthaginians,
> Nor sporting in the dalliance of love
> In courts of kings where state is overturned,
> Nor in the pomp of proud audacious deeds,
> Intends our muse to daunt his heavenly verse.
> Only this, gentlemen, we must perform
> The form of Faustus' fortunes, good or bad. (Prologue, 1–8)[19]

Once the Chorus leaves, Faustus enters alone and speaks. Unlike the Chorus, 'He nowhere acknowledges the presence of the playgoers. Instead, he explicitly and emphatically addresses himself' (p. 114):

> FAUSTUS Settle thy studies, Faustus, and begin
> To sound the depth of that thou wilt profess.
> Having commenced, be a divine in show,
> Yet level at the end of every art,
> And live and die in Aristotle's works. (1.1.1–5)

To this Hirsh adds the comment:

> Faustus communes only with himself. He is immediately and vividly dramatized as an isolated individual, radically cut off from communal life. Faustus does not know he is a character in a play, does not know he is being observed by playgoers, and so is alone in a way that no character in a medieval drama could have been. (p. 114)

Hirsh is clearly right about the change in register between Chorus and protagonist; but to attribute everything here to a change in dramatic

---

[19] *The Tragical History of Doctor Faustus* (A-Text), ed. David Bevington and Eric Rasmussen, *Doctor Faustus and Other Plays*, Oxford World's Classics (Oxford: Oxford University Press, 1995), 139.

mode between morality play and the new drama seems crude. The crucial signifier for us is probably shown by the stage direction: '*Enter Faustus in his Study*'. The Oxford editors surmise a 'discovery' in the standard manner of the Elizabethan stage, with Faustus revealed in a separate space behind a curtain, after which he perhaps comes forward into full view and occupies the whole stage himself.[20] The audience, that is, is caught between two ways of listening to Faustus: of eavesdropping on the private space of the study, and thus of private thought, or of listening in to a man in consultation with himself about matters of acute intellectual inquiry. Despite Hirsh's certainty, Faustus' mode of address (to self or other) is anything but clear.

According to Raymond Williams, there could be no such thing as a character talking to himself on the Shakespearian stage for the simple reason that it was physically impossible to produce the illusion that a character was alone.[21] At the Globe and other outdoor theatres the actor could always see the audience and the audience always recognized this. The illusion created by artificial light since the nineteenth century has changed this dynamic and allowed for the modern interpretation of the soliloquy as (to quote Margreta de Grazia) thought with the sound turned up. The Globe, de Grazia argues, 'allowed Hamlet no such illusion of exclusionary self-absorption'.[22] Elsewhere, indeed, de Grazia has argued at length that Williams's simple observation refutes the way that Hamlet's soliloquies have been received in modern theatre and criticism alike, as 'a chance to glimpse Hamlet's inner being, his mystery'.[23]

'To be or not to be' is the speech that perplexes de Grazia here. Contrary to its modern reception, she points out, this soliloquy has none of the characteristics of a modern sense of inner speech: 'deep subjectivity, profound self-revelation, intense introspection' (p. 76). It does not even use the singular pronoun 'I' a single time, and also lacks the deictic markers of personal experience—'here' or 'now':

> 'Tis a consummation
> Devoutly to be wished. To die, to sleep,
> To sleep, perchance to Dream; Ay, there's the rub,
> For in that sleep of death, what dreams may come,

---

[20] *Faustus* (A-Text), ed. Bevington and Rasmussen, 433.

[21] Raymond Williams, 'On Dramatic Dialogue and Monologue (Particularly in Shakespeare)', in *Writing in Society* (London: Verso, n.d.), 31–74.

[22] *Hamlet without Hamlet*, 185.

[23] Margreta de Grazia, 'Soliloquies and Wages in the Age of Emergent Consciousness', *Textual Practice*, 9.1 (1995), 67–92, this ref. p. 74.

When we have shuffled off this mortal coil,
Must give us pause. There's the respect
That makes Calamity of so long life (3.1. 63–9)

De Grazia concludes that 'the soliloquy is *generic* rather than *reflexive*' (p. 76). The speech, and soliloquy with it, she argues, is a rhetorical composition and is not to be confused with transparent introspection. It is only modernity's obsession with the idea of the birth of secular consciousness that has made us make this confusion. The speech itself is 'decidedly unmodern' (p. 81).

SOLILOQUY & SECULARITY

The emergence of consciousness, de Grazia argues, is coincident with Hegel's 'meditative introversion of the soul upon itself'. Or in Heidegger's account of 'The Age of the World Picture': 'the very essence of man itself changes, in that man becomes subject'. This emergence takes place long after Shakespeare; but since then, we have had to see Shakespeare in this light. Several things are combined in Heidegger's analysis of the historical shift into modernity: a scientific apprehension of the world as mechanism; a repositioning of the artwork as a realm of pure aesthetics; the redescription of human activity as culture; and finally, as the clinching gesture, the loss of gods and the emergence of atheism, so that Christian doctrine is revealed as one world picture among many. The Renaissance has been conceptualized precisely as an explanation for all these developments at once—scientific hypothesis as paramount, art for art's sake, the world as cultural artefact, and above all secularization. The Renaissance, in de Grazia's analysis, is necessary to us as an explanation of the point from which we have to have come in order to be where we are in modernity. The soliloquy is thus a topos of modernity: the space where Hamlet contemplates himself in isolation and from which he views the world as picture.

What happens if we remove secularization from this history of the soliloquy? Every commentator on the history of soliloquy notes that the word is derived from its use in Augustine, and every commentator avows that the etymology is irrelevant to the subject. Strictly this is true: there is no direct connection between the language of dramatic convention and the two books of *Soliloquia* which Augustine composed early in his career. On the other hand, there is (as we have seen) no application of the term 'soliloquy' to drama until Congreve in the late seventeenth century. Finding the right terminology, and the right rhetorical context, in which to understand Shakespeare's conventions of speech *solus* is a complex subject with no direct approaches. Hirsh complains that Augustine's form is strictly a dialogue (between the self and 'reason', who are given alternate speaking parts in Augustine's work)—and thus not soliloquy—and yet in the next breath he complains that the legacy of Augustine's terminology has been too much concentration on the concept of speech uttered alone, whereas many of Shakespeare's soliloquies occur when the speaker is not alone. Hirsh's confusions here should alert us to the myriad ways of interpreting interior monologue, or for that matter what Augustine calls (with obvious paradox) 'internal dialogue'. Evidently, if a monologue were literally interior, nobody else could hear it or interpret it. All soliloquy is a rhetorical device. It involves both a contrived (and artificial) speaker *and* (in a manner that is much less well observed) an implied (and artificial) listener.

Soliloquy is not a term of dramatic criticism in the sixteenth century but it is nonetheless a common enough word in English, often retaining its Latin form. The overwhelming majority of these references are to Augustine's work. Dwarfed now by the *Confessions* in literary history and memory, the *Soliloquies* were up to the seventeenth century one of the best-known of his works. Citation in recusant sources (such as Robert Persons and Robert Southwell) was very common. A century before the first *Oxford English Dictionary* citation for 'soliloquy', Sir Thomas Elyot's *Dictionary* contained the following definitions:

> *Soliloquus,* he that talketh beinge alone.
> *Soliloquium,* communication, which a man beinge alone, hathe with god in contemplation.[24]

This is a refrain taken up in word lists and dictionaries later in the century, such as the *Thesaurus linguae Romanae & Britannicae tam accurate congestus* (1578):

> *Soliloquium. Talke alone with god.*
> *Soliloquus. That talketh being alone.*[25]

There is an interesting elision here. When is a person alone, and when is he not alone? The *soliloquus* talks as it were in the condition of being alone, or inadvertently, while being alone; but as he does so he is overheard. Is it his own self that overhears, or is it God? And when he speaks, could he be trying to converse with God? In the opposite

---

[24] *The dictionary of syr Thomas Eliot knight* (London: Thomas Berthelet, 1538), sig. 2A1ᵛ.
[25] *Thesaurus linguae Romanae & Britannicae tam accurate congestus* (London: Henry Denham, 1578), sig. 6B3ʳ.

direction, though, Elyot also implies that the communication man has with God takes place as if without God being present: whatever takes place in the inner eye of contemplation, nevertheless takes place 'man beinge alone'.

Such uncertainties are especially prominent in *Huloets dictionarie* (1572), a compendium of both Latin and French idiom in English. A '*Babbler to hym selfe alone*' is a Soliloquus, it is said, and '*Babblyng to him selfe, and no body present*' is called *Soliloquium*.[26] On the other hand, '*Communication, or contemplatiue talking with God*' is equally to be identified as *Soliloquium*, which is also defined as '*Contemplatiue talking to God*' (sig. K1ʳ). This is the sense that is transferred to the English word 'soloquy' in a range of references which also comfortably pre-date the *OED* entry for 'soliloquy'. In Christopher Sutton's *Godly meditations vpon the most holy sacrament of the Lordes Supper* (1601), 'A Spirituall Soloquie or meditation of the Soule' is prescribed for every person contemplating taking the Eucharist.[27] Another Christian manual of 1603 describes

> their Soliloquie, that is, the talke which they vsed to haue alone by them-selues: That as men wearied, desire rest; so wee by the varietie and multi-plicitie of busines in this world, being troubled and distracted, may seeke ease to our mindes by meditation.[28]

In other works, such as the phenomenally popular *Practice of Pietie* of Lewis Bayly, a 'soliloquy' is a synonym for a prayer of any kind. A devout person is enjoined to say 'A short Soliloquie when one first wakes in the Morning'. Before Communion it is equally appropriate for 'A sweet So-liloquie to be said betwixt the Consecration and receiuing of the Sacra-ment'. Such prayers can also be forms of spiritual exercise, in narrative meditation on the life of Christ as applied to the self: 'The Soules Solilo-quie, rauished in contemplating the Passions of her Lord'.[29] In 1620, the word is used as an alternative to 'psalm', a song in which the soul medi-tates to itself: 'Metaphrased into words of one syllable of great Brittains

---

[26] *Huloets dictionarie newelye corrected, amended, set in order and enlarged, vvith many names of men, tovvnes, beastes, foules, fishes, trees, shrubbes, herbes, fruites, places, instrumentes &c.* (London: Thomas Marsh, 1572), sig. C6ʳ.

[27] Christopher Sutton, *Godly meditations vpon the most holy sacrament of the Lordes Supper With manie thinges apperteininge to the highe reuerenee* [*sic*] *of soe greate a mysterie.* (London: I[ohn] W[indet], 1601), sig. C6ʳ.

[28] Richard Rogers, *Seuen treatises containing such direction as is gathered out of the Holie Scriptures, leading and guiding to true happines, both in this life, and in the life to come: and may be called the practise of Christianitie* (London: Felix Kyngston, 1603), 236.

[29] Lewis Bayly, *The practise of pietie directing a Christian how to walke that he may please God* (London: Iohn Hodgets, 1613), 302; 753; 1017.

language, & are to be vsed by a devout Christian soule in his priuate soliloquies, & holy solaces with his god'.[30]

Such usages do not prove that soliloquy always has a religious frame of
reference, but they do pose the question of why the soliloquy has been so
rigidly secularized in its historical meaning. As always, the issue is how
secularization has been employed as an excuse for an exclusivity of meaning. If we do not assume a fixed boundary between the religious and the
secular, we can listen to a different register in the idea of solitary speech.
The Augustinian model, as recently illuminated by Brian Stock, is a highly
subtle one. The soliloquy encompasses not a single work by that title, but
a literary and philosophical form. Stock argues that it is present not only
in the *Soliloquia* but in a variety of other dialogues of Augustine's early
career, and also in his mature masterpieces, the *Confessions*, the *City of
God*, and *De trinitate*. The form arises, Stock believes, out of Augustine's
frustration with the limitations of the model of Cicero's *Tusculan Disputations* for the kind of philosophical enquiry he had in mind. Augustine
creates a tension between inner and outer forms of dialogue:

> we each have two sorts of selves: an outer mobile and malleable self, which
> corresponds to the transitory element in our makeup, and an inner, change-
> less, and true self, which corresponds to the permanence of God's 'image
> and likeness'.[31]

The latter self is not simply substituted for the former, however; rather the
work results from a friction between the two.

Augustine does not arrive at a dialogic form of soliloquy as a kind of
category mistake, then, as he has been represented by a series of Shakespearian critics. Rather, the form shows a number of sophisticated approaches to
the literary fiction of personal identity. First, the literary self is fundamentally rhetorical rather than literal. Second, it is fragmented and volatile
rather than singular and constant. And finally it is mediated rather than
transparent. The object of *soliloquium*, however, is philosophical as much as
literary. In Stock's words, 'the best way to do philosophy is not by talking to
others but by talking to oneself' (p. 5). Soliloquy is a way of apprehending
the truth as much as it is a form of autobiography. Indeed, Pierre Hadot,
among others, has argued that the modern sense of autobiography has tra-
duced but also narrowed its meaning in ancient sources. He used the term
'spiritual exercises' as a conscious attempt to escape this framework.

---

[30] William Loe, *Songs of Sion Set for the ioy of gods deere ones, vvho sitt here by the brookes
of this vvorlds Babel, & vveepe vvhen they thinke on Hierusalem vvhich is on highe. By W.L.*
[Hamburg: n.p., 1620], 27.
[31] Brian Stock, *Augustine the Reader: Meditation, Self-Knowledge and the Ethics of Interpretation* (Cambridge, Mass.: Harvard University Press, 1996), 20.

Hadot admitted that in a modern, secular context the word 'spiritual' was unfamiliar and jarring. It presupposed a Christian reference in many minds, and therefore also a closed discourse. In fact, Hadot applied the term to Jewish and pagan sources as well as Christian ones, and he specifically rejected the idea of a closed system. 'Spiritual' appeared to him the right term because it denoted not so much a set of doctrines (as the words 'moral' or 'intellectual' might imply) as a philosophical practice: 'it is thought, which, as it were, takes itself as its own subject matter'.[32] This was also his meaning of the word 'exercise':

> The Stoics, for instance, declared explicitly that philosophy, for them, was an 'exercise'. In their view philosophy did not consist in teaching an abstract theory—much less in the exegesis of texts—but rather in the art of living. (p. 83)

Soliloquy in this sense can be thought of as a literary form which gets at truth through its own process of enquiry.

Such a concept of philosophy is familiar to us in a Renaissance context by way of Montaigne's idea of the 'essay': the mind finds enlightenment not through apprehending a doctrine but by experiencing a way of thinking. It may be, indeed, that Montaigne's Stoicism is as much methodological as it is conceptual. This can then be applied back to Shakespeare and his ideal of the soliloquy. Instead of regarding the soliloquy as a transparent revelation of self, it is revealed as rhetorical and experimental. It is autobiographical in this mediated sense, as in Augustine's *Soliloquies* and *Confessions*.

Augustine describes the condition of soliloquy in the *Confessions*: *et cum ipso me solo coram te* ('with myself all alone in front of you'). It is a paradoxical phrase: all alone with another. The presence of God as a silent but contributory witness is understood as a given throughout the *Confessions*. In that sense, the work has been misinterpreted by a range of commentators throughout the twentieth century as a text of interiority. In a similar way the interiority of Shakespeare's soliloquies has been misunderstood. It was a natural language of the late sixteenth century to think of speech alone as also potentially a conversation. In many contexts this will be imagined directly as conversation with God. But we do not need to make this transference of divine 'presence' so directly to *Hamlet* in order to recognize the soliloquy as rhetorical, unfinished, and meditative. Some soliloquies have indeed been compared to the language and method of prayer; but just as Augustine also imagines a dialogue between

---

[32] *Philosophy as a Way of Life: Spiritual Exercises from Socrates to Foucault*, Eng. trans. ed. Arnold Davidson (Oxford: Blackwell, 1995), 81.

exterior and interior selves as constituting this debate between changing
and unchanging states, and as experimental exercises with the idea of
inner truth, so Hamlet, far from speaking his mind, confronts us with a
fragmentary repository of alternative selves, and searches within for the
limits of being.

MORTAL SPEECH

Richard III's second soliloquy comes at the end of the play:

> *Richard starteth up out of a dream.*

> k. rich. Give me another horse! Bind up my wounds!
> Have mercy, Jesu!—Soft, I did but dream. (5.3.178–9)

The peculiar stage direction frames the ambivalence of the scene. At first
it seems as if Richard is speaking to a bodily presence, a groom or knight
who can fetch him a horse. Then it seems he is praying, or cursing, or
talking to Jesus. The comparison of Richard with Jesus is a constant motif
of the play, but here Richard realizes he is imagining things.[33] He is on his
own, except he imagines himself in the third person, or as his own interlocutor, in the person of his incubus 'conscience':

> O coward conscience, how dost thou afflict me!
> The lights burn blue; it is now dead midnight. (5.3.180–1)

Conscience, we saw in Chapter 2, is frequently figured as an interior voice,
counterpointing or interjecting into the mind's ear. Here the sense of one
part of the self listening to another part is all the more accentuated:

> What do I fear? Myself? There's none else by;
> Richard loves Richard, that is, I and I.
> Is there a murderer here? No. Yes, I am!
> Then fly. What, from myself? (5.3.183–6)

It is a commonplace to assert in the history of selfhood the shift from reflexive grammatical forms such as the English pronoun 'self' (or the
German 'selbst') towards the emergence of abstract nouns such as 'the
self' or 'das Selbst', a phenomenon which has occurred in a number of
languages and is especially prevalent in the late seventeenth century. In
English the invention is usually attributed to John Locke. Neither Richard,

---

[33] On Richard as God's deputy, see Lily B. Campbell, *Shakespeare's Histories: Mirrors of
Elizabethan Policy* (San Marino, Calif.: Huntington Library, 1958), 194.

nor Hamlet, thus talks about his own 'self' as a noun. However, the inference of 'selfhood' could be said to be latent in the language itself, however important the philosophical moment of abstraction:

> language gives voice to reflectivity in the grammatical structure of the sentence, which assigns agency to the subject, thus designating the speaker as active even in making reference to the natural ground of his or her existence.[34]

Richard's self-questioning gives rise to a separate level of reflectivity, by referring to 'myself' in the third person, so that his grammar can no longer be thought of as strictly pronominal, and makes of 'self' an independent construction, a feature emphasized by the separation in early modern English grammar of 'my self', as is seen in any early text of the play such as Q1: 'What do I feare? my selfe'.[35]

Richard's last soliloquy was described by the actor Ian Richardson as talking not to audience or even to himself but to an 'alter ego', between 'I and I'. This is the reading in Q1; all of the subsequent early editions, quarto and folio, give instead 'I am I'. The tautology in the Q2 reading itself expresses a certain subjective confusion, and has been accepted by almost the entire editorial tradition, until Antony Hammond in Arden 2 followed a doubt first expressed by Edmond Malone, that what we might now call the schizophrenic vein of Richard's speech represents verbally 'the mutual encounter and alternation of these two selves'.[36] The speech becomes a virtuoso exercise in split personality, with the phrase 'my self' used as a kind of antanaclasis, repeating the same word as if in self-contradiction. Yet perhaps we should resist the modernizing rhetoric of a glib psychology of schizophrenia in favour of what Robert Miola calls (in more recognizably sixteenth-century terms) 'a crisis of conscience'.[37] Five verse lines in succession are built around the pronominal form, as Richard first sets himself against himself, then descends into self-loathing, and ultimately as it were loses contact with himself and literally denies himself ('I am not'):

> What, myself upon myself?
> Alack, I love myself. Wherefore? For any good
> That I myself have done unto myself?
> O no, alas, I rather hate myself
> For hateful deeds committed by myself.
> I am a villain—yet I lie, I am not! (5.3.187–92)

---

[34] Seigel, *The Idea of the Self*, 14.   [35] Q1, L4ᵛ.

[36] Antony Hammond, *Richard III*, Arden 2nd Series (London: Methuen, 1981), 184.

[37] *Shakespeare and Classical Tragedy: The Influece of Seneca* (Oxford: Clarendon Press, 1992), 89.

There is a way in which the speech acts as a counterbalance to the first soliloquy with which the play opens. Not surprisingly, actors prefer the first: it is the moment of maximum confidence and formidable self-display. Yet it has its own flair as a stage moment, as this most charismatic and unyielding of villains gives into the most extraordinary possible volte-face and attack of conscience. Except that nobody, least of all himself, is taken in: he is still acting himself as he pretends to divest himself of all acting and show himself how he is.

However, there is one sense in which Richard's last moment alone on stage amounts to a kind of self-revelation. It is that there is now finally nowhere to hide. This is not so much because he is alone and can no longer lie—lying to himself is perhaps his métier, and makes him all the better at convincing others—as that the person who is listening is not identical with himself. There is an open space between actor and audience into which self-address escapes as an area of contemplation, meditation, or analysis. Soliloquy has been misunderstood as a rendition of character, as it exists more as a special form of rhetorical self-performance. Indeed, Harold Fisch comments that 'religious meditation' is a distinctive feature of Shakespeare's style, especially in *Hamlet*.[38] Far from existing as a form of solipsism, we have seen how the rhetorical analogy for soliloquy, 'talking with oneself', is a form of colloquium with God as silent witness. In the post-medieval theatre, this is transferred to an implied presence beyond the self.

In Richard's second soliloquy this becomes a more specialized aural arena: the actor empties himself from the stage into the presence of death:

> I shall despair. There is no creature loves me,
> And if I die, no soul will pity me— (5.3.201–2)

Death and the soliloquy have a special relationship. In tragedy, soliloquy acts as final testament or case of conscience, but it always acts under witness. The audience can hear everything even if they are not formally auditing. There is thus a double view.

In *Richard III* this is still in experimental form. In *Romeo and Juliet*, Juliet confronts her mortal fears as she resolves to drink the potion in Act 4:

> JULIET How if, when I am laid into the tomb,
> I wake before the time that Romeo
> Come to redeem me? There's a fearful point! (4.3.30–2)

---

[38] *The Biblical Presence in Shakespeare, Milton, and Blake: A Comparative Study* (Oxford: Clarendon Press, 1999), 100–2.

Here, the thought of mortality is expressed in a paradox that living en-
tombed in the vault will be more fearful than death itself. Juliet makes no
disquisition on death, but instead takes the poison as if in preference to a
life. Romeo, in his turn, begins by looking at his surroundings within the
same tomb, an exercise in ekphrasis which makes it all the more a shock
when he remembers his own position:

> ROMEO For here lies Juliet, and her beauty makes
> This vault a feasting presence, full of light.
> Death, lie thou there, by a dead man interr'd.
> How oft when men are at the point of death
> Have they been merry! Which their keepers call
> A lightning before death. (5.3.85–90)

This 'lightning', the dictionary tells us, is 'That exhilaration or revival of
the spirits...supposed to occur...before death'.[39] But Wolfgang Clemen
comments that the phrase also adumbrates the more commonplace sense
of 'lightning', a suggestion which brings with it a sense of the fragility of
life and the proximity of death.[40] Clemen argues interestingly here that
the impact of this soliloquy is bound up in 'the disparity between Romeo's
reactions and those of the audience' (p. 108). The scene is tinged with a
doubled temporality: immediacy haunted by finitude. Romeo is crossing
the door from event and consequence into a void in which time has no
meaning.

The true meaning of soliloquy, therefore, lies not in some either/or (as
in Hirsh's account) of the actor's head or the audience's consciousness, but
in the mediation between the two. This is implicit in all theatre, but it is
brought into sharper focus by the convention of the soliloquy. This is a
register which is special by virtue of its reception by its auditors as much
as by its enunciation by its speaker. The stage is haunted by a voice which
has no proper endpoint. In that sense the voice is caught in the expression
of its own temporality and mortality. No wonder that mortality occasions
the most memorable soliloquies. Indeed, the direct address of death, such
as Romeo's final apostrophe, is the least remarkable feature of this theatrical effect:

> ROMEO Eyes, look your last.
> Arms, take your last embrace! And lips, O you
> The doors of breath, seal with a righteous kiss
> A dateless bargain to engrossing Death.

---

[39] *OED* vbl sb 2 b; the phrase is proverbial: Tilley L 277.
[40] Wolfgang Clemen, *Shakespeare's Soliloquies* (London: Methuen, 1987), 108.

Come, bitter conduct, come unsavoury guide,
Thou desperate pilot now at once run on
The dashing rocks thy seasick weary bark.
Here's to my love! [*He drinks.*] (5.3.112–19)

The most evocative moment here is not the stereotype invocation of death
as abstract lover or courier, but the liminal shock of 'The doors of breath'.
Breath, like time, is running out. For this, the finitude that is the ordinary
limit of the time of the stage is a powerful metonym. We will be out of
doors soon, but Romeo, we are made to imagine, will not.

This experimental use of the soliloquy as exteriorized mental meditation
reaches its formal zenith for the first time at the end of *Richard II*. Here, in
a soliloquy that is perhaps the strangest and most beautiful speech in a play
full of such poetry, Richard confronts his mortal self. Samuel Daniel in *The
Civil Warres* also opens his description of Richard's death with a soliloquy,
but here the comparison ends: there is no correspondence between the two
speeches.[41] In Shakespeare, the king has been deposed, imprisoned by Bolingbroke in Pomfret Castle, and now lies in a dungeon contemplating his
own death: with good reason, since unknown to him, but in view of the
audience, murderers are already on their way to the castle. The audience,
too, shares this sense of impending finitude. The world of the play is closing in, as the teeming world of medieval England is reduced to a bare stage.
Richard, crucially, is 'alone'; and yet we are still with him as he contemplates the limits of his being and of the world itself:

Enter RICHARD *alone.*[42]

RICHARD I have been studying how I may compare
This prison where I live unto the world;
And, for because the world is populous,
And here is not a creature but myself,
I cannot do it. Yet I'll hammer it out.
My brain I'll prove the female to my soul,
My soul the father, and these two beget
A generation of still-breeding thoughts;
And these same thoughts people this little world,
In humours like the people of this world,
For no thought is contented. The better sort,
As thoughts of things divine, are intermixed
With scruples, and do set the word itself

---

[41] *The First Fowre Bookes of the ciuile warres betweene the two houses of Lancaster and Yorke*
(1595), Book III, stanzas 64–71.
[42] The stage direction 'alone' appears in Q1 (1597) up to Q5 (1615); it is omitted in Folio.

Against the word, as thus: 'Come little ones';
And then again:
'It is as hard to come as for a camel
To thread the postern of a small needle's eye':
Thoughts tending to ambition, they do plot
Unlikely wonders—how these vain weak nails
May tear a passage through the flinty ribs
Of this hard world, my ragged prison walls,
And, for they cannot, die in their own pride.
Thoughts tending to content flatter themselves
That they are not the first of Fortune's slaves,
Nor shall not be the last, like silly beggars
Who sitting in the stocks refuge their shame
That many have and others must sit there;
And in this thought they find a kind of ease,
Bearing their own misfortunes on the back
Of such as have before endured the like.
Thus play I in one person many people,
And none contented. Sometimes am I king;
Then treasons make me wish myself a beggar,
And so I am. Then crushing penury
Persuades me I was better when a king;
Then am I kinged again, and by and by,
Think that I am unkinged by Bolingbroke,
And straight am nothing. But whate'er I be,
Nor I nor any man that but man is
With nothing shall be pleased till he be eased
With being nothing.[43]

I have quoted this speech at length, but it is not even here at an end: after the intervention of external music, perhaps by a single stringed instrument, Richard continues this breathtaking monologue on mortality and existence for another twenty-five lines. This speech is much longer in total than any of the soliloquies of Hamlet, and is a staggeringly long period in which to represent an actor in front of the audience alone.

For Kermode, the speech is crucial in the development both of Shakespearian soliloquy and of the distinctive language of interior thought process in the plays:

> The wonderful long soliloquy of the King in prison is truly transitional, for the occasion of such a lament resembles others in the earlier plays, until it

---

[43] Q1 (1597), 5.5.1–41, fol. I3ᵛ–I4ʳ, cited here from Arden edition.

becomes clear that something else is happening, that the elaborations of
figure are not simply prefabricated and laid out neatly before us but ham-
mered out (p. 43)

Yet if so, the speech is both profound and yet at some level quite unquan-
tifiable and certainly risks comprehensibility. And perhaps this is the
point: Richard seems himself mesmerized by the power of his own words
to express virtually anything, and yet at the same time embarrassed by
their vulnerability and virtual meaninglessness.

Richard is considering his deposition and his death: how he, the king,
no longer is king; and how he, his own self, is now, but may soon *be* no
more. Articulating this is, he realizes, a paradoxical activity. He invests
language with kingship ('Then am I kinged') and simultaneously divests
it of authority ('I am unkinged'); he uses words to express himself ('what
ere I be') and then also to efface self from words ('being nothing'). Yet at
the same time as trying to do these complex things in language he also
attempts to investigate the very processes by which language does these
things. The speech uses difficult metaphors but is also a study of the difficulties of metaphor: 'I have been studying how I may compare this
prison where I live unto the world'.

The speech is thus dizzyingly self-conscious and its reflections tortuously self-reflexive. Richard half suggests that by summoning up the
power of metaphor ('A generation of still-breeding thoughts') he will
somehow unlock the secret of language; and yet is beset by a sense of
knowing failure and self-ironizing doubt that these are mere words.
Alongside his conjuration of the metaphorical power not only to suggest
but to embody meaning, there is his admission, within his analysis of the
way in which metaphor works, of its tenuous illusions. Richard combines
in this space of time what Clemen has perceptively listed as 'narcissism',
'metaphorical embellishment', 'brooding reflection', and 'theatricality'
(p. 25). But Clemen is perhaps reductive in seeing this as an aspect of
Richard's character. More to the point, these features are the natural rhetorical territory of the mortal soliloquy in action, a meditation on being.

MORTAL MEDITATIONS

Richard's fragile and delicate imaginings of his own finiteness have been
readily assimilated to the critical tradition of the invention of the personal soliloquy. Indeed Hugh Grady finds in the speech a premonition
of modern subjectivity, an 'identity crisis' which he assimilates with
Louis Althusser's concept of 'interpellation' and the Hegelian tradition

of 'being-for-others'.[44] Grady's whole argument is a prime example of the secularization thesis, in which Machiavelli and Montaigne are appropriated as forms of 'predecessor text' (p. 3). Yet just as we saw in Chapter 1 how Montaigne does not fit this image, so here Richard's soliloquy, in form and meaning, resembles something quite contrary to a secularization thesis: it is a religious meditation in the face of death. This is a commonplace genre of the period, not in any way restricted to ministers or the extravagantly godly. John Hayward, whose *The First Part of the Life and Raigne of King Henrie IIII* (1599) dealt in depth with the deposition and death of Richard II, was imprisoned because of the implication that a corrected edition was favourable to Essex's rebellion (a charge also sometimes associated with Shakespeare's play). While in the Tower, Hayward wrote *The Sanctuarie of a Troubled Soule*, also published by John Wolfe in 1601. This saw a dozen editions and indeed has been said to have 'brought him more contemporary acclaim than his histories'.[45] Yet our surprise at this fact is also misplaced: it is only the secularization thesis that makes us reluctant to see a Tacitean historian as a Protestant devotional writer of equal gravity.

There are strong parallels between Richard's temporal and spiritual states. Of his earthly position, Richard says that when unkinged by Bolingbroke, I 'straight am nothing'. In Hayward's *First Part of the Life and Raigne*, the same conclusion is made, 'for in this case there is no meane betweene Caesar & nothing, betweene the highest honor & the deadliest downfall'.[46] However, when his prison surroundings cause him to expatiate on this 'With being nothing', it is Hayward's prison meditation which comes to mind:

> & now I am troubled, but thou art not with me. Alasse, better it were to bee nothing, then to bee without thee, without whom al things are nothing[47]

There is no doubt in Hayward's case of the presence of an interlocutor, Christ: 'Christ, my fainting soule groaneth and gaspeth for thy grace, but it is abashed at thy glory' (p. 8). That is the narrative form of the devotional treatise. On the stage, the liminal effect is more ambiguous. Richard speaks to nobody, so his verse has no locatable addressee. It is a prayer to Christ where Christ has hidden himself.

---

[44] *Shakespeare, Machiavelli, and Montaigne: Power and Subjectivity from Richard II to Hamlet* (Oxford: Oxford University Press, 2002), 106.

[45] John J. Manning, 'Hayward, Sir John (1564?–1627)', *Oxford Dictionary of National Biography*, Oxford University Press, 2004; online edn., January 2008 <http://www.oxforddnb.com/view/article/12794>, accessed 9 February 2012.

[46] *The first part of the life and raigne of King Henrie the IIII* (London: John Wolfe, 1601), sig. M2r.

[47] *The sanctuarie of a troubled soule written by I.H.* (London: John Wolfe, 1601), 11.

Yet it is in the register of the meditational colloquy that Shakespeare's Richard speaks. Like Hayward, he feels 'my very neerest friendes, not onely forsaking me, but reioycing and praysing God for his iustice in my damnation' (pp. 17–18). Indeed, he imitates Hayward imitating Christ, as he contemplates 'all the miseries of mortallitie: hunger, colde, griefe, pouerty, contempt, scorn, blasphemies, bandes, blowes, the crosse, woundes, death, and the graue' (p. 25). Hayward's reflections on mortality are always also a reflection on the condition of personhood:

> Alas, howe is my soule abandoned? how are all the powers thereof layd wast? comforte is no more ease vnto me, then is the handlinge of sore woundes. I am deuided in my selfe, how can I stand? I am ouerthrowne in my selfe, how shall I rise? (pp. 122–3)

The literature of preparation for death was one of the staples of the age. One of the main aims of this literature was to achieve what was called 'contentment of mind'.[48] The clergyman Christopher Sutton's *Disce mori* ('learn to die') was followed two years later with the more cheerfully titled sequel *Disce vivere* ('learn to live'), but the message was similar. The aim of a good life, as of a good death, is 'quiet and content in their estate, or without any desire of seeking superfluitie'.[49] Life in Christ consists in 'contentment of the soule' (p. 51). It is this state of mind which provides external evidence of the godly condition, when: 'we desire the content of our will, naturally to be well, and the exercise of our wit to haue a certaine end, and this end to be the particular good, benefit, and welfare of all our being' (p. 54).

'Contentment', as a subjective state, is a late sixteenth-century word. In fifteenth-century English it generally means the satisfaction of certain conditions in others. The *OED* dates the new sense of 'The fact, condition, or quality of being contented; contentedness' to 1597, in Richard Hooker's *Lawes of Ecclesiasticall Politie*. Other new senses of 'pleasure, delight, gratification', or of a source of such pleasure, it also finds in the 1570s and 1580s. A theological sense of fulfilment equivalent to an apprehension of God's grace or election as a subjective experience may come a little earlier. It appears to be present in John Knewstub's Good Friday sermon at Paul's Cross in 1577 preached against the Family of Love. Here he contrasts the feelings of the godly elect of 'ease, quiet, comfort and contentment' with the showy emotional gratification of the

---

[48] Christopher Sutton, *Disce mori. Learne to die A religious discourse, moouing euery Christian man to enter into a serious remembrance of his ende* (London: John Wolfe, 1600), sig. K1ʳ.

[49] Christopher Sutton, *Disce vivere* (London: E. Short, [1604?]), 48.

Family of Love.[50] For Knewstub there is a rule here of finding a truth within in the correct judgement of internal faculties and passions:

> For if thine heart be not setled in thine estate, with good liking & contentation, as in a good prouision: it is vnpossible, that euer thou shouldest become thankful for it. For to seeme to ioy without ioy, is to play yᵉ hypocrite, & to dissemble wᵗ God. (C2ʳ)

It is possible Knewstub found this word in a pair of Calvin's sermons published in the same decade. If so, he is in the process of formulating a distinctive Calvinist theory of the emotions, of feelings in proper accord with grace. We must not fake our feelings before God: or rather we cannot. This is the ultimate proof-test of subjective states.

This is the vocabulary of introspection which forms the background to Richard's last soliloquy, where he puzzles out how to describe his mortal condition in the solitude of his prison, and finds that he cannot, because 'no thought is contented'. His tone is meditational, but also confrontational, in that here there is no place to hide. Any subjective experience is set against the truth of mortality and of divine judgement. Richard is at the point where he can no longer 'dissemble'. The only person who is listening is the same person who is speaking. He therefore enters into a last, other-worldly self-examination. And just as Knewstub founds his discussion in a contrast of worldly measures of wealth and happiness with the divine calculus of election ('We must therfore take our selues to be riche already, and let goe this desire to be riche'), so Richard measures his eternal state against his earthly treasure.

In the midst of this disquisition, teeming with meaning, Shakespeare interpolates a commentary on two citations from the New Testament, which bristles with interpretative difficulty:

> The better sort,
> As thoughts of things divine, are intermixed
> With scruples, and do set the word itself
> Against the word, as thus: 'Come little ones';
> And then again:
> 'It is as hard to come as for a camel
> To thread the postern of a small needle's eye'

Richard's study in metaphor runs aground in the seeming intractability between the world and his words, an intractability which is to be discovered,

---

[50] *A sermon preached at Paules Crosse the Fryday before Easter, commonly called good Friday* (London: Thomas Dawson, 1579), sig. C2ʳ.

he suggests, not only in his own language but in the one text which would appear to be free from any linguistic obstruction, 'the word itself'. Exegetical difficulty is matched by a textual crux: 'set the word itself | Against the word' is a correction in Folio, repeating a phrase from 5.3.120, where it is spoken by the Duchess of York. In the Quartos, it is 'faith' that is set against 'faith'.[51] As will become clear, 'word' does indeed challenge 'faith' here.

At this point Richard's speech, already so compressed as to be virtually opaque to interpretation, compounds its own difficulties with a submerged argument about New Testament meaning. He makes two citations from the Bible, formulated in a manner which is in fact quite familiar in sixteenth-century theology. He juxtaposes texts which create an apparent conflict of sense, an exegetical trope which was known as *contradictio*. Equally characteristic of contemporary practice is the fact that the *contradictio* surrounds texts which are themselves interpretative cruces. Let us compare an example from Luther in 1538, who juxtaposed two citations from 1 John, 'Whosoever is born of God, doth not commit sin' and 'If we say that we have no sin, we deceive ourselves',[52] and then reacted as follows (he was writing in Latin but suddenly burst into demotic German to express his consternation):

> Quid hoc? Quomodo haec consentiunt?... Mira profecto res est. *Es is warlich ein fein ding. Reim da wer reimen kan.* Duo contraria in uno subiecto et in eodem puncto temporis.

> How is this? How may these texts agree? It is surely an extraordinary matter. A really fine pickle. Rhyme it who can. Two opposites in one subject and simultaneously.[53]

Richard, too, finds *duo contraria in uno subiecto*, and asks *Reim da wer reimen kan*. But in setting 'the word itself against the word', he creates a further problem. For his two texts are both sayings of Jesus, in whom *contradictio* is especially worrying. Can Jesus contradict himself? Or worse, can *God* contradict himself?

The two texts, indeed, are not only spoken by the same person but come in the same chapter, with three different gospels as textual witnesses. Richard's first citation is Matthew 19: 13–14:

> Then were brought vnto him little children, that hee should put his handes on them, and pray: and the disciples rebuked them. But Iesus saide, Suffer

---

[51] *Richard II*, ed. Peter Ure, Arden Series 2 (London: Methuen, 1956), 169.

[52] 1 John 3: 9 and 1 John 1: 8.

[53] *Die dritte Disputation gegen die Antinomer* (6 September 1538), WA 39: 1.507.18.

little children, and forbid them not to come to me: for of such is the kingdome of heauen.[54]

The second comes from the incident immediately following in the Gospel, when a man asks how he may enter into eternal life. He is told to keep the commandments, and when he replies that he has always done so, he is told to 'sel that thou hast, and giue it to the poore'. The young man departs bewildered, but Jesus has not finished. He turns his instruction into a general rule which combines legislative finality with gnomic inscrutability (verses 23–4):

> Then Iesus said vnto his disciples, Verely I say vnto you, that a rich man shall hardly enter into the kingdome of heauen. And againe I say vnto you, It is easier for a camel to go through the eye of a needle, then for a rich man to enter into the kingdom of God.

Not surprisingly, given the peculiar turn of Jesus' phrase, there has been a history of argument about the meaning of his words, and even about the text of his Greek. Richard has thus not only chosen to consider a *contradictio* between two texts. The second text is, additionally, a crux within itself, a word set against itself, a nexus of textual, linguistic, and hermeneutical controversies, throwing into instantaneous question the problem of how to establish an authoritative edition, an accurate translation, and an orthodox interpretation; in other words, about how to discover Jesus' true words, and the truth of his word.

FIGURING THE SELF

Far from being a distraction, Richard's moment of biblical exegesis takes us into the heart of his meditation on the self. This enquiry turns into a meditation on meaning, on how to make sense of his own being: and for this, Richard delves into the question of representation within meaning. 'I have been studying', he begins; and the object of his study is the most fundamental in the philosophy of language: how things are represented in words. He plays on this by asking how he can make his own solitary condition a metaphor for the world—because he has been left with nothing else but himself to compare anything with. The question underneath

---

[54] *The Newe Testament of Our Lord Iesus Christ, Translated out of Greeke by Theod. Beza. Whereunto are adioined briefe summaries of doctrine... by the said Theod. Beza, and also short expositions of the phrases and hard places, taken out of the large Annotations of the foresaid Author and Ioach. Camerarius, by Loseler. Villerius. Englished by L. Tomson* (London: Christopher Barker, 1597), Matthew 19: 13–14. The verse also occurs verbatim in Mark 10 and in Luke 18.

is how to describe himself in the first place. What kind of a thing is he himself?

There could be no stranger case study in metaphor than the one he chooses from the New Testament. The crux of Matthew 19: 24 involves in fact three poles of meaning. The first is the most literal: Jesus really does mean, however wildly, the difficulty of pushing a large ruminant quadruped, with a humped back and a long neck, through a hole approximately two millimetres square. However, Jesus appears here to stretch metaphorical rules to breaking point. At the very least this could be felt to be a catachresis, a mixed or clumsily artificial metaphor, at worst it could be said to be a failed metaphor. Biblical commentators have long baulked at it, and have been inventive in resolving the complexity. One solution has been to note that the Greek word κάμηλος is only one letter different from κάμιλος, which means a thick rope as used on a ship.[55] It would still be impossible to get this through a needle (that is the point, after all) but it makes a neater, more elegant visual analogy. The irony is that the word κάμιλος is only recorded in commentary on this verse of the Bible, and may have been coined for the purpose (although it is based on the Arabic word *Jammil* which does have this meaning). A third solution, on the other hand, lies not in the camel but in the expression τρυπήμα ῥαφίδος, 'the eye of a needle'. For in some middle eastern cities, there are two outer gates, one big and one small. The first is for camels and donkeys; the second, for foot-passengers, is called 'the needle's eye'. Unquestionably pedestrian, this again sounds more plausible than the literal reading.

How far was Shakespeare entering into these scriptural contestations of metaphor? The idea that Shakespeare is reflecting on the Tudor devotional art of meditation on death is supported by the fact that Thomas Lupset made the same exegetical and metaphorical connection in *A Treatise of Dieying Well* (1534): 'For as harde a thynge it is to plucke through the smale nedels eie a greatte caboull rope, as to brynge a ryche man in at heuens wycket'.[56] Ure's Arden 2 edition (p. 170) faithfully followed Shakespeare's creative exegetical interest, but his is a lone voice. Even the pioneer enthusiast of biblical sources in Shakespeare, Richmond Noble, showed a secularist bias here. Noble believed the interpretation of the city gate was only invented in the nineteenth century, while it has been around in the margins of commentary for a thousand years: it was universally available throughout the Middle Ages in the standard *Glossa ordinaria*, is

---

[55] See Liddell and Scott, *A Greek–English Lexicon*.

[56] *A compendious and a very fruteful treatyse, teachynge the waye of dyenge well written to a frende, by the flowre of lerned men of his tyme, Thomas Lupsete Londoner, late deceassed, on whose soule Iesu haue mercy* ([London]: Thomas Berthelet, 1534), sig. C3ʳ.

mentioned by Aquinas, and obliquely by Dante.[57] Most relevantly, it is found in Erasmus' edition of the New Testament, one of the most widely cited sources in the sixteenth century, via a variety of intermediaries.[58] It was certainly known in England not only in Lupset but later in the seventeenth century:

> there was a little *Postern Gate* in the *Wall* of *Jerusalem,* which was called *foramen acûs,* or the *Needles eye,* through which a *Camel* could not pass without Kneeling (which saith *Pliny* Camels are taught to do) so as by going on their *Knees,* a Camel might pass through that Gate, which otherwise it could not do.[59]

At a lesser scholarly level, in Erasmus' Paraphrases, a source used by church ministers for their weekly sermons and placed at hand for them to do so by visitation orders, the difficulty of the rich in entering heaven is compared with the camel going 'through the narowe gate'.[60]

As for the 'camel' as a synonym for a thick and heavy nautical rope, it is found in another commonplace biblical reference book of the late sixteenth century, Theodore Beza's bilingual Greek and Latin *Novum Testamentum.* He cites an Aristophanic scholiast as suggesting this reading, before going on to say that he has found no other reference to corroborate it.[61] Yet even as a rejected reading this lurks as a prompt to an imaginative mind; and from Beza it passed into a source known to, and even probably owned by, Shakespeare.

This is the revised version of the Geneva New Testament edited by Laurence Tomson, first published in 1576. From 1587 it was issued bound up with an ordinary Geneva Old Testament, an edition that in more educated circles began to oust the original Geneva in popularity. Tomson's revision of the text was not extensive, but he replaced the Geneva marginal annotations with more voluminous notes largely translated or adapted from Beza's Latin edition. In relation to Matthew 19: 24 in the margin of Tomson's text, there is a note marked 'p': 'Theophylact

---

[57] William L. Edgerton, 'Shakespeare and the "Needle's Eye"', *Modern Language Notes,* 66 (1951), 549–50.

[58] The Greek Text in Erasmus' 3rd edn. of 1522 reads as follows: πάλιν δὲ λέγω ὑμῖν, εὐκοπώτερόν ἐστιν κάμηλον διὰ τρυπήματος ῥαφίδος διελθεῖν ἢ πλούσιον εἰς τὴν βασιλείαν τοῦ θεοῦ.

[59] Lazarus Ercker, *Fleta minor the laws of art and nature, in knowing, judging, assaying, fining, refining and inlarging the bodies of confin'd metals: in two parts* (London: Thomas Dawkes, 1683), 93.

[60] Erasmus, *The first tome or volume of the Paraphrase of Erasmus vpon the Newe Testamente* ([London]: Edwarde Whitchurche, 1548), fo. cxlvi.

[61] *Iesu Christi Domini nostri Novum Testamentum, sive Novum foedus, cujus Graeco contextui respondent interpretationes duae* (Cambridge: Roger Daniel, 1642), 66.

noteth, that by this word is meant a cable rope'; indeed in a briefer form there is a reference to this interpretation in the ordinary Geneva edition, where the margin has 'Or, cable rope'.[62]

Noble argued, and Naseeb Shaheen has confirmed in the fullest analysis of biblical references in Shakespeare, that at some points the Geneva version is the closest to being a source.[63] Some scholars, in the wake of the 'Catholic Shakespeare' argument, have doubted this, on the basis that the Geneva was regarded as a sectarian Bible identified with a radical Calvinist stance. In fact, this is something of an anachronistic canard. While the 1560 edition was a Genevan exile version, from 1576 these bibles were produced by the Queen's printer, Christopher Barker. They were the most widely available, and in format the cheapest, text of the Bible in English. While historians often refer to the notes as virulently Calvinist, this is on the basis of James I's objections over the word 'tyrant'; the truth is that the vast majority of the annotations are etymological and explanatory. John Whitgift, Lancelot Andrewes, and indeed James himself (for whom as a Scots child this was the standard version) all used the Geneva Bible for private use. Any common reader, probably including many Catholics, will have used this version for ease of practice and clarity of explanation.

Noble nonetheless concluded that Shakespeare's use of the Geneva post-dated *Richard II*, and he cited the camel reference to back this: Shakespeare thought only of poetic exaggeration.[64] However, this, too, was an idea to be found in the second half of Beza's note in Tomson: 'Caninius alleageth out of the Thalmudists, that it is a prouerb, and the word Camel, signifieth the beast it selfe'. And the evidence that Shakespeare knew these two alternative textual solutions in Tomson is in *Richard II* itself: 'It is as hard to come, as for a Cammell | To threed the posterne of a small needles eie'. The 'threed' implies the 'cable rope' interpretation, while 'posterne' brings in the gate at Jerusalem. Indeed Richard's version is like a conflation of all *three* textual theories.

Contrary to Noble, Shakespeare seems to be aware of the exegetical controversies surrounding this verse, indeed is fascinated by them, and presents Richard as fascinated by them. Richard's rendition of the verse

---

[62] Tomson, marginal note to Matt. 19: 24. Geneva (first edition, 1560): *The Bible, Translated according to the Ebrew and Greeke... With most profitable Annotations vpon all the hard places* (London: Christopher Barker, 1589), marginal note to 'camel' (Matt. 19: 24, repeated at Mark 10: 25 and Luke 18: 25).

[63] Naseeb Shaheen, *Biblical References in Shakespeare's Plays* (Newark, Del.: University of Delaware Press, 1999), 31–2.

[64] 'Any intelligent person not misled by commentary would so take it and especially would this be true of a poet'; Richmond Noble, *Shakespeare's Biblical Knowledge* (London: SPCK, 1935), 96.

constitutes a poetic commentary on the textual arguments, a biblical interest not found in any of his historical sources.[65] But he is not interested in them as separate semantic glosses, in order to choose one over another. Instead he treats the verse as a confusion of glosses, a proliferation of different meanings. Whereas the biblical commentators try to reduce Jesus' meaning to a single simple metaphor, Richard multiplies it into four different metaphors, and then recombines them as a single complex one: a camel going through a gate, a thick rope threaded through a needle, a camel threaded through a needle, even a rope going through a gate. In other words, he creates a *mixed* metaphor. The effect is not one of catachresis so much as semantic density, a thick texture of meaning.

Richard treats the exegetical apparatus not as a commentary but as itself a text, an example of metaphorical process. Each word of Jesus' saying implies a complex set of referents which, when the words are put in sequence in a sentence, engenders ever new metaphorical correspondences. The very conflict of meaning among the scriptural exegetes is an exemplary case of Richard's more general sense of a problem over meaning. Words do not so much refer to things as *make things up*, conjuring into language a fantasy of camels, gates, ropes, needles. The commentators attempt to control the conjuration, abjuring them into submission, a recognizable reality of fixed proportion. Richard's own version, on the other hand, is a realistic impossibility, and works only as a pure linguistic fiction; through his still-breeding words he generates something which could not ever happen in the world. As he gropes to understand the limits of language, 'imagination breaks'.[66]

THE WEIGHT OF THE FLESH

The Shakespearian soliloquy does not arrive out of nowhere as the expression of a newly minted secular interiority. Hamlet is left on stage for the first time as the king's formal audience departs with a flourish. The stage is reduced from public to private chamber, and the prince is left in a colloquy with his own mortality:

Flourish. Exeunt all but Hamlet.

HAM. O that this too too sullied flesh would melt,
Thaw and resolve itself into a dew (1.2.129–30)

---

[65] Shaheen, *Biblical References in Shakespeare's Plays*, 361–2.

[66] Anne Barton, 'Shakespeare and the Limits of Language' (1971), collected in *Essays, Mainly Shakespearean* (Cambridge: Cambridge University Press, 1994), 56.

The lines have long held a textual crux. Q1 and Q2 both read 'sallied', while Folio reads 'solid'. Harold Jenkins's note on the line is characteristically comprehensive and formidable. 'Solid' he feels is only too obvious a correction for a metaphor which in its Quarto form is difficult to unravel. 'Sallied' is a variant spelling in Shakespeare for 'sullied', so it may not be necessary to accept Furnivall's sense of 'assailed' in order to accept a sense of bodily corruption. Yet perhaps the argument over the crux has hidden a simpler and yet reverberant range of reference. Hamlet naturally conflates a sense of his physical being as both overly material and ineluctably tainted, because both kinds of language here are associated with the genre of this speech, the contemplation of the body in the presence of incipient death.

This may be the reason why his metaphor twists itself so easily towards a trope of 'dissolution'. Jenkins feels the transference from 'solid' to 'melt' to be a cliché not quite worthy of the poet. But this is because the primary sense of 'dissolve' in modern English is so dominantly one of a chemical change of state. In early modern English, this may rather be a subjugate sense that the metaphor teases out. The first sense of the metaphor might rather be 'to destroy the physical integrity; to disintegrate, decompose'. Indeed, so strong was the association of the word 'dissolve' with the idea of the dissolution of the union of soul and body that might be enjoined by death that 'dissolve' was a synonym for death itself—as the dictionary puts it, 'To release from life; to cause the dissolution or death of'. This is derived from the Vulgate reading of Philippians, where the Latin verb used is the passive form *dissolvi*. In the Geneva version the verse reads as follows:

> For I am distressed betweene both, desiring to be loosed and to be with Christ, which is best of all. (Phil. 1: 23, Geneva)

This sense of being loosed or cut free from the cares and sins of a 'sullied' life merges in *Hamlet* with the metaphorical transferred sense of solid melting into liquid to form a powerful combined metaphor.

Such a concoction aligns Hamlet's first soliloquy with a characteristic Reformation language of the anticipation of death:

> the fleashe abhorreth naturally his awne sorrowful dissolucion, whiche death doth threaten vnto theim, and partely, by reason of sickenesses, and paynfull diseases, whiche be moste strong pangues and agonies in the fleshe.[67]

---

[67] 'An exhortation agaynst the feare of Death', *Certayne sermons, or homelies appoynted by the kynges Maiestie, to be declared and redde, by all persones, vicars, or curates, euery Sondaye in their churches, where they haue cure* (London: Richard Grafton, 1547), sig. O3ᵛ–O4ʳ.

Only, as the same homily on the fear of death goes on to recall, Paul himself, despite this overwhelming natural fear, 'declareth the desire of his heart, which was to bee dissolued and loosed from his body, and to be with Christ'. So here, Hamlet in a similar manner both accepts and reverses the language of death. Rather than abhorring or avoiding his own dissolution, he welcomes it, yearns for it, aspires for a release from corruption which will *also* be a dissipation of the burden of material being. It is a metaphor Montaigne uses in both directions in 'L'Apologie de Raimond Sebond': 'Je veux estre dissoult', in a passage where he is translating from Lucretius the same Latin verb *dissolvi*.[68] Elsewhere in the same essay Montaigne quotes once again from Lucretius: whatever changes, dissolves, and therefore dies:

> quod mutatur enim, dissolvitur, interit ergo[69]

Yet Montaigne in 'Divers evenemens de mesme Conseil' also recognizes well enough the opposite tendency: our nature shuns dissolution, 'elle fuit la dissolution'.[70]

A Lucretian element in Shakespeare's descriptions of mortality is most obvious in the diptych of speeches between the Duke and Claudio in *Measure for Measure*. What is so interesting about these speeches is that they have the character of monologue although uttered in dialogue: a sense of the soliloquy turning itself out into colloquy. In the first the Duke speaks as if for Claudio, in his presence, as a kind of confessor, that most private of audiences which stands in for an absent God. The confessor prepares the condemned man for death, and in this guise gives voice to an intense scepticism about the fortunes of the human material form:

> DUKE Thy best of rest is sleep;
> And that thou oft provok'st, yet grossly fear'st
> Thy death, which is no more. Thou art not thyself;
> For thou exists on many a thousand grains
> That issue out of dust. Happy thou art not;
> For what thou hast not, still thou striv'st to get,
> And what thou hast, forget'st. (3.1.17–23)

A discourse on death, often in dialogue form, marks out the Renaissance genre of 'consolation' literature, perhaps inspired by a Ciceronian rhetorical model, here freely mixing Stoic and Christian ideas. The Duke consoles Claudio with the idea of a sleep from which he might awake into eternal life. Yet he intersperses this with an account of human embodiment which

---

[68] *Essais*, II.xii.465, citing Lucretius, *De rerum natura*, iii. 613–15.
[69] *De rerum natura*, iii. 756; quoted in *Essais*, II.xii.547.
[70] *Essais*, I.xxiii.131; trans. Frame, p. 112.

instead is seemingly based on the atomic theories of Lucretius. Whether Shakespeare has read Lucretius at this point is a matter of dispute, but what is clear is that the thought is speculative, and as L. C. Martin comments, 'is hardly an ordinary commonplace'.[71] Claudio's body is a configuration of atoms which once dissolved will make him nothing: in this sense, 'Thou art not thyself', and Claudio's happiness hangs on the thread of his lifeline.

It is in this context that Claudio gives voice to his own reply, the most shocking description of the fear of death in Shakespeare. While implicitly a reply to the Duke's formal discourse, it is addressed instead to Isabella, and once again mixes pagan philosophy and Christian doctrine, the conception of death taking its Lucretian cue directly from the Duke:

> CLA. Ay, but to die, and go we know not where;
> To lie in cold obstruction, and to rot;
> This sensible warm motion to become
> A kneaded clod; and the delighted spirit
> To bath in fiery floods, or to reside
> In thrilling region of thick-ribbed ice (3.1.117–22)

Lucretius takes over but turns out to be less salutary than the consolatory Cicero, even though Lucretius writes in the spirit of the most logical response to the fear of death. Who is more alone, the Claudio who listens to the Duke, or the Claudio who replies to Isabella?

This may help us to understand a fundamental ambiguity in the most famous of all soliloquies. What does it mean for Hamlet to say that he might wish 'not to be'? For the moment the question here is not that of whether suicide is desirable or unconscionable—that is a question for another chapter. Because of the Christian ban on suicide it has often been assumed that Hamlet's notorious question must be secular in origin. But it is not, and indeed occurs in Augustine, *De libero arbitrio*: whether it is better to be unhappy than not to be at all (Nemo vere dixerit se malle *non esse quam miserum esse*).[72] To which Augustine gives the reply:

> *Non ideo mori nolo, quod malim miser esse quam omnino non esse, sed ne post mortem miserior sim*

> It is not because I would rather be unhappy than not be at all, that I am unwilling to die, but for fear that after death I may be still more unhappy.[73]

---

[71] 'Shakespeare, Lucretius, and the Commonplaces', *The Review of English Studies*, 21 (1945), 174–82, this ref. 176.
[72] Augustine, *De libero arbitrio*, III.vi.
[73] Augustine, *De libero arbitrio*, III.vi.19; *Patrologia Latina*, 32.1280.

The question that is still open, then, is whether it is possible to 'not be' at all, a question to which I return in Chapter 7.

The modern and secular assumption here is that the idea of an afterlife is consolatory and that 'not being' is the worst of all options. Yet the meaning of Augustine, and perhaps of *Hamlet*, too, is the precise opposite. It is the continuation of existence after death that is the most frightening possibility. Non-existence is the release, the dissolution, of the body from its torments of being. It is in peril, or better hope, of this that Hamlet stands at the beginning of Act 3:

HAM. To die—to sleep,
No more; and by a sleep to say we end
The heart-ache and the thousand natural shocks
That flesh is heir to: 'tis a consummation
Devoutly to be wish'd. To die, to sleep;
To sleep, perchance to dream—ay, there's the rub:
For in that sleep of death what dreams may come,
When we have shuffled off this mortal coil,
Must give us pause— (3.1.60–8)

Soliloquy reaches out once more to contemplate what a man meditates as he finds himself alone with his creator or himself: what it means to be a creature, to have existence.

Hamlet's first response is to equate death, as in the cliché of the literature of *memento mori*, with sleep. Death is a form of rest or recreation from the trials of mortality, 'the thousand natural shocks | That flesh is heir to'. Sleep mollifies the trials and aches of daytime. But Hamlet comes to a halt on a word he cannot quite give a meaning to: 'consummation'. It is a word he first appears to enjoy giving voice to: it has a satisfyingly completing sound, as a tetrasyllable that fills out almost half a line. He longs for it as he longs for death: it is something 'Devoutly to be wish'd'. Yet once uttered the word seems to give him pause; he lingers over it, as if wondering what it really means.

The word 'consummation' appears only one other time in the whole of the First Folio. This is also in the context of death, where it is used in *Cymbeline* at the end of the dirge sung over the grave of Imogen by Guiderius and Arviragus, 'Fear no more the heat of the Sun':

BOTH. Quiet consummation have,
And renowned be thy grave! (4.2.280–1)

The natural primary meaning of the word in this context is a final ending, a conclusion. This is the sense in Christ's words on the cross (John 19: 30) which in the Vulgate reads *consummatum est* ('It is finished'), a reference given immediate resonance in Hamlet by its citation at a famous moment in Marlowe's *Doctor Faustus*. But the meaning is not so clear-cut. 'Consummation' (the Q2 reading is in fact 'consumation') is strongly related to the word 'consumption', a word which has also changed substantially from its principal early modern sense of 'The action or fact of destroying or being destroyed; destruction'.[74] Indeed the 1609 Quarto of *King Lear*, when Lear gives his misogynistic vision of the pains of hell, gives 'consumation' where the Folio reads 'consumption':

> LEAR. There's hell, there's darkness, there is the sulphurous pit, burning, scalding, stench, consumption! Fie, fie, fie! Pah, pah! (4.6.123–5)

Lear, then, like Hamlet, opposes material to immaterial states with a fear bordering on paranoia.

Haunting Shakespeare's meditation on the meaning of non-being is a sense of the word he may acquire from Montaigne's French, for instance in 'De la Physionomie':

> Si c'est un aneantissement de nostre estre, c'est encore amendement d'entrer en une longue et paisible nuit. Nous ne sentons rien de plus doux en la vie, qu'un repos et sommeil tranquille, et profond sans songes.

> If it is an annihilation of our being, it is still an improvement to enter upon a long and peaceful night. We feel nothing sweeter in life than a deep and tranquil rest and sleep, without dreams.[75]

'Consummation' is the word Florio used to translate Montaigne's *aneantissement*. This coincidence has long persuaded commentators that Shakespeare in this instance from 'De la Physionomie' knew Florio's version before it was published in 1603:

> *If it be a consummation of ones being, it is also an amendment and entrance into a long and quiet night. Wee finde nothing so sweete in life, as a quiet rest and gentle sleepe, and without dreames.*[76]

Imagining death as gentle sleep is so commonplace that it is hard to be precisely sure about the citation here. However, *aneantissement* is an important word for Montaigne. More than the English word which replaces it in Florio, *aneantissement* signifies a bringing to nothing, literally an 'annihilation' of being. The verb 'annihilate' is a sixteenth-century coinage in English, and does not yet have its widespread associations; 'consume' does

---

[74] *OED* CONSUMPTION, 1.　　　　[75] III.xii.1099; Frame, p. 981.
[76] *Essays vvritten in French by Michael Lord of Montaigne*, 593.

some of the same work.[77] Montaigne uses the same word *aneantissement* in the same crucial passage in the 'Apologie de Sebond', where he quotes Lucretius on 'dissolving':

> les commoditez ou peines corporelles, qui nous attendent encore après la ruine et aneantissement de nos corps

> the bodily comforts and pains that still await us after the destruction and annihilation of our bodies[78]

Florio here translates, 'the commodities or corporall paines which even after the ruine and consumption of our bodie, waite for vs', so that the semantic link between 'consummation' and 'consumption' is reinforced.[79] But it seems the English cannot quite capture the precise denotation of nothingness. To be 'consumed' is to be destroyed or alternatively to be eaten up, but it is not necessarily to become nothing. Indeed in this same passage, Florio uses 'consummation' (a word he uses only three times in the whole of the *Essayes*) as an equivalent for Montaigne's *ruyne*:

> Car nous sommes bastis de deux pieces principales essentielles, desquelles la separation, c'est la mort et ruyne de nostre estre.[80]

Florio writes: 'for we are builte of two principall essentiall parts, the separation of which, is the death and consummation of our being'.[81] The distinction between soul and body thus gives rises to the extinction of the self itself.

Elsewhere in the 'Apologie' Montaigne turns his attention to what it might be like to feel this state of nothingness. He cites Epicurus' concept of 'l'indolence', a favourite topic of his, the capacity to be insensible of the material things around us.[82] Even when he is sick, Montaigne says, he likes to feel what is happening to him; likewise when the doctor cuts him open. The only true sensation of insensibleness would be, as Cicero described, to remove the entire capacity for sensation: 'De vray, qui desracineroit la cognoissance du mal, il extirperoit quand et quand la cognoissance

---

[77] *OED*, ANNIHILATE, *v.* 1a. The *OED* gives 1599 as the first reference for 'annihilate' to mean 'To reduce to non-existence' a physical object, in a medical handbook; the theological sense of reducing to non-being, of destroying the soul as well as the body, it dates to 1635 ('Death ... not annihilates, but uncloudes the soule').

[78] II.xii.546; Frame, p. 467.

[79] *Essays vvritten in French by Michael Lord of Montaigne*, 289.

[80] II.xii.548 ('For we are built of two principal essential parts, whose separation is death and destruction of our being', Frame, p. 469).

[81] *Essays vvritten in French by Michael Lord of Montaigne*, 290.

[82] On 'indolence' and 'nonchalance' in Montaigne, see Felicity Green, *Montaigne and the Life of Freedom*, 141–84.

de la volupté, et en fin aneantiroit l'homme' ('In truth, he who would eradicate the knowledge of evil would at the same time extirpate the knowledge of pleasure, and in fine would annihilate man').[83] Such would be a true *stupor in corpore*.[84] This is the death of sensation itself (literally 'the knowledge/consciousness of the senses/pleasure'), and is a figure for the death of self.

The passage from 'De la Physionomie' makes sense as a source for Hamlet's soliloquy not only because of verbal reminiscence, which we could explain away, but because of the structure of his thinking. Indeed, it appears that Hamlet is thinking as much about Montaigne's *aneantisse-ment* as Florio's 'Consummation', although he could not have said 'anni-hilation', since the word did not yet exist. Montaigne cites in that moment the supreme scepticism of Socrates, in the face of something that he is certain exists, but about which he can say nothing for certain. Montaigne here paraphrases a long passage from Plato's *Apology*.[85] Socrates, alone with his examiners, admits to his ignorance in the face of death:

Je sçay que je n'ay ni frequenté, ny recogneu la mort, ni n'ay veu personne qui ait essayé ses qualitez, pour m'en instruire

I know that I have had no association or acquaintance with death, nor have I known anyone who has had experience of its qualities to inform me about it (III.xii.1099, Frame, p. 981)

He has no experience to draw on for knowledge, either at first or second hand. Fear of death is irrational, since they who fear would claim to know what it is that they fear, but they cannot know this. As for Socrates (and now it is Montaigne who begins to speak in his own voice, as he speaks 'à moy'), he does not know either what death is, or what it would be like in another world, another world he cannot enter without already being dead: 'quant à moy, je ne sçay ny quelle elle est, ny quel il faict en l'autre monde' (III.xii.1099, Frame, p. 981). In this sense death is a thing truly 'indifferent', perhaps even 'desirable': 'A l'avanture est la mort chose indif-ferente, à l'avanture desirable' (III.xii.1099, Frame, p. 981). He calls it, in a manner where the word truly fits the man and the occasion, a 'noncha-lant' kind of death: 'une si nonchallante et molle consideration de sa mort' ('such a nonchalant and mild way of considering his death').[86]

---

[83] II.xii.520; Frame, p. 442.

[84] Quoting Cicero, *Tusculan Disputations*, III.vi.12: *Nam istuc nihil dolere non sine magna mercede contingit, immanitatis in animo, stuporis in corpore* (ed. J. E. King, Loeb Classical Library (Cambridge, Mass.: Harvard University Press, 1960), 238–40).

[85] Plato, *Apology*, 29A and following; ed. and trans. H. N. Fowler, Loeb Classical Library (London: Heinemann, 1977), 140–4.

[86] III.xii.1101; Frame, p. 983.

This is what Hamlet means by 'a consummation | Devoutly to be wish'd'. He is thinking of what Richard II is thinking of in his final soliloquy, 'being nothing', and like Richard, he is thinking about what it would be to wish such a thing. For to desire such a state is still to be in a state of being, still to feel the knowledge or consciousness of sensation or of pleasure. I desire therefore I am. Hamlet's momentary hiatus at the enjambement between 'consummation' and 'Devoutly' perfectly expresses the bridge he cannot cross, what Montaigne calls 'une transmigration d'une place à autre' (III.xii.1099), the transference from desiring to not desiring, from feeling to not feeling, from being to non-being. Hamlet pauses at what he cannot know without himself not being.

LAST SYLLABLE

Waiting for the end of a tragedy is like watching your own death. We await an end which is known but not yet upon us. Audience and actor become engaged in a strange transaction in which the lines blur as to who is speaking for whom. In Shakespeare's plays it is not always clear that the actor is alone even when nobody else is on stage; or else it can appear that even when in company, he speaks to nobody else but himself:

> MACB. To-morrow, and to-morrow, and to-morrow,
> Creeps in this petty pace from day to day,
> To the last syllable of recorded time;
> And all our yesterdays, have lighted fools
> The way to dusty death. (*Macbeth*, 5.5.19–23)

Macbeth speaks more, as it were, *to death*, than he does to Seyton, who has just entered to announce his Lady Macbeth's end. Seyton overhears Macbeth's speech even though it is spoken alone, much like the audience overhears in a soliloquy. And Macbeth speaks of his own death as much as he does of that of his wife. His meditation on time and mortality is therefore characteristic of Shakespearian soliloquy in showing thought in the process of its own composition, and yet also in its own unmaking. It combines epigrammatic grandeur with extreme figurative complexity. The verse is readily remembered but not easy to explain. This sense of linguistic difficulty is not counter-productive, however; one of the features that makes the lines memorable is that it is not possible to catch the sense straightaway, so that it remains mysterious and complex in the same way that the idea Macbeth is expressing is mysterious and complex. His mind is caught at the moment of the most intense effort to explain and understand what his life has been like and how it is going to end, yet it cannot complete its thought or comprehend its own sense. His meaning, like his premonition of death, is haunted by an apprehension of incompleteness.

Macbeth, like Richard II and like Hamlet, apprehends his own finitude by trying to give expression to the mystery of his embodiment in words, in ways which also draw attention to the mystery of language and of metaphor. What makes his sentence hard to comprehend is the figurative sequence, rather than the syntax or diction. None of the words individually is difficult or philosophical. Macbeth's meditation presents instead a concatenation of figures which pile quickly on top of each other. His speech refers overtly to the mathematical reckoning of time, measured in terms of speed ('this petty pace'). Time passes by inexorably, indifferent to the course of a single life. Macbeth longs for the space to mourn his wife but time will not let him. This is conflated with a figure of an individual lifetime made up like a book with 'syllables', in particular the book of record which the angel keeps at the last judgement. Time itself seems infinite but each life within it is limited, like a sentence that must end in its own period. These are perhaps the primary figures we have to keep in mind. Yet no explicit connection is made between them. The figure transfers itself from one referent to the other without elucidation. Time measured in relation to speed and time imagined as a book of words are conflated together, but the link between them is left to the auditor to make out. To cloud the picture further, there are other figurative undercurrents. The phrase 'creeps in' can be interpreted in two different ways, one in terms of slow progress and the other in terms of a narrow space.[87] This suggests a new connection with a third figure of a passageway, a sense supported by the Elizabethan meaning of 'pace' as a narrow road, passage, or strait.[88] Although submerged as a meaning the connection is natural in that it associates the finitude of time with burial, perhaps in a catacomb beneath the ground. In turn, this creates a link with a fourth, final figure that emerges at the end of the sentence, where a person's past is represented as a funeral procession ('The way to dusty death'), lit by torches held by fools.

In this process the difficulty of trying to capture the sense of the words matches the difficulty in trying to capture the shape of a life as it comes to an end. Shakespeare's characteristic figure of speech here is metalepsis: a

---

[87] This reading of 'creeps' is suggested in *The Tragedy of Macbeth*, ed. Nicholas Brooke, The Oxford Shakespeare (Oxford: Oxford University Press, 1990), 205 (5.5.20).

[88] *OED*, PACE, 2.a and fig. ('a road or passage through dangerous territory'); it is possible that 3. ('In a church: a passage between the pews or seats') may be relevant, as applying to a burial site within a church.

figure in which the middle term is left out, so that we have to guess the full sense. His figures appear to link themselves in replicating chains, doubling up on themselves, inverting themselves, or merging into each other. It is a figure that can end only in death.

In *Macbeth*, soliloquy is a subtle and ambiguous literary form. Whereas Hamlet finds his most natural form of speech in the long soliloquy when he is left alone on stage, Macbeth, from his very first scene, finds his own speech rhythm much harder to discover. He struggles to find space on stage to be alone, he is crowded out. His resource is to cut across the rules of the stage to insist on his own identity in the 'Aside'. Of all the theatrical conventions of solitary speech this is perhaps the oddest. Somewhere between a social gaffe and an interior monologue uttered aloud, it enacts a rupture between the world on stage and the world of the witnesses in the audience. Macbeth's first exercise in the aside is very brief, like an interjection—'Glamis, and Thane of Cawdor: | The greatest is behind' (1.3.116–17)—an exclamation of pure ambition which might pass others by. But his next aside, almost immediately afterwards, takes Macbeth into a characteristically ambivalent social space of invented privacy. Typically, this is also the space of Macbeth's imagination, the place where he conjures forbidden ideas into being. Macbeth himself comments on this rule of the imagination, and as if in afterthought or else in horrible premonition (it is hard to say which) he becomes the first to utter the word 'murder' in the play:

MACB. [*Aside.*] Present fears
Are less then horrible imaginings:
My thought, whose murther yet is but fantastical,
Shakes so my single state of man,
That function is smother'd in surmise,
And nothing is, but what is not. (1.3.137–42)

Is 'murther' here a figure? And if so, is it a tortured ellipsis ('a thought of murder') or a terrifying prolepsis (an inadvertent prophecy)? The borderline between imagining terrible things ('but fantastical'), and doing them, is the great ethical and political crux of the play.

The word 'fantastical'—an unusual word already used by Banquo of the witches earlier in the scene—seems to mean 'imaginary'. But Macbeth is now setting in train a line of thought in which language itself sets the limits to action, rather than the other way round. His being is brought into being by his capacity to imagine himself. The sense that this is an individual form of speech is reinforced by the fact that the last three lines, as lineated in the Folio (the only text of the play), are metrically short: but despite attempts to re-lineate as blank verse by various editors, Kenneth Muir remarked that 'as nearly every actor speaks them thus and, I think, correctly' it seems better to interpret Macbeth here as speaking his own idiolect.[89] He is trying to assemble 'my single state of man' as if such a concept is in doubt. By 'single', perhaps, he means the conjunction of soul and body, the fragile balance which makes him alive, or, in Montaigne's words, 'deux pieces principales essentielles, desquelles la separation, c'est la mort' (II. xii.548). For the rest of the play it is a struggle to keep himself intact. His intellectual faculties no longer seem synchronous with the world around him, but are bounded only by his imagination: 'function is smother'd in surmise'. Reality and the fantastic now change places: 'nothing is, but what is not'.

Macbeth cannot help imagining things, and once imagined, cannot stop himself doing them. The explanation for this is caught between a traditional tragic canopy of fate and a complex motivational psychology of moral behaviour. This culminates in his only true soliloquy in the play, a magnificent and terrifying imagination of what it is to be alive:

> MACB. If it were done, when 'tis done, then 'twere well
> It were done quickly: if th' assassination
> Could trammel up the consequence, and catch
> With his surcease success; that but this blow
> Might be the be-all, and the end-all—here,
> But here, upon this bank and shoal of time,
> We'd jump the life to come.— (*Macbeth*, 1.7.1–7)

'The meanings', William Empson said, 'cannot all be remembered at once, however often you read it.'[90] The lines are like a metalepsis in explanation of metalepsis, in a recognition of the way that every life is lived in an interplay between language and action. In the play's continuous passage between *figura* and *res* it finds its 'be-all, and...end-all'. The words are coinages. The boundaries of a fantasy happening on stage and the actors and spectators who are caught in the apprehension of their own mutual mortality are never more fragile than here. Muir says of the hiatus suggested by the dash 'The pause is the most powerful of which blank verse is capable.'[91] Yet the figures provide fictive pleasure and relief as well as remorseless self-commentary. As the figures double up on themselves, they provide for us at least an illusion that in the act of making up our own language we can (at least fleetingly) anticipate the shape of our existence and 'jump the life to come'.

---

[89] *Macbeth*, ed. Kenneth Muir, Arden Series 2 (London: Methuen, 1951), 21.
[90] *Seven Types of Ambiguity* (London: New Directions, 1930), 50.
[91] *Macbeth*, ed. Muir, 37.

6

Hamlet's Luck

Shakespeare & the Renaissance Bible

Why do things turn out the way they do, in one way rather than another? At the end of *Hamlet,* in the space of perhaps two minutes of stage time, four people die. Hamlet is the last. Although he has suffered a mortal injury, he still has a little more to say. But he can hardly get the words out. He speaks in grammatical fragments, and barely finishes a sentence:

I am dead *Horatio*, wretched Queene adiew,
You that looke pale, and tremble at this chance,
That are but Mutes or audience to this acte:
Had I but time (as this fell Sergeant death
Is strick'd in his Arrest) oh I could tell you.
But let it be.[1]

Just one word he can get out in time to explain his life and death, and that word is 'chance'. I am not sure the word seems quite right to us. Is it chance that has brought Hamlet to this pass? Does he live, or more to the point, does he die, by chance? Yet when Horatio begins the task in the play's stark denouement of absenting himself from felicity awhile to tell Hamlet's story (as he is bidden to do) he echoes Hamlet's metaphysical analysis of what has just taken place:

And let me speake to th' yet vnknowing world,
How these things came about. So shall you heare
Of carnall, bloudie, and vnnaturall acts,
Of accidentall iudgements, casuall slaughters,
Of death's put on by cunning, and forc'd' cause,
And in this vpshot, purposes mistooke,
Falne on the Inuentors heads. All this can I
Truly deliuer. (F3874–81)

---

[1] Quotations from *The Tragedie of Hamlet* are taken from the First Folio, using Charlton Hinman's facsimile edition (*The First Folio of Shakespeare* (New York: Norton, 1968)) and citing his line numbers. This instance F3817–22; further citations appear in the text in parentheses.

Horatio's vocabulary here is redolent of a philosophy of chance. The acts he has to recount are against nature, criminal and bloody, but they are also the result of what he characterizes as strange mischance or 'purposes mistooke'. His choice of words is as precise as it can be: justice has been achieved only by 'accidentall' process; intention has been mismatched with result; cunning plots have had the opposite effect; malicious motives have succeeded only in redounding upon themselves. The key word is that interesting case 'casual', a word that has over time been reduced to meaning a kind of attire to wear at parties but here is used in its root sense: subject to chance, something that just happens.

The last scene of *Hamlet* is famously confused. Nothing quite goes to plan. Gertrude takes the wrong cup; Hamlet and Laertes swap swords; both receive a killing blow. It is at this point, apprehending the full enormity of what has happened, that Hamlet finally is spurred into doing what he has been promising to do throughout the play, and kills his uncle. It makes for a shock ending, some people feel a slightly schlock ending, cheap thrill and trashy melodrama, blood all over the stage. The Elizabethans liked this kind of thing, we are told. Yet in this hammiest of revenge endings we come face to face with a metaphysical conundrum. Hamlet at last in killing Claudius achieves full human agency. He is in control of his own destiny, he seizes his moment, and defines himself by taking unilateral action. And yet at the very same point he loses his life, through a series of events entirely outside of his control, coincidences haphazardly heaped together, a conspiracy compounded by a mistake compounded by an accident. He is the victim of a freak set of circumstances. He calls this process, not unjustly, 'chance'.

A HISTORY OF CHANCE

What are the odds on Hamlet dying? The question is not entirely facetious. Osric, turning bookmaker in Act 5, reports that the king has 'laid a great wager' on Hamlet's head in the fencing match with Laertes.[2] Claudius is said to have gambled that, in a dozen passes, Hamlet 'shall not exceed you three hits': 'He hath laid on twelve for nine'.[3] Claudius stakes six Barbary horses on the result, and Laertes six French rapiers and poniards,

---

[2] On the nature of the swordfight, see James L. Jackson, '"They Catch One Another's Rapiers": The Exchange of Weapons in Hamlet', *Shakespeare Quarterly*, 41 (1990), 281–98.

[3] A mathematical analysis of the wager was attempted by Evert Sprinchorn in 'The Odds on Hamlet', *Columbia Forum* 7.4 (1964), 41, reprinted in *The American Statistician* 24.5 (1970), 14–17. He calculated that the probability that Laertes will win is 0.443, which is very close to the probability 0.429, corresponding to the king's odds of 9 to 12.

with some other expensive bits of fencing merchandise thrown in. Hamlet quips that this is 'the French bet against the Danish'. Horatio gloomily predicts 'you will lose this wager, my Lord'. Hamlet is more upbeat: 'I shall win at the odds'. He appears to feel that the handicap of 'twelve for nine' may give him the edge. Of course, the odds are far worse than he realizes. The king has no intention of a fair bet. At the end of Act 4, he has already fixed the arrangements for the swordfight with Laertes, giving him the opportunity to revenge his father Polonius. Claudius loads the dice by making one of the blades unblunted. Laertes joins in, promising to envenom the points with a poison so powerful that no cataplasm under the moon can serve as an antidote, if the victim is only scratched. If all else fails, the king has a poisoned chalice up his sleeve. Perfectionist that he is, the king plots to kill Hamlet three times over, just to make sure. At this reckoning, the odds are not, as they appear, four to one against, but a dead certainty.

The meaning of this wager is vexed, and has occasioned one of the longest footnotes in an edition of the play which is itself notorious for the longest notes in Shakespearian history (Muriel Bradbrook uncharitably dubbed the 1982 Arden by Harold Jenkins as *Hamlet* edited by Polonius).[4] In February 2004, the matter was reopened in a staged quarrel in *The Times Literary Supplement*, in which Frank Kermode debated the wager with a novelist, a poker player, an expert on the mathematics of probability, and an Olympic swordsman.[5] Faced with such expertise, we may regard this particular book as closed. In the following, there is no new calculation of the odds, whether at 4/1, 5/1, or 9/12. But why is it that Shakespeare, in the last scene of his play, makes so many references to Hamlet's death in terms of odds, wagers, and the calculation of chance? This involves delving deeper into the language and philosophy surrounding chance, both in the play and in the culture of Elizabethan England.

As is well known, the mathematics of chance did not yet exist at this point. According to Ian Hacking in *The Emergence of Probability*, 'Probability began in about 1660'.[6] This is a curious historical fact, since gambling is one of the earliest inventions of organized human societies, and fortunes were there to be won by an enterprising scientist from the

His argument was refuted by James A. Kilby, 'The Odds on Sprinchorn's "The Odds on Hamlet"', *Notes & Queries*, 16 (1968), 133–6, on the basis that 'to exceed you three hits' cannot possibly mean 'to achieve three hits in a row'.

[4] *Hamlet*, ed. Harold Jenkins, The Arden Edition of the Works of Shakespeare (2nd series) (London: Methuen, 1982). The notorious footnote is at pp. 561–5.

[5] Frank Kermode, Anthony Holden, Robin Marris, Ken Follett, Linden Stafford, and Daniel Marciano, 'The Odds against Hamlet', *The Times Literary Supplement*, No. 5262 (6 February 2004), 11.

[6] *The Emergence of Probability: A Philosophical Study of Early Ideas about Probability, Induction and Statistical Inference* (Cambridge: Cambridge University Press, 1975), 18.

ancient Egyptians on. Hacking argues in a sophisticated way for the emergence of probability at the precise time and in the precise form that it did. This involves him in cumulative essays on the history of economics, science, and logic, on concepts of evidence and opinion, bills of mortality, and the first calculation of the peculiar statistic that the chances of a male child being born are about 18 in 35. All these matters have a bearing on *Hamlet*, along with another factor which Hacking argues is central to the development of a science of probability: theology. Here Hacking says something provocatively counter-intuitive. Before Hacking, it was often assumed that the prevalence of ideas of fate both in ancient pagan societies and in Christianity was one of the clearest inhibitions to a science of chance. Hacking dismisses such a view, indeed calls it an 'absurdity':

> Europe began to understand concepts of randomness, probability, chance and expectation precisely at that point in its history when theological views of divine foreknowledge were being reinforced by the amazing success of mechanistic models. (pp. 2–3)

It might even be, Hacking says, that a mechanical model of determinism was a precondition of a scientific concept of chance. Hacking's observation is important for two reasons. One is that he implies that we have been driven by modern philosophical doctrines of determinism to understand earlier, theological models (both pagan and Christian) in more rigid ways than may be the case. The other is in what we can glean of an understanding of randomness or chance *just before* the development of a proper mathematics.

Conventionally, the appearance of chance in *Hamlet* would seem to be part of the play's secular outlook. But Hacking's analysis suggests there is a closer relation between ideas of chance and ideas of divine providence than we might have believed. This is one of a number of ways in which human identity in *Hamlet* can be seen as part of the penumbra of Reformation controversy, rather than as a route out of it. For Hamlet's sense of his own life as being surrounded by 'chance' is embedded in religious language, visible in the daily routines of the liturgy. In the Collects after the Offertory at Communion in the Elizabethan *Book of Common Prayer*, often also said at Morning and Evening Prayer, salvation itself is imagined in the context of life's 'chances':

> dispose the way of thy servauntes, towarde the attainement of everlasting salvation, that emong al the chaunges, and chaunces of this mortal lyfe, thei may ever be defended by thy moste gratious, and redy helpe.[7]

[7] 'Communion (1559)', *The Book of Common Prayer: The Texts of 1549, 1559, and 1662*, ed. Brian Cummings (Oxford: Oxford University Press, 2011), 139.

The word 'chances' appears first in Cranmer's 1549 version, and was retained in every version of the Prayer Book afterwards, including the 1662 text after the Restoration.[8] Thus English-speaking communities prayed for divine aid in a world given over to chance for four centuries. The survival of this idea in the face of puritan sensitivities is striking, and will form a large part of what follows. In the Bible, as we will see, the vocabulary of 'chance' and related words is carefully chosen and often censored. Yet here the *Book of Common Prayer* speaks for a moment like Hamlet in the face of 'al the chaunges, and chaunces of this mortal lyfe'. As often, it is the human apprehension of mortality which gives rise to the most urgent speculation into the peculiarity of human subjectivity.

The subject of this chapter is a kind of philosophical prehistory: a history of chance before the discovery of chance. Its focus is a particular word, one that plays a central part in the everyday language of chance and fortune: 'luck'. The word 'luck', as opposed to 'chance' and 'fortune', does not appear in *Hamlet*. There is no particular reason why this should be: it appears thirty-six times elsewhere in Shakespeare. Perhaps this is just bad luck for the argument. However, the point is not purely lexicological. The aim is to enquire into a particular version of a history of 'chance' via a history of this word, one that illuminates the vexed understanding of chance in Hamlet, what his odds are, how 'lucky' he is.

In the process it will be shown how theology intersects with ideas of fortune in the century before a mathematics of probability took hold. The first book on games of chance was written by Girolamo Cardano in around 1560, not published until 1663.[9] This notorious and obnoxious Milanese doctor, astrologer, occasional gambler, and father of a convicted murderer, spent several years studying dice throws and a precursor of modern Italian football, developing a theory about frequency in relation to repeated trials.[10] More prosaically, in England a general lottery was proposed in 1567 to raise money for building ships and developing ports.[11] This is the first known coinage of the word 'lotterie' in English. It is one of many new words that interested Shakespeare: the curious procedure for determining Portia's husband is called a 'lotterie', and Octavia is described as potentially a 'blessed Lottery' for the heart of Antony.[12] Over all such speculations into

[8] *Book of Common Prayer*, ed. Cummings, pp. 37 and 405.
[9] Hacking, *Emergence of Probability*, 54.
[10] *Liber de Ludo Aleae* ('The Book on Games of Chance'), ch. 11; in *Hieronymi Cardani Mediolensis opera omnia* (Lyons: J. A. Huguetan and M. A. Ravaud, 1663).
[11] A royal proclamation was issued in 1567 advertising England's first national lottery (*Tudor Royal Proclamations*). Tickets cost ten shillings each; the first prize was an astonishing £5,000.
[12] *The Merchant of Venice*, 1.2.32; *Antony and Cleopatra*, 2.2.348.

predicting the future, however, hung a threat of theological or perhaps divine intervention. Cardano was condemned by the Inquisition in 1571 for delving into divination and making a horoscope of the life of Christ.[13] When Thomas Gataker developed a philosophical enquiry into the nature of lots in 1619, despite his credentials as a puritan divine, he was accused by other Calvinists of promoting games of hazard and of looking too closely into the mind of God.[14] Which returns us to *Hamlet*, since the mention of bets and wagers is juxtaposed with the most serious theological discussion of divine providence in the play, perhaps in all Shakespeare.

THEOLOGY IN HAMLET

The doctrine of providence makes its entrance in Act 5 scene 2. What is more, it does so via a precisely identifiable biblical quotation. In the scene following Ophelia's burial, on being offered the king's bet, Hamlet replies:

> Not a whit, we defie Augury; there's a speciall Prouidence in the fall of a sparrow. If it be now, 'tis not to come: if it bee not to come, it will bee now: if it be not now; yet it will come; the readinesse is all, since no man ha's ought of what he leaues. What is't to leaue betimes? (F3668–73)[15]

As has been noted by all Shakespearian scholars who have looked at the citation, it is possible to identify the exact sixteenth-century version involved, the Geneva Bible of 1560. It is quoted here from a copy printed in the decade the play was written (1590):

> Are not two sparrowes sold for a farthing, and one of them shal not fall on the ground without your Father? 30. Yea, and all the haires of your head are nombred. 31. Feare ye not therefore, ye are of more value then many sparowes. (Matthew 10: 29–31)[16]

---

[13] Anthony Grafton, *Cardano's Cosmos: The Worlds and Works of a Renaissance Astrologer* (Cambridge, Mass.: Harvard University Press, 1999), 4.

[14] Gataker, *Of the nature and vse of Lots; A Treatise historicall and theologicall* (London: Edward Griffin, 1619). In 1623 James Balmford reprinted his 1594 diatribe against card-playing, adding criticisms of Gataker's work.

[15] Not for the last time in the current discussion, a line associated with providence turns out to be a difficult textual crux.

[16] *The Bible: That is, the Holy Scriptvres conteined in the Olde and Newe Testament: Translated according to the Ebrew and Greeke, and conferred with the best translations in diuers languages* (London: Christopher Barker, 1590). This edn., like other Roman letter copies, in the new Testament uses the annotations in the version of Laurence Tomson: *The Newe Testament of our Lord Iesus Christ, translated out of Greeke by Theod. Beza. And also short expositions on the phrases and hard places, taken out of the large annotations of the foresayd Authour and Ioach. Camerarius, by P. Loseler Villerius. Englished by L. Tomson* (London: Christopher Barker, 1590).

It is equally well known that Hamlet's gloss of the verse ('a speciall Proui-dence in the fall of a sparrow') is Calvinist in language. In Book I, chap-ter 17 of the final edition of the *Institutio*, Matthew 10: 29 is cited as a prime example of God's *singularis providentia*, also called elsewhere his *specialis providentia*, or in the French edition of 1560 'la providence sin-gulière' or 'la providence spéciale'.[17] In an English context, the distinc-tion between 'general' and 'special' providence is fundamental to the standard Calvinist discussion in William Perkins's *Exposition of the Sym-bole or Creede*.[18] Perkins, in ways that seem particularly relevant to Hamlet, says that providence should teach us 'contentation of minde', which he further glosses 'a patterne of quietnesse of minde' (p. 160). In a late sixteenth-century Calvinist treatise we even find the word 'read-ines' for the same psychological point.[19]

So a second question is, what does theology have to tell us about Ham-let's death? Here, we might expect to say something about Shakespeare's religion. But what happens if we work outwards from the language of the play rather than inwards from what we might think we know about Shake-speare's biography? What follows is not at all inconsistent with the possi-bility that Shakespeare had a recusant background and even recusant sympathies. But the play confronts us with competing and often contra-dictory theological languages, perhaps best captured by Stephen Green-blatt's aperçu of 'a young man from Wittenberg, with a distinctly Protestant temperament, ... haunted by a distinctly Catholic ghost'.[20] This contradic-toriness is not incompatible with sixteenth-century thinking on provi-dence, and undercuts the way Shakespearian criticism has been so anxious about the references to predestination in the play and at the same time so determined to censor it from the play's central meanings. Harold Bloom,

---

[17] Jean Calvin, *Institutio Christianae religionis*, cited here from the 1559 text edn. in *Opera selecta*, ed. P. Barth and W. Niesel, 5 vols. (Munich: Kaiser, 1928), iii. 191 and 197. French text from *Institution de la religion chrestienne*, ed. Jean-Daniel Benoit, 5 vols. (Paris: Vrin, 1957), i. 223 and 231. Further references in text.

[18] *An Exposition of the Symbole or Creed of the Apostles, according to the tenour of the Scrip-ture, and the Consent of Orthodoxe Fathers of the Church*, in *The Workes of that famous and worthie minister of Christ, in the Vniuersitie of Cambridge, M. W. Perkins*, 3 vols. (Cam-bridge: Iohn Legate, 1608–9), 160.

[19] 'Sith of what things soeuer come to pas, our minde, albeit it perceiueth not the out-ward causes, and which we vsually terme next or neerest, yet hath it at all times in a readines and vnderstandeth the principall woorking cause, to witte, the prouidence and good will of God'; Andreas Hyperius, *A speciall treatise of Gods prouidence and of comforts against all kinde of crosses and calamities to be drawne from the same With an exposition of the 107. Psalme. Heerunto is added an appendix of certaine sermons & questions, (conteining sweet & comfortable doctrine) as they were vttered and disputed ad clerum in Cambridge. By P. Baro D. in Diui.* ([London]: Iohn Wolfe, [1588?]), sig. H6r (see also H5v).

[20] Stephen Greenblatt, *Hamlet in Purgatory* (Princeton: Princeton University Press, 2001), 240.

on several occasions, magisterially states that 'Hamlet is no mystic, no stoic, and hardly a Christian at all' displaying 'a radically new mode of secular transcendence'.[21] Alan Sinfield is more modulated but still strangely doctrinaire when he says that the play 'takes us to the brink of a Protestant affirmation' but then 'encourages us to question divine justice'.[22]

Eamon Duffy has asked the question of what happened to English culture when it rejected a centuries old social practice in living with death, when (as it were) it lost faith in the dead. In the world of the 1552 revised *Book of Common Prayer*, he says, 'the dead were no longer with us'.[23] Yet in some ways he has missed the answer that is staring us in the face. The doctrines of grace, providence, and predestination found in Luther, Calvin, Beza, and their English followers are often so abstractly theological that we forget that they, too, are doctrines in the face of death. If Duffy sometimes implies that Protestants were simply in denial, that they had forgotten how to deal with death, he is conveniently ignoring an overwhelming body of evidence that suggests the opposite.

When Hamlet is confronted by preening Osric he knows that he is implicated in a wager with death. He also knows that it is a wager for which, although he can calculate the odds, he cannot foreknow the outcome. Horatio says that if he feels any bad premonition here, he can always walk away. But Hamlet replies that life is like that: he may be lucky or he may not, but he can't know now, and there is nothing he can do to change the luck he is about to have. The reference to 'speciall Prouidence' is precisely to that, to a future that is both certain yet unknowable. (The First Quarto has an alternative reading, fascinating in this context: 'theres a predestinate prouidence in the fall of a sparrow'.) It is in this nexus of the knowability and the unknowability of the future, of certainty and uncertainty, that the play is situated. This nexus is part of the ordinary language of sixteenth-century Protestantism. To understand this, we need to rediscover the religious implications of sixteenth-century luck.

BIBLICAL LUCK

Seventy years before *Hamlet*, luck enters the first printed translations of the Bible into English. The citation is Judges 2: 15 in Matthew's Bible of 1537, commonly attributed to the hand of William Tyndale, published

[21] Harold Bloom, *Shakespeare: The Invention of the Human* (Newark, Del.: University of Delaware Press, 1987), 429 and 430.

[22] Alan Sinfield, 'Hamlet's Special Providence', *Shakespeare Survey*, 33 (1980), 89–97, this ref. 97.

[23] *Stripping of the Altars*, 475.

covertly the year after his death. As usual in the book of Judges, the Israelites are having it bad:

> Wherfore the Lorde waxed angry with Israel, & vnto whatsoeuer thynge they went, the hand of the Lorde was vpon them wyth euyl lucke, euen as the Lord promysed them, and as he sware vnto them. And they were sore vexed.[24]

The phrase 'euyl lucke' was retained by the Great Bible in 1539, but dropped in other versions. It is the same story with good luck. In Genesis 30, after Jacob has slept with Leah, and with her younger sister Rachel, and with Rachel's maid Bilhah, and now has three sons by Leah and two by Bilhah, although none yet by poor Rachel, he gets to sleep with Leah's maid Zilpah. Zilpah, too, bears Jacob a son. At which point in Tyndale's version of the Pentateuch, Leah (perhaps forbearingly in the circumstances) says, 'good lucke: and called his name Gad'.[25] Tyndale's word 'luck' survived longer in this case, through Coverdale right up to the Bishops' version in 1569. There, 'luck' runs out. These, and every other instance of 'luck' and its cognates, 'lucky', 'luckily', 'good luck', 'evil luck', are excised totally from the many editions of the Geneva translations, a prohibition reinforced by King James's translators and not lifted until the New English Bible. For 400 years, from 1560 to 1960, there is no new luck, good or bad, to be found in the English scriptures.

It is not difficult to hazard an initial explanation for this taboo over 'luck' in Elizabethan England. A belief in chance or fortune was a prime object of opprobrium among Calvinist divines. Alexandra Walsham's study of *Providence in Early Modern England* provides abundant instances of theological impatience with the 'heathenish' metaphysics of fate or the goddess Fortuna.[26] A vocabulary of luck was held to be endemic in such

---

[24] *The Byble which is all the holy Scripture: In whych are contayned the Olde and Newe Testament truly and purely translated into Englysh by Thomas Matthew* (Antwerp?: 1537). Thomas Matthew is commonly understood to be the pseudonym of John Rogers, Tyndale's close associate. Rogers is believed to have acted largely as an editor. The text of the Pentateuch and of the New Testament closely follows Tyndale's published translations of these texts. The portion from Ezra to the end of the Apocrypha is substantially that of Miles Coverdale's *Biblia*, the first complete English printed Bible of 1535. The text from Judges to Chronicles, however, deviates considerably from Coverdale, and corresponds to no other surviving printed text. It is now regarded as most likely the work of Tyndale, left in manuscript after Tyndale's execution in 1536. See the revised version of T. H. Darlow and H. F. Moule's *Historical Catalogue of Printed Editions of the English Bible 1525–1961*, ed. A. S. Herbert (London: British and Foreign Bible Society, 1968), 18; a view confirmed in David Daniell, *Tyndale's Old Testament* (New Haven: Yale University Press, 1992), pp. xxv–xxvi.

[25] *The fyrst boke of Moses called Genesis* ([Antwerp: Martin de Keyser?], 1530), G1ᵛ.

[26] *Providence in Early Modern England* (Oxford: Oxford University Press, 1999), 20–32.

beliefs. William Gouge, rector of St Anne, Blackfriars, complained in a sermon on the text of Matthew 10: 29–31 in 1623, 'How frequent in mens mouths are these phrases good luck, ill luck…good fortune…ill fortune'.[27] Such words struck at the heart of divine providence. Perhaps most prevalent was the widespread tradition of lucky days, or their opposite, often known as 'dismal' or 'Egyptian days': days on which it was considered ill-advised to set out on a long journey or begin any great undertaking, such as the harvest, or a meeting of the privy council.[28] Lord Burghley counselled his son to avoid business on the first Monday in April (the anniversary of the death of Abel), the second Monday in August (the date of the destruction of Sodom and Gomorrah), or the last Monday in December (the birthday of Judas Iscariot).[29] Puritan divines despaired of such practices. It is in such a pejorative context that the word 'luck' finds its only citation in the whole of the Geneva Bible, and even then only in a marginal note to Leviticus 19: 26.[30] Here the common lay tendency, 'To measure luckie or vnluckie dayes', is berated as pagan superstition.

There we might be tempted to leave it: luck is just one of those many things, along with dancing, throwing dice, wedding rings, football, strong cheese, Christmas, which puritans disapproved of. In such a picture, 'luck' emerges as part of a distinctively secularized view of life standing in stark opposition to the world of the Elizabethan godly, an opposition we perhaps too readily identify with the eventual clash between cavalier and roundhead. However, this is too simple a contrast. Let us instead outline a brief history of luck. How is it that 'luck' got into Tyndale in the first place? It is a surprising word to find in Tyndale, when we know from his biblical prefaces that he is hardly soft on questions of free will or election. Yet the legacy to Calvinism was ambiguous. To recognize this, we need to understand the rich lexical history the word was acquiring: for 'luck' is a strange and precious English word. Philological history impinges on profound philosophical issues, with which sixteenth-century culture was in general struggling to come to terms. This helps to explain not only

---

[27] William Gouge, *The extent of Gods prouidence, set out in a sermon, preached in Black-fryers Church, 5. Nov. 1623, On occasion of the downe-fall of Papists in a Chamber at the said Black-fryers, 1623. Oct. 27* (London: George Miller, 1631), 380.

[28] M. Förster, 'Die altenglischen Verzeichnisse von Glücks- und Unglückstagen' in K. Malone and M. B. Ruud (eds.), *Studies in English Philology: A Miscellany in Honor of Frederick Klaeber* (Minneapolis, 1929), 258–77.

[29] William Cecil, *Precepts, or, Directions for the well ordering and carriage of a mans life, through the whole course thereof: left by William, Lord Burghly, to his Sonne, at his death* (London: Thomas Jones, 1636), D2ᵛ.

[30] The reference to witchcraft and the practice of 'observing times' is glossed as 'To measure luckie or vnluckie daies', *The Bible and Holy Scriptures conteyned in the Olde and Newe Testament. Translated according to the Ebrue and Greke, and conferred with the best translations in diuers languages* (Geneva, 1561), fo. 55ʳ.

Tyndale's brief flirtation with luck but also, in a darker way than mere verbal self-censorship or care over words, Elizabethan and Jacobean England's unquiet desire to suppress every remnant of it. It also suggests some new explanation of the strange metaphysical world of Elsinore.

What does Tyndale mean by 'luck'? After all, how can there be 'luck' in the Bible? This is not a simple question to answer. In the case of Judges 2: 15, 'euyl lucke' is not a matter of pure chance. It is a consequence of the Israelites' own actions. Tyndale is in two minds on this subject. In the Prologue to Genesis, he recalls God's benevolence to the foibles of the patriarchs, such as Noah the drunk, Lot undone by his daughters, David the adulterer turned murderer. Why does God keep giving them a second chance? Tyndale extracts a moral: these chequered characters are forgiven so that next time they might do better. The moral looks more awkward in reverse, however, when Tyndale asks Plato's question, why do bad things sometimes happen to good people, or, in Tyndale's quainter, homely style, why do chaste virgins sometimes end up in brothels?

> Why? The iudgementes of god are bottomlesse. Soch thinges chaunced partely for ensamples | partely God thorow synne healeth synne. Pryde can nether be healed nor yet appere but thorow such horrible deades.[31]

Tyndale's answer is not satisfactory: far from bottomless, God's motives are transparent: he punishes some people to help others along. Perhaps seeing a difficulty, Tyndale changes tack, inferring the virgins might not be so pure after all. For a moment Tyndale speculates that the virgins had perhaps had popish thoughts or believed in the doctrine of meritorious works, and so God punished them until they consented to the truth. The logic is not edifying. Even if Tyndale believes this is true of some virgins in brothels he presumably cannot think it's true for them all.

These passages show the difficulties Tyndale runs into with ideas of chance and of accident. In the Prologues he wants to rationalize chance into a moral lesson, but his work as a translator takes him in a quite different direction. It is as if Tyndale discovers in the old Hebrew stories an unaccountable surplus, an inexplicable metaphysics, a narrative of risk and uncertainty, which he struggles to put back in its place. Such is the story of Joseph in Egypt:

> Ioseph was brought vnto Egipte | and Putiphar a lorde of Pharaos: and his chefe marshall an Egiptian | bought him of ye Ismaelites which brought him thither. And the LORde was wyth Ioseph | and he was a luckie felowe and continued in the house of his master the Egiptian.[32]

---

[31] *The fyrst boke of Moses called Genesis* ([Antwerp: Martin de Keyser?], 1530), A6^v.
[32] *The fyrst boke of Moses called Genesis*, H8$^{r–v}$.

The description of Joseph as 'a luckie felowe' is one of those felicitous details which prove that Tyndale is a master storyteller. It was a reading striking enough to survive in every version of the mid-century through Coverdale and the Great Bible ('a luckye man'), to the Bishops' version.[33] The Bishops, however, were worried enough to supply a gloss: 'Men are neuer luckie in dede, but when God is with them. For the felicitie of the wicked is cursed.'[34] This gloss sounds a note of warning, one confirmed with heavy moralization in the Geneva translation a year later: 'And the Lord was with Ioseph, and he was a man that prospered'.[35] A marginal note adds: 'The fauour of God is the founteine of all prosperitie'. By the time of the King James, Tyndale's 'luckie felowe' has smartened up and joined the middle classes: 'And the LORD was with Ioseph, and hee was a prosperous man'.[36]

THE LUCK OF THE ENGLISH

It is one of those extraordinary features of the semantics of everyday language that these two words, 'lucky' and 'prosperous', while almost identical in dictionary content, nonetheless mean something completely different. A 'luckie felowe' has got away with something, life has given him more than he deserves, whereas a 'prosperous man' is full of merit and more than a hint of self-satisfaction. Whatever its appropriateness in relation to the Hebrew which it translates, 'luckie' seems true to Joseph, to his qualities as a chancer, a risker, a man of the moment. Where, then, did Tyndale find the inspiration for this word? Here we encounter something interesting, for 'luck' was a very recent addition to the English language. It is not found in the Wycliffite Bible, or even in Chaucer, who in similar contexts uses 'chaunce' or often 'cas', ancestor of the modern word 'casual' but otherwise obsolete.[37] 'Were it by auenture or sort or cas', the

---

[33] *The Byble in Englyshe that is to saye, the content of all the holye scrypture, bothe of the olde and newe Testament, truly translated after the veryte of the Hebrue and Greke textes* (London: Thomas Berthelet, 1540), fo. Xvii[r].

[34] *The holie Bible conteynyng the olde Testament and the newe* (London: Richard Jugge, 1568), O2[v].

[35] *The Bible and Holy Scriptures conteyned in the Olde and Newe Testament* [Geneva], fo. 20[v].

[36] *The Holy Bible conteyning the Old Testament, and the New | newly translated out of the originall tongues, and with the former translations diligently compared and reuised, by His Maiesties speciall commandement* (London: Robert Barker, 1612), C1[v].

[37] Compare the incidence of *cas* and *chaunce* in Christopher Cannon, *The Making of Chaucer's English: A Study of Words* (Cambridge: Cambridge University Press, 1998), 257 and 259.

Knight is chosen to tell the first tale in the General Prologue to *The Can-terbury Tales*.[38] As Pandarus persuades Criseyde to take a chance with love, he tells her, 'Lo neyther cas ne fortune hym deceyven'.[39]

In fact, 'luck' is an example of something very special in lexicographical terms. It comes into being at a fairly precisely dateable moment. Almost immediately it is very widespread in use, and is found in a huge range of registers and social contexts, from the poetic to the throwaway, in cheap print and in learned books, in the city and the country, among ladies at court and among ploughboys. The *Middle English Dictionary* gives its first definitive citation as 1500, only a generation before Tyndale's Pentateuch. A song preserved in Lambeth Palace Library, MS 306, preserves the greeting: 'lucke and good hanssell, my hert, y sende you'.[40] The word seems to be voraciously successful, and within a century acquires most of the associations we might give it today. You can have luck in early modern England at dice or in other games. There is hunter's luck, and luck at fishing. To be 'lucky in love' is already a commonplace in both George Peele's *The araygnement of Paris* and Robert Greene's *Mamilia*.[41] You can find 'pot luck' in Thomas Nashe.[42]

What was it that gave 'luck' its evolutionary advantage, so that 'cas' dropped out of the language in a few decades? What meanings were displaced onto related words such as 'fortune' or 'chance' so that 'luck' found its proper home? These are subtle questions to answer. Yet it is possible to identify straightaway some odd charm, even benevolence, which the word seems to convey. To wish 'good luck' to someone quickly becomes one of the most benign and familiar forms of English greeting. There is also something interesting about the degree of contingency felt to be involved in luck. Even now, when we can measure odds or risk, we can't quite measure 'luck'. To be either lucky or unlucky is clearly not a permanent or stable state of affairs, yet it is not so arbitrary or momentary or precise as 'chance'. You can be unlucky for a long time; some people seem to be 'born lucky'. It is just my luck to be writing, and just your luck to be reading. Yet 'luck'

[38] *Canterbury Tales*, A844; *The Riverside Chaucer*, ed. Larry D. Benson, 3rd edn. (Oxford: Oxford University Press, 1988), 36.

[39] *Troilus and Criseyde*, ii. 285; *Riverside Chaucer*, 493.

[40] *Political, Religious, and Love Poems*, ed. F. J. Furnivall, Early English Texts Society 15, repr. edn. (Oxford: Oxford University Press, 1965), 66–7. See *Middle English Dictionary*, LUK; <http://quod.lib.umich.edu/cgi/m/mec/med-idx?type=id&id=MED26310>, accessed 11 March 2008.

[41] *The araygnement of Paris a pastorall. Presented before the Queenes Maiestie, by the Children of her chappell* (London: Henry Marsh, 1584), sig. E1ʳ; *Mamillia. A mirrour or looking-glasse for the ladies of Englande* (London: Thomas Woodcock, 1583), sig. G8ᵛ.

[42] *Strange newes, of the intercepting certaine letters, and a conuoy of verses, as they were going priuilie to victuall the Low Countries* (London: John Danter, 1592), A2ʳ; *A pleasant comedie, called Summers last will and testament* (London: Simon Stafford, 1600), D1ᵛ.

does not involve a judgement on you as a person: wherever luck comes from, it is not down to you.

The meaning of luck is given fuller context by considering related vernaculars. The *Oxford English Dictionary* traces 'luck' to Middle High German, and detects the influence of gambling terms.[43] The geography is nearly right, although perhaps Dutch or Flemish merchants' talk is a better bet, since the Dutch word *luk* is a frequent variant for *geluk*; the online version of the *OED* now cites Caxton (who lived in Bruges for twenty years) as the first user of the word, in an example that antedates the *MED*. The suspicion of gambling, however, may be wrong, perhaps betraying a certain residual Calvinism in the Dictionary's nineteenth-century editors. The Dutch words, like the German word *Glück*, had a wide resonance, and were in common use. It is from Luther's German that Tyndale's usages of 'luck' and 'lucky' derive.[44] So do most of the usages, in Coverdale and elsewhere, which use the word where Tyndale does not, or in biblical books that he did not live to translate.[45] In Job 30: 15, Coverdale gives 'my prosperite departeth hence like as it were a cloude', where Luther has 'mein glückseliger Stand'. While *glückselig* commonly means 'blessed', here Luther seems to mean the 'state of his luck'.

This brings into view the fact that there is something potentially theological about luck. What is present in Luther's German is a sense that the Christian life can quite properly be held to contain elements of the unexpected, the unlooked-for, perhaps even the uncanny. The coming of luck into life is unpredictable, contingent, in the way that the human body, its motion and its experience, is contingent. From the 1530s to the 1550s it is therefore quite normal for biblical and liturgical translations to use the everyday phrase 'good luck' as a form of greeting (usually following Luther's habitual *Glück zu*), in a way that sounds too casual and dressed-down to ears trained on the lugubrious tones of the *Revised Standard Version*.[46]

In Hermann von Wied's Reformed liturgy in Cologne of the 1540s, for which the Lutheran theologian Martin Bucer was one of the consultants, this vocabulary enters the service for burial, in ways that have an intriguing resonance with *Hamlet*, the quintessential play of the burial of the dead. Hermann's German order was one of the principal sources for Cranmer's

---

[43] 'Probably it came into English as a gambling term; the LG. dialects were a frequent source of such terms in 15–16 centuries', *OED*, 2nd edn. (Oxford: Oxford University Press, 1989), LUCK.

[44] Judges 2: 15: 'da war des HERRN Hand wider sie zum Unglück'; Gen. 39: 2: 'der HERR war mit Joseph | daß er ein glücklicher Mann ward'.

[45] For instance, 1 Sam. 25: 6, where Coverdale translates 'Good lucke, peace be wᵗ the & thine house, & with all yᵗ thou hast', Luther has 'Glück zu | Fried sey mit dir vnd deinem Hause | vnd mit allem das du hast'.

[46] For instance Zech. 4: 7, 'Glück zu | Glück zu'.

1549 *Book of Common Prayer*, and was issued in an English translation by John Day in 1548. In the English translation, it is considered idiomatic for God to be prayed to grant a 'luckie' life:

> Hereunto lette an exhortation be added for them that stande by, namely that they shoulde dayly dye more and more to synne, and prepare them selues to the heauenly life that is to come, and so praye God continually, that he wyll graunt them a luckie, and good end of this lyfe.[47]

The word 'luckie' here translates what in the German liturgy is given as 'ein seligs end', a 'happy end'.[48] In the Latin text (probably used by Cranmer), the equivalent to 'luckie' is the standard Latin word for fortune (whether in love, politics, or gambling), *felix*: 'ut foelicem ac salutatem sibi vitae huius exitum'.[49] *Salus*, 'salvation', is *felix*, lucky. Life is a matter of God's luck, of sublimely, or even providentially, 'good luck'. This is not a verbal one-off in Hermann. In the service for Confirmation, entry into the godly life for young Christians is once again a lucky break:

> Grant them that they luckily springinge up in thy sonne our Lorde Jesu Christe, the heade of us all, may grow into him tyl they come to mannes age fuly, and perfectly in al wysedome, holiness and ryghtuousnes.[50]

Perhaps most striking of all is the phrasing of the marriage service: 'this copulacion of man, and woman is without doubt acceptable to God, and therefore holye, and luckie' (2I1ᵛ).

These strokes of luck are not among the materials used by Cranmer in his 1549 *Book of Common Prayer*, although, as we saw earlier, the Collect for his Communion service did frame salvation in relation to 'all the chaunges and chaunces of thys mortall lyfe'.[51] Luck did come into the Prayer Book by another means however, in the form of the psalter used in the daily and weekly offices of the parish church. On three occasions, Miles Coverdale used 'we wish you good luck' as a blessing in the Psalms— here in fact going beyond the authority of Luther, who preferred the more obviously pious register of *segnen*.[52] It was Coverdale's readings of the

---

[47] *A simple, and religious consultation of... Herman by the grace of God Archebishop of Colone* (London: John Day, 1547), 2I8ᵛ–2K1ʳ.

[48] *Einfaltigs bedencken warauff ein Christiche in dem wort Gottes gegrünte Reformation an Lehrbrauch der Heyligen Sacramenten vnd Ceremonien Seelforge vnd anderem Kirchen dienst ... verbesserung* (Bonn: Laurentius von der Müllen, 1543), Y1ʳ.

[49] *Nostra Hermanni ex gratia Dei Archiepiscopi Coloniensis, et principis electoris, &c., simplex ac pia deliberatio* (Bonn: Laurentius von der Müllen, 1545), S8ᵛ.

[50] *A simple, and religious consultation*, 2B6ᵛ.

[51] 'Communion (1549)', *Book of Common Prayer*, ed. Cummings, p. 37.

[52] Coverdale, *Biblia* (1535), Psalm 44: A: 'we wish you good lucke'; see also Psalm 117: C; Psalm 128.

Psalms which entered into the Great Bible of 1539, subsequently used in the psalters printed with the *Book of Common Prayer* in 1550, and indeed even after 1662.[53] In the Tudor mid-century, in fact, it was still possible for theological hard-liners such as Hugh Latimer to use the word 'luck' quite unselfconsciously, if a little glumly: 'the more wicked, the more lucky'. Lady Elizabeth Howard wrote to the dowager Queen Katherine Parr in 1548, praying 'the Almighty God to send you a most lucky deliverance'.[54] In one remarkable phrase, John Bradford wrote to Erkinald Rawlins and his wife, in the midst of the Marian persecutions:

> My dearely beloued, looke not vppon these dayes and the afflictions of the same here with vs, simplye as they seeme vnto you, that is, as dismall dayes, and dayes of Gods vengaunce, but rather as lucky dayes.[55]

Whatever the shibboleth which later applied to the term 'dismall dayes', Bradford gives resonant voice to the contingencies of experience. It is a phrase which reads the more movingly when we remember that Bradford went to the stake, whereas the Rawlinses escaped a few months later to the safety of the continent.

In the 1560s these things became more difficult to utter. Unlike the *Book of Common Prayer*, the Geneva Bible excised 'luck' from the entire text of scripture, allowing it in only one footnote in order to banish its usage from our mouths. There is a similar, if more complex, process with the words 'chance' and 'fortune'. There are two occasions in the text of the Geneva Old Testament where 'chance' is used: 1 Samuel 6: 9 and Ecclesiastes 9: 11. On both occasions there are stern annotations in the Geneva margin, warning us against dangerous doctrinal solecism: 'The wicked attribute almost all things to fortune and chance, where as in deede there is nothing done without Gods prouidence and decree.'[56] Twice further in the Old Testament notes we are given similar rebukes, with almost superfluous zeal. One is at Leviticus 26: 21. At Psalms 148: 8, in an innocent descriptive passage of hail and snowstorms, we are given the heavy lesson that stormy weather, too, 'come[s] not by chance or fortune, but by Gods appoynted ordinance'. In the New Testament there is no reference to 'chance' in the text of the Geneva version, but in Laurence Tomson's

[53] The numbering in the Great Bible (1539) follows the Vulgate order: Psalms 45: A; 118: D; 129: A.

[54] *OED*, LUCKY 1 a and c.

[55] Letter cited in John Foxe, *Actes and Monuments*, 2 vols. (London: John Day, 1583), ii. 1632.

[56] *The Bible: That is, the Holy Scriptvres conteined in the Olde and Newe Testament: Translated according to the Ebrew and Greeke* (London: Christopher Barker, 1590), 1 Sam. 6: 8–9, note [f].

notes, translated from Theodore Beza, there are no fewer than eight occasions when 'chance' is raised in the margins as a false reading requiring specific refutation. At Luke 10: 31 the Greek verb συγκυρίαν had been translated by Tyndale as 'by chaunce', a reading repeated in Matthew's Bible and the Great Bible.[57] The Geneva emends to 'it fell out', and warns against the imputation of 'chance' in the margin. Chance here appears as in dialectical opposition to the interpretation of divine providence, as at Acts 8: 32: 'Those things which seeme most to come by chance or fortune (as men terme it) are gouerned by the secret prouidence of God'. Only in the Apocrypha, where there are no marginalia, do two references to 'chance' occur without comment.[58]

We can take this (if we like) as Calvinist heavy-handedness, but there is more to it. There are suggestions within the text of scripture which it takes some effort to suppress, and the surplus of comment in the Geneva is an indication that silence is not enough. It becomes even clearer in the extraordinary fate which overcomes the use of 'fortune' as a verb, especially in the past tense, in sixteenth-century versions of the New Testament. Chance and fortune in the New Testament are all the more problematic than in the Old; even Tyndale never uses 'luck' in the New Testament. But 'fortuned' is used 384 times in bibles up to the Bishops' version of 1568. There are none in Geneva, and none in the King James. Tyndale uses the verb twenty times in Luke alone, and eleven more times in Acts. This is because of the characteristic Lucan idiom, καί ἐγένετο. It is in such everyday, unnoticeable habits of language that we find perhaps the most telling signs of a personal philosophy in action. The Greek word is a prosaic narrative filler found ubiquitously in Herodotus or Xenophon to mean 'it happened, it took place'. Tyndale finds it absolutely normal to say 'it fortuned', or 'it chaunsed'. In the Geneva Bible and the King James Version, it is replaced with that familiar phrase, the orotund, archaic sound that makes the 1611 Bible so beloved, 'And it came to pass'. It is almost an epitome of the difference in style between Tyndale and the King James Version, that while Tyndale uses 'it came to pass' twenty-four times in all of his translations, the King James Version does so seven times more frequently (171 times), counting only the books which Tyndale himself translated.

It is in these references to the narrative of everyday life, to the weather, to unexpected meetings, to the potluck of circumstance or the accidental turnout of events, that we find the most persistent signs of theological pressure. It is into the metaphysics of events and accidents that we will now trespass.

---

[57] Liddell and Scott, *Greek–English Lexicon* give as the root meaning 'to come together by chance', also 'meet with an accident'; Tischendorf's commentary glosses *fortuito*.

[58] 2 Esdras 10: 49 and Esther 16: 8.

DEEP PLOTS

The question of how to interpret a sequence of events within experience, and of how to understand the shape of a person's life in relation to those events and that sequence, is something that regularly punctuates the action of *Hamlet*. In Act 5, it threatens to overwhelm the play altogether. On his return to Denmark from his escapade on the way to England, Hamlet takes the time to enter into a philosophical discussion on the subject with Horatio. It comes at a crucial point in the action, a philosophical interlude between the terrifyingly beautiful graveyard scene and the shattering holocaust that is the play's denouement. It contains one of the most quoted and least understood phrases in the play: 'There's a divinity that shapes our ends, rough-hew them how we will'. The reason this line gets quoted so often, is that on its own it seems clear what it means, whereas it comes from a single complex sentence of about twenty lines containing about sixteen subordinate clauses, almost impossible to unravel on the spot. I will quote just the first few, concatenated clauses, up to the point where Horatio interrupts him in mid-sentence to say (with that supernatural ability he has to state the obvious and the obviously untrue at the same time) 'That is most certain':

> Sir, in my heart there was a kinde of fighting,
> That would not let me sleepe; me thought I lay
> Worse than the mutines in the Bilboes, rashly—
> (And praise be rashnesse for it) let vs know,
> Our indiscretion sometimes serues vs well,
> When our deare [Q2 deep] plots do paule,
> and that should teach vs,
> There's a Diuinity that shapes our ends,
> Rough-hew them how we will— [F3503–10]

This is one of those speeches which, as Kermode has well said, shows that Shakespeare has no equal when it comes to representing the haphazardness and intensity of complex thought process. Hamlet is recounting how, on his sea voyage to England, he discovered, by accident, in letters hidden on the persons of the hapless Rosencrantz and Guildenstern, proof of Claudius' deadly conspiracy to have him done away with on debarkation. The discovery is made, he says, only because of his restlessness at night, because of an unconscious anxiety about his erstwhile fellow-students, and because of, well, for this there seems no better word than luck. Hamlet, characteristically, puts this in the form of an epigram that is both idiomatic and obscure: 'Our indiscretion sometimes serues vs well, | When our deare [Q2 'deep'] plots do paule [some copies of Q2, 'falle']'.

The sense is not easy: sometimes when we're not thinking very hard about what we're doing, things work out better; or we succeed better in our aims; or perhaps we actually think better, than when we're really concentrating on our actions with a fully realized intention.

The meaning of this brilliant and difficult remark is readily captured by that twentieth-century Hamlet, John Lennon, in one of his last songs, 'Birthday Boy': 'Life is what happens to you while you're busy making other plans'.[59] It is a sentiment given greater resonance by the fact that Lennon was shot dead before the song had been released, denying him the chance to sing the lullaby to his infant son. This should remind us, too, of the exquisite irony of Hamlet's excited recitation of his recent voyage. What he is describing, clearly, is luck, but is it good luck or bad that brings him back to Denmark? We know, as we have known all along, that he is coming back to die. Would he have died anyway, if he hadn't found the packet in the night, and had gone to England instead? Sooner, perhaps, or then again maybe later. This is the kind of counterfactual question which lurks like a promise or a premonition behind Hamlet's urgent reminiscence. To which the obvious answer, of course, is *God knows*: 'There's a divinity that shapes our ends'. Beckett's *Waiting for Godot*, as so often, provides the best commentary on the play at this point, as when he was asked why he had called his character Lucky: 'I suppose he is lucky to have no more expectations.'[60]

Barbara Everett has commented that it is only with the disappearance of the ghost in Act 3 that Hamlet properly comes into being, and that as he does so, he is 'already a dead man'.[61] Yet we could add to this that Hamlet is always dying, always already dead, by virtue of the plot which contains him and prefigures him. It is the particular quality of the revenge plot that the revenger is doomed to die through the act of revenge. This is his expiation, from Aeschylus onwards. Hamlet's end is already shaped, then, whether he knows it or not. This is what rendered the story of Hamlet already familiar, long before it became all too familiar through its exposure to endless commentary from philosophers to school syllabuses. *Hamlet* the play was hackneyed before *Hamlet* the play we know was written: Thomas Nashe in 1589 and Thomas Lodge in 1596 already write as if sick of Hamlet and his always not quite yet completed revenge. Shakespeare seems to be the first writer of a revenge play to make this familiarity of the plot part of the plot. The end is there in the beginning.

[59] John Lennon, 'Birthday Boy' (1980).

[60] *Beckett in the Theatre*, ed. Dougald McMillan and Martha Fehsenfeld (London: John Calder, 1988), 64.

[61] *Young Hamlet: Essays on Shakespeare's Tragedies* (Oxford: Clarendon Press, 1990), 126.

This foreknowledge is central to the play. In a series of speeches Hamlet prefigures his own end, so much so that his life seems to become commensurate with the act of imagining his death. In this way, the workings of the theatre become coterminous with living a life. Spectators and actors alike participate in this mimesis of their own mortality.

Alongside this sense of repetition and pre-enactment, however, is the knowledge that in the end Hamlet will only have *one* moment to die. The action of Hamlet is therefore caught between extreme narrative certainty and a radical fragility of the moment, of time caught in its singularity. Perhaps because of the endless speculation about the character of the hero, and the seemingly existential dimension of the hero's experience of subjectivity, we have become less alive to the terrific narrative economy of even so long a play. Even T. S. Eliot, in calling Hamlet an 'artistic failure', admitted the first scene was as perfect a piece of writing as any in the history of drama. Despite the fact that we seem to know exactly what is going to happen, the events of Acts 3 and 4 overtake us with an intensity of surprise—the Mousetrap, Polonius caught behind the Arras, Ophelia's madness and apparent suicide, Hamlet's escape, the death wager—each event lurching the action into a spasm of new direction. Scene changes, despite the flood of verbiage, are rapid and often confusing.

At the beginning of Act 5, abruptly, the play's action distils into perfect stasis. With Hamlet back, no further inhibition to his uncle's death remaining, and Laertes spoiling for a fight, Shakespeare presents us with two clowns, sitting by a freshly dug grave, exchanging morbid humour. Hamlet's whole life, its pattern and meaning, are laid out in front of us: in a dazzling exchange with the prince, the clown reveals that it is thirty years exactly since he took up grave-digging, the same thirty years since Old Hamlet fought old Fortinbras, the same thirty years since young Hamlet himself was born. As G. R. Hibbard has suggested, the effect of the flashback is to suggest that the paths of the gravedigger and of the prince have been set in motion to converge at this very moment. The grave contains the skull of the old king's jester, Yorick, who raised the prince like a father. Yorick's resting-place waits to welcome Ophelia, although Hamlet does not yet know it; the obvious inference is that the grave might as well be for Hamlet himself.

I have gone over this ground at some length in order to show that Hamlet's speech about the divinity that shapes our ends does not come out of the blue. It is a moment of layered meaning, in which many strands in the play have come together. The pattern of coincidence, of significant repetition in events, has been carefully constructed to justify Hamlet's sense of wonderment at how everything in his life is locking into place. Horatio offers him the chance to escape his destiny, but Hamlet refuses:

it is too late to back out now. Yet here the ironies begin to proliferate. For the narrative which Hamlet subsequently presents as proving the benefits of rashness, and showing the height of his own indiscretion, is the least rash, least indiscreet set of actions he has been guilty of in the whole play. The episode shows meticulous cunning rather than impetuous risk-taking. He takes the letters from Guildenstern's pocket, reads them, produces a forged copy of his own, puts it back in the pocket, all of which he manages without stirring his companions by so much as a whisper. So Rosencrantz and Guildenstern go to it. Hamlet's declaration about having the royal signet ring to hand, 'Why, euen in that was Heauen ordinate', is another piece of kidology: it seems positively boy-scout preparedness to have red wax in your purse.

Of all the events in the play this is the least improvisatory, yet it raises, by way of emphasis in reverse, significant questions about a series of other events. *Hamlet* as a play contains a collection of narrative accounts, usually involving violent death, which create complex difficulties of contingent explanation. Take the curious, clumsy, embarrassing casual violence of the death of Polonius. Here, surely, if anywhere, we have an example of Hamlet's indiscretion. Does he kill Polonius thinking it is the king? That is how he rationalizes it, almost immediately. And yet, Hamlet knows, and he knows he knows, that he cannot know for sure that it is the king he is killing. His first reaction, when asked by Gertrude what he has done, just after the fatal stab, is to say 'Nay, I know not', and then to ask, 'Is it the king?' How would this play in a law-court? Does he lash out, in instinct, perhaps in self-defence? Or is it a case of mistaken identity? Should he have looked first? The arras is a key: Hamlet kills without looking, and without seeing the person he kills. When he calls Polonius a 'wretched, rash, intruding fool' it is as if he is displacing onto Polonius words that apply better to him, something confirmed by the later repetition of the word 'rashly' in Act 5. The wildness of fortune at this point of the play is confirmed by a verbal pattern in the First, Bad Quarto, which repeatedly uses the words 'chance' and 'mischance' in variants that do not appear in the later editions. Asked by the king where the body can be found, Hamlet replies:

> In heau'n, if you chance to misse him there,
> Father, you had best looke in the other partes below
> For him, and if you cannot finde him there,
> You may chance to nose him as you go vp the lobby.

Polonius' death lies somewhere uncomfortably between accident, culpable homicide, manslaughter, and plain cock-up. The queen in Q1 calls it tellingly 'this mischance'. Within the initial premiss of the revenge plot, it is a violent spasm, a misdirection of juridical energy and emotion, and it sends the plot off in a violent new direction, from which everything else flows in ugly consequence. As a result, not only Claudius, but Ophelia—and therefore Laertes, and Gertrude, and others—and Hamlet himself—all die.

These deaths, too, although inevitable from the logic of the revenge plot, also turn out to result from peculiar forms of 'mischance'. Ophelia appears to commit suicide—thus depriving her of Christian burial—but the detail of the evidence is not so clear cut.[62] A branch she is lying on falls from a tree, and she fails to save herself, 'As one incapable of her owne distresse'. Is this self-murder, or misadventure? This occasions from the clowns some topical musing on the legal definition of suicide, apparently drawn from a contemporary coroner's conundrum: 'if the water come to him and drown him, he drowns not himself'. In a fantastic line, straight out of Beckett, it is said that Ophelia 'drowned herself in her own defence'.[63]

The Elsinorean law of unintended consequences extends most of all into the final scene. Claudius, just to make sure, decides to kill his nephew not once or even twice over, but three times: using blades of the swords that are unbated, dousing them with poison, and giving Hamlet a spiked drink as well, just in case. Theatre once again makes a visual metonym for the complexities of life's chances. There is no need to labour the point here that despite the overkill, things turn out rather differently. The action at the end of the play is notoriously rushed, confused, and even farcical, and the stage finishes up littered with bodies.

THE ENDS OF LIFE

The philosopher Martha Nussbaum, in a highly influential study of Greek tragedy, argues that the Greek concept of τύχη, which she calls in English 'luck', was central to tragedy's moral meaning. It is worth dwelling at this point in the argument on her powerful philosophical definition of the idea of 'luck':

> I do not mean to imply that the events in question are random or uncaused. What happens to a person by luck will be just what does not happen through his or her own agency, what just *happens* to him, as opposed to what he does

---

[62] On Ophelia's suicide, see R. M. Frye, *The Renaissance Hamlet* (Princeton: Princeton University Press, 1984), 298–304.

[63] On the clown's jokes concerning *se offendendo*, see de Grazia, Hamlet *without Hamlet*, 176–7.

or makes. In general, to eliminate luck from human life will be to put that life, or the most important things in it, under the control of the agent (or one of those elements in him with which he identifies himself), removing the element of reliance upon the external and undependable.[64]

Nussbaum's discussion, in turn, is highly dependent on a 1976 paper by the late Bernard Williams entitled 'moral luck'.[65] Luck in this Greek sense, Nussbaum several times emphasizes, is not the same as 'randomness' or an 'absence of causal connections' (p. 89). It is rather 'what just happens'; 'the element of human existence that humans do not control'. She draws attention to a central phrase in Sophocles' *Antigone*, where it is said by Tiresias that mankind lives ἐπὶ ξυροῦ τύχης (on 'the razor's edge of luck').[66] Creon and Antigone in their diametrically opposed ways both attempt to construct an ethical law of unyielding certainty—a straight path between ineluctable laws of right and wrong, whether political and legal, or else familial and religious. But life is not like that: it happens in ways that cannot be predicted by these laws, and does not conform to them.

It is not difficult to see how Nussbaum's account of Sophocles or of Aeschylus' *Oresteia* might be applied to *Hamlet* (to paraphrase her argument): how much luck do we think we can humanly live with? How much luck should we live with, in order to live a life that has meaning and value? What kind of ill-luck makes a life unbearable, or more to the point, incapable of any ascription of meaning or value? I have tried to show that these are questions that the action of *Hamlet* forces us to consider, and that Hamlet himself in the last act of the play, and especially in his speeches on divine providence, poses the questions directly. Yet here we encounter one last problem. For it is equally an explicit part of Williams's and of Nussbaum's polemic that the idea of 'luck' is inimical to the Judaeo-Christian ethical system, even that this is a central weakness in Christian moral thinking. A world with God in it, they assume, is a world without luck.

Yet luck, in Elizabethan literary examples, shows no such rigid secularizing bias, even or perhaps especially in relation to pagan classical sources. The spate of translation in the 1580s of Greek and Roman arch-texts of destiny is perhaps at some level a reaction to public awareness of the Calvinist doctrine of predestination. Richard Stanyhurst's translation of the

[64] Martha C. Nussbaum, *The Fragility of Goodness: Luck and Ethics in Greek Tragedy and Philosophy* (Cambridge: Cambridge University Press, 1986), 3–4.
[65] Bernard Williams, *Moral Luck* (Cambridge: Cambridge University Press, 1981), 20–39.
[66] Sophocles, *Antigone*, line 996; ed. and trans. F. Storr, Loeb Classical Library (London: Heinemann, 1962), 390.

first four books of the *Aeneid*, for example, uses 'luck' five times in Book II alone, applied to the mechanism of divine destiny. As Aeneas finds his true resolve to follow his path to Rome, he remarks:

> What luck shal betide vs, wee wil be in destinie partners,
> Or good hap, or forward.[67]

Rather as in the biblical translations of the same period, 'luck' is here used to translate a verb meaning 'this is how things fell out': *Quo res cunque cadent.*[68] Turning to Elizabethan translations of tragedy, we find a similar pattern. John Studley, in his translation of Seneca's *Hippolytus*, has the Chorus wish the hapless hero, 'God send thee better lucke'.[69] Theologically, Stanyhurst and Studley stand at opposite poles: Studley, a staunch puritan, was forced in 1573 to vacate his fellowship at Trinity College, Cambridge, because of a charge of nonconformity; while Stanyhurst was a recusant exile in the Low Countries. The controversial background makes the reference to divine luck all the more complex: it can be used equally for Calvinist and anti-Calvinist purposes. One man's chance is another man's providence. Luck oscillates easily between divine and profane contexts. In a biblical play of 1568, *Jacob and Esau*, Esau's bad luck, it is said, will not last forever. In Arthur Golding's Calvinist play, *Abraham's Sacrifice*, translated from Beza in 1575, Abraham recognizes the one God, and his own insignificance in relation to that God, by referring to man's 'happy lucke' since the world was made.[70]

There is some reason for thinking that by the 1590s the ease of reference to 'luck', at least in tragedy, was becoming problematic. This is a period of intense theological self-consciousness, as an anti-Calvinist rearguard action was fought in Cambridge and in London, and the Calvinists responded with renewed predestinarian fervour. After the Lambeth articles of 1595, it became much more difficult to adopt a public position on the matter without attracting unwanted attention. 'Luck' becomes more easily acknowledged in comic than in tragic circumstances. Certainly that is the lesson of the Shakespeare concordance. We could be in the London streets, where Ben Jonson in *Every man out of his humour* has one cry out 'God send me good luck'.[71] Jonson is a prolific and pointed writer of luck.

---

[67] Richard Stanyhurst, *The First Foure Bookes of Virgils Aeneis, Translated into English Heroicall Verse, by Richard Stanyhurst* (London: Henrie Bynneman, 1583), D3ᵛ.

[68] Virgil, *Omnia opera: diligenti castigatione exculta: aptissimisque ornata figuris* (Venice: B. Zannis de Portesio, 1510), fo. 177ᵛ.

[69] [Jasper Heywood, Alexander Neville, John Studley, T. Nuce and Thomas Newton], *Seneca his tenne tragedies, translated into Englysh* (London: Thomas Marsh, 1581), fo. 67ʳ.

[70] Arthur Golding, *Abrahams Sacrifice* (1577), 9.

[71] *The comicall satyre of euery man out of his humor*, sig. F2ᵛ.

'Luck' is especially prodigal in *Bartholomew Fair*, where the word is used nine times, including 'wonderful ill lucke'.[72] There is 'damn'd luck' in *The Case is Altered*; 'good luck' in *The Devil is an Ass* and *Every man in his humour*. In *The Alchemist*, first performed in 1610, Jonson twice slyly refers to a luck that cannot be resisted, making luck a secular version of divine grace, which the Calvinists in the same decade declared to be 'unresistable'.[73] By the end of the decade, as the Arminian crisis broke out in the Netherlands, 'irresistible grace' was one of the most controversial phrases in Europe.

Hamlet bears the traces of these different kinds of source in its thinking on life's luck. The Senecan influence is too well known to need comment. The second book of Virgil's *Aeneid* provides the source of the first of the plays that Hamlet gets the players to rehearse, with its powerful cultural memory of the fall of princes. Yet in the same scene, Hamlet also cryptically quotes to Polonius from a popular ballad of the story of Jephthah from the Bible. How Jephthah vowed to sacrifice the first person he meets, and then encountered his own daughter, is one of the key texts for divine providence. As so often with Hamlet, we cannot be sure what is going on in his mind when he quips to Polonius, 'And as by lot, god wot | It came to pass, most like it was'. But could it be that just like Jephthah, we don't know what's just round the corner, and who the next person will be who will come through the door; and like Jephthah's daughter, we can't know if the person crossing the threshold does not prognosticate our own death? A couple of scenes later, Hamlet, too, kills the first person he comes across in a room, only this time it is the father not the daughter.

Early modern thinking about providence is much broader and more widespread, and yet also more complex and more ambiguous, than we have got used to thinking. Literary commentators refer to Seneca as if there is only one strain of Senecan thought; and to the theology of providence as if there is only one available theory, and that a pretty crude one. It certainly was possible around 1600 to give a crude account of the workings of providence in a literary source. John Reynolds in 1621 retold the story of Middleton and Rowley's *The Changeling* as if it were a clear-cut case of 'The Trivmphs of Gods revenge, against the crying, and execrable Sinne of Murther'.[74] In 1597, in *The Theatre of God's Judgements*, Thomas Beard extracted a providential moral from the case of the Duchess of

---

[72] *Bartholmew fayre: a comedie, acted in the yeare, 1614 by the Lady Elizabeths seruants, and then dedicated to King Iames, of most blessed memorie* (London: Robert Allot, 1631), sig. E4ᵛ.

[73] *The alchemist. VVritten by Ben. Ionson* (London: Thomas Snodham, 1612), sig. C1ʳ and G4ᵛ.

[74] Reynolds, *The Trivmphs of Gods revenge* (London: Felix Kyngston, 1621), 105–6.

Malfi, fifteen years before Webster's play of that name, citing it as an example of 'Whoredomes committed vnder colour of Mariage'.[75] God's hand is as evident, it is a relief to discover, in the strangling of the Duchess as it is in the eventual come-uppance of her nasty catholic brother the Cardinal: 'Gods iustice bare the sway, that vsed him as an instrument to punish those, who vnder the vaile of secret marriage, thought it lawfull for them to commit any villany'.[76] It is not difficult to imagine what Beard would make of the tragedy of the prince of Denmark. No doubt it would be much like the opinion of William Gouge, the vicar of Blackfriars, who when the roof fell in, in a neighbouring parish, during a secret sermon by a recusant priest in October 1623, commented that God would not kill ninety-one catholics for nothing, and when one of the priests escaped, reported in a satisfied tone that the priest drowned in the Thames a week later.[77] Taking as his text the fall of a sparrow in Matthew 10: 29–31, he observes that fortune is a mere fiction: 'I know not any one other thing, whereunto, more of those things which are done by God, are attributed, then to *fortune, chance*, or *lucke*' (p. 380).

Yet there is more than one voice in Calvinism. Thomas Gataker was a learned divine, one of the first fellows of Sidney Sussex College, Cambridge, and later at the time of *Hamlet* a lecturer at Lincoln's Inn. Fastidious enough to decline the mastership of Trinity College, Cambridge, he was a moderate puritan in ecclesiastical polity but a proper Calvinist in theology, publishing refutations of Arminianism and other clarifications of the doctrine of justification.[78] Nevertheless, he wrote a treatise on the use of lots, a pioneering study of the metaphysics of causality on the eve of the mathematics of probability. Here he demonstrated a strict carefulness about the theological meaning of chance, elucidating the occurrence of the word in biblical contexts such as Ecclesiastes 9: 11, Matthew 12: 42 and Luke 10: 31. He considered the various etymologies of Hebrew and Syriac terms, of the Greek word $\tau \acute{\upsilon} \chi \eta$, and the Latin verbs *euenire, contingere*, and *occurrere*. Augustine, he argued, while rigorously countering

---

[75] Thomas Beard, *The Theatre of Gods Ivdgements: Wherein is represented the admirable iustice of God against all notorious sinners, both great and small* (London: Adam Islip, 1612), Book II, ch. xxiv.

[76] Thomas Beard, *The Theatre of Gods Iudgements: or, a collection of histories out of Sacred, Ecclesiasticall, and prophane Authours, concerning the admirable Iudgements of God vpon the transgressours of his commandements* (London: Adam Islip, 1597), 322–3.

[77] William Gouge, *The extent of Gods prouidence, set out in a sermon, preached in Blackfryers Church, 5. Nov. 1623, On occasion of the downe-fall of Papists in a Chamber at the said Black-fryers, 1623. Oct. 27* (London: George Miller, 1631), 393–401.

[78] Brett Usher, 'Gataker, Thomas (1574–1654)', *Oxford Dictionary of National Biography*, Oxford University Press, 2004; online edn., Jan 2008 <http://www.oxforddnb.com. ezproxy.york.ac.uk/view/article/10445>, accessed 8 November 2012.

the idea of fortune, noted the proper sense of the '*casuall euent of things*' (*fortuitum rerum euentum*).[79] God's world indisputably contains contingent events, he asserted, meaning by contingent something that is '*vncertaine or variable*' (p. 11). Some events are contingent and yet 'not casual': these events are what we call now counterfactual, 'such as are so done one way, as they may or might haue bene done some other way'. Yet here a person with due knowledge or forecast may determine which is the most likely to transpire and act accordingly. Other events, however, are 'Contingent and casuall', beyond any divination or skill in pre-deliberation. Such was the killing of Achab in 1 Kings 32: 34. Gataker at this point mounts a legal defence of the crime of 'casual slaughter', something that is said to be done *sodainly, inconsiderately, not out of enmitie, not of set purpose* (p. 13). Is this what Horatio means by 'casual slaughters' right at the end of *Hamlet*? Is this how we are to take the killing of Polonius?

Gataker half retracts, half eggs himself on to take further risks with the uncertainties of God's providence. He brings back in by way of comparison 'an act of the Creator, a prouidence or assistance either in generall or speciall' (p. 15), with the mandatory reference to the falling of a sparrow. Surely no man is 'slaine without Gods prouidence'? Then he twists again, quoting for a third time Ecclesiastes 9: 11, and adding a series of citations from Petronius' *Satyricon*, Menander, Plutarch, and Cicero, to the effect that things often turn out against the grain of what we expect or intend. No sooner has he said this than he turns right round, quoting St Bernard to the effect that what we call chance is God's way of showing what he is up to (*suam nobis indicans voluntatem*).[80] Yet if we follow this too much, we will give in to the superstition of deciding what to do on the basis of seeing a bird fly in front of us. In seeming desperation, his final definition of providence is so general that it perforce includes all possible definitions of subspecies of chance or fortune: '*Prouidence is the cause of all things that are done.*'

Gataker concludes that '*That* (say they) *which to the wise and godly is Gods singular Prouidence, to the foolish and prophane is Fortune or Chance.*' Yet if so, we note that this is a reversible proposition: as well as renaming chance as providence, we can also rename providence as chance. Gataker's tergiversations attest not to vacillation but to a consciousness of philosophical complexity. If they show also a little public cowardice, it was not misplaced: he was immediately accused of advocating games of hazard. Calvinists were inclined to ban the use of dice (or we might say betting on swordfights) and they had good cause to be worried. As often, we are

---

[79] Gataker cites Augustine, *Retractiones*, l.1.c.1 (*Caput Primum, Contra academicos, libri tres*), *Patrologia Latina*, 32, col. 585.

[80] Bernard of Clairvaux, *Sermones de diversis*, 26 (Sermo XXVI, *De voluntate nostra divinae voluntati subjicienda*), *Patrologia Latina*, 183, col. 611B.

mistaken if we assume their prohibitions result from a simple lack of fun-spiritedness. There is a theological nervousness at work here, shown also in the textual nuances and polemics of the Geneva Bible. Gataker is a Calvinist on predestination, but he is also a philosopher of chance.

Perhaps Gataker will be taken as an exception. Yet we could be forgiven for thinking that Hamlet would have enjoyed reading him, whether in Wittenberg or in Geneva. As for Calvin himself, he was at pains to contradict the blasphemous presumption involved in the kinds of judgement made by Thomas Beard, as if we could read God's will into everyday events, like a message on a tea-towel. Calvin's writing on chance shows exceptional subtlety and ambiguity, if we are prepared to read carefully enough. Everything can be ascribed finally to the will of God, yes; but then that is also the case in Aquinas, Boethius, even in some sense in Plato. That does not mean that it is easy to interpret divine intention in everyday events. As his test-case, Calvin, like Aristotle, like Hamlet in his adventures with the pirates, presses his closest attention to accidents at sea. Even in the case of a shipwreck, he says, or when a man miraculously reaches harbour having been entirely at the mercy of the wind and the waves, escaping death by a hair's breadth—whatever the temptation to call this an effect of fortune, we must see that all such fortunes are governed by the secret purpose of God ('le conseil secret de Dieu').[81] This is a refutation of chance, but it is nonetheless constructed on a classic exposition of the grounds for believing in chance. Even at the moment of refutation, he makes a fascinating theological observation. Events are governed by secret processes beyond chance, but they still *look like* chance (quoted here from Thomas Norton's English translation of 1561):

> I say therfore, how soeuer al things are ordeined by the purpose and certayne disposition of God, yet to vs they are chaunsable, not that we thynke that fortune ruleth the world and men, and vnaduisedly tosseth all thynges vp and down (for such beastlynesse ought to be farre from a Chrystyan harte) but because the order, meane, ende and necessitie of those thynges that happen, doeth for the moste parte lye secrecte in the purpose of God, and is not comprehended wyth opinion of man, therfore those thinges are as it were chaunsable, which yet it is certaine to come to passe by the wil of God.[82]

Even though every moment of our lives is in the hands of God—here, naturally, Calvin cites Matthew 10: 31, Hamlet's own sermon text, even the hairs of our heads are numbered—to us all of these moments appear

---

[81] *Institutes*, 1.16.2; Jean Calvin, *Institution*, ed. Benoit, i. 222.
[82] John Calvin, *The Institution of Christian Religion, wrytten in Latine by maister Ihon Caluin, and translated into Englysh according to the authors last edition* (London: Reinolde Wolfe & Richard Harison, 1561), fo. 60ᵛ.

quasi fortuita, 'quasi fortuites'.[83] Norton struggles to find an English word that will do, and comes up with the unusual word 'chaunsable'. It is as if Calvin, by the back door, or through the other end of the telescope, has rediscovered the accidentality of life.

Life in Hamlet is 'chaunsable' in the profoundest sense. Yet we should resist the idea that in this it is out of sympathy with the philosophical assumptions of its time. We do not have to reinvent the history of theology to make sense of it. We began with a moment of verbal censorship. We might have thought that this censorship somehow involved the elimination of the idea of luck in Elizabethan England. But instead it shows the opposite: that the idea of luck was the source of anxiety and ambiguity. The verbal scruple of the Geneva translators is only one end of the spectrum: at the other, we find a proliferation of interest in 'luck' and in related words such as 'chance'. Shakespeare, in creating such a complex world of chance in Hamlet, was not reacting against this theological sensitivity, he was participating in it. The Protestant obsession with providence created a rich and complex philosophical language. Shakespeare could draw on pagan and Christian narratives without feeling that there was some unbridgeable chasm between them. For, *pace* Williams and Nussbaum, there are cases in the Hebrew scriptures which speak in a similar way to Aeschylus or Sophocles of this sense of 'moral luck'. At some level Luther, and the early English translators, recognized this. Joseph is 'lucky' in the sense that he might as easily not have succeeded. He is lucky in the way meant shortly before his death by the Jewish composer György Ligeti, who, on reaching his eightieth birthday, said beautifully of his own life, in which as a young man he survived the holocaust: 'Somehow I am still living today, by a mistake, by chance'.[84] In Luther and sometimes in Tyndale grace is like that, it is something that involves *Glück*. Calvin half knew this, and half chose to suppress it. After his death, Calvinist theology struggled to overwhelm this desperate possibility, and strove to prove that luck has absolutely nothing to do with grace. Yet luck, in some unfathomable divine sense, might have everything to do with it.

---

[83] *Institutes*, 1.16.9; Calvin, *Institution*, ed. Benoit, i. 234. Latin text quoted from *Opera selecta*, ed. Barth and Niesel, iii. 200.

[84] 'Prelude for Pygmies', Interview in *The Guardian* with Tom Service to coincide with the Barbican concert in London 'Ligeti at 80', 17 October 2003, <http://arts.guardian.co.uk/fridayreview/story/0,12102,1064091,00.html>, accessed 3 March 2008.

7

Freedom, Suicide, & Selfhood
Montaigne, Shakespeare, Donne

Suicide is central to the psychological and sociological turn that has overtaken ideas of selfhood in the twentieth century. And Hamlet, as well as
being the prince of arguments linking modernity, identity, and secularity,
is modernity's favourite early modern would-be suicide. Yet what does
Hamlet mean when he makes the most famous of all Renaissance confessions of the temptation to suicide?

> HAM. To be, or not to be, that is the question:
> Whether 'tis nobler in the mind to suffer
> The slings and arrows of outrageous fortune,
> Or to take arms against a sea of troubles
> And by opposing end them. (3.1.56–60)

The idea that Hamlet is speaking here of 'self-murder' goes back at least as
far as William Warburton in his contributions to Lewis Theobald's notes
on the play in his edition of the 1720s. This view then passed into the
mainstream of Shakespearian interpretation, through Malone to Bradley
and down to Dover Wilson and modern annotation. Since the nineteenth
century, the idea of self-murder in this speech has been assimilated to a
view that Hamlet is in some sense prey, by this stage in the play, to a form
of mental disorder. As Margreta de Grazia remarks, 'After Coleridge, criticism will increasingly look for psychological explanations for Hamlet's
"strange and odd behaviour", attributing it to various kinds of psychic
disturbances, disorders, pathologies, neuroses.'[1] Suicide is at the heart of
this modern, neurotic Hamlet. The argument is neatly circular. Suicide is
defined as a form of mental disturbance; Hamlet is assumed to be discuss-
ing his own proneness to a suicidal inclination; and Hamlet then in turn
has acquired the status of the quintessential dramatic type of the neurotic.
Coleridge at one point himself used the vogue term 'psycho-analytic' to

---

[1] Hamlet *without Hamlet*, 12–17 and 163–5.

describe his approach to the problem of Hamlet's character, and the engine of Freud's methodology has completed the pattern. What begins with the Oedipus Complex ends in the Death Drive. Hamlet is modern psychic man.

The logic of this argument has nonetheless been disputed in several respects. While the psychoanalytic bent in Hamlet criticism has always been controversial, de Grazia has argued that a whole tradition of interpreting *Hamlet* has grown up in which the play, as it were, awaited a psychological explanation to bring it into life. More specifically, in what may be the longest ever footnote even on this most annotated of dramatic soliloquies, Harold Jenkins has commented on how the idea of suicide has been exaggerated to create an extreme sense of Hamlet's mental confusion. Such interpretations have especially 'shared the error of applying the speech to the speaker's personal problems'. Yet nothing in the speech, Jenkins insists, relates it to Hamlet's individual case. He interprets the meaning of 'To be, or not to be' somewhat differently:

> The 'question', then (crudely paraphrased as 'Is life worth living?') is essentially whether, in the light of what *being* comprises (in the condition of human life as the speaker sees it and represents it in what follows), it is preferable to have it or not. There is no reference here to suicide, nor even as yet to death.[2]

Jenkins therefore concludes that we should resist interpretations of the speech 'which distort the general proposition by irrelevant metaphysics'. De Grazia has built on Jenkins's scepticism about psychologizing Hamlet in order to create what we might call an anti-metaphysical *Hamlet*, not so much the play within the play as the play before the play. Suicidal Hamlet is just one more example of the abundance of philosophical Hamlets who have sprung up in the image of their philosophical creator: Hamlet as Schopenhauer, Hamlet as Nietzsche, Hamlet as Kierkegaard, Hamlet as Freud.

Yet formally, Jenkins is surely wrong: not only is Hamlet patently referring to taking one's own life, at least in some sense, but also the play refers frequently to the question, both directly and obliquely. Ophelia's death is analysed in both complex and comic terms as self-induced, and Horatio, too, offers to end his own life: 'I am more an antique Roman than a Dane', he says, avowing the Stoic fashion for choosing death over ignoble

---

[2] *Hamlet*, ed. Harold Jenkins, Arden series 2 (London: Methuen, 1982), 3.1.60, Long Note.

life.[3] But perhaps Jenkins is also wrong, philosophically. It may be instead that, rather than philosophy being the problem, we have mistaken one form of philosophy for another. Suicide is exactly the issue, not because we have placed too great an emphasis on suicide, but that we have assumed that a modern understanding of suicide is the only one.

SUICIDE & MODERNITY

When John Donne wrote *Biathanatos* in around 1608, often called the first modern formal defence or justification of the act of taking one's life, he could not use the word 'suicide'. The term of definition favoured by Donne is 'self-homicide', which is added as a subtitle to the work: 'A Declaration of that Paradoxe, or Thesis, That Selfe-homicide is not so naturally Sinne, that it may never be otherwise'.[4] However, there was no stable term in English. As well as 'self-homicide', Donne used the word 'self-murder', which was rather older, occurring in Foxe's Book of Martyrs in 1563 and Raphael Holinshed's *Chronicles* in 1587.[5] Sir Philip Sidney referred to the act of 'self-destruction' in *Arcadia* in the 1580s; Milton later used the same composite word in *Paradise Lost*.[6] In *Hamlet*, the word used by Shakespeare is 'self-slaughter'. This is also the word in the account of the suicide of Lucretia in his 1594 poem: 'Till Lvcrece Father that beholds her bleed, Himselfe, on her selfe-slaughtred bodie threw'.[7] Shakespeare seems to have made this word up.[8] There is a sense, indeed, that the early modern word is a neologism, in which the only common factor is the reflexive prefix 'self-'. *Selbstmord* is both inherently self-referential and yet also paradoxical, in that it involves the destruction of the very thing

---

[3] On 'the Roman question', see Martin Dodsworth, *Hamlet Closely Observed* (London: Athlone Press, 1985), 114.

[4] *ΒΙΑΘΑΝΑΤΟΣ a declaration of that paradoxe or thesis, that selfe-homicide is not so naturally sinne, that it may never be otherwise: wherein the nature and the extent of all those lawes, which seeme to be violated by this act, are diligently surveyed | written by Iohn Donne* (London: John Dawson, [1644]), title-page.

[5] Cited here from the revised edition, *Actes and monuments*, 2 vols. (London: John Day, 1570), ii. 2300. Raphael Holinshed, *The Third volume of Chronicles, beginning at duke William the Norman, commonlie called the Conqueror* (London: Henry Denham, 1587), 1385. There is one other occurrence by 1600 in Sir William Cornwallis's *Essays* (1600).

[6] *The Countess of Pembroke's Arcadia* (1590), II.xii, in *Complete Works of Sir Philip Sidney*, ed. Albert Feuillerat, 4 vols. (Cambridge: Cambridge University Press, 1912), i. 227; Milton, *Paradise Lost*, x. 1016.

[7] *Hamlet*, 1.2.132; *Lucrece* (London: Richard Field, 1594), sig. M2.

[8] *OED*, SELF-SLAUGHTER. The 1619 translation of Annaeus appears to be the first usage after Shakespeare. The word confused the compositor of the 1604 *Hamlet* Q2, which reads 'seale slaughter'.

it is. As a term it feels forever strange, a compound noun that has to be put back together each time anew, rather in the way the action is unmentionable or intrinsically difficult. David Hume in the late eighteenth century wrote an essay forthrightly entitled 'Of Suicide', but thought better of publishing it, so that it only appeared, posthumously, in 1783.[9]

To unravel this we have to uncover some of the modern mystique that surrounds the subject. It is not too much to say that in the twentieth century the idea of suicide was reinvented. Indeed for many people suicide appears to be a thoroughly modern problem, and its philosophical discussion a thoroughly modern debate. In that sense, early modern discussions, such as in France in Michel de Montaigne, or in the Netherlands in Justus Lipsius, or in England in Shakespeare or Donne, appear as staging posts on the route to modernity. Suicide is a psychological or even neurological condition. Misunderstood and condemned for centuries, especially by Christian doctrine, it has been rehabilitated only gradually by the throwing off of religious taboo. Modern philosophical approaches, while still recognizing the unique difficulty of the idea, are part of this humanitarian rationalization.

There is something clearly wrong with this thesis: suicide is a standard topic in ancient philosophy, especially in Plato, Cicero, and Seneca. Plato's attitude to the death of Socrates, especially in the *Phaedo*, is deeply anxious on the issue as to whether Socrates chooses death or has it forced on him.[10] Nevertheless, in the *Laws*, he rejected suicide as a moral evil except in specific circumstances.[11] Even so, he allowed for the intervention of the state, some terrible misfortune ($\tau \acute{\upsilon} \chi \eta$), or a shame beyond endurance. Cicero, on the other hand, made suicide a part of a rational assessment of a moral view of the self:

> When a man's circumstances contain a preponderance of things in accordance with nature (*secundum naturam*), it is appropriate for him to remain alive; when he possesses or sees in prospect a majority of the contrary things, it is appropriate for him to depart from life.[12]

---

[9] *Essays on Suicide and the Immortality of the Soul, ascribed to the late David Hume, Esq., never before published* (London: M. Smith, 1783).

[10] e.g. the question asked of Socrates by Cebes in *Phaedo*, 61E: 'on just what grounds do they say it's forbidden to kill oneself' (trans. Gallop, p. 5). The Greek verb is simply the reflexive form: $\kappa \alpha \tau \grave{\alpha} \ \tau \acute{\iota} \ \delta \acute{\eta} \ o\mathring{\upsilon}\nu \ \pi o\tau \epsilon \ o\mathring{\upsilon} \ \phi \alpha \sigma \iota \ \theta \epsilon \mu \iota \tau \acute{o}\nu \ \epsilon \mathring{\iota}\nu \alpha \iota \ \alpha \mathring{\upsilon}\tau \acute{o}\nu \ \acute{\epsilon}\alpha \upsilon \tau \grave{o}\nu \ \mathring{\alpha}\pi o\kappa \tau \epsilon \iota \nu \acute{\upsilon}\nu \alpha \iota$; Plato, *Phaedo*, ed. C. J. Rowe (Cambridge: Cambridge University Press, 1993), 28.

[11] Plato, *Laws*, IX.873C–D; ed. and trans. R. G. Bury, Loeb Classical Library, 2 vols. (London: Heinemann, 1926), ii. 264–7.

[12] *De finibus*, III.xviii.60; ed. and trans. H. Rackham, Loeb Classical Library (London: Heinemann, 1931), 279.

Stoic philosophy made the strongest case for justifying suicide. Seneca made the argument that the quality of a life forms the only criterion for life's continuation. The resonance of his arguments have been the more powerful because of his own death by suicide, ordered by Nero.

Like many kinks in intellectual history, the hiatus in the moral attitude towards suicide is attributed to the secularization thesis. What stopped modernity becoming modernity is Christianity, and suicide illustrates this issue like no other: once the everlasting 'Cannon 'gainst Selfe-slaughter' got unfixed, Renaissance humanism opened the way to modernity. 'As the humanists freed men to live, they brought them the right to die', S. E. Sprott's history of early modern attitudes to suicide asserts.[13] Christian theology has been taken to be a negative counterweight between pagan sympathy and 'liberalized Enlightenment attitudes'.[14] Indeed, in the fullest account of early modern suicide in England, *Sleepless Souls*, suicide is given its own history of 'secularization'.[15] In brief, this version of secularization asserts that the repression of suicide in Christianity gave way in time to a rationalist view. This view was more tolerant in relation to religious taboo because it removed suicide from the realm of sin and reinterpreted it within a non-religious framework of 'illness', a form of mental disorder. Scepticism in relation to religion is the key to this moral transformation.

Decriminalization is central here. Only with the Suicide Act in 1961 was suicide finally removed from statute in England and Wales. In the eighteenth century juries were already found to be reluctant on this point. William Blackstone commented, with disdain, that the reluctance to convict a case of suicide was making a mockery of the rational discussion of motive and evidence. Only a plea of insanity could protect the suicide from the weight of the law's opprobrium, so that insanity was becoming a universal form of defence: 'the very fact of suicide is an evidence of insanity; as if every man who acts contrary to reason, had no reason at all'.[16] These legal battles were fought across the sanction of religious piety and morality. Allowing lenience for suicide was a natural response against a law that seemed draconian in its rigidity. Greenblatt beautifully calls this

---

[13] *The English Debate on Suicide from Donne to Hume* (La Salle, Ill.: Open Court, 1961), 1.

[14] Michael Cholbi, 'Suicide', *The Stanford Encyclopedia of Philosophy*, ed. Edward N. Zalta (Fall 2009 Edition) <http://plato.stanford.edu/archives/fall2009/entries/suicide/>, accessed 23 June 2011.

[15] 'The Secularization of Suicide' is the title of Part II in Michael MacDonald and Terence R. Murphy, *Sleepless Souls: Suicide in Early Modern England* (Oxford: Clarendon Press, 1990).

[16] *Commentaries on the Laws of England* (Oxford, 1769), iv. 186.

the 'boundary disputes' of funeral rites. In Shakespeare's *Hamlet*, concern over the correct ritual redress for Ophelia expresses a disruption of 'rituals for managing grief, allaying personal and collective anxiety, and restoring order'.[17] In 1823 burial at the crossroads was abolished; in 1870 property was no longer confiscated when death by suicide was proved.[18] Yet such acts of human tolerance were interpreted as a descent into depravity and an encouragement of an act that was emotionally as well as ethically to be deplored. Christian theology, the criminal law, and the medical debate about the causes of suicide, are therefore intimately linked. Yet it is still open to question whether a teleological interpretation of progression from religious taboo to medical enlightenment is meaningful.

That Christian doctrine in all its forms condemned suicide is beyond doubt. The first systematic argument for prohibition was given by Augustine, who took a ban on suicide (*Nullam esse auctoritatem quae Christianis in qualibet causa ius voluntariae necis tribuat*) as a simple extension of the fifth commandment: 'In fact, we must understand it to be forbidden by the law' where it says "You shall not kill".'[19] Suicide is murder like any other. Augustine's forcefulness on the issue reflects the way that *De civitate Dei* is a response to classical moral philosophy, and for a late Latin rhetorician especially, a rejoinder to the reputation of Seneca. Within the moral enquiry of the scholastics, suicide is given sympathetic treatment but is nonetheless rejected unequivocally. Aquinas gave three reasons against suicide: first, suicide is against nature, since the love of the self is natural to all beings (*naturaliter quaelibet res seipsam amat*). Second, since every part affects the whole, suicide is a sin against the community, which is affected by the death of the individual. Third, and most significantly, suicide is an offence against God.[20] Aquinas's reasoning is subtle here: life is a gift (*donum*) given by God, and nobody has the right to throw away such a gift. A person has *usus* of her body (possession, employment), but to God belongs the body's *dominium* (dominion, authority).[21]

Protestant theology in the sixteenth century added little to this tradition, although it did not in any way remove the bar. Calvin does not mention suicide anywhere in the *Institutes*, and discusses the question only briefly, on two occasions, in his biblical commentaries, on suicides in

[17] *Hamlet in Purgatory*, 247.

[18] Sprott, *English Debate*, 157–8.

[19] *De civitate Dei*, I.20, Benedictine Edition (Paris: Gaume, 1838), cols. 29–30; ed. David Knowles and trans. Henry Bettenhouse, *Concerning the City of God against the Pagans* (Harmondsworth: Penguin, 1972), 31.

[20] *Summa theologiae*, 2a2ae, q. 64, art. 5; *Summa Theologica diligenter emendata*, ed. de Rubeis, Billuart et al., 6 vols. (Turin: Typographia Pontificia), iii. 376–8.

[21] This argument originates in Augustine, *De civitate Dei*, I.26.

the Old Testament.[22] The deaths of Saul and Achitophel he interprets as
showing divine justice, in adding a sinful death to a sinful life. By way of
moral commentary, he adds only 'Let us wait for the highest commander,
who sent us into the world, to call us out of it.'[23] This view, despite Calvin's
phrasing in terms of his own concept of the sovereignty of God's power,
is more or less a quotation from Augustine, who is himself quoting from
Plato's *Phaedo*.[24] It is therefore something of a misnomer to repeat, as
historians of suicide so often do, a deep theological antipathy to a topic
tolerated in antiquity. Christian moral apologetics is not greatly concerned with any special remonstration towards suicide, just as pagan accounts, with the exception of Stoicism, surround any justification with
some severe caveats. The outrage expressed towards suicide is found, in
fact, in Christian social attitudes more than in its doctrine. Canon Law
prohibited suicide, and denied Christian burial where it could be proved.
This remained the case in Calvinist Geneva, where the defamation of the
body of the suicide was commonplace, and perhaps more especially in
Protestant England.[25] Yet it also needs to be said that most ancient Greek
city states also criminalized suicide.[26]

Humanists such as Erasmus in one of his apophthegms and Thomas
More in *Utopia* showed sympathetic knowledge of the classical traditions
on suicide. More allows suicide in Utopia when life is no longer worth
living.[27] This is commonly taken, as with Montaigne, as evidence of a stirring of revolution against Christian intolerance.[28] In a contrary direction,
however, Macdonald and Murphy argue that humanist sympathy is out
of step with its times: if anything, early modern England stepped up the

---

[22] Jeffrey R. Watt, 'Calvin on Suicide', *Church History*, 66 (1997), 463–76, this ref.
p. 464.

[23] Sermon on 1 Sam. 31; *Ioannis Calvini opera quae supersunt omnia*, ed. Wilhelm
Baum, Edvard Cunitz, and Edvard Reuss, Corpus Reformatorum, XLVI (Braunschweig,
1891), 718–19.

[24] Augustine, *De civitate Dei*, I.21; Plato, *Phaedo*, 62c. The idea of humans as the senti-
nels of bodies which owe their allegiance to the creator as a general originated with Pythagoras and was a classical commonplace; it is used by Cicero in the *Tusculan Disputations*,
I.xxx.74 (ed. King, p. 87), and in *De senectute*, xx.72 (ed. and trans. W. A. Falconer, Loeb
Classical Library (London: Heinemann, 1964), 82–4).

[25] See on Geneva, Jeffrey R. Watt, *Choosing Death: Suicide and Calvinism in Early
Modern Geneva*, Sixteenth Century Essays & Studies (Kirksville, Mo.: Truman State University Press, 2001); and on England, MacDonald and Murphy, *Sleepless Souls*, 138.

[26] J. M. Cooper, 'Greek Philosophers on Suicide and Euthanasia', in B. Brody (ed.), *Suicide and Euthanasia: Historical and Contemporary Themes* (Dordrecht: Kluwer, 1989), 10.

[27] *Utopia*, II; ed. Edward Surtz and J. H. Hexter, in *Complete Works of Thomas More*, iv.
186 (trans. p. 187). The marginal gloss (which may not be More's own) terms suicide as
mors spontanea.

[28] MacDonald and Murphy, *Sleepless Souls*, 87; and Cholbi, 'Suicide', *Stanford Encyclopedia of Philosophy*.

antipathy to suicide in the courts and in the popular imagination.[29] More made his tolerant gesture only in fiction: in *A Dialogue of Comfort against Tribulation*, he made a clear stance against taking the idea into practice.[30] *Sleepless Souls* can only account for the eventual overthrow of these attitudes with the Enlightenment emergence of anti-theological and rational explanations of suicide as a form of mental illness. My argument is rather different. It is that suicide belongs to a sceptical philosophical train of thinking which should not be confused with anti-Christian polemic.

Indeed, there is in this way a more profound sense in which suicide has been reinvented in the twentieth century, which indeed puts us on the other side of a divide from the early modern. Arguments about suicide in modern society centre on the act itself, conceived principally as a medical condition or a sociological problem. Indeed suicide is a primal moment in the history of the social sciences. Émile Durkheim's *Le Suicide: étude de sociologie* of 1897 is a classic of methodology as much as of material, using comparisons of suicide rates in Catholic and Protestant countries to formulate a general thesis. It was a breathtaking piece of work because suicide seemed such unlikely material for a social analysis up to this point. The act of self-killing had always been described in individual terms, relying on psychological theories. Durkheim showed that suicide could not be fully explained by psychologists. Sociology explained aspects that were beyond psychological explanation. Primary among these were what could cause the statistical evidence Durkheim acquired that suicide was more prevalent in Protestant communities than Catholic ones. Durkheim tried to establish social causes and social types of suicide, and used his analysis to develop his theory of *anomie*, the experience of social alienation from a sense of prevailing norms. For Durkheim, *anomie* stems from a mismatch between personal or group standards and wider social standards, or from the lack of a social ethic, which produces moral deregulation and an absence of legitimate aspirations.

While Durkheim conceived social research as an antidote to psychological studies of suicide, he probed in his introductory section the relationship of social causes to those based on the individual—what he called 'psychopathic' explanations.[31] It is possible to see here a link between what are seemingly opposed theories of human behaviour. While sociology and psychology were completely different in their methodologies,

[29] MacDonald and Murphy, *Sleepless Souls*, 103–4.
[30] More describes as the worst possible sin 'where the devill temptith a man to kyll and destroy hym selfe', *A Dialogue of Comfort against Tribulation*, ed. L. L. Martz and F. Manley, in *Complete Works of Thomas More*, xii. 122.
[31] *Le Suicide: étude de sociologie* (Paris: F. Alcan, 1897), 46.

they shared this in their conceptual structuring of the idea of suicide, that it is an act that implies pathological behaviour. The suicide responds to forces beyond his control. He is the victim either of his own mind or his social context. The 'cure' to this behaviour lies in restoring a sense of voluntary empowerment.

We are here only a step away from the medicalization of psychology within which the modern condition of suicide has come to be understood. Suicide is linked inherently to ideas of clinical depression and their treatment. There are now neurological theories which try to explain why suicide happens, what makes one person more prone to the instinct than another, and treatment may be pharmacological as well as therapeutic. There is no doubt that this context has in turn influenced the philosophy of suicide. As early as 1922, Albert Bayet's *Le Suicide et la morale* appropriated Durkheim's legacy for a sociological interpretation of history. For Bayet, a lapsed Catholic, when theology is taken away, all that is left of suicide is a social problem, requiring social explanations and solutions.[32] The anti-clerical and anti-theological edge in Bayet creates a form of historical determinism. Overthrowing the negative association of suicide within Christianity releases a modern view of neutrality.

Jonathan Glover in his classic *Causing Death and Saving Lives* has stated that suicide nowadays is 'thought of as an irrational symptom of mental disturbance and so as a "medical" problem'.[33] As a result, indeed, some people have a problem in seeing it as a topic in moral philosophy at all:

> the reaction against responding to suicide with horror and condemnation has made widespread the view that the question is not in any way a moral one. (p. 171)

Suicide is the modern sin, perhaps the sin of modernity. It is secular, social, and psychological. It therefore stands as a test-case of moral philosophy, probing the limits of the law's enquiry into the realm of the self, as perhaps also the self's responsibility to itself. In the law of nature, the self at least has a stake in taking good care of itself, and the moral law of society has a duty to encourage this stake. But the law should not go too far. The presumption of guilt in relation to suicide is a prime example of an archaic or outdated principle. It belongs to a society which assumes that God has the final jurisdiction of the soul. In a society which no longer, at least collectively or officially, believes in the soul, we no longer

---

[32] *Le Suicide et la morale* (Paris: F. Alcan, 1922), 21–2.
[33] 'Suicide and Gambling with Life', *Causing Death and Saving Lives* (London: Pelican, 1977), 171.

have any right to condemn the suicide. This is the ultimate claim of a private sphere.

There are counter-currents in modern thought about suicide. The principal is that of existentialism, where suicide is used as a strong form of theory in relation to a concept of human freedom. This works in complex ways. On the one hand, Sartre defined human freedom as the opposite of a life determined by external forces. Suicide could in that sense appear as a model of existential freedom: I can choose whether to live. Yet in Camus's *Le Mythe de Sisyphe* this freedom is condemned as illusory. Sisyphus is a hero because he accepts the absurdity of his own condition and chooses life: 'il s'agit de vivre'.[34] The developed version of suicide in Sartre is therefore to reject it, as in his analysis of Meursault in Camus's *L'Étranger*, 'L'homme absurde ne se suicidera pas':

> The absurd man will not commit suicide; he wants to live, without relinquishing any of his certainty, without a future, without hope, without illusions...and without resignation either. He stares at death with passionate attention and this fascination liberates him. He experiences the 'divine irresponsibility' of the condemned man.[35]

Yet we could say that while Sartre appears to restore an idea of agency to suicide in making of it an essential question of existence, he does so against the grain of twentieth-century assumptions about what the act of suicide is really like. Here, too, we feel in reverse the draw of a pathological concept of suicide. He also makes a strong claim for freedom in relation to suicide which will bear comparison with early modern arguments, but which will also show how far those arguments are from the twentieth-century understanding of suicide as a form of mental illness.

This chapter is not the place for an assessment of the modern debate over suicide, either in relation to theories of mental depression or the legal ramifications of euthanasia and assisted suicide. Rather, it attempts a revision of the way in which pre-modern discussions of suicide are reconstructed retrospectively to fit a modern paradigm. While currents can be found of an understanding of suicide in terms of a neurosis or mental breakdown, the overwhelming burden of explanation is in terms of suicide as a rational act, even when it is seen as the result of a religious

---

[34] Camus, *Le Mythe de Sisyphe*, in *Essais*, ed. R. Quilliot and L. Faucon, Bibliothèque de la Pléiade (Paris: Gallimard, 1965), 146.

[35] Jean-Paul Sartre, 'Explication de l'Étranger', in *Situations: essais de critique, I* (Paris: Gallimard, 1947), 96; trans. in *Literary and Philosophical Essays* (London: Rider & Co., 1955), 27.

'despair'.[36] In this respect, Montaigne is quite explicit: 'combien improprement nous appellons desespoir cette dissolution volontaire, à laquelle la chaleur de l'espoir nous porte souvent, et souvent une tranquille et rassise inclination de jugement' ('how improperly we call "despair" that voluntary dissolution to which we are often borne by the ardour of hope, and often by a tranquil and deliberate inclination of our judgement').[37] Montaigne is here commenting on the considerable discussion in Aristotle of what it means for something to be 'voluntary'.[38] Also, while prudential arguments are made about suicide in relation to the quality of life, assisted suicide and voluntary death are formulated in terms of the politics of freedom rather than a calculus of social benefits.[39] It is my desire here to discuss early modern arguments in their own context and against the grain of modern preoccupations.

DONNE'S 'SICKELY INCLINATION'

Donne's *Biathanatos* is a prime case in the creation of a lineage of the secularizing and psychologizing of suicide. It is a work which has rather baffled historians and critics alike. Its obvious importance as a formal defence of an act commonly regarded as anathema has been submerged in complaints about its pedantic style.[40] In compensation, the work has been combed for some personal frame of reference to explain it. Donne can only have written it through some autobiographical yearning for confession. The opening sentence of the work indeed refers to his 'sickely inclination' for death:

> *BEZA*, A man as eminent and illustrious, in the full glory and Noone of Learning, as others were in the dawning, and Morning, when any, the least sparkle was notorious, confesseth of himself, that only for the anguish of a Scurffe, which over-ranne his head, he had once drown'd himselfe from the Millers bridge in *Paris*, if his *Uncle* by chance had not then come that way; I have often such a sickely inclination.[41]

---

[36] Nicholas Watson, 'Despair', *Cultural Reformations: Medieval and Renaissance in Literary History*, ed. Brian Cummings and James Simpson (Oxford: Oxford University Press, 2010), 350.

[37] 'Coustume de l'Isle de Cea', II.iii.380; Frame, p. 316.

[38] Aristotle, *Nicomachean Ethics*, III.1109ᵇ–11ᵇ; *Nicomachean Ethics Books II–IV*, trans. C. C. W. Taylor (Oxford: Oxford University Press, 2006), 16–19.

[39] Green, *Montaigne and the Life of Freedom*.

[40] Georges Minois, *History of Suicide: Voluntary Death in Western Culture* (Baltimore: Johns Hopkins, 1999), 88.

[41] *Biathanatos* (1644), 17.

The sentence has a beguiling quality of self-reflection combined with impersonal statement. It is anecdotal, whimsical, novelistic, and yet auto-biographical. It has seemed natural to look to this work, as to so many of Donne's writings, for subjective speculation and even introspection. Donne, we say, 'was much possessed by death'. In a letter to his friend the courtier Sir Henry Goodyer (or Goodere), probably contemporary with his treatise on suicide, he described the desire in pathological terms, admitting that 'a thirst and inhiation after the next life' could readily become 'envenomed, and putrefied, and stray into a corrupt disease'.[42] This turns quickly into a more complex personal meditation:

> With the first of these I have often suspected my self to be overtaken; which is, with a desire of the next life: which though I know it is not meerly out of a wearinesse of this, because I had the same desires when I went with the tyde, and enjoyed fairer hopes then now: yet I doubt worldly encumbrances have encreased it. (*Letters*, 49)

In a letter to 'my Lord G.H.' he wrote, perhaps at the same time:

> I am now in the afternoon of my life, and then it is unwholesome to sleep. It is ill to look back, or give over in a course; but worse never to set out. I speake to you at this time of departing, as I should do at my last upon my death-bed. (*Letters*, 94)

It has been difficult not to make every reference to death in Donne's prose an autobiographical reflection, and to give in to the temptation of seeing Donne in a permanently morbid light.

This is clearly a pose Donne himself delights in:

> THis advantage you, and my other friends have, by my frequent Fevers, that I am so much the oftener at the gates of heaven, and this advantage by the solitude and close imprisonment that they reduce me to after, that I am thereby the oftener at my prayers. (*Letters*, 241–2)

The jokiness of the sentiment is soon confirmed in this letter (undated and without a recipient in the text we have): 'It hath been my desire, (and God may be pleased to grant it me) that I might die in the Pulpit; if not that, yet that I might take my death in the Pulpit, that is, die the sooner by occasion of my former labours'. This is not unlike Montaigne's stated desire to be caught by death while planting his cabbages, while having a

---

[42] *Letters to severall persons of honour written by John Donne Sometime Deane of St Pauls London. Published by John Donne, Dr. of the civill law* (London: J. Flesher for Richard Marriot, 1651), 49.

distinctive donnish and clerical twist.[43] The sight of his congregation in his mind's eye is part of the deliciousness of the conceit.

The mode of autobiographical reflection, I have been arguing in this book, is a natural affect of writing on human mortality. The death of the person is hardly a non sequitur to the abstract idea of death. In Donne's case, there is the added knowledge that he twice created innovative autobiographical writings out of the imagination of his own death. In the first, in 1623, he described his suffering and recovery from a seemingly mortal illness. Then as he prepared for the death which indeed finally overtook him, he created an elaborate fiction around himself involving both his own funeral monument in stone, and a mock funeral sermon in his own honour. Yet neither work should be read too easily in the guise of a modern personal confessional. The *Devotions upon Emergent Occasions* (1623) are a spiritual exercise in prayer and meditation, and *Deaths Duell* (1631) was a sermon on the subject of death for the edification of his cathedral, and not a solipsistic indulgence.

Such caveats are all the more important in relation to Donne's treatise on suicide. *Biathanatos* is a scholastic, not personal work. It consists of exhaustive analyses of canon law, of natural law theory, and of moral philosophy, in order to contradict the universal ban on suicide. There are cases, he argues, where Christian theology has made death the lesser of two evils: martyrdom is the principle and most obvious:

> For certainly the desire of Martyrdome, though the body perish, is a Selfe preservation, because thereby out of our Election our best part is advaunc'd.[44]

Within natural law, too, suicide cannot be said to be against nature, for the simple reason that it occurs naturally:

> Another reason which prevayles much with me, and delivers it from being against the Law of Nature, is this, that in all *Ages*, in all places, upon all occasions, men of all conditions have affected it, and inclin'd to do it. (p. 49)

Indeed, the proof that it is a natural condition is that it cannot be explained by self-interest. It is this kind of paradox that animates Donne's whole work. Nature works against its own interests, and thus ratifies such an unnatural practice as explicable only by natural means: 'since being contrary to our sensitive Nature, it hath not the advantage of

---

[43] 'que la mort me treuve plantant mes choux': 'Que philosopher est apprendre à mourir', I.xix.91; Frame, p. 74.

[44] *Biathanatos*, ed. E. W. Sullivan (Newark, Del.: University of Delaware Press, 1984), 48.

pleasure and delight, to allure us withall, which other sinnes have'. A sin
for the sake of opportunism could be held against the law of nature, but
not one that conduces only to self-harm. Yet Donne also appeals to a
rational principle: there are circumstances in which the continuation of
life is itself contrary to nature: where the body is too weak to enjoy its
own goods, or where pleasure or happiness has become impossible. The
law of self-preservation, he says, is applied to 'that which conduces to our
ends, and is good to us' (p. 48). So in certain circumstances, when the
continuation of life inhibits the conduct of a life properly lived, a life
may be brought to an end by my own hands without violating the law of
nature. Moral philosophy abounds with examples of the preference of an
honourable death over a dishonourable life, such as one subject to tyranny or enslavement or moral turpitude. A 'greater Good' (p. 49) takes
precedence. Yet how do we take such remarks? Eric Langley has argued
suggestively how Donne's treatise is too easily taken at face value, as if it
were recommending suicide per se. It is, rather, a work constantly aware
of its own self-contradiction.[45]

Yet despite its philosophical seriousness, *Biathanatos* within modern
commentary is more likely to be seen inside a modern lens of personal
conflict or agonistic self-realization. Donne yearns for death and argues
himself into accepting it:

> how much more may I, when I am weather beaten, and in danger of betray-
> ing that precious soule which God hath embarqued in me, put off this bur-
> denous flesh, till his pleasure be that I shall resume it? For this is not to sinck
> the ship but to retire it to safe Harbour, and assured Anchor.[46]

Montaigne, too, is assessed in these terms. Jean Starobinski, in one of the
subtlest accounts of Montaigne's personal style, *Montaigne en mouvement*,
nonetheless risks the speculation (punctuated by a question mark) that in
approaching the topic of suicide ('L'être ultime'), Montaigne himself perhaps embarks on this path: 'Montaigne s'engage-t-il lui-même sur cette
voie?'[47] Starobinski adds his own wild surmise at this point—'He tries it
out vicariously (*par personne interposée*), out of curiosity' (although he
surely does not mean this literally)—and then quickly makes his own
sceptical rejoinder—that Montaigne's trial is partly at the malicious expense of his readers, 'denouncing the ultimate vanity and failure of the

[45] *Narcissism and Suicide in Shakespeare and his Contemporaries* (Oxford: Oxford University Press, 2009), 221.
[46] *Biathanatos* (1644), 110–11.
[47] *Montaigne en mouvement* (Paris: Gallimard, 1982), 91.

enterprise'.[48] Yet this is not Montaigne's own death we are talking about, it turns out, but the death of Cato the Younger.[49] Something else must be going on.

'À mourir il ne reste que le vouloir', says Montaigne in 'Coustume de l'Isle de Cea'; 'to die all that is needed is the will'.[50] The comment suggests philosophical depth but is inscrutable in surface meaning: it is poised between an axiom in metaphysics and a self-reflexive meditation. Does he express a wish to die, or only a general statement on the fragility of life? Like many sentences in Montaigne, it is less an assertion than a concealed set of questions. What kind of argument is Montaigne making in this curious essay towards the beginning of Book II? It is tempting to call it an argument about suicide. Yet equally obviously, it does not call itself an argument about suicide. It does not even call itself an argument. The essay begins with the hypothesis 'Si philosopher c'est douter' (II.iii.368; 'If to philosophize is to doubt', Frame, p. 305), but then places its own enquiry lower than doubt, making it sub-philosophical, indistinguishable from fantastical ravings ('niaiser et fantastiquer, comme je fais', II.iii.368; 'to play the fool and follow my fancies, as I do', Frame, p. 305). Only a scholar can debate important issues; only a theologian can resolve them. Montaigne is neither: he reserves any authority in the matter to the inalienable truth of divine will ('l'authorité de la volonté divine'; II.iii.368). As for his own essay, it describes rather than comments; its object is not a principle nor even a belief, but a 'coustume', a 'custom' or a 'habit'. Perhaps the essay has no proper subject, still less a conclusion. It is positioned between an essay on drunkenness and one on procrastination. The writer keeps writing, the reader keeps reading. We will die, assuredly, but not yet.

The uncertainty surrounding the essay extends to its subject. Patrick Henry has rightly commented that Montaigne could not have called the essay, 'Du suicide', since the word did not yet exist.[51] The French word, like the English 'suicide', is mid-seventeenth century.[52] For Patrick Henry,

---

[48] *Montaigne in Motion*, trans. Arthur Goldhammer (Chicago: University of Chicago Press, 1985), 71.

[49] 'De la cruauté', II.xi.445.

[50] II.iii.369; Frame, p. 306.

[51] Patrick Henry, 'The Dialectic of Suicide in Montaigne's "Coustume de l'Isle de Cea" ', *Modern Language Review*, 79 (1984), 278–89, this ref. p. 280.

[52] *OED*, SUICIDE, 1.a. ascribes the first reference to 1651 in William Charleton's *Ephesian and Cimmaronian Matrons*. This was first published in 1668. The first printed reference I have found is Edward Philips, *The new world of English words, or, A general dictionary containing the interpretations of such hard words as are derived from other languages* (1658), which refers to 'suicide' as an example of a barbarous loan-word (or 'inkhorn' term) from Latin. Philips evidently regards it as of very recent occurrence, and not in general use.

this is explanation enough for Montaigne's reticence.[53] Montaigne's method is partly aesthetic and partly defensive. 'Coustume de l'Isle de Cea' is an exemplary piece of humanist rhetoric, coming across its point sidelong; and it is an exemplary piece of philosophy, because it knows its subject is dangerous and even forbidden, so it has to tread carefully.

The obliquity of Montaigne's argument is a challenge not only to the historical understanding of suicide but to philosophical method concerning death in general. Is this a subject beyond philosophy, either because it is too difficult to talk about or even because it is too paradoxical to understand? Montaigne's essay, like other accounts of suicide, has been reduced to a manifesto for or against. Is suicide permissible, or even justifiable in some circumstances; are there occasions when it may be the best, or the least worst, action available? One way of reading the essay is an exercise in the rhetorical figure of 'paradox'.[54] Superficially, indeed, the essay on Cea (in Henry's reading) even divides itself into such rhetorical sections, which Henry dubs 'Arguments in Favour of Suicide' and 'Arguments against Suicide'. These two sections aggregate undigested examples from the classical and modern past, such as, in favour of suicide, the Spartan child facing slavery under Philip of Macedon, who exclaims: ' "it would be shameful for me to be a servant, with freedom so ready at hand". And so saying he threw himself from the top of the house.'[55] Or, in the opposite direction, Montaigne cites Virgil's dire warnings in the *Aeneid*, VI (later quoted by Dante) of the fate in the afterlife of the violent against themselves, *Proxima deinde tenent maesti loca*, 'the next place in hell those gloomy souls hold').[56] Into the midst of these literary and historical examples are freely interpolated various philosophical remarks, rather in the manner of the later Wittgenstein, tossed in front of us as self-evident, requiring no further analysis. First among these, placed in silent juxtaposition to the strange story of a child refusing life under tyranny, is the phrase, 'C'est ce qu'on dit, que le sage vit tant qu'il doit, non pas tant qu'il peut ('That is what they mean by saying that the sage lives as long as he should, not as long as he can').[57]

---

[53] Henry, 'Dialectic of Suicide', 279.

[54] Margaret McGowan, *Montaigne's Deceits: The Art of Persuasion in the Essais* (London: University of London Press, 1974), 72–3.

[55] Frame, p. 305: 'ce me seroit honte de servir, ayant la liberté si à main: et ce disant, se precipita du haut de la maison'; II.iii.368.

[56] *Aeneid*, vi. 434; ed. R. G Austin (Oxford: Clarendon Press, 1977), 14; also cited in Augustine, *De civitate Dei*, I.xix.

[57] II.iii.368; Frame, p. 305.

Montaigne presents this without any source; but a careful reader will remember that it is not only a citation but a word-for-word translation of a well-known line from Seneca, *Ad Lucilium Epistulae Morales*: *Itaque sapiens vivit, quantum debet, non quantum potest.*[58] Indeed, Pierre Villey called the essay 'un tissu de centons traduits de Sénèque'.[59] The notes in the revised Pléiade edition (2007) reveal that of the eight arguments for suicide, seven are derived from Seneca, and are encrusted with seventeen direct translations from Book II of the letters, ten of which come from a single letter to Lucillus, *Epistola* LXX.[60] Nature has left us 'the gift of the key to the fields' (Frame, p. 306).[61] She has 'ordained only one entry into life, and a hundred thousand exits' (Frame, p. 306).[62] Or the sentiment with which I began, 'To die all that is needed is the will' (Frame, p. 306): *ad moriendum nihil aliud in mora esse quam velle* (*Ep*. LXX, ii. 68). The epigrams pile up unabated: '*Death is a remedie against all evils* ...The voluntariest death, is the fairest. *Life dependeth on the will of others, death on ours* ...To live is to serve, if the libertie to die be wanting.'[63] The eighth argument in favour of suicide Henry attributes not to Seneca directly but to a general Stoic view: that God gives permission, when life is worse than death, for us to depart in peace. In fact, Stoicism often involves a calculus of how to estimate when the 'undesirable' (ἀποπροηγμένα) factors in a life predominate over the 'desirable' (προηγμένα), in order to make life itself no longer worth living, putting the life of the person directly at stake.[64] Even here a direct source in Seneca is easy enough to find: *Non enim vivere bonum est, sed bene vivere.*[65] Indeed a wise man may decide to leave his life even when in an apparent state of happiness, just as a fool is determined to prolong his life even when he is the midst of misery. Suicide was permitted 'when the advantages of living were outweighed by the disadvantages of living'. Henry finds in this a reworking of Plato in the *Phaedo*, although with a different slant: 'one should not kill oneself until God

---

[58] Seneca, *Ad Lucilium Epistulae Morales*, ed. and trans. Richard M. Gummere, Loeb Classical Library, 3 vols. (London: Heinemann, 1917–25), ii. 58. All references to Seneca's letters from this edition, citing number (e.g. *Ep*. LXX) and page number.

[59] Pierre Villey, *Les Sources et l'évolution des Essais*, 2 vols. (Paris: Hachette, 1908), ii. 17.

[60] *Essais*, ed. Balsamo, Magnien, and Magnien-Simonin, p. 1510.

[61] *In aperto nos natura custodit, Ep*. LXX (ii. 68–70).

[62] *unum introitum nobis ad vitam dedit, exitus multos, Ep*. LXX (ii. 64).

[63] *Ep*. LXXVIII (ii. 184); *Ep*. LXIX (ii. 54); *Ep*. LXX (ii. 62); *Ep*. LXXVII (ii. 176). Florio's English is given here to convey a sense of the epigrammatic.

[64] Miriam T. Griffin, *Seneca: A Philosopher in Politics* (Oxford: Clarendon Press, 1976), 376.

[65] *Ep*. LXX (ii. 58).

sends some necessity': nevertheless, sometimes God does do exactly that.[66]

One way of reading the essay, then, places Montaigne within a rhetorical tradition of commonplace wisdom, tacking together classical citations in one direction then another. The avowed object of this is a defence of the indefensible. Yet whereas the identification of a pattern of Senecan references is a fine piece of scholarship, we might wonder if it quite catches the literary and philosophical flavour of the result. The 'Coustume' is more than the sum of its parts. It sets out citations for and against self-killing, but it also moves beyond them. A final section does not fit the rhetorical strategy of the first two: it forms neither a reply nor a conclusion. Yet it is much the longest part of the essay, and between the first printed edition of 1580 and the last of 1595, it doubled in length. The additions consist entirely of new examples, without any philosophical analysis. Moreover, Montaigne's interest in suicide goes way beyond the act itself. It seems as if modern readers cannot see beyond suicide as such: but for Montaigne, suicide is a subject inherently related to questions of human freedom. The Stoic context itself proclaims this: suicide in Seneca, and in the neo-Stoics of Renaissance Europe who read him as a model, is a form of resistance to tyranny, both in the political sense, of refusing to obey a ruler who acts against justice, and in the ethical, as a means of mastering the passions and thus acting within a personal rule of reason. Freedom for the Stoic is 'total independence of the person from all passions and all wrong desires'.[67] For Montaigne, this principle is so cardinal that it lies at the heart of his thinking. Death frees the human from mastery: it is a premonition of a final freedom of being. 'La premeditation de la mort, est premeditation de la liberté. Qui a apris à mourir, il a desapris à servir' he says in his essay on death in Book I.[68] Suicide is thus for Montaigne a highly specialized form of moral debate; not so much in the cliché of whether it is ever justifiable to take one's life, as in the more general question of in what sense human life is ever completely free. Yet Montaigne's thoughts on suicide do not suggest any easy resolution of this question. Montaigne's essay seemingly recedes into mystery: like death, it refuses summation.

---

[66] Plato, *Phaedo*, 62c; trans. David Gallop (Oxford: Clarendon Press, 1975), 6.

[67] Suzanne Bobzien, *Determinism and Freedom in Stoic Philosophy* (Oxford: Clarendon Press, 1998), 339.

[68] I.xix.88 ('Premeditation of death is premeditation of freedom. He who has learned how to die has unlearned how to be a slave'; Frame, p. 72).

THE DEATH OF SENECA

Writing backwards into history, it is within a twentieth-century construction that early modern arguments about suicide have been contained. Histories of suicide, unconsciously or not, place it within an epistemological category all of its own: an instinct outside our control, almost outside us. This is true both of sociological and psychoanalytic explanations of suicide, even though in other ways those methods seem opposite. 'From sin to insanity' goes the title of one recent book.[69] Alexander Murray, in his exhaustive study of medieval suicide, consciously marginalizes any cases where the act is described as being done in equanimity or joy: 'A wish to die can only result from the strongest negative impulses from life: loss, incapacity, failure and pain.'[70] Henry Fedden's demographic study purportedly proved suicide was on the up in the sixteenth century. All of his explanations, stereotyped as they are, assume that suicide is a depressive illness: the 'birth of melancholy', 'fascination with death', 'an obsession with the role of the individual', and finally, 'the depressing nature of the doctrines of Calvin'.[71] This last explanation appears everywhere: religious grief and melancholy, the tendency to despair, was turned by Calvinism into the figure of the 'depressive predestinarian'.[72] This was the subject of an influential book, *The Persecutory Imagination*, by John Stachniewski.[73]

We attempt to align early modern thinking with this history of liberating secularity. If Donne is a hesitant or even reluctant emancipator, clinging to the Christian framework even as he attempts to find freedom of conscience for the suicide, Montaigne in the *Apologie de Raimond Sebond* is a hero in this narrative of enlightenment. He plays with the idea of a natural theology, in which he imagines a religion of natural desires. If we believed in an eternal life in the same fashion as a philosophical principle, he speculates, we would have no fear of death. 'Je veux estre dissoult, dirions nous, et estre aveques Jesus-Christ' ('I would be dissolved, we would say, and be with Jesus Christ').[74] In this view of Montaigne, his sentiment

---

[69] *From Sin to Insanity: Suicide in Early Modern Europe*, ed. Jeffrey Watt (Ithaca, NY: Cornell University Press, 2004).

[70] Murray, *Suicide in the Middle Ages*, vol. i: *The Violent against Themselves* (Oxford: Oxford University Press, 1998), 9.

[71] Henry Fedden, *Suicide: A Social and Historical Study* (New York: Blom, 1972), 155–67.

[72] Sprott, *English Debate*, 48.

[73] *The Persecutory Imagination: English Puritanism and the Literature of Religious Despair* (Oxford: Clarendon Press, 1991).

[74] II.xii.465; Frame, p. 395.

gently mocks Christian belief in the immortality of the soul while assimilating it with a general desire for death. The essay on Cea briefly risks blasphemy in this regard: 'Je desire, dict Sainct Paul, estre dissoult, pour estre avec Jesus Christ' (II.iii.380).

What Montaigne himself thought in this way is open to dispute. He made no rigid distinction between classical and Christian approaches to death. In the 1588 edition of the *Essais*, Montaigne interpolated next to his reference to Christ a long quotation from Lucretius, Book III, in line with a habit he shows elsewhere not only in the 'Apologie' but in the 'Coustume de l'Isle de Cea': *Non iam se moriens dissolvi conquereretur* ('He would not now complaine to be dissolved dying').[75] All through these works, he cites Seneca in the *Epistulae ad Lucilium* expressing the view that a death instinct is universal. Montaigne's frequent comments on preparedness for death easily align what now are taken to be the contrary forces of religion and secularity. In this respect, the topic of suicide is central. For contrary to a modern view of suicide as a form of mental disorder and pathological instinct, suicide in early modern thought raises fundamental issues about freedom and agency.

What, then are the lineaments of an early modern view of suicide that is not constructed as part of a narrative of secular emancipation and the history of a neurosis? To gain a sense of Montaigne's context it is possible to compare a contemporary and at least superficially very similar argument in Justus Lipsius. The 'Coustume de l'Isle de Cea', in its initial form, can be attributed to the earliest phase of Montaigne's writing, 1572–4.[76] In a letter of 1575, Lipsius asked, *Mentem enim istam liberam quis tyrannus mihi artat?* ('What tyrant constrains this free mind of mine?')[77] His answer came in the form of a Greek Stoic epigram: 'Who is slave when he is scornful of death?', citing a series of ancient political suicides: Socrates, Seneca himself, Helvidius. Aristotle discussed whether a person constrained by a tyrant can truly be said to act 'voluntarily'.[78] *Libertas* indeed in Roman thought was a negative concept—the opposite of being a *servus* and thus enslaved.[79] Both in this and a related letter Lipsius discussed suicide as a defence of the idea of *libertas* or 'freedom'.[80] In this way he made

---

[75] II.xii.465; see the 'Coustume', II.iii.371, 372.

[76] Villey, *Les Sources et l'évolution des Essais*, ii. 158.

[77] *Iusti Lipsii Epistolarum selectarum chilias* (Cologne: Antonius Meraldus, 1616), 4; Cent. I, Epistola IV, Gerarto Falkenburgio, 1575 (1 August 1575).

[78] *Nicomachean Ethics*, 1110ᵃ; ed. J. Bywater (Oxford: Clarendon Press, 1975), 40.

[79] Matthew B. Roller, *Constructing Autocracy: Aristocrats and Emperors in Julio-Claudian Rome* (Princeton: Princeton University Press, 2001), 220.

[80] Cent. II, Ep. XXII, Petro Regemortero.

suicide exemplary of the Stoic political ethic: for 'liberty, the freedom attained by the individual by submitting to reason, is in effect the cornerstone of Neostoic psychology and ethics'.[81] The self that is free is beyond the influence of fortune, or his own passions, or subjection to the external tyranny of the ruler. He takes possession of himself and thus constitutes his own world. In this, his choice whether to live or die is the final test of freedom.

Lipsius' researches into Tacitus led him to many examples of ancient suicide in the face of tyranny, his personal favourite being Publius Clodius Thrasea who opposed Nero to the point of self-inflicted death. The point to make here is that suicide appears in humanist thought primarily as a political argument.[82] This goes back to the way that freedom in classical Stoic thought is an 'internalization of a social and political reality'.[83] Suicide sets the limits to tyranny by giving the individual a right which cannot be reached by tyranny: the right to decide whether to endure such a life.[84] Lipsius constructs suicide as a defence of political subjectivity as defined by its own sovereignty of autonomy. If a man can overcome his last final attachment to the passions and control even the fear of death, he is a free agent. In the last decades of the sixteenth century this appears to be the standard position on suicide in late humanism. It is in this context that Montaigne declares 'À mourir il ne reste que le vouloir', and not one of morbid anxiety. 'Le vivre, c'est servir, si la liberté de mourir en est à dire' ('Life is slavery, if the freedom to die is wanting', II.iii.369; Frame, p. 306), he quotes from Seneca.[85] This is also the immediate context for understanding Hamlet's soliloquy. Freedom from the tyranny of Claudius' corruption ('Something is rotten in the state of Denmark') gives him self-mastery.

Lipsius discussed suicide at some length here and on several other occasions: briefly in the classic *De Constantia* of 1584, and substantially in a pair of chapters in the later *Manuductio ad Stoicam philosophiam*. Indeed, he planned a whole monograph on suicide, a promised sequel to

---

[81] Freya Sierhuis, 'Autonomy and Inner Freedom in Early Modern England: Lipsius and the Revival of Stoicism', in Quentin Skinner and Martin van Gelderen (eds.), *Freedom and the Construction of Europe: New Perspectives on Religious, Philosophical and Political Controversies* (Cambridge: Cambridge University Press, 2013).

[82] Mark Morford, *Stoics and Neostoics: Rubens and the Circle of Lipsius* (Princeton: Princeton University Press, 1991), 150–1.

[83] Brad Inwood, 'Seneca on Freedom and Autonomy', collected in *Reading Seneca: Stoic Philosophy at Rome* (Oxford: Clarendon Press, 2005), 303.

[84] Richard Sorabji, *Emotion and Peace of Mind: From Stoic Agitation to Christian Temptation* (Oxford: Oxford University Press, 2000), 214.

[85] *Ep.* LXXVII (ii. 176).

De Constantia, in a dialogue entitled *Thrasea sive de contemptu mortis* ('Thrasea or the contempt of death'), for which there is an incomplete draft plan in manuscript. Lipsius thus outlines the full humanist case on suicide. He refers to Pythagoras and Protagoras as well as Plato, to Epictetus and the Latin Stoics as well as later collections such as Diogenes Laertius. Together they form a kind of Stoic humanist poetic anthology of suicides that is clearly generally dispersed. As well as his treatises, Lipsius showed his fascination with the topic in his edition of Seneca, which included as a frontispiece an engraving of Seneca in the act of committing suicide; Rubens was one of the artists.

Is Montaigne in 'Coustume de l'Isle de Cea' a neo-Stoic, and is he encouraging us to be one? One way of reading the text certainly leads us that way. Or is Montaigne just playing the Stoic, and agitating us into some further more troubling reflection? Does he, like Lipsius, see the ideal citizen as a man who acts according to reason, is answerable to himself, is in control of his emotions, and is ready to go to war for the right cause; and does he think of the suicide as conforming to this example, even as representing it (in Jan Papy's paraphrase in his study of Lipsius as a Christian stoic) as the 'affirmation *par excellence* of liberty'?[86] Perhaps this seems too extreme a phrasing. Yet at least in the case of Seneca, the idealization of suicide as an act of freedom as a proof test of individual autonomy is of critical importance. For John Rist this indeed makes Seneca an aberration in relation to the mainstream of Stoic thought. Seneca's wise man is 'in love with death', Rist says.[87] But for Miriam Griffin this trivializes Seneca's philosophical seriousness on suicide, and at the same time underestimates its importance to the concept of freedom. Suicide is the ultimate proof of autopragia, 'self-determination'.[88] 'Are you asking for the road to freedom?', Seneca asks in *De ira*; 'Take any vein you like in your body'.[89] While in the main, Seneca uses suicide as a philosophical account of what we might call a last resort in the face of overwhelming suffering or else as an answer to remorseless despotism, he also makes of suicide the most elegant proof of human autonomy. I can choose whether to live or die,

---

[86] Jan Papy, 'Lipsius's Stoic Reflections on the Pale Face of Death: From Stoic Constancy and Liberty to Suicide and Rubens's Dying Seneca', *LIAS: Journal of Early Modern Intellectual Culture and its Sources*, 37.1 (2010), 35–53, this ref. p. 45.

[87] *Stoic Philosophy* (Cambridge: Cambridge University Press, 1969), 249.

[88] *Seneca: A Philosopher in Politics*, 379.

[89] *Quaeris quod sit ad libertatem iter? Quaelibet in corpore tuo vena*; *De ira*, III.xv.3, Seneca, *Moral Essays*, ed. and trans. John Basore, Loeb Classical Library, 3 vols. (London: Heinemann, 1928–35), i. 294 (quoted here in the translation of John Procopé, cited in Inwood, *Reading Seneca*, 310).

therefore I am. In that sense suicide is the most fundamental confirmation of human agency.[90]

This argument enables us to see Montaigne both as a kind of neo-Stoic, and yet not in any simple sense a Lipsian neo-Stoic. But perhaps it is also too easy to use Lipsius as Montaigne's straight man. Lipsius himself deviates from the classic account of suicide in Seneca in an important sense as well. Indeed, the *Manuductio* shows that Lipsius' method and argument in relation to suicide is not at all simple. Suicide occupies the last two chapters of Book III, the culmination of twenty chapters of what Lipsius calls the Stoic 'Paradoxes'. The *paradoxa* represents for Lipsius a formal demonstration of truth by means of rhetoric: what appears improbable or even logically impossible is revealed to be the truest form of reality. The Stoic wise man can appear to be enslaved but is a king in reality; he can have no money but be rich, he can suffer life's worst tragedies and yet be happy, inside himself. That is, his wisdom does not concur with external forces or values, but has subjective validity. In his own self he is always free. At first it seems as if suicide is the ultimate test of truth as *paradoxa*. In the final reckoning, a wise man demonstrates his own liberty in life by taking his own life away.

The wise man (in the Senecan cliché) lives as long as he ought not as long as he can. Taking one's own life is reasonable on behalf of one's country, or friends, or if one is suffering intolerable pain or an incurable disease. We remember all this material from Montaigne. Yet at this point, Lipsius' argument is overtaken by a different sense of 'paradox'. First, and uniquely in this part of the *Manuductio*, he finishes his argument with a citation that appears to undercut what has gone before. Plato at the end of the *Laws*, he recalls, says that a man who kills himself when he is not ordered to by the state, or when he is not compelled by some intolerable misfortune, so that he is beyond remedy or endurance—such a death Plato calls a kind of 'sloth and unmanly cowardice'.[91] Even more strikingly, the next chapter begins with a straightforward question addressed to Lipsius as part of his dialogue form: *Heus tu, an non aliquid inclinas?* ('Alas, do you not somewhat incline to the argument for suicide'). Lipsius replies: *Absit: respuo*, as if to say, 'God forbid'.[92] It is a unique moment of recoil in Lipsius, a self-rejection, a turn on the self in defiance of his own

---

[90] On the importance to Seneca of suicide for an argument concerning agency, see Inwood, *Reading Seneca*, 312.

[91] Plato, *Laws*, IX.873D; trans. Bury, ii. 267.

[92] *Iusti Lipsii Manuductionis ad Stoicam philosophiam libri tres* (Antwerp: Officina Plantiniana, 1604), 204.

logic. The moment of repentance is forced out of him, as it were, by Christian conscience; Lipsius had returned to the Catholic church in 1591. Yet as well as quoting Augustine's denunciation of Stoic suicide, in which Augustine equates suicide with murder, Lipsius also quotes liberally from Stoic sources against suicide. The assumption that it is Augustine who provides the antidote to suicide in early modern thought may have been exaggerated; alternatively, Lipsius may wish to downplay the problematic heritage of Christian thought in this context.

This may explain the complexity of Montaigne's essay. It is a mistake to think that it is Christian censorship which is the cause of his philosophical uncertainty in relation to suicide. Scepticism in Montaigne reaches much further than this, it is the centre of his writing style, and more than that, a kind of form of life. Perhaps our rush to create a simple divide between Christianity and scepticism also makes us underestimate Lipsius' capacity for ambiguity. Lipsius was a careful reader of Montaigne; he surely noted 'Coustume de l'Isle de Cea' in writing the *Manuductio*.[93] This essay, as we have seen, creates a montage of examples and arguments about suicide, yet it also casts the reader adrift on this sea of allusion, by taking away the reference points for the citations. It gives almost no indication of its formal logic. Citations in favour of suicide are given no heading or analysis or even synopsis, or any framing warnings. We follow blithely a chain of references to our own mortality and voluntarism, until the chain abruptly stops, with the words, in mid-paragraph: 'Mais cecy ne s'en va pas sans contraste'.[94] The argument then slips into reverse gear, as it were, but without telling us; until once again this thread of thinking also closes, with the barest announcement, 'Entre ceux du premier advis, il y a eu grand doubte' (II.iii.372; 'Among those of the first opinion there has been much doubt', Frame, p. 309). In both directions, the transition is both abrupt and concealed. It is as if Montaigne is thinking aloud.

He goes first this way, and then that, he tacks back and forth, as if improvising his way along. We are reminded of his description of his own writing style in 'De la vanité': 'nonchalant et fortuit'.[95] Yet there is philosophical method here as well as literary grace. In the 'Apologie de Sebond' he gave an indication of a perfect kind of argument, if he had 'the health, and enough leisure':

---

[93] Jeanine De Landtsheer, 'Montaigne en Lipsius', in Paul J. Smith (ed.), *Een Ridder van groot oordel: Montaigne in Leiden* (Leiden: Universiteitsbibliotheek Leiden, 2005), 39–66.
[94] II.iii.370; 'This does not pass without contradiction', Frame, p. 307.
[95] *Essais*, III.ix.1041 ('casual and accidental', Frame, p. 925).

pour ramasser en un registre, selon leurs divisions et leurs classes, sincere-
ment et curieusement, autant que nous y pouvons voir, les opinions de
l'ancienne philosophie sur le subject de nostre estre et de nos moeurs, leurs
controverses, le credit et suitte des pars, l'application de la vie des autheurs
et sectateurs, à leurs preceptes, ès accidens memorables et exemplaires! (II.
xii.614)

to compile into a register, according to their divisions and classes, as honestly
and carefully as we can understand them, the opinions of ancient philosophy
on the subject of our being and our conduct; their controversies, the credit and
the sequence of the schools, the relations of the lives of the authors and followers to their precepts on memorable and exemplary occasions. (Frame, p. 529)

His ideal writer for such a project would be, he affirms, Justus Lipsius.
'Coustume de l'Isle de Cea' is an example of this kind of ideal of writing,
taken to an extreme form.

Why is this? It has to do with the very subject matter in hand. The
subject of Montaigne's enquiry shifts from suicide as an affirmation of
political freedom to a more puzzling and insoluble question of what it is
to want something, and what it is to do something. In this sense the essay
goes beyond mere 'paradox'.[96] This is the occasion of his third and longest
section, which is also the most confusing. It abandons argument and Stoic
sententiousness, quoting from Seneca and other authorities much less
readily, and instead allowing human stories to speak for themselves. At
times it is pure narration, a novelistic delight in oddness of detail or circumstance. There is an extreme attention in particular to what we might
call narrative syntax, to how events fall out. Montaigne lumps examples
(what in the 'Apologie de Sebond' he calls 'accidens memorables et exemplaires', II.xii.614) together, making a kind of accidental writing through
attention to exemplary storytelling. In the process he makes his argument
subject to the accidentality of life. 'Coustume de l'Isle de Cea' is above all
a study in voluntarism. This is a key point in what I am calling his coun-
ter-attack on the idea of the sovereign subject. Suicide appears to make
the self free to make its own destiny, to choose its own state. Montaigne
first encourages us to believe in this idea of sovereignty, as Lipsius does;
but then in a second move he undercuts the very idea that he has nur-
tured. Freedom of the will is sacrosanct; but freedom is not quite what it
looks like. Felicity Green has recently argued that as well as the idea of
liberty as freedom from external constraints or the interference of external
agents, Montaigne constructs a more personal ideal of freedom as 'lacheté',

---

[96] McGowan, *Montaigne's Deceits*, 73.

or 'carelessness': the self disengages itself from perturbation.[97] But it needs to be stressed that this second form of liberty is much less under voluntary control than the first. Both the will, and the idea of the voluntary, are prone to many forces at once, and not all of them are we in any position to have cognitive power over.

The death of Cato, described in 'De la cruauté', presents at first an image of the Stoic as hero:

> Quand je le voy mourir et se deschirer les entrailles, je ne me puis contenter, de croire simplement, qu'il eust lors son ame exempte totalement de trouble et d'effroy: je ne puis croire, qu'il se maintint seulement en cette desmarche, que les regles de la secte Stoïque luy ordonnoient, rassise, sans esmotion et impassible: il y avoit, ce me semble, en la vertu de cet homme, trop de gaillardise et de verdeur, pour s'en arrester là. Je croy sans doubte qu'il sentit du plaisir et de la volupté, en une si noble action, et qu'il s'y aggrea plus qu'en autre de celles de sa vie. (II.xi.445)

> When I see him dying and tearing out his entrails, I cannot be content to believe simply that he then had his soul totally free from disturbance and fright; I cannot believe that he merely maintained himself in the attitude that the rules of the Stoic sect ordained for him, sedate, without emotion, and impassible; there was, it seems to me, in that man's virtue too much lustiness and verdancy to stop there. I believe without any doubt that he felt pleasure and bliss in so noble an action, and that he enjoyed himself more in it than in any other action of his life. (Frame, p. 374)

Cato was not only free from fear, he embraced death with joy and willingness. He undertook the action for the beauty of the thing in itself. Starobinski comments on this, 'In committing suicide, Cato sets his own limit and gives proof of absolute possession. His entire being is in his hands, within his reach and at his mercy' (p. 71). We are reminded here of Sartre's use of suicide as a proof of the inviolability of human freedom. But is death in Montaigne existential in this sense? Even in his narrative of Cato, Montaigne expresses some perplexity. This is shown only in a mirror, through his astonishment at Cato's language of the emotions. None of this narrative is presented straightforwardly; it is mediated through the awkward interpretative matrix of Montaigne's uncertainty: 'je ne me puis contenter, de croire simplement'; 'je ne puis croire'; 'il y avoit, ce me semble' (p. 403). This culminates in Montaigne's reverse expression of exaggerated certainty: 'Je croy sans doubte qu'il sentit du plaisir et de la volupté, en une si noble action, et qu'il s'y aggrea plus qu'en autre de celles de sa vie'.

---

[97] 'Freedom and Self-Possession in Montaigne's *Essais*', in Skinner and van Gelderen (eds.), *Freedom and the Construction of Europe*.

We know from 'Des boyteux' that these syntactic reservations, 'je ne puis croire', 'je croy sans doubte', these nervous tics of Montaigne's style, are not there by accident:

> J'aime ces mots, qui amollissent et moderent la temerité de nos proposi-
> tions: à l'avanture, aucunement, quelque, on dit, je pense, et semblables: Et
> si j'eusse eu à dresser des enfans, je leur eusse tant mis en la bouche, cette
> façon de respondre: enquestente, non resolutive: Qu'est-ce à dire? je ne
> l'entens pas; il pourroit estre: est-il vray? (III.xi.1076)

> I like these words, which soften and moderate the rashness of our propositions:
> 'perhaps', 'to some extent', 'some', 'they say', 'I think' and the like. And if I had
> to train children, I would have filled their mouths so much with this way of
> answering, inquiring, not decisive—'What does that mean? I do not under-
> stand it. That might be. Is it true?' (Frame, p. 959)

More than a habit of style, these are representations of the perplexity inherent in experience. No experience comes to us unmediated. We trust to our senses ('Les sens sont nos propres et premiers juges, qui n'apperçoivent les choses que par les accidens externes').[98] But even our senses are at one remove: they need interpreting. His hesitation at the death of Cato respects the gulf of imagination which lies between his own experience and that of another. He cannot enter Cato's mind, even as he attempts to imagine it. Cato kills himself in an eruption of self-violence which causes Montaigne to shudder, even if it is a shudder of warped admiration. Starobinski in translating this into an ethical proposition, the 'proof of absolute possession', does a kind of violence in turn to Montaigne's strict sense of ethical refusal. Cato's suicide is precisely beyond his own experience. He can only stare in wonder at other human lives: the peculiar suffering (or for that matter the peculiar joy or rapture) that leads another human being to suicide.

No death raises this question more acutely than the death of Seneca. Seneca's end is such a cliché of Stoic moral philosophy that it is hard to rescue it from the banality of gruesome parody. This is, perhaps, the effect of the pseudo-objectivity rendered in Rubens's festival of incision and blood-letting in his second version of the episode (Fig. 16), the oil paint-ing now in the Alte Pinakothek in Munich. Montaigne approaches it al-together more obliquely. The account comes not in 'Coustume de l'Isle de Cea' but in 'Des trois bonnes femmes'. It is not Seneca's narrative at all: but that of his wife. It is through the lens of her courage and fortitude, and her empathy with her husband, that we approach Seneca, the Stoic master, himself.

---

[98] 'De l'art de conferer', III.viii.975.

Après avoir dit ces paroles en commun, il se destourne à sa femme, et l'embrassant estroittement, comme par la pesanteur de la douleur elle def-failloit de coeur et de forces, la pria de porter un peu plus patiemment cet accident, pour l'amour de luy; et que l'heure estoit venue, où il avoit à mon-trer, non plus par discours et par disputes, mais par effect; le fruict qu'il avoit tiré de ses estudes: et que sans doubte il embrassoit la mort, non seulement sans douleur, mais avecques allegresse. (II.xxxv.786)

After having spoken these words to all, he turned to his wife and, embracing her tightly, since her heart and strength were giving way under the weight of her grief, asked her to bear this accident a little more patiently for the love of him, and said that the time had come when he had to show, no longer by arguments and discus-sion but by action, the profit that he had derived from his studies, and that he really embraced death not only without sorrow but cheerfully. (Frame, p. 687)

After this seemingly conventional opening of the loving encounter be-tween the hero and his wife in the face of death, Montaigne's narrative is full of strange turns, however. Paulina offers, beautifully, to die with him: 'et quand le pourroy-je ny mieux, ny plus honnestement, ny plus à mon gré qu'avecques vous?' (II.xxxv.786; 'when could I do so either better or more honourably or more to my own desire, than with you?', Frame, p. 687). Now the scene unfolds, retold from Tacitus' familiar account in *Annals*, graphically represented in Rubens.[99] The veins of both their arms are cut, so that they will bleed to death. Yet the narrative is radically trans-posed from Tacitus by a change in point of view. Tacitus gives us a picture of Seneca in complete control of his circumstances. In Montaigne, this control slips. The incisions do not work; he has to ask his doctor to inter-vene and give him poison to help the process along. Does the presence of these assistants in some way ambiguate the act of suicide?

'Des trois bonnes femmes' subtly rewrites the genre of the Stoic suicide narrative. Thrasea, who in Lipsius is the very topos of the virtuous man, is reduced to a bit part in a story which makes his wife the protagonist. In a savage episode she hits her own head against a wall until she is nearly unconscious. Thrasea's suicide is made an afterthought:

Et en mesme instant, s'en estant donné un coup mortel dans l'estomach, et puis l'arrachant de sa playe, elle le luy presenta, finissant quant et quant sa vie. (II.xxxv.784)

And at the same moment, having given herself a fatal blow in the stomach and then torn the dagger out of her wound, she presented it to him, at the same time ending her life. (Frame, p. 686)

---

[99] *Annales*, XV.lxii–lxv; ed. and trans. J. Jackson, Loeb Classical Library, 4 vols. (London: Heinemann, 1962), iv. 314–20.

Fig 16. Rubens, *Death of Seneca* (*c.*1610); oil on panel.

It is to Thrasea's wife that Montaigne attributes the political philosophy that makes suicide the last bulwark against tyranny and slavery. Thrasea seems meek in comparison. In a similar way, Montaigne's narrator supplies a philosophical coda to Seneca's story, giving it a neo-Stoic gloss, but introduces by means of the coda a sly counter-narrative running against Seneca, as if implying he was too fond of living:

> En ce dernier couple, cela est encore digne d'estre consideré, que Paulina offre volontiers à quitter la vie pour l'amour de son mary, et que son mary

avoit autre-fois quitté aussi la mort pour l'amour d'elle. Il n'y a pas pour nous grand contre-poix en cet eschange: mais selon son humeur Stoïque, je croy qu'il pensoit avoir autant faict pour elle, d'alonger sa vie en sa faveur, comme s'il fust mort pour elle.

In regard to this last couple, this too is worthy of consideration: that Paulina willingly offers to give up life for the love of her husband, and that her husband had once also given up death for the love of her. For us there is not a very even balance in this exchange; but from his Stoic attitude, I believe he thought he had done as much for her in prolonging his life for her sake as if he had died for her. (Frame, p. 689)

It is Paulina who is the hero of this story of 'Des trois bonnes femmes', not the masculine virtue displayed in Tacitus and in Lipsius. The story is translated from Seneca's perspective to Paulina's; or rather the reader learns to see things from her point of view rather than his. Yet the act of empathy is incomplete. We cannot finally enter her state of mind. She resists us, and never more so than in choosing death. 'La mort volontaire' is a mystery, not only in its motivations, but also in the radical uncertainty it renders in relation to other human minds and hearts. Montaigne constantly changes tack in his essays on suicide; often merely by a juxtaposition of narratives, without moral annotation or sententious comment of his own. The change of view comes in the silence provided by a citation from a classical source, a moral dictum or a fragment of verse, as if he becomes lost in thought. He sees what another says, but he gives no endorsement. The experience of Seneca is beyond him. Paradoxically, this happens most clearly at the end of the essay, as he quotes a whole paragraph from the *Epistulae ad Lucilium*.[100] Listening to the voice of Seneca from beyond the grave only leaves us full of questions: whether he or his wife is the braver; or whether the desire for life is weaker than the desire for death. Oddest of all, it seems as if Seneca mourns with longing for life even as he chooses death.

VOLUNTARY DEATH

Self-killing raises the question of self-reflection in the most acute way, in such a way indeed that cuts out any other viewpoint but that of the self. This is true in specific ways, which can be seen in the intricate heart of

---

[100] *Ep.* CIV.1–2 (iii. 190–1).

Hamlet's language. The first goes back to the reflexive form of 'self-slaughter':

> HAM. O that this too too sullied flesh would melt,
> Thaw and resolve itself into a dew,
> Or that the Everlasting had not fix'd
> His canon 'gainst self–slaughter. (1.2.129–32)

This form is also used by Imogen in *Cymbeline* as she contemplates the necessity of her own death.[101]

The self comes into being in the grammar of reflexive language. This is present but occluded in the Latinate form 'sui-'. Jerrold Seigel has commented in his history of the philosophy of selfhood how in most European languages, such as 'the self' in English and 'das Selbst' in German, the abstract noun for the concept is derived from a grammatical form.[102] But the word 'self' as a noun is a late seventeenth-century invention, first found frequently in Locke; as with other pre-modern languages, English made do at an earlier stage with a purely grammatical language with which to confront problems of the self. This can be seen in that peculiar subset of actions which a person does *to herself*. Suicide above all, in the recognition of the mortal self, brings an intense concentration on the agency of the person. The modern inclination to see Hamlet's suicide in terms of a disorder, of a pathological desire to do something which comes from some psychological reservoir so deep inside himself that he does not recognize it as his own action, is highly misleading in this context. Suicide in Hamlet does not deflect attention away from voluntary agency, and towards some form of pathological compulsion, but precisely back towards it.

The other question raised intensely by 'self-murder' in *Hamlet* is one of necessity versus freedom. It may be that the most important word in Hamlet's most famous line is the one that is least commented on: 'or'. This most unnoticed of conjunctions contains within it a metaphysical grammar of incalculable consequence. What most troubles Hamlet about the question of being is the fact that it is a question at all: there is an alternative. But it is a choice which only comes into operation at the moment of death. No person has the choice about whether 'to be': by definition, a person already *is*, and her birth now lies in a prehistory beyond her choice. But in death, choice comes (paradoxically) into being: non-existence is revealed as an alternative state.

---

[101] 'Against self–slaughter | There is a prohibition so divine | That cravens my weak hand' (3.4.77–9).
[102] *Idea of the* Self, 13.

Suicide in neo-Stoic thinking is a final proof-test for human autonomy, for a subjectivity that is sovereign.[103] Self-control is subject to no external constraint. This form of political suicide is present in Hamlet, maybe in some of Hamlet's soliloquies, and certainly in Horatio's unfulfilled promise to follow Hamlet to the grave. It is also beautifully captured by Cleopatra after the death of Antony:

> CLEO. We'll bury him; and then, what's brave, what's noble,
> Let's do it after the high Roman fashion,
> And make death proud to take us. Come, away.

Yet in Montaigne's version there is also equally a sense of suicide as setting the limits to human subjectivity, revealing the transience and contingency of selfhood. Montaigne moves beyond Seneca, even as he quotes him: 'À mourir il ne reste que le vouloir'. For what does it mean to 'want' death? To wish to die is not quite the same as to wish no longer to live. At the same time, it is not possible, logically, to choose life. Life is not something in my control or at my command. I am alive by virtue of the fact that I was born. It is not something I ever asked for or willed into being. By contrast, I can choose not to live. But can I choose death, exactly? Is death something I can *do* (like eating apples, opening a door)? Death is a negative quality: the absence of life. And yet: I cannot exactly choose not to live, in the sense that it takes more than an effort of will. I can't close my eyes and think to myself, now I die. I have to kill myself, or persuade someone else to kill me, in order no longer to live.

This is what haunts Donne's account of martyrdom in *Biathanatos*; death does not come upon the martyr, so much as the martyr seeks death. Christ sacrificed his own life and so provided such a death as the model. For the early church, the eschatological proximity of death created a culture in which voluntary death seemed the only way out for the body of Christian believers:

> So heaven had no doore from this world but by fires, Crosses, and bloody persecutions: And presuming Heaven to be at the next step, they would often stubbornly, or stupidly winke, and so make that one step. (Sullivan, p. 56)

How, then, could martyrdom be explained but as a form of 'a disease of this naturall desire of such a death'? Yet such an argument only placed the more burden on the question of what 'voluntary' death might be.

---

[103] Inwood, *Reading Seneca*, 316.

Suicide relies upon a strong test of intentionality in law, shown in a second model from *Hamlet*, what we might call the Ophelia complex. Ophelia appears to commit suicide but the detail of the evidence is not so clear. A branch she is lying on falls from a tree, and she fails to save herself, 'As one incapable of her owne distresse'. Is that self-murder, or death by accident, or misadventure? Many of Montaigne's examples hinge on this uncertainty, making the relationship between the desire and will of the agent and the circumstances of the agent's action extremely difficult to interpret. I can will something, and the opposite happens; or the thing I wanted happens, but not at all because of me wanting it or putting my will into action. This applies both to our best wishes and to our worst fears. 'Et puis y ayant tant de soudains changemens aux choses humaines, il est malaisé à juger, à quel poinct nous sommes justement au bout de nostre esperance' (II.iii.373; 'And then, there being so many sudden changes in human affairs, it is hard to judge, just at what point we are at the end of our hope', Frame, p. 310). A Sicilian, to escape being conquered by the Turks, first kills his daughters, then runs into the midst of his enemies, assuring his death (II.iii.374). Nicanor in the Bible runs himself through with his own sword, but it does not work; so he falls off a high building hoping to complete the job (II.iii.375). As Montaigne puts it, borrowing from Augustine, it seems to him 'que la force soit meslée à quelque volonté' ('force meets with a certain willingness').[104] His heroes rush to death or await it patiently, but in the end death must come to them and not they to death, since death itself is not finally an action or event within our control.

We do not, it appears, finally own our own stories. Even at the moment of decision in taking charge of our own destiny, something else intervenes. Montaigne plays constantly on the activity or passivity of an action, on just what it means to be the agent of one's own actions. And this is also, I think, the point of Donne's strange beginning to *Biathanatos*. Modern eyes fall on Donne's self-description of his 'sickely inclination' to death, but just as intriguing is the presence in the first sentence of the celebrated Calvinist theologian, Theodore Beza. Beza, he says, escaped death by the skin of his teeth, moreover, in a strange concept, he escaped his own suicide. The incidental details of this story—a chance encounter with an uncle, a morbid anxiety about a skin disease, the geographical specificity of the 'Millers bridge' (the ancient ramshackle Pont-aux-Meuniers, a wooden inhabited construction with thirty to fifty houses on two

---

[104] II.iii.375, Frame, p. 312; cf. *De civitate Dei*, I.xxv and xxvi.

storeys, not unlike old London Bridge, nowadays replaced by the Pont-au-Change just by Châtelet)—all of these things invite the reader into a reverie of imaginative sympathy. Yet this beguiling narrative style has perhaps precisely inhibited readers from asking the question that may be the key not only to this passage, but to the work as a whole. Why, in this introduction to suicide, does Donne choose as his main character the *doctor profundus*, perhaps the *doctor fundementalis* of Calvinist predestination, Beza?

Theodore Beza, as the hardest of hardliners, is the unlikeliest of sources for such a story. Indeed, this is part of the shock of Donne's opening. However obscure to a modern reader, Beza is a sensational choice. There is, though, a literary source for the Parisian anecdote cited in the margin of *Biathanatos*, 'Epistola ante confessionem'. It is part of a long Latin letter addressed to Melchior Wolmar, the Swiss humanist and Hellenist who taught Greek to Calvin as well as Beza in Orléans.[105] The letter contains extended autobiographical references, including the only surviving record of his childhood, and is confessional in more than one sense.[106] Beza placed it very self-consciously at the head of his *Confessio christianae fidei* in 1558. Subsequently it was reprinted in his theological *summa*, the *Tractationes theologicae* of 1570. The letter was therefore highly visible among the best known and most reprinted of all of the Calvinist master's works.

The boy Theodore suffered from an infectious skin rash and even more from the violent remedies applied by the doctors, which, he says to Wolmar, he still trembles to recall thirty years later. Theodore was sent each day with his cousin, a little older than himself, from his uncle's home on the Left Bank to cross the Seine to the doctor's residence near the Louvre. Passing over the Pont-aux-Meuniers, the cousin suggests to Theodore a desperate remedy: 'we can't take any more of this suffering. Let's throw ourselves in the water by the bridge.' Is it a death wish or a youthful dare? At first Theodore refuses, but then he promises his cousin one day to follow him into the water. He approaches the appointed day with trepidation as if it is a day of execution; they arrive at the bank and watch the river, slow and yellow, beneath them. Between the motion and the act lies the shadow. Completely out of the blue, crossing from another street, the uncle turns up. He realizes exactly what the boys have in mind, returns with them straight back to his house, and arranges in future for the surgeon to pay home visits.

---

[105] Paul-F. Geisendorf, *Théodore de Bèze* (Geneva: Alexandre Julien, 1967), 5–9, discusses the authenticity of the letter as the sole source for Beza's early life.
[106] On Wolmar, see Geisendorf, *Bèze*, 10–11.

In his letter to Wolmar, Beza leaves no doubt how to interpret his story. His deliverance by his uncle is the direct intervention of divine providence. At moments like this, he says, we feel the firm hand of God's goodness leading us away from the temptations of the devil, even though our own will would willingly follow the wrong way. So does this context clear up Donne's citation of it a generation later? Hardly. In fact, what we notice immediately is that he makes the citation entirely *against the grain* of its origin. Beza is horrified at the thought of self-slaughter; God has provided a remedy for it by a gratuitous interruption of human will. God cannot allow himself to stand by, and will not let his servant take his own life.

There is no such providential narrative in Donne. God does not intervene, indeed he is not present. In Beza's text of *Confessio christianae fidei* which follows the letter, almost immediately there is an articulation of the doctrine of predestination in its developed Calvinist form. I quote from the English translation which first appeared in about 1565: 'NOthing is done at auenture or by chaunce, or without the most iust ordinaunce and appointment of God'.[107] In Beza, then, there is an explicit denial of the existence of the concept of chance. In Donne, however, his uncle only arrives 'by chance'. Far from the clarity and unambiguity of doctrine in the *Confessio*, Donne confesses to suspecting 'a perplexitie and flexibility in the doctrine it selfe'. Whereas Beza's God 'sustaineth and gouerneth all according to his eternal prouidence, by his infinite and substaunciall power', Donne, by contrast, finds in the imagination of his own death that 'mee thinks I have the keyes of my prison in mine owne hand'. Rather than predestination, no event could show to him more clearly the potentiality, and at the same time restrictedness, of human free will. Beza's luck, rather like Hamlet's luck in the last chapter, is a revelation of the complexity of human circumstance and human agency.

Outlandish as Beza's brief autobiography may seem, there are enough references to the suicide of distinguished Protestant theologians as to constitute a literary topos. These circulated, mainly orally, for several decades after the first generation of Protestant leaders began to die in the 1540s. Tommaso Bozio, the Oratorian and controversialist, collected together a number of these rumours in *De signis ecclesiae* in 1591.[108] Luther had hanged himself using a sheet tied to his bed-post. This story was repeated by the Franciscan Sedulius in 1606, in a book to which Lipsius also con-

---

[107] *A briefe and piththie summe of the Christian faith made in forme of a confession, vvith a confutation of all such superstitious errours, as are contrary therevnto. Made by Theodore de Beza. Translated out of Frenche by R.F.* (London: Richard Serll, [1565?]), 4.
[108] *De signis ecclesiae*, 2 vols. (Rome: Ascanio, 1591), ii. 514.

tributed.[109] Johannes Oecolampadius is mentioned by Bozio in the same paragraph as another suicide by strangulation. Indeed, Calvin is also added to this list: not as a suicide as such, but as having died a very bad death, leaving the world in desperation and misery, unreconciled with God.

The circumstances of Luther's death were fought over almost as soon as he died; Melanchthon's account of Moses leaving the earth in earnest prayer was quickly disputed by Cochlaeus in 1549, who satirized Protestant attempts at hagiography. Cochlaeus, however, recounted a version in which Luther died in the living room on a leather bench, not in bed; when the suicide story circulated, the leather bench was triumphantly exposed by Protestants defending their master. For the life of Oecolampadius printed in 1592 along with that of Zwingli, Capito commissioned Simon Grynaeus to answer the charge of suicide in detail.[110]

Perhaps these quarrels appear a little unseemly, but they conceal a theological debate which repositions the reference to Beza in Donne. For the calumny of the deaths of the Reformers is not just aimed at denigrating opponents or disputing their piety. It takes us straight to the centre of Reformed theology, to its insistence on the grace that is certified for the elect and the experience of assurance that is said to accompany it. It is this which makes the idea of suicide so powerful in relation to Luther, Calvin, or Beza. Bozio makes Calvin's despair on leaving life the final proof of the emptiness of the Calvinist doctrine of certainty of salvation. Despair is the phenomenological contradiction of certainty.

Beza, Donne asserts, was on the point of throwing himself into the Seine as a young child, 'if his Uncle by chance had not then come that way'. Suicide, we know, is only suicide when it can be shown that we intended to die by our own action; but what does it mean when we have the intention but the act is not fulfilled? The desire for death places the contingency of life ever in view. And so, like Hamlet's, 'To be or not to be', Donne's syntax is overcome by the curious signifier of metaphysical uncertainty, the little word 'or'. The first two sentences of *Biathanatos* are stretched out to breaking point by tenuous relative clauses; in the second sentence, divided no fewer than six times by the conjunction 'or', finishing:

> Or that there bee a perplexitie and flexibility in the doctrine it selfe; Or because my Conscience ever assures me, that no rebellious grudging at Gods

---

[109] *Praescriptiones Adversus Haereses* (Antwerp: Officina Plantiniana, 1606), 208.
[110] Irena Backus, *Life Writing in Reformation Europe: Lives of Reformers by Friends, Disciples and Foes* (Aldershot: Ashgate, 2008), 52–3.

gifts, nor other sinfull concurrence accompanies these thoughts in me, or
that a brave scorn, or that a faint cowardlinesse beget it, whensoever any
affliction assailes me, mee thinks I have the keyes of my prison in mine owne
hand, and no remedy presents it selfe so soone to my heart, as mine own
sword.

Donne has 'the keyes of my prison in mine owne hand' just as Montaigne
has 'the key of the fieldes'. Nature 'hath appointed but one entrance vnto
life, but many a thousand wayes out of it'.

Yet 'voluntary death' is so difficult a concept as to be virtually a self-
contradiction. No case tests the limits of voluntarism more than the death
of Christ. 'There was nothing more free, more voluntary, more spontane-
ous then the death of *Christ*', Donne says, in *Deaths Duel*.[111] Yet he immediately backtracks. What Christ wished was also what he had to do: 'yet
when we consider the contract act that had passed betweene his Father and
him, there was an *oportuit*, a kind of necessity vpon him. All this Christ
ought to suffer.' This conflict of interpretation is embedded in the grammar of Christ's action of suffering. He suffers death, that is death happens
to him. Death strains the limits of language. We reach unto death, but
death in the end comes in its own time. We can want it, but we cannot
make it happen. Death meets us halfway, even in the action of suicide.

THE LIMITS OF SUBJECTIVITY

In Shakespeare, Antony after his defeat at Actium feels his identity slip-
ping away from him. There is nothing left for him but to die:

> Nay, weep not, gentle Eros. There is left us
> Ourselves to end ourselves.[112]

So he says, but it is not quite what he means. Suicide in Shakespeare, odd
though it is to say it, does not happen alone. Antony in wishing for his
own death, does not take it, but requests the intervention of another, his
servant. Suicide in Shakespeare is always assisted: it is always the ultimate
sympathetic act of a noble servant or friend. Brutus at Philippi calls this
the ultimate act of friendship:

> BRUTUS Hence; I will follow.
> [*Exeunt Clitus, Dardanius and Volumnius.*]

---

[111] *Deaths duell, or, A consolation to the soule, against the dying life, and liuing death of the body* (London: Thomas Harper, [1632]), 33.
[112] *Antony and Cleopatra*, 4.14.21–2.

I prithee, Strato, stay thou by thy lord.
Thou art a fellow of a good respect:
Thy life hath had some smatch of honour in it.
Hold then my sword, and turn away thy face,
While I do run upon it. Wilt thou, Strato?
STRATO Give me your hand first. Fare you well, my lord.
BRUTUS Farewell, good Strato— [*Runs on his sword.*]
Caesar, now be still.
I killed not thee with half so good a will. *Dies.*[113]

Brutus finds closure, it seems. But in *Antony and Cleopatra*, the act is further shrouded in human failure. Antony's death, far from raising him above the iniquities of life, subjects him to his own humiliation. He pleads with his servant, Eros, to kill him ('Do't. The time is come'). But Eros refuses to kill Antony (4.14.70–2), then shows up his master by killing himself (4.14.95). When Antony attempts to commit suicide himself, he fails:

ANTONY Thrice nobler than myself!
Thou teachest me, O valiant Eros, what
I should and thou couldst not! My queen and Eros
Have by their brave instruction got upon me
A nobleness in record. But I will be
A bridegroom in my death and run into't
As to a lover's bed. Come then!
And, Eros,
Thy master dies thy scholar. To do thus
[*Falls on his sword.*] (4.14.96–105)

The scene is painfully drawn out, subjecting Antony to the humiliation of stage time. He will not die, cannot it seems bring himself to his own action:

I learned of thee. How? Not dead? Not dead?
The guard, ho! O, dispatch me. (106–7)

But the guards will not do it either.

Antony is hidden in 'the secret house of death'. He attempts to use death to escape himself. But he cannot find anything beyond his own bounds. It is as if he is reduced to his own words about himself, and he can find redemption only in Cleopatra's memory of him. Perhaps in both Montaigne and Donne suicidal argument only appears on the surface to be one about self-murder, because the real subject is even more painful

---

[113] *Julius Caesar*, 5.5.43–53.

and troubling. What it is to die conceals the underlying question, what is it to live? They use the case for and against suicide not only to examine the limits of subjectivity, but also what we might call a subjectivity of limits.

In the conventional history of ideas about suicide, Christian reticence and repression is overcome by a superior moral sympathy towards suffering and misfortune. Into this picture some have tried to fit Montaigne's reception of Seneca, as suggesting a more humane and finer moral sentiment. Yet this is to ignore how Montaigne rejects Seneca's version of suicide, even as he is attracted towards it. What he rejects is the Stoic's assumption that humanity can, in its ends, evade the accidentality of life. In Seneca, the human mind is muddled by its passions, so that it cannot see clearly. But when you understand fortune, he says, she ceases to have power over you. *Quae sit libertas, quaeris? Nulli rei servire, nulli necessitati, nullis casibus, fortunam in aequum deducere* ('What is freedom, you ask? It means not being a slave to any circumstance, to any constraint, to any chance; it means compelling Fortune to enter the lists on equal terms').[114] This is how philosophy confers freedom, Seneca says.[115] But Montaigne replies that no life is like that. Suicide gives an illusion of freedom. We never escape our own limits, least of all, of course, the limits of our own mortality.

This is not to say that Montaigne provides some homily against suicide, like a Christian moralist. But nor does he give some simplistic anti-Christian humanist panacea. While in the twentieth century scepticism came to be seen as coterminous with a rejection of theology, in Montaigne there are other, more primary, ways of being sceptical. Indeed we could say that in secularizing suicide and in reducing it to an illness, we have lost sight of the way (understood in both classical and early modern philosophy) that suicide confronts us with ultimate questions of mortality. In one of the most extraordinary twists and turns in Montaigne's 'Coustume de l'Isle de Cea', he makes the desire for death and the desire for life almost interchangeable. 'Voire quelquefois la fuitte de la mort, faict que nous y courons' (II.iii.371; 'Sometimes flight from death makes us run into it', Frame, p. 308), he says; before quoting Martial at his most paradoxical, *Hic rogo, non furor est ne moriare mori?* ('I ask, is this not madness, dying to avoid death?')[116] Montaigne continues, without pausing for breath: 'like those who, for fear of a precipice, throw themselves over it'.

At this point, he introduces two different quotations. The first, from Lucan, repeats the Stoic moral:

[114] *Ep.* LI.9 (i. 340–1).   [115] Inwood, *Reading Seneca*, 317.
[116] *Epigrams*, II.lxxx.2; ed. and trans. D. R. Shackleton Bailey, Loeb Classical Library, 3 vols. (Cambridge, Mass.: Harvard University Press, 1993), i. 190–1.

Qui promptus metuenda pati, si cominus instent,
Et differre potest.

Those who are ready to suffer fearful things, if they face them head on, can yet delay them.

But next, as so often when Montaigne is at the edge of his most pressing concerns, he quotes Lucretius:

usque adeo mortis formidine, vitæ
percipit humanos odium, lucisque videndæ,
ut sibi consciscant mærenti pectore letum,
obliti fontem curarum hunc esse timorem. (III.79–82)

through fear of death so deeply does the hatred of life and the sight of the light possess men, that with sorrowing heart they compass their own death, forgetting that it is this fear which is the source of their woes.[117]

There could be no more puzzling example of Montaigne using one citation to challenge rather than buttress another. Admiring the Stoic lack of regard for life as a good in itself, Montaigne then quotes Lucretius as if to show Stoicism's own self-contradiction. Overtaken by a morbid consciousness of the misery of the human condition, the suicide enacts the very thing which limits his life and makes it fearful and loathsome.

While this part of the essay has been assigned to the arguments against suicide, Montaigne's increasingly volatile citation shows there is no such stable method of arguing. Mortality rebuffs argumentation. For, in another volte-face, he asks how we could disdain our life in the first place. 'Car en fin c'est nostre estre, c'estre nostre tout' (II.iii.372). 'For after all, life is our being, it is our all' (Frame, p. 308); how can I want what makes me not? He goes on:

mais c'est contre nature, que nous nous mesprisons et mettons nous mesmes à nonchaloir; c'est une maladie particuliere, et qui ne se voit en aucune autre creature, de se hayr et desdaigner. C'est de pareille vanité, que nous desirons estre autre chose, que ce que nous sommes. (II.iii.372)

it is against nature that we despise ourselves and care nothing about ourselves. It is a malady peculiar to man, and not seen in any other creature, to hate and disdain himself. It is by a similar vanity that we wish to be something other than we are. (Frame, p. 308)

Montaigne reaches the point of resistance. His philosophy of self is one of nonchalance, of carelessness, of disengagement from things outside oneself. But what does it mean to be *nonchalant* of the self itself?

[117] *De rerum natura*, ed. Bailey, i. 307.

This is the third and most dangerous version of suicide, what we might call Hamlet's own, the mortal self. For the desire for death puts into question the very personhood that defines the idea of 'desire' in the first place. 'Le fruict d'un tel desir ne nous touche pas, d'autant qu'il se contredit et s'empesche en soy' (II.iii.372; 'The object of such a desire does not really affect us, inasmuch as the desire contradicts and hinders itself within', Frame, pp. 308–9). A desire to die is a desire that reaches outside and beyond the desiring subject. The subject disappears. This makes nonsense of the idea of a sovereign will. Not only is the will not sovereign, but the self that wills is itself contingent.

We cannot know our own end without understanding where we come from. And where we come from was never within our power. Lucretius comes once more into view:

> debet enim, misere cui forte ægreque futurum est,
> Ipse quoque esse in eo tum tempore, cùm male possit
> Accidere. (III.861–3)

for if, by chance, there is to be grief and pain for a man, he must needs himself too exist at that time, that ill may befall him.

For personhood to be relieved by its own finitude, the person must survive his own death. For Lucretius this is an absurdity, as Book III is a conclusive rejoinder to the idea of an afterlife. Montaigne refuses to utter an opinion on this most unutterable of concepts. The mortality of the soul is the definitive heresy of Epicureanism. But he creates a piece of pure Epicureanism of his own, some of his most beautiful writing in the *Essais*: 'La securité, l'indolence, l'impassibilité, la privation des maux de cette vie, que nous achetons au prix de la mort, ne nous apporte aucune commodité' (II.iii.372; 'The security, the freedom from pain and suffering, the exemption from the ills of this life, that we purchase at the price of death, bring us no advantage', Frame, p. 309). We bring ourselves no relief by ending the burden of our own lives, for in the ending we cease to feel anything for ourselves. This is the final self-contradiction of suicide. Yet in this place Montaigne also discovers a form of relief.

For a life with limits also contains its own plenitude, the space within which we have the one form of self-possession that is open to us. This is the theme of a series of citations from *De rerum natura*, Book III, found throughout his work, going back to the essay in Book I (which itself is derived from Cicero, and then from Socrates via Plato), 'That to philosophize is to learn how to die'. [118] *Iam fuerit, nec post unquam revocare licebit.*

---

[118] *Essais*, I.xix.82; Frame, p. 67. See Cicero, *Tusculan Disputations*, I.xxx.74 and Plato, *Phaedo*, 67E.

'In a moment, the present will have gone, never to be recalled'.[119] The life we have is the only life we get. The last citation from Book III in 'Coustume de l'Isle de Cea' comes at a point of maximum personal meaning to Montaigne, immediately after the passage marked in his own copy of Lucretius, discussed in Chapter 1, where the younger Montaigne made a note in the flyleaf. The annotation sums up his sense of the contingency of his being, as he reads the moment where Lucretius imagines, and then rejects, the possibility of his own atoms being reformed at some future point. In Montaigne's Latin, *ut alius nascatur Montanus*, if another mountain should be born, punning on his own name, another Montaigne, might yet come into the world.[120] Yet would he know himself again? The new self is cut off from the old self, irrecoverably lost across the gulf of space and memory. He is who he is now, he cannot be another. He is bound to the exclusivity of his body and to the fortuitousness of his making. Thus the imagination of his own death sets the limits of his enquiry into himself. Suicide is a false solution, since it offers an idea of a personal autonomy which is an illusion. Subjectivity is both more fragile and more materially resistant than we had thought. Yet to show this he asks, what kind of philosophical problem is suicide? Suicide tests the very concept of philosophy or of philosophical argument. And what is philosophy if it cannot go there?

[119] *De rerum natura*, III.915.
[120] Screech, *Montaigne's Annotated Copy of Lucretius*, 135.

8

Soft Selves: Adam, Eve, & the Art of Embodiment

Dürer to Milton

They stand naked before us, God's animate machines. Adam and Eve in Albrecht Dürer's 1504 engraving of *Adam and Eve* (Fig. 17) are in every sense exemplary human bodies.[1] In Erwin Panofsky's words, they are 'two classic specimens of the nude human body, as perfect as possible both in proportions and in pose'.[2] Adam, with his splendid curly locks, looks sideways towards Eve, seeking her eyes, yet holds his body outwards toward the viewer, one leg stock still while the right leg behind is caught in exquisite forward-leaning equilibrium. His chest is full in view, muscles taut, the abdomen slightly arched, pectorals nicely vibrant. On either side, his arms stretch out to complete his confident pose; in his right hand he grasps, as if holding it aloft as a staff, the branch of an ash tree, on which a parrot perches with impeccably delicate balance. Eve meanwhile is looking downwards at the forbidden fruit, which she holds at the fingertips of her right hand, her right forearm in mirroring diagonal parallel with Adam's left. A serpent, coiling itself seductively around the trunk of the fatal tree in the centre of our view, is beginning to take a nibble at the fruit.

The Renaissance saw an explosion of interest in the figures of Adam and Eve. This is hardly surprising, since arguments about original sin and human redemption were central to the conflicts of the Reformation. Both Luther and Calvin wrote voluminous commentaries on Genesis. In the following generations, Protestant exegesis pored over every detail of the story of the Fall, whether in commentaries on the whole book, such as by Peter Martyr and David Pareus, or in expositions of only the first two chapters, such as by Hieronymus Zanchius.[3] Meanwhile Catholic

---

[1] Schoch et al., *Das druckgraphische Werk*, No. 39.
[2] Panofsky, *Life and Art of Dürer*, 85.
[3] Arnold Williams, *The Common Expositor: An Account of the Commentaries on Genesis* (Chapel Hill, NC: University of North Carolina Press, 1948), 7.

Fig. 17. Albrecht Dürer, *Adam and Eve* (1504); engraving.

theologians worked hard to reassess Augustine's magnificent legacy on the scriptural story (not only in his various writings on Genesis, but also in *De civitate Dei*) in riposte to the Protestants.[4] The Spanish Jesuit Benedictus Pererius produced the *Commentariorum et disputationum in Genesin* between 1589 and 1598; it was printed separately in Rome, Lyon, and Cologne, and in further seventeenth-century editions, becoming the most widely known work on Genesis in Europe.[5]

But precisely because of this theological and controversial interest, there is another side to the imaginative life of Adam and Eve that may have become obscured from our view. Artists and poets are as much part of the Edenic revival as theologians. If we consider only the great masters, examples come easily to mind. Masaccio painted a temptation of Adam and Eve on the outer wall of his series of frescos of the life of St Peter in the Brancacci chapel at the Carmelite church in Florence in 1424. Most celebrated of all, Michelangelo incorporated two scenes of Adam and Eve in paradise in the ceiling of the Sistine Chapel in Rome between 1508 and 1512, just a few years after Dürer. Further north, in Ghent, Jan van Eyck painted a pair of matching portraits of a naked Adam and Eve to form the outer shutters of his extraordinary altarpiece in the church of Sint Baaf. At least in Germany (where iconophobia was less strong than in England, Scotland, or Switzerland) this was a form of church art which survived the Reformation: the naked flesh of Adam and Eve commonly provided the outer doors of altarpieces representing the crucifixion or annunciation.[6] Perhaps it was an image like this that suggested to Dürer the diptychal form of his 1504 composition. In the wake of this outstandingly popular engraving, Dürer created an oil panel of Adam and Eve in 1507 (now in the Prado in Madrid), and a further woodcut in 1509. Following Dürer, Lucas van Leyden produced a series of very high-quality engravings of Adam and Eve over a period of twenty years from 1510 to 1530. Outside church contexts, Adam and Eve were a staple of Protestant art from Lucas Cranach to Rembrandt van Rijn.

The image of Adam and Eve raised questions that went way beyond curiosity about humankind's origins. Genesis 1: 26 declares that God made man in his image, after his 'likeness'. As Philip Almond acutely comments, this verse, while so often repeated, most often raised consternation and hostility rather than pride or empathy. For in reverse it

---

[4] Augustine produced two finished commentaries on Genesis, the *De Genesi ad litteram* and the *De Genesi contra Manichaeos*; and an unfinished third work, the *Opus imperfectus*, all collected in vol. 34 of *Patrologia Latina*.

[5] Williams, *The Common Expositor*, 8.

[6] Joseph Leo Koerner, *Reformation of the Image*, 214.

suggested that 'God was shaped in the form of a man'.[7] As early as the fourth century, in the condemnation of Audius, this was regarded as a heresy. For even Aristotle argued that God must be single and cannot be 'like' something else.[8] People who believed that God had a bodily form were known as 'Anthropomorphites'. Augustine argued in a number of places that man was 'like' God not in the faculties which he shared with other animals (that is, the body) but only in the faculty which sets the human apart (the intellect). In *De trinitate*, he defined the image of God as consisting in the three powers of the soul as defined by Aristotle: memory, mind, and will.[9]

Luther, on the other hand, while quoting and approving Augustine's analysis, went further in stating that Adam also possessed a power of body and a beauty of limb which surpassed all other created things. The eyes of Adam were so clear, Luther said, that his vision exceeded that of the lynx. In a fight he could handle a lion or a bear. As his power excelled, so did his sensitivity: when he ate a fruit, it tasted far sweeter than anything we can now feel, after the Fall.[10] Calvin backtracked on Luther. His main insistence was a renewed attack on the Anthropomorphites: God could not be understood as corporeal, which was altogether too gross an idea.[11] But via synecdoche, allowing man God's image in part but not as a whole, prelapsarian Adam could be understood to have not only a right judgement but well-ordered passions and emotions and senses. The seat of the divine image in him was not only the head but the heart.[12]

Embodiment thus becomes a crux for understanding the nature of the human as well as the fundamentals of theology . Yet this is not to be seen as the gradual secularizing emergence of a scientific and philosophical interest at the expense of the scriptural. As Peter Harrison has argued, the literal interpretation of the biblical text led directly to intense interest in the natural world, including the human. The natural science of the seventeenth century needs to be understood in the context of an explanation of hermeneutic practice, not in spite of or in contradistinction to it.[13] Nor should the body be seen in any simple sense as the 'villain' in an

---

[7] Philip C. Almond, *Adam and Eve in Seventeenth-Century Thought* (Cambridge: Cambridge University Press, 1999), 9.

[8] *Nicomachean Ethics*, 1154^b; ed. Bywater, p. 154.

[9] *De trinitate*, x. 12 (*Patrologia Latina*, 42, col. 998) and xiv. 7 (*Patrologia Latina*, 42, col. 1043). See also *De civitate Dei*, xi; *Contra manicheos*, 1.17.28; and *Confessions*, 1.32.47.

[10] *Lectures on Genesis*, ed. Jaroslav Pelikan, 4 vols. (St Louis, Mich.: Concordia, 1961), i. 26.

[11] Almond, *Adam and Eve*, 10.   [12] Calvin, *Genesis*, 95.

[13] Peter Harrison, *The Bible, Protestantism, and the Rise of Natural Science* (Cambridge University Press, 1998), 265.

intellectual and literary history of Protestantism.[14] Most especially in Milton's treatment of embodiment we can see what Christopher Tilmouth has called 'passion's triumph over reason'.[15]

HUMAN NATURE

In Dürer's Eden the garden is crammed with animals: at Adam's feet lie a sleeping cat and a rabbit, safely single. A mouse to the cat's right is oblivious to any danger. The parrot above Adam's head is caught in uncanny stillness; an elk wanders broodingly across the scene behind the fatal tree; an ox is slumped lethargically behind Eve to her left, beneath a second apple which she cups in her left hand, ready to proffer to her husband when she has finished with her own. What are the animals doing there? Visually they represent the copiousness of animal nature, and at the same time the mutual interdependence and equality of human and animal bodies in original creation. The animals coexist in a moment of tense equilibrium, cat with mouse, parrot with serpent. Symbolically, in a theory first presented by Panofsky, the four animals grouped closest to the human couple represent, in addition, the four humours of classical and humanist medical philosophy. The elk is melancholic, the rabbit sanguine, the cat choleric, and the ox phlegmatic.[16] Animal bodies manifest to the viewer the synergy of human passions.

This animal symbolism thus confirms that the true subject of the engraving is not original sin alone, but the human body and its meaning in creation. Indeed, Panofsky suggests that the preparatory drawings which Dürer made for *Adam and Eve* indicate that he originally intended to present 'the perfect male' and 'the perfect female' in two separate engravings.[17] Inherent in this exercise was a study of the human nude.[18] These were based on classical prototypes derived from ancient sculptures: principally, perhaps, the recently discovered *Apollo Belvedere* (in the Vatican collections) and the *Medici Venus* (now in the Uffizi in Florence), which Dürer probably knew from prints or drawings. A further exemplary parallel

---

[14] Richard Strier, 'Against the Rule of Reason: Praise of Passion from Petrarch to Luther to Shakespeare to Herbert', in Gail Kern Paster, Katherine Rowe, and Mary Floyd-Wilson (eds.), *Reading the Passions: Essays in the Cultural History of Emotion* (Philadelphia: University of Pennsylvania Press, 2004), 23.

[15] *Passion's Triumph over Reason: A History of the Moral Imagination from Spenser to Rochester* (Oxford: Oxford University Press, 2007).

[16] Panofsky, *Life and Art of Dürer*, 86. Dürer's study of the elk is in the British Museum, Winkler 242.

[17] Panofsky, *Life and Art of Dürer*, 86.

[18] Peggy Grosse, 'Bild des Nackten', in Hess and Eser (ed.), *Der frühe Dürer*, 373–82.

was the legendary *Cnidian Aphrodite* by Praxiteles, of which Roman copies proliferated throughout Europe, including one now in the Vatican Museum. This marble torso, to be viewed equally from behind as well as full frontal, enjoyed a literary fame equal to its visual reputation, being discussed in commentary by Pliny the Elder, Valerius Maximus, and Lucian. This mythical portrayal transmuted into a hermetic Renaissance tradition all of its own.[19]

Aphrodite's pose, in which she subtly shields her genitals with one hand while resting her other, away from her body, on a drape cast over a large urn, metamorphosed readily into the iconography of the Renaissance Eve, who, as in Dürer's monumental version, employs a variety of manual means to protect her modesty as if with unaffected inattention, while using her other hand to pick up the deadly fruit. At the same time, Dürer's Eve and Adam take on other capacities from classical precedent. Panofsky's phrase, 'two classic specimens', is true also in the literal sense. Dürer's nude studies from the mid-1490s onwards are part of a conscious project in idealizing the human form. His washed pen and ink drawing of a *Female Nude with Staff and Drapery, Seen from Behind*, dated to 1495, makes a clear reference to classical sculpture (the *Cnidian Aphrodite* being a prime model), while encompassing also the tradition of viewing the model in the studio.[20] Another example from the same period (1498), a pen drawing now in the Crocker Art Museum, shows a study of the female nude caught in motion.[21] She seems unaware of being observed, indifferent to the presence of the artist, in ways that become a classic feature later of the tradition of representing Eve. A reference to the Bible, 'they were both naked, the man and his wife, and they were not ashamed' (Genesis 2: 25), is visually implicit. They do not know they are naked, or observed, until after the Fall.

Human nature is Dürer's object of interest. The bodily proportions of the human form were laid down in a famous passage in the third book of Vitruvius' *De architectura* (as in Leonardo da Vinci's now celebrated drawing). Dürer was now entering the height of his fame, expanding his painting production with major altarpieces such as those now in Munich and Florence.[22] His workshop was expanding, where he was joined by

---

[19] Berthold Hinz, *Aphrodite: Geschichte einer abendländischen Passion* (Munich: Hanser, 1998), 17.

[20] Paris, Louvre: Département des arts graphiques, Inv. 19058; Winkler 85.

[21] *Female Nude with Drapery and Caduceus* (1498), Sacramento, Calif., Crocker Art Museum: Inv. 1871.3; Winkler 947.

[22] The *Paumgartner Altarpiece* (now in the Alte Pinakothek in Munich) was created for the Katharinenkirche in Nuremberg in 1498–1502; the *Adoration of the Magi* (now in the Uffizi in Florence) for the Schoßkirche in Wittenberg in 1504. See Fedja Anzelewsky, *Albrecht Dürer: Das malerische werk* (Berlin: Deutscher Verlag für Kunstwissenschaft, 1971), 50–1 and 82.

three young artists, Hans von Kulmbach, Hans Schäufelein, and Hans Baldung, who worked with him on a burgeoning portfolio of commissions for devotional woodcut books by Nuremberg printers.[23] The Munich *Self-Portrait* marks this formation of his artistic self, accompanied by a preoccupation with the mathematics of human organic life.[24] As early as 1500, in a drawing in the Berlin Kupferstichkabinett, Dürer created a female figure from geometric forms.[25] Using a compass, he composed the upper part of the body as a pair of concentric circles, with the breasts formed as a pair of smaller circles poised at the circumference of the inner of the two; even the nipples are geometrical, joined by a line drawn with a ruler, on an axis which then reaches back at an angle to match the extension of the tilted head. Further ruled lines create the balancing form of the lower body, with the compass coming back into employment to create the outlines of the abdomen, the knees, and the outline of the movement of the right leg, which is in free motion while the left leg is pivoted, standing in tension. With an almost comic effect of the mathematician's eye, two crossed strokes of the compass form the folds of the woman's genitals. The navel alone is free from geometry, a single looped curl of the pen, the artist's doodle freeing itself from the rule of number.

The verso of the page is the same image in directly copied reverse, only now revealed as a stylized anatomical study, a white female figure finely criss-crossed with shading against a trademark, starkly contrasted, blackish brown wash.[26] The head is only vaguely formed, and all of Dürer's attention—and of the implied viewer—is placed on the human form. The genealogy of this (in every sense) experimental preparatory study towards the ultimate rendition of the 1504 Eve is clear. One leg is standing, the other caught in movement; one arm is raised, the other droops and rests, grasping an object. It needs only for the human body to find an apple as its object of desire to complete the pose. In the meantime, however, Dürer developed these human studies in other iconographic formulations. There are related drawings of standing female figures, recto and verso with mathematical annotations, in Dresden, Hamburg, and the British

[23] Bartrum, *Albrecht Dürer and his Legacy*, 135.

[24] Dürer's concept of mathematical 'Norm' is discussed by Jaya Remond in Hess and Eser (ed.), *Der frühe Dürer*, 499–507.

[25] *Geometrical Construction of a Female Nude Holding an Escutcheon and a Lamp*, pen drawing, Berlin, Staatliche Museen zu Berlin, Stiftung Preußischer Kulturbesitz, Kupferstichkabinett, KdZ 44; Winkler 413.

[26] *Anatomical Study of the Same Figure Holding an Escutcheon*, pen and wash, Berlin, Staatliche Museen zu Berlin, Stiftung Preußischer Kulturbesitz, Kupferstichkabinett, KdZ 44; Winkler 414.

Museum in London.[27] Mathematical measurements are again used in two engravings made in the years leading up to the *Adam and Eve*: the female nude *Nemesis or Large Fortune* (*c*.1501–2), and the male and female pairing of *Apollo and Diana* (*c*.1503–4).[28] His preparatory studies for these engravings show him using squares to mark out proportions, pricked to enable an exact transfer to the final image, making the head an eighth of the size of the body and the face a tenth.[29] In *Nemesis*, a winged nude female figure stands on a globe, her shoulder carrying a huge if redundant drapery, her hands fully occupied in holding large and significant objects, all above a verdant Tyrolian landscape of a city on a river.[30] In facial features as well as body, Nemesis anticipates Eve.

The figure of Apollo in the later engraving, on the other hand, is clearly Dürer's model for Adam. Dürer sketched Apollo and Sol in a variety of poses in the three years before the Eden print. In the drawing with brown and black ink now in the British Museum (Fig. 18) the name 'APOLO' is inscribed in reverse, suggesting a model for an engraving which was never completed.[31] If we reverse the image, Apollo's pose in this drawing is an almost exact precedent for Adam: the left (right in Adam) arm is raised to hold an object, here the sun; the right (left) hangs diagonally downwards. The standing leg of Apollo is the right, of Adam the left, while the following leg is caught in virile balancing suspense of movement. Only the direction of the face is not reversed, although in each it has a similar bearing and feature, in imitation of a classical sculpture. Indeed, this is Dürer's most clearly classically inspired human figure to date: the male of the Apollo drawing has been said to derive from drawings or prints of the Apollo Belvedere.[32] The seated figure of Diana is thought to have been influenced by an engraving of the same subject by Jacopo de' Barbari. At around this time, Dürer produced a small engraving of Apollo and Diana, again in imitation of Jacopo.[33]

---

[27] Bartrum, *Albrecht Dürer and his Legacy*, 137–8, including plates of the British Museum study, cat. 70.

[28] *Das druckgraphische Werk*, Nos. 33 and 38; see also Bartrum, *Albrecht Dürer and his Legacy*, cat. 72 and 85.

[29] Bartrum, *Albrecht Dürer and his Legacy*, 140 and 149.

[30] Frankfurt am Main, Städel Museum, Graphische Sammlung, Inv. 31391; British Museum 1895-9-15-346; *Das druckgraphische Werk*, No. 33. *Die Nemesis* is Dürer's title in the Netherlands daybook of 1521. The subject, first identified by Panofsky, comes from a poem by Angelo Poliziano printed by Aldus Manutius in 1498; see Bartrum, *Albrecht Dürer and his Legacy*, 140.

[31] *Apollo and Diana* (*c*.1501–4), London, British Museum, Sloane 5218-183; Winkler 261. See Bartrum, *Albrecht Dürer and his Legacy*, cat. 84.

[32] Bartrum, *Albrecht Dürer and his Legacy*, 149.

[33] London, British Museum 1868-8-22-189; *Das druckgraphische Werk*, No. 38. For illustration and comment, see Bartrum, *Albrecht Dürer and his Legacy*, cat. 85, p. 150.

Fig. 18. Albrecht Dürer, *Apollo and Diana* (1501–4); pen and ink.

Dürer also made a series of studies of Eve at the same period in pencil and in ink. Once again, the classical model is clear, and Eve could as easily be Venus, since the apple in the hand is equally part of the iconography of the Helleno-Roman goddess of love (in the Judgement of Paris) as it is of the Hebraic first parent. In these drawings, Eve is entirely naked, with no encumbrance of leaves; her hair flows easily in the breeze. One of these, in the Ashmolean Museum in Oxford, shows a central vertical line of composition and pricked points made by mathematical calculation.[34] A second, now in the British Museum (Fig. 19), an exquisite drawing in pen and brown ink with a brown wash, builds on the proportions established in the Ashmolean drawing.[35] This is one of the most finished studies of the female nude ever executed by Dürer, with subtle shading of the musculature on both arms, and a finesse of attention to the athletic pose of the legs in motion. It bears comparison with Dürer's full nude self-portrait in ink and wash (Fig. 1), discussed in Chapter 1, which dates perhaps from the same year.[36]

When Dürer turned to work on the complete engraving of *Adam and Eve*, the exemplary status of the first human beings is brought to fruition. Panofsky surmised that the artist intended originally to render two separate mythological subjects, on separate sheets. Perhaps Panofsky wondered at a classical ideal of human proportion being represented by a biblical subject.[37] The Vitruvian does not appear to him a suitable model for Christian ideals. Yet if so, Panofsky is working against the apparent equanimity of Dürer in relation to Eve and Venus, Adam and Apollo. For Dürer there is no project of secularization here. Indeed, the biblical text allows him an analysis in human nature of a peculiarly objective kind. The subject of the image allows him to present the male and female forms of the species in perfect symmetry, like God's robots. They are aligned in a single plane. The strong central line of the tree reinforces the harmonious match: around this fold, the human pair may be interpreted as two sides of the same coin, or a diptych in flesh. Indeed, in this respect, the genital modesty of the image, and Eve's unpronounced breasts, help to engender the couple as human first and foremost, and sexually different only as an afterthought. While Dürer is faithful to distinctions in masculine and

[34] Oxford, Ashmolean Museum, WA 1855.101; Winkler 334. Description in Bartrum, *Albrecht Dürer and his Legacy*, cat. 89.

[35] London, British Museum, Sloane 5218-182; Winkler 335. Description in Bartrum, *Albrecht Dürer and his Legacy*, cat. 90. A monogram and date in Dürer's hand of 1507 is incorrect and perhaps refers to another drawing on the same sheet, now lost. Other preparatory drawings survive in the Albertina, Vienna, and the Pierpont Morgan Library, New York.

[36] See Nadeije Laneyrie-Dagen, *L'Invention du corps: la représentation de l'homme du Moyen Âge à la fin du XIXe siècle* (Paris: Flammarion, 2006), 155.

[37] Panofsky, *Life and Art of Dürer*, 86.

Fig. 19. Albrecht Dürer, *Study for the Figure of Eve* (1504); pen and ink.

feminine anatomy in the shoulders and hips, in philosophical terms he is happy to present us with a pair of hermaphrodites.

The mirroring between male and female is reproduced in another form of mirroring between artist and image. The branch which Adam holds in his hand suspends a placard which declares a signature, the artist's signature, ALBERTUS DVRER NORICVS FACIEBAT 1504 ('Albrecht Dürer of Nuremberg made this 1504'). It was the first time Dürer had used a Latin signature for one of his works, and the longest inscription he ever made in any of his engravings.[38] Pride in his handicraft was natural. Yet there is all the more significance that he gives Adam the personal honour of brandishing it aloft. Adam and Albrecht are joined in common humanity. Albrecht the author of Adam is also himself the son of Adam. His own body is adumbrated in the depiction, as indeed all humankind is contained in it. The great master of the self-portrait attempts in his *Adam and Eve* another form of portrayal of the self, the self as other, or the subject as object. The viewer of the engraving then completes this mirroring. The viewer, too, is on view: the viewer's reflection is seen as if in obverse in front of the self who views it. Here the gendered doubling of the image becomes its central meaning. For whereas half the viewers of either an Apollo or a Venus are excluded by sexual difference, any viewer of Dürer's 1504 masterpiece immediately identifies with it, male or female, since the image represents both halves of mankind. This is the uniquely universal meaning of the story of Adam and Eve: it bodies forth all our stories at one and the same time.

SEXUALITY & THE FALL OF MAN

Behind the serene surface, something darker lurks. The surface of the skin of the humans shines pellucidly. But the garden at their backs is an impenetrable forest. The contrast in light is part of the astonishing virtuoso technique of Dürer's workshop, but opposition is also part of the structure of meaning. We are presented with a dialectic: good and evil, knowledge and innocence, before and after the Fall, as in the biblical story, of course. Craig Harbison has commented on a conflict between 'inner and outer man, spirit and flesh' in the engraving.[39] But above all, the image is poised in a startling rendition of the burden of the moment. All is in equilibrium, because all is about to change. Panofsky noted this especially in the perturbingly quiet pose of the cat, less than a yard from the mouse (pp. 84–5). The pose of Adam's hand on

[38] Bartrum, *Albrecht Dürer and his Legacy*, 150.
[39] *Symbols in Transformation: An Exhibition of Prints in Memory of Erwin Panofsky* (Princeton: Princeton Art Museum, 1969), 17.

the branch of the mountain ash, or of Eve's with the fruit, is of the moment before the moment after. The scene is shot through with a sense of its own temporality, and therefore of life as flux. Flesh itself is caught in the apprehension of its life in time. Bodies as perfect as this will not last. The picture exudes, in that sense, a paradox of embodiment: the curse of the organic exposed to the inevitable touch of morbidity.

In this more troubled direction, the generation of Adam and Eve tells another exemplary human narrative, another mirror stage. Dürer here stands on the edge of a different iconographic tradition. His paradise is a serene location, the Tree of Knowledge providing not only a visual axis but a sense of intellectual structure. The first parents are statuesque and monumental, if also soft and athletic. The world of order has not yet been surprised by sin. In the work of his pupil, collaborator, friend, Hans Baldung Grien—*traddutore, traditore*—a startlingly new theme emerges. Baldung, born in Swabia in around 1484, was from a learned and humanist family; a relative was imperial physician, and his brother Caspar was rector of the University of Freiburg.[40] In 1503 Hans Baldung entered the workshop of Dürer in Nuremberg, and his hand is seen in some of the productions of this period; but by 1509 he was working independently in Strasbourg, where he was noted for his woodcuts and especially his experiments with colour printing techniques. From 1512 he was working on a commission for the high altar in the cathedral at Freiburg; in Strasbourg in the 1520s his workshop was in demand for work of a wide variety—including nudes, historical and classical works, and madonnas. His astonishing originality is most evident in his woodcuts, often polychrome, of witches, horses, and curious self-portraits as a stable groom. In all this work he was the renowned inheritor of Dürer, a lock of whose hair was given to him on his master's death in 1528.[41] This curious memento of artistic mortality is still preserved in the Albertina in Vienna. Koerner describes it as the first relic of the modern religion of the artist. Yet if Baldung is Dürer's most remarkable follower, he has also been described by Anthony Grafton as the worm in Dürer's apple.[42]

Dürer's treatment of Adam and Eve works subtly to suppress any sexual allure in the image. As was traditional in the representation of paradisal

---

[40] Bodo Brinkmann, *Hexenlust und Sündenfall: Die seltsamen Phantasien des Hans Baldung Grien / Witches' Lust and the Fall of Man: The Strange Fantasies of Hans Baldung Grien*, Exhibition Catalogue, Städel Museum, Frankfurt am Main (Petersberg: Michael Imhof Verlag, 2007), 19.

[41] The origin of this story lies with Sebald Bühler in the late sixteenth century; for full discussion, see Koerner, *Moment of Self-Portraiture*, 249–50.

[42] *Bring Out Your Dead: The Past As Revelation* (Cambridge, Mass.: Harvard University Press, 2001), 70.

nakedness, Adam and Eve are not flagrantly nude: with seemingly miraculous precision, they have been caught by the viewer in a position where a spindly twig with just the right number of leaves protects their privacy. In other respects, there is little to hint at the ominous suggestion of a history of sinfulness. Other treatments of the Genesis story clearly imitate Dürer in both structure and meaning. Lucas Cranach in a woodcut dated 1509 recalls Dürer both in the position of the tree and the positioning of his monogram in a plaque on the tree.[43] Adam and Eve coexist with nature in a world teeming with animals. They are unaware of their nakedness. In a very large woodcut closely copied from an original by Hans Burgkmair, the couple exchange the apple with gestures of intelligent consent. There are animals aplenty here, too, although the most prominent aspect of the image is the collection of specimen-style exotic trees and foliage. The only suggestion of sinfulness lies in the placing of a monkey between the first parents, an iconography which suggested the presence of evil.[44]

The outline of a new treatment of the Fall can be seen in Baldung's polychrome chiaroscuro woodcut from his first Strasbourg period, *The Fall of Man* of 1511 (Fig. 20).[45] This image both vividly recalls Dürer in the use of a woodland setting, yet transforms the sexuality of the scene. Eve is at once more demure and more lascivious. She holds the gaze of the viewer directly, even pertly; the serpent, with an anthropomorphic face that recalls the painted iconography of Hugo van der Goes, coils its entire length around the tree. In imitation once again of Dürer, Eden has other animal presences. But here we require no dictionary of mythological meaning: the pair of hares (a common symbol of lust) clearly only have copulation in mind, and the viewer immediately thinks of rampant sexual reproduction. The human pair are no less obviously preoccupied. Adam stands behind Eve, their bodies touching, and with his left hand he handles her breast, pressed outwards uncomfortably between left forefinger and thumb. She hides her genitals in a gesture borrowed directly from Dürer, although here she has gone so far as to tear off the twig and leaf necessary for her purpose: she knows she is naked, and is leading the viewer and voyeur on. Adam meanwhile stares intently at the fruit Eve holds in her hand; as their arms cross, he holds her breast as if

[43] Washington, DC, National Gallery of Art, Lessing J. Rosenwald Collection, 1943.3.2884; described and illustrated in Diane H. Russell, *Eva/Ave: Woman in Renaissance and Baroque Prints* (Washington, DC: National Gallery of Art, 1990), 120.

[44] Washington, DC, National Gallery of Art, Lessing J. Rosenwald Collection, 1946.21.203; Russell, *Eva/Ave*, 122.

[45] *Der Sündenfall*, woodcut with tone block in brownish grey, Dresden, Staatliche Kunstsammlungen, Kupferstichkabinett, Inv. A 2150.

Fig. 20. Hans Baldung Grien, *Fall of Man* (1511); chiaroscuro woodcut.

in conscious mirroring of the fruit.[46] His right arm reaches behind her; for all intents and purposes like a branch of the tree, merging with nature, he is groping unseeingly for another forbidden fruit. Oblivious to anything beyond her world and his, he does not so much conceal his genitals as press them into her behind. Giulia Bartrum surmises that this is the first time in art that the Fall was 'represented by an overtly sexual gesture'.[47]

In a further citation from Dürer, once again with a twist, Baldung caps his image with a framed plaque. In place of Dürer's self-proclamation as artist, instead we have the print's title, telling all and sundry what is going on: LAPSUS HUMANI GENERIS, 'the fall of humankind'. A second plaque in the lower left corner provides the artist's mark. This contains Baldung's monogram (in imitation of the master's epochal 'AD') 'HBG', but surmounted by another self-reference, a vine leaf. Baldung was in the habit of using this motif as a visual pun on his nickname 'Grien'. But Bodo Brinkmann suggests that it also echoes the leaf held by Eve to cover her modesty. The artist, he says, wears a leaf, just like our original mother, marking how in the year 1511 and in the body of the contemporary human 'original sin is alive and well'.[48]

For Baldung, Brinkmann argues, 'the original sin is sexuality, the Fall of Man to be equated with the first coitus' (p. 158). If Baldung is original in artistic terms, this was nonetheless a theological commonplace. John Cassianus, the fifth-century ascetic, believed that Satan introduced Adam and Eve to the sexual act after first observing it among the animals.[49] This radical iconography, suggested by the account in Genesis in its reference to nakedness and sexual shame, is carried into a highly charged world of erotic suggestion in two other images by Baldung in different media. In a painting now in the Thyssen-Bornemisza collection in Madrid, Eve suggestively caresses the trunk of the tree with her right arm while holding the fruit casually in her left.[50] Adam fondles her breast with one hand and loosely holds her thigh with the other. He looks sidelong at the viewer. In the absolute centre of the image, covered with a totally transparent veil similar to ones used by Cranach in depictions of Venus, is Eve's vagina. If Adam and Eve are here on the point of foreplay,

---

[46] The analogy between fruit and breast is pointed out by Brinkmann, *Hexenlust und Sündenfall*, 163.

[47] Giulia Bartrum, *German Renaissance Prints 1490–1550* (London: British Museum Press, 1995), 72.

[48] Brinkmann, *Hexenlust und Sündenfall*, 163.

[49] Harrison, *Bible, Protestantism, and the Rise of Natural Science*, 215.

[50] *The Fall of Man*, oil and tempera on spruce, Madrid, Museo Thyssen-Bornemisza, Inv. 1929.17.

Baldung goes further still in a drawing which survives only in a contour copy.[51] Eve leans back into the tree, like a pillow on a bed. The fruit in her hand looks like a post-coital snack. Adam is reaching his hand towards it, but he does not get that far: instead his hand has strayed lingering on her crotch—in Brinkmann's interpretation, even stimulating her.[52] The drawing could be an image from an erotic library of the nineteenth century, if it were not for the delicate tracing of hands in perfect artistic balance, a small symphony of consent. This is sexuality not as titillation but as frank mutuality. The Fall is a fall into humanity, not away from it.

In a later woodcut of 1519 (Fig. 21), Baldung's treatment is even more suggestive and disturbing in meaning. Adam approaches Eve from the rear, but there is none of the passive affection and mutuality of the 1511 version. There, his feet recede in a docile gesture. Here, he strides aggressively into Eve's space, placing his right foot in front of hers, perhaps even stamping on her toes. This is an act of invasion. His thrusting of a leafy branch across Eve's naked abdomen, buds upturned, it has been said imitates the image of the uterus in an anatomy lesson, and may 'suggest sexual penetration and conception'.[53] Adam's facial expression, which is in shadow, is 'dark and brutish'.[54] Eve meanwhile, far from seducing him (as in Baldung's earlier print), looks away in distress at her imminent rape.

THE PHILOSOPHY OF EMBODIMENT

The narrative of temptation, sin, and shame combines in the story of Adam and Eve with another, equally complex, form of human engagement. As we see in Dürer's 1504 engraving, artist, subject, and viewer are held in mutual reflection. Adam and Eve provide a prime example of the self-reflexive human body. However, the process of reflection is by no means transparent. The bodies are ours but also not ours, they are subjective and objective. As many commentators have observed, the bodies are statuesque rather than naturalistic. They seem to be composed of a mixture of marble and flesh, as if caught between organic matter and its idealization in sculpted form. Yet the classicization, too, is not complete. Eve, particularly, has the facial features not of an Italian Venus but of a German *Frau*, rather like *Nemesis* in Dürer's earlier engraving.

---

[51] *Contour Copy after Hans Baldung Grien*, with a monogram 'HBG' by Sebald Bühler, Veste Coburg, Kunstsammlungen, Kupferstichkabinett, Z. 10.
[52] Brinkmann, *Hexenlust und Sündenfall*, 162.
[53] Russell, *Eva/Ave*, 126.   [54] Russell, *Eva/Ave*, 126.

Fig. 21. Hans Baldung Grien, *Adam and Eve* (1519); woodcut.

Just as Adam and Eve are naked yet not quite naked, they are like us and yet not quite like us. And this captures something about the original story in Genesis. Adam and Eve are incipiently human but not yet completely human: they are captured in adult bodies but without full possession of them. They are innocent as yet of their own selves: it is only in possession of such selves that they will be fully realized in relationship to their own bodies. They do not know they are naked and so do not know who they are.

One of the wonderful things about Dürer's image, which has helped to make it so lasting an image of the human condition, is that it understands this ambiguity about the story of Adam and Eve. Adam and Eve are surprised by their own embodiment, and make us share that surprise with them. They make us ask, who are we? Why are we formed in this way? The engraving offers us an image of our own embodiment, and at the same time leaves all kinds of question open about it. As so often with Dürer, the image teems with objects and personifications that convey a sense of the possibility of making meaning from them, yet also renders a sense of that meaning being finally beyond comprehension or completeness. It is an image on the point of philosophy.

The philosophy of the human body is poised at a particularly volatile moment in the sixteenth and seventeenth centuries, before and after the appearance of René Descartes. Vitruvius' mathematical study of the body (which was widely copied in manuscript in the later Middle Ages) was available in print from 1486 and in an increasing number of editions beginning in Florence in 1496 and Venice in 1497.[55] Dürer's own fascination with the precise dimensions of the human form eventually culminated in his full-scale theoretical study in the four books of human proportions (*Vier Bücher von menschlischer Proportion*) which he produced between 1507 and 1528.[56] In the meantime, an anatomical understanding of the body was recommended by Leon Battista Alberti in *De pictura* and put into practice by Leonardo in his drawings. The fashion for an extreme rendition of such forms in the *écorché*, semi-dissected mixtures of exterior and interior renditions of musculature and the nervous system, found its ultimate expression in Andreas Vesalius' extraordinary book of 1543, the *De humani corporis fabrica*. Published in Basle by Johannes Oporinus in seven books, the work contains a grand theatre of human corpses, skeletons propping themselves up on elaborate statuary plinths or adopting a melancholy pose in the apprehension of another person's abandoned skull. Elsewhere, half-living bodies divest themselves of the outer layers of

[55] Laneyrie-Dagen, *L'Invention du corps*, 271.
[56] Laneyrie-Dagen, *L'Invention du corps*, 128.

their own skin to reveal the membrane, tendon, cartilage, and nerve which lie beneath. Later in the century, a similar attention was paid to the physiognomy of the face and the physiology of the passions, a predilection especially evident in France, with a plethora of seventeenth-century works by Coeffeteau, Cureau de la Chambre, Descartes himself (*Les Passions de l'âme*) and (in visual form) in the encyclopedic study of facial expressions by Charles le Brun.[57] Yet these questions lead not only to a focus on embodiment, but to a more perplexed confrontation of the juxtaposition of the bodily with the cognitive: '*Que la chaleur & le mouvement des membres procedent du corps, et les pensées de l'ame*'.[58] The passions were the main context in the seventeenth century for discussion of the boundaries between mind and body.[59] Such issues are at the heart of Descartes's project, as in the First Meditation, when he wonders about the difference between feeling and dreaming a feeling: *nec forte etiam nos habere tales manus, nec tale totum corpus* ('and that perhaps we do not even have hands or the rest of a body like what we see').[60] In that sense we associate Descartes with dualism or 'the incorporeal "I" of the *cogito*' in too glib a sense: he is ultimately interested in 'the unity of the human being'.[61]

What part does the myth of human origin play in this acute attention in the early modern period to the philosophy of embodiment? At this point I will shift the focus of attention from the visual arts to the verbal. Literature as well as painting shows a fascination with the figures of Adam and Eve. In France, Guillaume Saluste, Sieur Du Bartas, published his version of the creation myth in *La Sepmaine ou la Création du monde* in 1578. This was translated by Joshua Sylvester in 1605 as *The Divine Weeks and Works*. Later in the seventeenth century, John Milton's *Paradise Lost* eclipsed all other literary versions. *Paradise Lost* is perhaps the ultimate narrative of embodiment, encompassing as it does a comprehensive mythology of the story of creation. Milton's poem is nothing less than a narrative of the embodiment of the world and of the first human beings within it. In addition to this continuous imaginative engagement with the physical processes of creation, the poem also contains a fascinating

---

[57] Jennifer Montagu, *The Expression of the Passions: The Origin and Influence of Charles le Brun's Conférence sur l'expression générale et particulière* (New Haven: Yale University Press, 1994).

[58] Descartes, *Les Passions de l'âme*, ed. Geneviève Rodis-Lewis (Paris: Vrin, 1994), 67.

[59] Stephen Glaukoger, 'Descartes' Theory of the Passions', in John Cottingham (ed.), *Descartes*, Oxford Readings in Philosophy (Oxford: Oxford University Press, 1998), 211.

[60] *Meditationes de prima philosophia*, ed. Geneviève Rodis-Lewis (Paris: Vrin, 1978), 20; *Meditations on First Philosophy*, trans. Michael Moriarty, Oxford World's Classics (Oxford: Oxford University Press, 2008), 14.

[61] Geneviève Rodis-Lewis, 'Descartes and the Unity of the Human Being', in Cottingham (ed.), *Descartes*, 197.

series of soliloquies in which Eve and Adam are represented as reflecting on their own embodiment and its history. With fierce and philosophically complex reminiscence, they retell in narrative form their own first moments, their creation, their entering into consciousness, their first engagement with other bodies, their first apprehension of the possibility of the dissolution of those bodies in death. This has a peculiar aesthetic about it, since (of course) they are born fully formed as adults. As a consequence of the telescoping of consciousness there is a brilliant alternation of bafflement with intense metaphysical speculation, as Adam and Eve struggle to make sense of their bodies, their emotional instincts, their perceptual capacities, and their system of knowledge. To make sense of this they have to talk things through; what we might call a form of occupational therapy, coping with life by telling their story from the start. These narratives occur sometimes in dialogue with each other, sometimes in debate with a sympathetic angel. In the case of the creation of Eve, this involves a double retelling, since Adam and Eve are both made to remember her birth, from very different perspectives.

NARRATING SUBJECTIVITY

Milton presents the act of creation as a second order narration, something that is told over, in different ways and by different people, as a narrative within the narrative.[62] Something of the effect of this can be seen immediately by comparing the method of narration with Milton's ultimate source: the depiction of the creation in Genesis chapters 1 and 2. Unlike the third-person narrative of creation in Genesis, *Paradise Lost* recalls creation, both earthly and bodily, only through the filter of a first-person, unreliable witness. Even in Genesis, though, the creation of Adam and Eve is told twice, in slightly different formulations. In the documentary hypothesis developed since the nineteenth century, the differences have been put down to the idea of different authorship, dubbed by biblical scholars as J and P.[63] Although the identification of distinct authorship is a recent development, discrepancies were often noted in the Rabbinic commentary traditions.[64] Christian interpretation sometimes exacerbated the problem as well as attempting to resolve it.[65] In Milton's time, Protestant commentary worked

---

[62] William Poole, *Milton and the Idea of the Fall* (Cambridge: Cambridge University Press, 2005), 168.
[63] J. M. Evans, *Paradise Lost and the Genesis Tradition* (Oxford: Clarendon Press, 1968), 11.
[64] Examples are given in Evans, *Genesis Tradition*, e.g. p. 41.
[65] See Evans, ch. III.

hard to assimilate all the strands of Genesis into a single theological har-
mony, but Mary Nyquist has nevertheless suggested that Milton himself
privileged the J text over the P text, beginning in the divorce tracts of the
1640s, and then more urgently in *Paradise Lost*.[66]

First there is the general account of creation (the authorship of P) in
chapter 1:

> So God created man in his own image, in the image of God created he him;
> male and female created he them. (Genesis 1: 27)[67]

In this telling there is no suggestion of a distinction in time or in hierarchy
between the two genders, they are two parts of the same creative action,
two reflections of the same divine blueprint. Some rabbinic commentators
even surmised from this that the original human being was androgynous,
a theory certainly known in the seventeenth century.[68] In the seventeenth-
century polemic of Rachel Speght, which Nyquist carefully calls a forerun-
ner of 'feminist' readings, the singularity of human creation is taken to
imply equality and mutuality between Eve and Adam.[69] Indeed, Speght
interprets Genesis 1: 27 as inferring both a distinctive view of God's bodily
image, and a revisionary account of the relationship between genders: 'in
the Image of God were they both created; yea, and to be brief, all the parts
of their bodies, both externall and internall, were correspondent and meete
each for other'.[70]

In the second account, now attributed to the Yahwist J, which follows
in chapter 2, however, Adam comes first, and is definitively male:

> And the LORD God formed man of the dust of the ground, and breathed into
> his nostrils the breath of life; and man became a living soul. (Genesis 2: 7)

When Eve arrives, she is late, and she is secondary. She is created, of
course, out of the stuff of Adam's body.

> And the LORD God caused a deep sleep to fall upon Adam, and he slept:
> and he took one of his ribs, and closed up the flesh instead thereof; And the
> rib, which the LORD God had taken from man, made he a woman, and
> brought her unto the man. (Genesis 2: 21–2)

---

[66] Mary Nyquist, 'The Genesis of Gendered Subjectivity in the Divorce Tracts and in
Paradise Lost', in Mary Nyquist and Margaret W. Ferguson (eds.), *Re-Membering Milton:
Essays on the Texts and Traditions* (London: Methuen, 1988), 103.

[67] Quotations from the Bible in this chapter are taken from the Authorized Version (1611).

[68] Almond, *Adam and Eve*, 6; Harrison, *Bible, Protestantism, and the Rise of Natural
Science*, 216.

[69] Nyquist, 'Genesis of Gendered Subjectivity', 108.

[70] Rachel Speght, *A Mouzell for Melastomus, the cynicall bayter of, and foule mouther
barker against Evahs sex* (London, 1617), 11.

In the characteristic manner of Genesis, the narration is both full of extrinsic detail—the dust, the sleep, the rib, the closing up of the wound—and yet reticent in the extreme in terms of outside explanation. If we put aside theology for a moment we may wonder here about the internalized psychology: what would it have felt like for Adam and Eve to be born in this way?

Milton in this way was touching on a problem that was emerging as one of the most intractable in the new philosophy of the seventeenth century. Milton's lifetime saw the rise of the three great system builders of mechanist philosophy: Pierre Gassendi, Descartes, and Thomas Hobbes. While the three disagreed on many points of detail and often also on fundamental issues of principle, all were of the view that material objects could only be understood in mechanical terms. This included the human body, which in Descartes is equivalent to a complex machine. Such a view was at least implicitly contradictory to traditional Christian teaching and to the interpretation of the biblical version of the creation. Of the three, Gassendi attempted most thoroughly to reconcile the atomist ideas of Epicurus and Lucretius with Christian doctrine.[71] Descartes paid lip service to orthodoxy but privately expressed bewilderment that anyone should take the stories of Genesis seriously any more. Hobbes's violation of Christian doctrine was more aggressive, although he too was careful to protect himself with surface pieties.

It was in Hobbes's *Leviathan* that a mechanical and materialist argument was asserted most intransigently:

> every part of the Universe, is Body, and that which is not Body, is no part of the Universe.[72]

The most obvious line of defence against Hobbes open to Christian writers was the one adopted by the Cambridge Platonists: a reassertion of dualism. Yet here too, there was danger, since Descartes had reinvented dualism as well, and Cartesian dualism was in no sense contradictory of his view of the body as a machine. The incorporeal substance of mind (the *res cogitans*), according to Descartes' unfinished treatise, *La Description du corps humain*, could not be understood according to the laws of physical bodies.[73] But equally, the body was alien to the processes of mind. The Cambridge Platonists were here put in a quandary: attracted to Descartes as a way of refuting Hobbesian materialism, which saw the mind and soul

---

[71] Daniel Garber and Michael Ayers, *The Cambridge History of Seventeenth-Century Philosophy*, 2 vols. (Cambridge: Cambridge University Press, 1998), i. 570.

[72] Hobbes, *Leviathan*, ed. Richard Tuck, Cambridge Texts in the History of Political Thought, rev. edn. (Cambridge: Cambridge University Press, 1996), 463.

[73] *The Philosophical Writings of Descartes*, ed. John Cottingham, Robert Stoothoff, and Dugald Murdoch, 2 vols. (Cambridge: Cambridge University Press 1984–5), i. 314.

as cumbersome and puerile fictions, they found in Descartes little to support the Christian concept of the soul.[74]

It is not my intention here to isolate Milton's precise philosophical position on the issues of the day. His intellectual engagement and controversy with Hobbes in particular is well documented. Put briefly, in his early writing, up to the late 1640s, he appears to be dualist.[75] This is the sense in which Milton understands 'embodiment' in the masque *Comus*, which he wrote in the 1630s:

> The soule growes clotted by contagion,
> Imbodies, and imbrutes, till she quite loose
> The divine propertie of her first being.[76]

Yet it is important to see that this dualism is pre-Cartesian rather than Cartesian. It harks back to Aristotle's puzzlement about how to define the body's movement in terms of the soul or as an act of will.[77] The soul here becomes contaminated with the physical substance of the body, indeed in time it turns into body ('Imbodies, and imbrutes'). Such an idea is quite foreign and indeed perfectly illogical to Descartes, for whom mind and body are separate if commensurate states. The soul in its 'first being' in *Comus* is not in Milton's eyes a substance, a *res cogitans*; indeed it is in becoming substantial that it finds its downfall.

At some point by the late 1650s Milton had become a monist.[78] This was despite his continuing antipathy, philosophical and political, to Hobbes, who was the principal, indeed notorious, monist of the day. Indeed Milton's monism, in complete contradistinction to Hobbes, appears to be anti-materialist. Perhaps the clearest definition of Milton's mature but distinctly peculiar position is this statement in the *De doctrina Christiana*, a work he left unpublished and which cannot be dated with certainty:

> Man is a living being [*animal*], intrinsically and properly one and individual. He is not double or separable: not, as is commonly thought, produced from and composed of two different and distinct elements, soul and body. On the contrary, the whole man is the soul, and the soul the man [*totum hominem*

---

[74] C. A. Patrides, *The Cambridge Platonists* (Cambridge: Cambridge University Press, 1969), 29–31.

[75] Stephen Fallon, *Milton among the Philosophers: Poetry and Materialism in the Seventeenth Century* (Ithaca, NY: Cornell University Press, 1991), 79.

[76] Milton, *A Maske Presented at Ludlow Castle, 1634* (London: Humphrey Robinson, 1637), 16.

[77] *De anima*, 406ᵇ25; ed. and trans. W. S. Hett, Loeb Classical Library (London: Heinemann, 1964), 36.

[78] Fallon, *Milton among the Philosophers*, 79.

esse animam, et animam hominem]: a body, in other words, an individual substance, animated, sensitive and rational.[79]

For Hobbes, the mind only makes sense as a component of a body. Thought processes are therefore as mechanical as any other motion of the body, as he declares in *De homine*:

> *Conceptions* and *apparitions* are nothing *really*, but *motion* in some internal substance of the *head*.[80]

Milton, by contrast, almost puts this in reverse, a position which for Hobbes defies reason and is radically incoherent. For Milton, the human body is 'animated, sensitive and rational'. There is some connection here, perhaps, with hylozoism, the pre-Socratic doctrine (revived by Giordano Bruno) that life inheres in all material objects. The Cambridge Platonists Henry More and Ralph Cudworth were attracted to this concept, although in time Cudworth came to reject it passionately. Milton does not make himself clear on this point. An alternative case has recently been made for aligning Milton with a theory known as 'animist materialism'.[81] His adherence to such an idea has been compared with contemporaries such as Anne Conway.

It is probably mistaken to attempt to find in *Paradise Lost* any philosophically rigorous system. The poem works in a very different way, although its method is itself perhaps not thereby unphilosophical. Rather than define the relationship between mind and body, *Paradise Lost* attempts a series of representations of the relationship in action. In this sense it addresses one of the central conundrums of mid-seventeenth-century mechanist theory in all its forms. For while Hobbes asserts that a conception in the mind is a form of motion, he cannot quite find a formula which explains how matter actually thinks; any more than Descartes quite succeeds in explaining what kind of substance mind is. How does the mind move the body; how does a body produce non-material thought processes? This is the problem posed by the passions in Hobbes:

> For though judgment originates from appetite out of a union of mind and body, it must proceed from reason... Therefore appetite perturbs and impedes the operation of reason; whence it is rightly called a perturbation.[82]

---

[79] *Complete Prose Works of John Milton*, vol. vi, ed. Maurice Kelley (New Haven: Yale University Press, 1973), 317–18.

[80] *The Collected Works of Thomas Hobbes*, ed. Sir William Molesworth, 12 vols., repr. edn. (London: Routledge/Thoemmes Press, 1992), iv. 31.

[81] Fallon, *Milton among the Philosophers*.

[82] Thomas Hobbes, *Man and Citizen (*De Homine *and* De Cive*)*, ed. Bernard Gert (Indianapolis: Hackett, 1991), 55.

What Hobbes calls 'perturbations' (following a line of description of the passions that goes back to Augustine and beyond him to Cicero and the Stoics) turn out to be some of the central puzzles of Milton's poem, something the creation narrative impels him to imagine.[83]

In particular, Milton creates two parallel passages, in which Adam and Eve recount their own births. The two passages are separated by thousands of lines of verse; but in the first edition of the poem in 1667 they are more or less symmetrically placed, one-third from the beginning and one-third from the end of the poem. Typically, in true epic style, Milton reverses the order (just as in the poem as a whole Milton begins in hell and only later tells the story of the creation, in flashback). Eve tells her story first. Here, however, in order to develop an argument about how embodiment is imagined in the poem, I will restore the natural narrative order by quoting first Adam's side of the story. In the middle of a long dialogue with Adam, the angel Raphael gives Adam a crash-course in mathematics, cosmology, epistemology, dialectic, ethics, angelology. And like the perfect academic that he is, he persuades Adam to talk a lot in return in these tutorials, to ask questions, to articulate the structure of the problems for himself.

So Adam reflects on his own origins. This is the opening of Adam's reply:

> For Man to tell how human Life began
> Is hard; for who himself beginning knew? (*Paradise Lost*, VIII.250–1)[84]

The reflexive phrasing ('himself') puts it in a nutshell: what does it mean to understand the body from within the body, what does it mean to be a mind within a body? And he goes on:

> As new wak't from soundest sleep
> Soft on the flourie herb I found me laid
> In Balmie Sweat, which with his Beames the Sun
> Soon dri'd, and on the reaking moisture fed.
> Strait toward Heav'n my wondring Eyes I turnd,
> And gaz'd a while the ample Skie, till rais'd
> By quick instinctive motion up I sprung,
> As thitherward endevoring, and upright
> Stood on my feet (*Paradise Lost*, VIII.253–61)

First he describes himself in the passive voice ('I found me laid') as if this is happening to someone else. Then he looks around and upwards, and

---

[83] Augustine, *De civitate Dei*, XIV.9; Augustine himself cites Cicero, whose central discussion of the passions as *perturbationes animi* comes in *Tusculan Disputations*, ed. King, p. 402.

[84] All references to *Paradise Lost* are taken from Milton, *Paradise Lost: A Poem in Twelve Books*, 2nd edn. (London: S. Simmons, 1674).

discovers the motions of his own body, unaware of the mental or physical processes that make him do it ('By quick instinctive motion'). Immediately, though, in a very compressed way, Milton turns from the question of perceptual and muscular explanation to the issue of language which embraces both. Did Adam, all of a sudden, find himself with a language with which to describe himself, even know himself? Did he acquire all his neural networks in one go?

> My self I then perus'd, and Limb by Limb
> Survey'd, and sometimes went, and sometimes ran
> With supple joints, as lively vigour led:
> But who I was, or where, or from what cause,
> Knew not; to speak I tri'd, and forthwith spake,
> My Tongue obey'd and readily could name
> What e're I saw. Thou Sun, said I, faire Light,
> And thou enlight'nd Earth, so fresh and gay,
> Ye Hills and Dales, ye Rivers, Woods, and Plaines,
> And ye that live and move, fair Creatures, tell,
> Tell, if ye saw, how came I thus, how here? (*Paradise Lost*, VIII.267–77)

The question of Adamic language was one of the great philosophical quandaries of the age.[85] The Genesis story of Adam naming the animals was used as a way of explaining the origins of language itself, and its relationship to things.[86] Leaving aside the issues in this approach to the problem of naming, Milton suggests that it is only by naming other things that Adam can identify himself; and also that to identify himself fully he needs the other creatures to reply, to name and describe him in return. There is an interesting reciprocity here which comes to preoccupy the poem. First, that it is in the nature of Adam's embodiment that it involves an interface between its inner and its outer, that it cannot be understood in its entirety either from the point of reference of a controlling internal consciousness or of an external observer. Second, that embodiment implies otherness, and therefore implies something else outside itself which it is not; and thus that the embodied body immediately yearns for some interaction with that otherness in order to explain itself.

Of course even in paradise the animals cannot answer back. It turns out that for this purpose only Eve will do. But first, in a moment of wonderful philosophical realization, Adam is made to recognize that his own existence predicates the pre-existence of some other being who made him: he

---

[85] Barbara Shapiro, *John Wilkins, 1614–1672* (Berkeley and Los Angeles: University of California Press, 1969), 47.

[86] John Leonard, *Naming in Paradise: Milton and the Language of Adam and Eve* (Oxford: Clarendon Press, 1990), 263–4.

surely cannot have come out of nothing. Without any prior indication of his origin, he nonetheless rejects any possibility of self-replication. He calls out to his maker, who he assumes must be nearby; but 'answer none return'd'. This is a disturbing moment, as the conceptual possibility of true solipsism occurs to him: he falls asleep in shock. Once again, Milton makes an interesting observation at this point: as Adam drifts into unconsciousness, he wonders if he is passing back again into non-existence. Instead he begins to dream, for the first time. Perhaps he is dead, and imagining that he is alive. Mortality, still an abstract concept, begins to limit the horizons of his subjectivity. Either way, in his dream he comes after all into the presence of his maker, who walks with him through paradise. In the midst of his dream, he wakes to find external reality is the same as his inward imagination. His first conversation with God is also a paradigm for what turns out to be a fundamental ethical ideal for embodied personhood within the poem: the reciprocity of dialogue brings Adam's identity into full realization, completeness, by enabling him to see himself as both subject and object. To understand himself as embodied he needs to be recognized as such by another being.

COMING INTO EMBODIMENT

Let us now consider the parallel passage in which Eve recounts her coming into embodiment. This takes place in a very different context in the poem. It comes after the reader's first introduction to paradise, and first view of its human protagonists. This is complicated by the fact that this description is told through the eyes of Satan, who is watching on with bitter resentment at the blissful scenes in front of him. He sees (and we see through his eyes) two figures ('Godlike erect', 'the image of their godlike creator'). Then he listens (and we listen through his ears) to their first conversation in the poem.[87] Adam, rather characteristically, gives Eve some self-important advice about a tree they should try to keep away from. Eve, again characteristically for this early phase of the poem, concurs with perfect sheepishness: 'what thou hast said is just and right'. She agrees what a model husband he is and what a lovely mind he has, and then to prove the point recalls their wedding day, also of course her birthday. This charming memory, however, turns out to have a psychological and emotional complexity which comes as a complete surprise:

---

[87] Stanley E. Fish, *Surprised by Sin: The Reader in Paradise Lost* (Berkeley and Los Angeles: University of California Press, 1971), 100–3.

That day I oft remember, when from sleep
I first awak't, and found my self repos'd
Under a shade of flours, much wondring where
And what I was, whence thither brought, and how.
Not distant far from thence a murmuring sound
Of waters issu'd from a Cave and spread
Into a liquid Plain, then stood unmov'd
Pure as th' expanse of Heav'n; I thither went
With unexperienc't thought, and laid me downe
On the green bank, to look into the cleer
Smooth Lake, that to me seemd another Skie.
As I bent down to look, just opposite,
A Shape within the watry gleam appeard
Bending to look on me, I started back,
It started back, but pleas'd I soon returnd,
Pleas'd it returnd as soon with answering looks
Of sympathie and love; there I had fixt
Mine eyes till now, and pin'd with vain desire,
Had not a voice thus warnd me, (*Paradise Lost*, IV.449–67)

Like Adam, the memory of her birth brings the memory of the confusion that first consciousness brings, the questions of origin that it entails: 'much wondring where | And what I was, whence thither brought, and how'. She too emerges out of the deep sleep of non-being fully embodied and fully sentient.

Yet unlike Adam, hers was not the first body in existence; her embodiment is connected immediately to another body like itself. The prior assumption is that it is this body, Adam's body, which Eve sees appearing before her, and giving her 'answering looks | Of sympathie and love'. But she is not looking at Adam, she is looking at herself. This wonderful premonition of the mirror stage comes not from Freud or Lacan, but from Freud's great forebear: the Latin poet Ovid. This passage is a fantastic interleaving of one of the most celebrated episodes in Book III of Ovid's *Metamorphoses*, the myth of Narcissus.[88] Eve sees her own image in the lake and falls in love with it.

The story of Narcissus brings with it an erotic charge as well as a complex psychology. To anyone brought up thinking that Milton was a puritan, and that puritans are against sex, this may come as a pleasant surprise. But it is not a mistake: it is exactly to Milton's purpose. The Narcissus myth produces a critical moment in the construction of identity within the newly created human universe. What distinguishes human beings in

---

[88] Poole, *Milton and the Idea of the Fall*, 169.

the cosmology of *Paradise Lost* is that they are beings with bodies. In the hierarchy of different forms in the universe, God has pre-eminence. He exists, as do the other members of the Trinity, in some quasi-physical form—all three have voices, minds, wills. The angels, even more so, are identified in physical space: they move from one world to another, they can be seen, hailed from a distance; Raphael has dinner with Adam and Eve.[89] But angels do not have bodies in the full sense. The precise physical form of angels is discussed in detail later in the poem, in fact, in a passage where Adam asks Raphael whether angels can experience love in a full physical way. Raphael answers that angels communicate and interrelate in an altogether superior fashion, although he is vague on precise mechanics:

> Whatever pure thou in the body enjoy'st
> (And pure thou wert created) we enjoy
> In eminence, and obstacle find none
> Of membrane, joynt, or limb, exclusive barrs:
> Easier then Air with Air, if Spirits embrace,
> Total they mix, Union of Pure with Pure (*Paradise Lost*, VIII.622–7)

Adam and Eve, on the other hand, are stuck with 'membrane, joynt, or limb'. Raphael infers that human bodies form an encumbrance in comparison to the pure communion of angelic love. Yet as well as constraint and inhibition, in Milton's theology the human body also conveys a special dignity of status. The bodies of Adam and Eve entail special ethical responsibilities but they also derive from them special benefits and peculiar pleasures.[90]

Having seen her own image in the pond and fallen in love with it, Eve, in a redemption of the Narcissus myth, is called away by a voice beyond herself to find her true erotic fulfilment in a body distinct from her own, that of Adam her husband. This partner is not the same as herself but is as like to hers as a body can be to another; he is 'her image', or at least she is his. This brings into focus the issue concerning embodiment which is essential to the story the poem is trying to tell. In Genesis it is said that God created man in his own image. Yet what does it mean to be the 'image' of another? Clearly Adam and Eve are not identical with God. Indeed one fundamental difference is that they, unlike God, have bodies, as almost everyone agreed in the seventeenth century.[91] At the same time it is their bodies that constitute for them (unlike for God)

[89] Michael Schoenfeldt, *Bodies and Selves in Early Modern England* (Cambridge: Cambridge University Press, 1999), 138.

[90] Tilmouth, *Passion's Triumph over Reason*, 195.

[91] Almond, *Adam and Eve*, 9–10.

their unique identities. Indeed, in the *De doctrina Christiana*, Milton shows the influence of new philosophical approaches to the body in denying the possibility of identity existing outside the physical extension of the bodily person:

> the idea that the spirit of man is separate from his body, so that it may exist somewhere in isolation, complete and intelligent, is nowhere to be found in scripture, and is plainly at odds with nature and reason.[92]

This is just one of the many ways in which theology after Descartes and Hobbes had no way back to previous ways of imagining the soul and body problem. Adam and Eve here are only capable of existence as embodied beings.

The problem of identity and likeness was nonetheless a very old one, and long pre-dated Christian commentary on Genesis. At the end of the *Timaeus*, Plato wrote in a beautiful if opaque passage:

> learning the harmonies and revolutions of the universe, should correct the courses of the head which were corrupted at our birth, and should assimilate the thinking being to the thought, renewing his original nature, so that having assimilated them he may attain to that best life which the gods have set before mankind.[93]

This passage, Peter Harrison argues, lies behind the hermetic tradition which attempted to explain Genesis.[94] Redemption of the Fall might then be a restoration of knowledge to the mind of God.

There are still further paradoxes here which concern identity and gender. In Genesis chapter 1 it seems as if male and female are equally the image of God; but in chapter 2 Eve is like God but at one remove, as a reflection of a reflection of God: she is like Adam, and he is like God. This is a theological problem which Milton does not attempt to resolve doctrinally. But he does suggest a resolution within the narrative, through the representation of the two protagonists as separate bodies. Adam and Eve are inseparably similar, like identical twins, yet they have distinct and distinguishable bodies. They are alike and yet different. Most importantly of all, they are sexually different, of identical species but different gender. In sexual union, however, they become one again, 'one flesh', as the text of Genesis promises, and through this union they are destined also to reproduce further images of themselves who will be almost identical yet physically distinct.

---

[92] *Prose Works of Milton*, vi. 319.
[93] *Timaeus*, 90D; *The Collected Dialogues of Plato*, ed. Edith Hamilton and Huntington Cairns (Princeton: Princeton University Press, 1982), 1209.
[94] Harrison, *Bible, Protestantism, and the Rise of Natural Science*, 59–60.

> hee
> Whose image thou art, him thou shalt enjoy
> Inseparablie thine, to him shalt beare
> Multitudes like thy self (*Paradise Lost*, IV.471–4)

Through merging with his body she will be able to replicate the species, and multiply her image, the image of her body. Eve is captivated by this promise and follows the voice in the direction of the promised partner.

Yet even here Milton has another irony in store: for it turns out that although attracted to her mate, Eve finds him, after all, something of a disappointment after her own image in the water:

> what could I doe,
> But follow strait, invisibly thus led?
> Till I espi'd thee, fair indeed and tall,
> Under a Platan, yet methought less faire,
> Less winning soft, less amiablie milde,
> Then that smooth watry image; (*Paradise Lost*, IV.475–80)

This is further proof of the ambiguity that Milton attaches to the idea of bodily identity. Eve's narcissism has deep roots, and she finds it hard to let it go. Part of this is a narrative prefiguration of the Fall: Eve's predisposition to an attachment to self eventually leads her to the forbidden fruit. Yet there is another reason for her uncertain grasp of identity. Her bodily matter is hard to distinguish from Adam's not only because they share the same humanity, but also because she is, literally, made of the same sample of stuff. Half an hour earlier she was still his rib: it is hardly surprising if she does not yet know what is what.

At this point in the narrative, Milton merges the myth of Narcissus with another potent classical myth of the erotic status of the human body: the myth told by Aristophanes from Plato's *Symposium*. Aristophanes, asked to explain ἔρως (*eros*) at his turn in the dialogue, describes how every pair of lovers was originally one body, which was then cleft in two. After this, all human beings are only one half of their original body, and spend their lives searching for the other half, whether as a male for a male, a female for a male, a male for a female, or a female for a female.[95] In a brilliant conflation of classical and Hebrew mythology, Milton uses the image in Genesis of Eve body-morphing out of Adam to create a metonymic synthesis of the idea of Platonic love:

> back I turnd,
> Thou following cryd'st aloud, Return faire *Eve*,

---

[95] *Symposium*, 189C–193D; ed. and trans. W. R. M. Lamb, Loeb Classical Library (London: Heinemann, 1961), 132–46.

> Whom fli'st thou? whom thou fli'st, of him thou art,
> His flesh, his bone; to give thee being I lent
> Out of my side to thee, neerest my heart
> Substantial Life, to have thee by my side
> Henceforth an individual solace dear;
> Part of my Soul I seek thee, and thee claim
> My other half: with that thy gentle hand
> Seisd mine, I yielded, (*Paradise Lost*, IV.480–9)

Several kinds of poetic language are grafted here with extraordinary compression and exactness. The Ovidian language of ravishment and flight is conflated with the words in the Hebrew of Genesis ('His flesh, his bone') which are quoted over and over again in the liturgy of the marriage ritual. Ideas of out-of-body experience from the Christian mystical tradition (the idea known as *exstasis*) are merged with a standard trope from the commentary tradition on Genesis (known to seventeenth-century puritans and also to Rabbinic commentary) that the rib is taken from the place closest to Adam's heart.[96] All of this comes to a meeting place in the idea of erotic sublimation in Plato, where Milton's words 'My other half' are a literal translation of the Greek of the *Symposium*.[97]

MORBIDITY & TEMPORALITY

However, Adam and Eve are created not only in body but in time. Time, it could be said, is the true human fall. To understand this aspect of the narrative of Adam and Eve, I return to the visual tradition. In Dürer's engraving, Eve's right hand is frozen in a moment burdened by the rest of human history. There is no going back. In taking the fruit from the serpent's mouth, she enters into temporality. Lucas van Leyden placed this into more explicit context by presenting the Fall not, as in Dürer or Baldung, by whom he is visibly influenced, in a single frame, but as a sequence of different temporal states.[98] In an early print, dated in a monogram at the foot of the image to 1510, Lucas shows Adam and Eve as travellers on the road after their expulsion from paradise. Adam carries a spade; Eve places her first-born son Cain in a kind of pouch at her bosom ready for a long journey. It is a skilful exercise in the narrativization of the Fall, an interest which Lucas then takes to a whole new level in his

---

[96] Williams, *The Common Expositor*, 90–1.

[97] *Symposium*, 192D; see Dover's commentary on 'the desire and pursuit of the whole' (ed. Kenneth Dover (Cambridge: Cambridge University Press, 1980), 119).

[98] Lucas's place in Dürer's circle is confirmed by Dürer's drawing of him in 1521, Winkler 816.

1529 series of six complex engravings. In the first, *The Creation of Eve*, God, firmly corporeal, pulls Eve bodily from Adam's sleeping form. In the next, *The Prohibition*, God admonishes the couple, pointing to the tree of knowledge. Temporal continuity between the moments of crisis is shown by an elaborate iconography of gesture. Hands are highly expressive: in Eve's creation in the first engraving, her hand reaches towards Adam's head in proleptic desire. In the *Prohibition*, her hand now rests on Adam's shoulder while she stares with rapt attention towards a fruit dangling from the tree above them. The next two images show the moment of the Fall itself, in the sharing of the fruit in *The Fall*, and then in a highly expressive account of the *Expulsion from Eden*, Adam and Eve in full running panic at the onset of the angel from the clouds. The final pairing of engravings shows Cain's murder of Abel and then the mourning of the first parents for their younger son.

Larry Silver and Susan Smith emphasize the sexual suggestion of the images, and Eve's particular role in this.[99] They find Eve's sexuality present even in her creation. This is further represented in the images, surely, by the iconographic trope of the branch of the tree which hides Adam's genitals. In the *Creation of Eve*, the convenient leaves sprout from the ground of their own accord; but in the *Prohibition*, Eve has snapped the branch off as a handy piece of equipment, we might even say a sex toy, as she holds it playfully in front of him, he firmly grasping her wrist in consent. In the *Fall*, their hands meet, fingertips touching, the fruit performing a kind of coitus between them.

Yet as well as erotic charge, the engravings present a striking understanding of temporality. The two qualities are surely not unconnected. The bodies of Adam and Eve are caught in time, and as such prone to change. Indeed, embodiment is philosophically connected to temporality, as location is only to be understood as happening within a specific time frame, a definition standard from Aristotle.[100] Such a reading lends itself to Lucas's final rendition of *The Fall of Man* (Fig. 22) in an engraving of around 1530, a year after the series of six.[101] This image is about twice the size of its predecessors. Silver and Smith comment on the physicality of the nudes: 'their beauty is quintessentially that of the flesh, not of the spirit'.[102] Diane Russell comments on the contrast in pose between Eve at the left and Adam at the right: Eve's body is 'dynamically frontal and

---

[99] 'Carnal Knowledge: The Late Engravings of Lucas van Leyden', *Nederlands Kunsthistorisch Jaarboek*, 29 (1978), 239–98, this ref. p. 255.

[100] *Physics*, III (205ᵃ) and IV (223ᵇ).

[101] Washington, DC, National Gallery of Art, Lessing J. Rosenwald Collection, 1943.3.5611; Russell, *Eva/Ave*, 121.

[102] 'Carnal Knowledge', 250.

Fig. 22. Lucas van Leyden, *Fall of Man* (c.1530); engraving.

open'; Adam's is 'more equivocal and conveys his hesitancy to take the forbidden fruit'.[103] What the wide span of the image also conveys is a distinctive narrative.[104] As in Dürer's 1504 engraving, clearly the starting point for Lucas's design, the image is divided in two by the trunk of a tree at the centre, against the bark of which the fruit is etched. The fruit, as in Dürer, is the midpoint of our gaze, as it is also (within the image) the focus of the implied gaze of the two original humans. However, the tree at the centre of Lucas's image is not the tree of knowledge. This has been moved to the extreme left, behind Eve's torso; the serpent is coiled around an upper branch, almost out of sight, but with an unmistakably malevolent stare. The effect is to render a sense that the climactic event has already happened. While Eve in Dürer's design is poised on the point of falling, Eve in Lucas's version has eaten her own fruit and is now offering another to Adam. The kinetic energy of the bodies is powerfully conveyed by the fruit which she holds in outstretched grasp while Adam's fingers reach towards it but as yet do not find it. He is a fraction of a second away from sin. Russell comments that the centre of the image is 'supercharged by their gestures' (p. 121). Lucas had been working on the expressive meaning of human hands in the relationship of Adam and Eve for twenty years by now: here he distils powerful meaning into the space between two hands that reach for one another but fail, by a fruit's breadth, to meet. The moment is fraught with yearning but it is also an expression of time itself. As they look backward to the moment preceding this one, they find a future that is now past. It is expressed also by the strong contrast of light in the image—the sunlit verdancy of the background against the heavy shade of the foreground. The eternity of innocence which had awaited them is replaced with the urgency and burden of the present. For Eve there is no going back, while Adam's future is already fixed by the momentum engraved into the image by the movement of her body and his. His hand must now find the fruit, whatever he may desire. The body has a contingent force conveyed by the physics of motion. His will is done.

The implication of flesh in time is an obsession in the work of Lucas's contemporary and Dürer's pupil, Baldung Grien. Baldung worked on the theme of the representation of the Fall for many years. We have already seen in his woodcuts of 1511 (Fig. 20) and 1519 (Fig. 21), that what Bodo Brinkmann calls 'the sexualized Fall' is conveyed by what he calls an 'analogy between the fruit of paradise and the female breast'.[105]

---

[103] Russell, *Eva/Ave*, 121.
[104] See Peter Parshall, 'Lucas van Leyden's Narrative Style', *Nederlands Kunsthistorisch Jaarboek*, 29 (1978), 185–237.
[105] *Hexenlust und Sündenfall*, 163.

The analogy is not only morphological. Flesh shares with fruit an organic process associated with time: it is born, it ripens and grows, and it dies and decays. This consideration of the perishability of human flesh, and especially of female flesh consumed by a male figure of death, preoccupies half a dozen surviving versions of a topos Baldung made his own in the same decade as his images of the Fall: the ancient theme of *Der Tod und das Mädchen*—'death and the maiden'. Once again, Baldung was consciously following Dürer, as in the early copper engraving *Young Girl Threatened by Death* of 1495.[106] There are three painted panels on this theme by Baldung, one in the Bargello in Florence, and two in the Öffentliche Kunstsammlungen in Basle. There are also two drawings in Baldung's characteristic chiaroscuro medium with black and white paint on a brown background, both now in Berlin; and also a brilliantly powerful preparatory drawing (Fig. 23), now in the Uffizi, for one of the panel paintings. While the chronology is not precisely known of this collection of images, one of the Basle paintings is dated to 1517 and the two chiaroscuro drawings are both monogrammed with the date 1515. Much of the iconography is in common. There are two figures, a young woman with long hair, elaborately curled; in one of the chiaroscuro images she is caught in the midst of her coiffure, mirror in hand. Behind her is a *Knochenmann*—a 'bone man', a personification of death. The background in the paintings is black, perhaps alluding to the grave, Brinkmann suggests (p. 168). In all of the images, one or other of the figures is draped with a cloth, an evident representation of a shroud. In the first of the Basle panels, the message of the motif is provided in an inscription: 'HIE · MVST · DV · YN'—*Hier mußt Du hin*—'here you must go'. Death points downwards; the woman clasps her hands in prayer but no prayer can change her destiny.

Like Adam in the Baldung engravings of the Fall, Death holds the woman in an embrace. In the Uffizi drawing, a draft for the second Basle panel but executed with more skill and iconographic finesse, the embrace becomes an immolation. The *Knochenmann*'s legs incorporate her, consume her. She lifts the shroud over her, to protect herself from his advance, but the shape of the shroud merges with the shape of death, his decaying skin indistinguishable from the cloth. If in Cranach's and Baldung's depictions of Venus or Eve, cloth evanesces into transparency, leaving them all the more exposed, here the winding cloth is made a visual metaphor for human skin. The impermanence of flesh gives way to the permanence of death. Meanwhile, the Death-man's fingers dig into her

---

[106] Munich, Staatliche Graphische Sammlung, 1920: 157 D; cat. 32 in Hess and Eser (eds.), *Der frühe Dürer*, 309.

Fig. 23. Hans Baldung Grien, *Death and a Woman* (1515); chiaroscuro drawing.

side by her left breast, and it is as if they sink in without resistance, her flesh already morbid. Meanwhile Death caresses her, holding her head tenderly with his right hand. Her head tilts out to meet him, expectant, desiring, and yet also holding back, reluctant. If she anticipates his kiss, she is disappointed. His lips have disappeared and her lips encounter his teeth. Koerner has suggested death is biting her.[107] But perhaps he is not a necrophage but only necrophiliac: his body has disappeared in senectitude. As lover, he is willing but not able.

If the figure here is female, the strangest of all Baldung's graphic works (Fig. 24) shows a male. *Der behexte Stallknecht*—the 'bewitched stable groom'—is a title that betrays the uncertainty and even opacity which surrounds the interpretation of the image. The title refers to a witch in the window who raises a torch, perhaps in the act of hexing him—but there is no consistent pictorial narrative to confirm this. The heavily foreshortened perspective is divided in two by the threshold of the stable. Filling the doorway is a horse—a powerful symbol of animal sexuality familiar from elsewhere in Baldung's work, most strikingly the series of 'Wild Horses' from the 1530s. In this image (dated from a related drawing to 1544) the horse is paralleled by the prostrate figure of a man, feet thrust so far into the view of the onlooker that they obtrude outside the edge of the room and appear to escape the boundaries of the image altogether. Has the groom been kicked by the horse? Is he unconscious or even dead? His pitchfork and curry comb (for grooming the horse's coat) lie discarded, his fingers useless and even lifeless.

The face of the victim is so distorted by the perspective that he cannot be made out precisely. He has been identified on the basis of other Baldung images as a self-portrait, and the monogram lying by his feet lends substance to the identification. But it might be preferable to see in his unconscious form a kind of oblivion of individuation. Bewitched or plain dead, he is in the process of identity being drained from him. His head is far less prominent than his extravagantly obscene codpiece. Like Dürer's uncanny nude self-portrait, to which Baldung's late work is an inverted and reclothed homage, the bewitched corpse has been reduced to its constituent: mortal flesh. The image is reflexive. Koerner saw it as 'the death of the artist'.[108] Yet rather than being coupled too closely with the artist himself, we perhaps should see in it a representation of human identity, any old body. Like the images of the Fall of Man, this is humankind, not the individual.

---

[107] Koerner, 'The Mortification of the Image: Death as a Hermeneutic in Hans Baldung Grien', *Representations*, 10 (1985), 52–101, this ref. p. 85.
[108] Koerner, *Moment of Self-Portraiture*, 411.

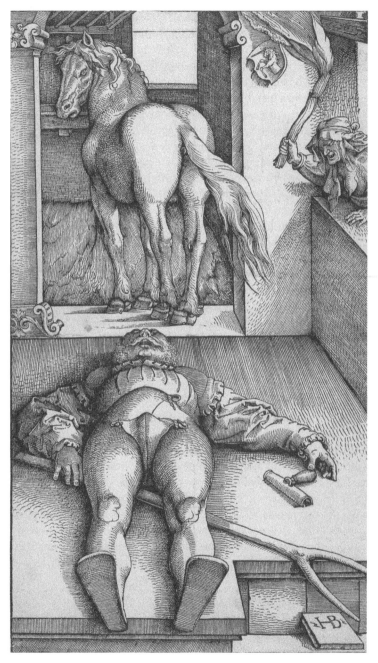

Fig. 24. Hans Baldung Grien, *The Bewitched Stable Groom* (1544–5); woodcut.

The assimilation between Baldung's figurative conceptualization of death and his idea of the Fall is evident from the most famous of all his works, the highly idiosyncratic *Eve, the Serpent and Death*, now in the National Gallery of Canada in Ottawa. It creates a violent juxtaposition of the two genres. The tree of knowledge frames the right side of the oil panel, and a metallic serpent coils round it. Eve, to the left, flauntingly naked and with a simpering smile, reaches out to clutch the tip of the tail of the snake in a suggestive gesture. Meanwhile Death, once again a *Knochenmann*, but with his flesh atrophying and putrefying in front of us, lurks behind the tree, placing his left hand emphatically on Eve's forearm. The serpent's head spirals to bite into Death's wrist. Death holds a blood red fruit aloft; Eve hides a second fruit behind her back.

Dieter Koepplin has traced Baldung's complex imagery of death and sexuality to the *danses macabres* of the fifteenth century, including the trope of the kiss of death.[109] Such wall paintings are often found in southern German churches and sometimes, the other side of the Alps in northern Italy in the Dolomites, on the outside. As Brinkmann comments, Eve is flesh of our flesh and thus corresponds to the Renaissance rhetorical theory of art: *Tua res agitur*, 'this concerns you'.[110] The modern cliché of the medieval *ars moriendi* tradition, that it is a flesh-creeping *memento mori*, sometimes conceals from us what is also a more philosophical interest: subjectivity as reflection of the image in front of us and as the image in the mirror. Mortality conveys the necessity of self-reflection, in the consciousness of finitude.

Thomas da Costa Kaufmann calls Baldung's work a 'negative transformation of Dürer'.[111] One final engraving of Adam and Eve has also been commonly seen as an inversion of the tradition formed by the 1504 image. This is Rembrandt van Rijn's 1638 etching on ivory laid paper (Fig. 25). The sexuality of the image is often remarked on. Russell calls it 'one of the most atavistic images of Adam and Eve ever created', and describes the two figures as 'almost simian'.[112] Perhaps a little exaggeratedly, James Grantham Turner calls them 'a pair of primitives so distinctively ugly that they seem to issue from a private obsession rather than from

---

[109] 'Baldungs Basler Bilder des Todes mit dem nackten Mädchen', *Zeitschrift für Schweizerische Archäologie und Kunstgeschichte*, 35 (1978), 234–41.

[110] *Hexenlust und Sündenfall*, 174.

[111] 'Hermeneutics in the History of Art: Remarks on the Reception of Dürer in Sixteenth- and Early Seventeenth-Century Art', in J. C. Smith (ed.), *New Perspectives on the Art of Renaissance Nuremberg: Five Essays* (Austin: University of Texas Press, 1985), 22–39, this ref. p. 33.

[112] Russell, *Eva/Ave*, 121.

Fig. 25. Rembrandt, *Adam and Eve* (1638); etching.

the contemplation of divine creation'.[113] Their 'pendulous and gaping torsos', he says, make us identify with them 'as fallen, brutalized humanity' (p. 141). Such comments register the disturbance that Rembrandt's image readily evokes. Animal nature, however, is conveyed in a complex manner, here, and psychologizing needs to be seen in the context of the theory of animal and human passions and the hermeneutics of the Old Testament story.

The composition of Eve's bodily gesture, as Christopher White first showed, changed radically as Rembrandt worked on the preparatory drawings for the etching.[114] Whereas in Lucas's traditional psychology of the Fall, Eve openly proffers the fruit and Adam displays gestures of hesitancy and delay, in Rembrandt, Eve in the sketches manifestly tempts Adam, but in the finished version, Adam participates in his own sin. While Eve holds the fruit and looks towards him, Adam stares outright at the fruit and caresses the top of it lost in thought. In this way, the critical responses which have concentrated on brutishness have missed the point. Adam and Eve are distinctively human in the combination of animal desire and complex cognition. They share their responses to the temptation intersubjectively, their hands forming a beautifully composed concentric circle around the object of their desire. Adam's one free hand matches his thought process, with forefinger upraised in the direction of his eyes and brain. His right thumb mirrors Eve's left thumb in a mimesis of corporeal volition. Whereas in Lucas (Fig. 22), the movement of Adam's legs is meanwhile away from Eve, here in Rembrandt he leans into her.

In other respects, Rembrandt continues the line of iconography in Lucas that emphasizes the temporality of the moment. The sunlit background, in which an elephant sportively romps with trunk in forward display, contrasts with the heavy shading in the foreground. The serpent has transformed into a giant winged dragon who merges with the tree so completely that at first it is hard to make him out. The meaning of the metamorphosis is difficult to extract. Russell remarks that it 'adds a further primeval note' (p. 127). This is contrasted by Russell with the elephant, who perhaps represents the statement in the Old Testament that God creates the other animals so that man might not be alone (Genesis 2: 18–20). A different interpretation is possible. Rembrandt's image shows Adam and Eve coming into being as fully human in their combination of embodiment and cognition. Rather than falling into brutal and undifferentiated sexualized life, as in Turner's

---

[113] James Grantham Turner, *One Flesh: Paradisal Marriage and Sexual Relations in the Age of Milton* (Oxford: Clarendon Press, 1987), 140.

[114] *Rembrandt as Etcher: A Study of the Artist at Work*, 2 vols. (University Park, Pa.: Penn State University Press, 1969), i. 43; see also ii (pl. 36–7).

stereotype, they display consciousness of human desire. The image represents both a light and a dark side of this. Above all, it is an image which places life in the context of mortality. Adam and Eve know they are naked but also know, of a sudden, that they are mortal. Death enters the image in the form of the dragon-like serpent, who casts all into shadow, even what before seemed light. Eve's body is deep in gloom. But it is also a fully realized human form, and in her hands she holds the fruit raptly, as a source of nutrition, appetite, and also incipient morbidity. She is engaged in an organic process which gives life but also brings her death.

IMAGINING DEATH

In Milton, too, the fruit is linked to death not only as the theological origin of sin, but as a material signifier of morbidity. Eating, as Michael Schoenfeldt points out, fascinates Milton: it is a source both of physiological and ethical speculation, and reveals what Schoenfeldt has called Milton's 'deeply embodied psychology'.[115] More than this, eating is associated intricately with death. Imbibing and excreting food are not just a reminder that life is organic, these processes, as well as enabling us to live, make us die. As Eve consumes the fruit, the narrator knowingly tells us she 'knew not eating Death' (IX.792). Quite how the alimentary organs would have survived a prelapsarian diet is not properly explained. Jakob Böhme, the Lutheran theologian, held that Adam's body was mystical and only became fleshly after the Fall.[116] John Pordage, described by Richard Baxter as Böhme's most faithful English follower, held that Adam before the Fall ate 'magically, yet with mouth, lips and tongue'.[117] He did not excrete. But the allegorized figure of Death in the poem knows better what he is about when he uses the sense of smell to find his quarry, as Schoenfeldt notices: Death 'snuffed the smell | Of mortal change on earth' (X.273).[118]

Death is the great metaphysical contradiction at the centre of the poem. Life without sin is life without death. But can such a thing be imagined?

---

[115] Schoenfeldt, *Bodies and Selves*, 135.

[116] Harrison, *Bible, Protestantism, and the Rise of Natural Science*, 214.

[117] *Mundorum explicatio, or, The explanation of an hieroglyphical figure wherein are couched the mysteries of the external, internal, and eternal worlds, shewing the true progress of a soul from the court of Babylon to the city of Jerusalem, from the Adamical fallen state to the regenerate and angelical* (London: Lodowick Lloyd, 1661), 61. The book is attributed to John Pordage's son, Samuel, on its title-page; the authorship is still disputed. Harrison (p. 216) gives it to Samuel, whom he describes as the 'English Behmen', but this title was given by Baxter to John, not Samuel. Böhme's influence on this passage is clear in either case.

[118] Schoenfeldt, *Bodies and Selves*, 155.

On the other hand, can life without death truly imagine what an awful consequence death is? Adam and Eve are in continual confusion as to what the terrible punishment stated in the prohibition against eating the fruit really means.[119] At the point of the Fall, Adam is surprised by Eve's continued life, and Satan's: shouldn't they be dead? He is caught wondering if God had got it wrong: 'Perhaps thou shalt not die', he posits (IX.928). Indeed, by Book X he is so perplexed he begins to long for death to resolve the philosophical burdensomeness of living:

> Why am I mockt with death, and length'nd out
> To deathless pain? how gladly would I meet
> Mortalitie my sentence, and be Earth
> Insensible (*Paradise Lost*, X.774–7)

Mortality is a hard condition, but at least it finds its consolation in its own finitude.

Indeed, as Rachel Trubowitz has commented, Adam in his great soliloquy on death is caught in a kind of hopelessly repressed denial of death.[120] He can only imagine the state of death in terms of a variety of continuations of living. The prime of these, of course, is of a kind of sleeping unconsciousness ('sleep secure', X.779). But there is a fear worse than death: life without death, immortality:

> Yet one doubt
> Pursues me still, least all I cannot die,
> Least that pure breath of Life, the Spirit of Man
> Which God inspir'd, cannot together perish
> With this corporeal Clod (*Paradise Lost*, X.782–6)

Flesh longs after all for finitude. Yet the body cannot quite understand its own limits. Perhaps it is not surprising Adam is confused. Raphael, too, in Book V, does not quite know what will happen to the body long term: 'Your bodies may at last turn to spirit', he speculates (V.497). This is what Trubowitz calls 'the unthinkable thought of death'.[121]

Yet perhaps the real mystery is not imagining death, but imagining life. It is in this context that we can understand the parallel narrative in which Adam describes the creation of Eve a second time. For this final primal scene we move to Book VIII where Adam is discoursing with the archangel Raphael. By now we have seen how complex and layered

---

[119] Tilmouth, *Passion's Triumph over Reason*, 198.

[120] 'Sublime/Pauline: Denying Death in *Paradise Lost*', in Elizabeth Jane Bellamy, Patrick Cheney, and Michael Schoenfeldt (eds.), *Imagining Death in Spenser and Milton* (Basingstoke: Palgrave Macmillan, 2003), 131.

[121] Trubowitz, 'Denying Death in *Paradise Lost*', 142.

Milton's narrative method is. The story of Adam and Eve is told in anything but a linear way. It is an act of memorial reconstruction. Milton
uses the techniques of flashback and prolepsis liberally and artfully.
Like any act of memory the narrative is fragmentary and evanescent.
Memory is interspersed with fantasy and fiction, indeed it is impossible to say which is which. In this we see also that Milton uses a method
of multiple narration. He tells the story of Eve's birth out of the body
of Adam all over again, this time from the point of view of the body
that is split rather than the body that is emergent. As Poole comments,
his memory is strikingly different from Eve's.[122] For instance, Eve makes
no mention of the rib, or of Adam's wound which (of course) she
cannot remember. Whereas Adam assumes the priority of his own creation, with the easy superciliousness of an elder sibling, Eve has no such
natural assurance of her own inferiority. This shows us that there is no
single stable point of narration or of interpretation in *Paradise Lost*,
whatever the subsequent efforts of the poem's editors and commentators to find one. There is no objective point from which to view the
body in Milton, only a series of intersecting subjective points.

Adam's long narration to the archangel Raphael of Eve's embodiment is prefaced by a wildly fanciful account of the conversation between Adam and God which precedes it. Adam's sensation on waking
into the world as a single man is one of bewildering loneliness and lack.
He does not even know why he feels alone in paradise, indeed he is not
sure yet what the concept of aloneness might be. But the primordial
apprehension is strong enough for him to pluck up courage to ask God
if he can do something about it. It is a witty passage, in which God is
not uninclined to make rather highbrow jokes and tease Adam about
his bodily urges.[123] He asks if the animals will not suffice for Adam's
purposes, to which Adam replies that they are lovely in their own way,
but do not do much for company. Then God changes tack, saying that
if companionship is so necessary to happiness, he himself must be insufficient in some way. Adam retorts that it is different for God, for
whom loneliness is a rather unique concept. God enjoys delaying Adam
so much that he keeps stretching the jokes out further. But eventually
he says that he was only pretending, and that he intended Adam to
have a partner all along. In granting Adam his wish, indeed, God goes
so far in showing his approval as to couch it in the same Platonic language used by Eve earlier:

---

[122] Poole, *Milton and the Idea of the Fall*, 172.
[123] Turner, *One Flesh*, 183–4.

> I, ere thou spak'st,
> Knew it not good for Man to be alone,
> And no such companie as then thou saw'st
> Intended thee, for trial onely brought,
> To see how thou could'st judge of fit and meet:
> What next I bring shall please thee, be assur'd,
> Thy likeness, thy fit help, thy other self,
> Thy wish, exactly to thy hearts desire. (*Paradise Lost*, VIII.444–51)

'Thy other self', once again, is translated from the Greek: ἕτερος αὐτός.

By this stage Milton has created a mythopoeic language of such sophistication that he can do almost anything he likes by shorthand. Indeed the finesse of his philosophical method is such that we might take it for granted, not realizing how far every word is weighed for its purpose. By now the business of the poem and of the poet are as one: Milton is bringing Eve into being just as God is, in an act of imaginative autonomy. Adam is subject to this act of creation just as the reader is: it all happens in the mind's eye, in the realm of the imaginary, the dream, of what Milton calls (with huge consequences for the Romantic movement) 'fancie':

> As with an object that excels the sense,
> Dazl'd and spent, sunk down, and sought repair
> Of sleep, which instantly fell on me, call'd
> By Nature as in aide, and clos'd mine eyes.
> Mine eyes he clos'd, but op'n left the Cell
> Of Fancie my internal sight, (*Paradise Lost*, VIII.456–61)

The processes of embodiment and metaphorization are now in reverse mode, or perhaps more properly, interchangeable. In a dream within a dream, Adam cannot make sense of what the boundaries of his fictive world are. He cannot, either, tell what are the boundaries of language: what is literal and what is metaphorical.

The problem of metaphor lurks behind every seventeenth-century attempt to create a new reconciliation of the claims of mind and body. The closest analogy here is the concept of 'plastic nature' conjured up by Cudworth to explain the corporeal motion of living things. Plastic nature has 'no *Animal Fancie*, no Express *Con-sense* or *Consciousness* of what it doth'.[124] This is not the same as Descartes's *res cogitans* but it is incorporeal, since for Cudworth all life is in essence incorporeal. Struggling for ar metaphor which will fit, he calls it 'the mere *Umbrage* of *Intellectuality*,

---

[124] *Collected Works of Ralph Cudworth*, ed. Bernhard Fabian, facsimile edition, 2 vols. (Hildesheim: Georg Olms, 1977–9), i. 159.

a faint and shadowy *Imitation* of *Mind* and *Understanding*'.[125] Cudworth is sailing close to hylozoism here, but instead rejects it because of its clumsy mixed metaphors. Hylozoism wishes to explain everything via matter, Cudworth says, but keeps bringing back a thin version of mental conceptions to explain how matter moves, 'spreading them all over upon Matter, just as Butter is spread upon Bread, or Plaster upon a Wall'.[126] Yet he has the same problem in reverse, wanting to make incorporeal spirit 'plastic', or to give it an 'umbrage' that we can see or feel.

Milton puzzles over some of the same linguistic conundrums. However, he finds the problem of metaphor not his fatal flaw but his creative opportunity. Indeed rather than attempting to find some exact philosophical definition of the status of the body we can see him straining to find some language to express the subtlety of the problems involved. Issues of corporeality and incorporeality are left behind in the search for a concept of self which can encompass both mental and bodily explanations. Perhaps there is an affinity here with some of the attempts in cognitive philosophy to redefine embodiment, such as in Andy Clark's pregnant phrase 'soft selves'.[127] Adam and Eve in Milton are indeed 'soft selves', selves that are emergent, indefinite, thinking and speaking, yet also intrinsically bodily. This becomes most apparent in the dazzling description of Eve emerging out of Adam's body:

> by which
> Abstract as in a trance methought I saw,
> Though sleeping, where I lay, and saw the shape
> Still glorious before whom awake I stood;
> Who stooping op'nd my left side, and took
> From thence a Rib, with cordial spirits warme,
> And Life-blood streaming fresh; wide was the wound,
> But suddenly with flesh fill'd up and heal'd:
> The Rib he formd and fashond with his hands;
> Under his forming hands a Creature grew,
> Manlike, but different sex, so lovly faire,
> That what seemd fair in all the World, seemd now
> Mean, or in her summ'd up, in her containd (*Paradise Lost*, VIII.461–73)

The process of metonymic inversion stretches the imagination almost beyond its limits in the idea of Adam's 'wound', borrowed directly from the Hebrew of Genesis but now turned back on itself to form the most

[125] *Works of Ralph Cudworth*, i. 172.
[126] *Works of Ralph Cudworth*, i. 173.
[127] Andy Clark, *Natural-Born Cyborgs: Minds, Technologies, and the Future of Human Intelligence* (Oxford: Oxford University Press, 2003), 137.

explicit sexual metaphor in the whole poem: 'wide was the wound, | But suddenly with flesh fill'd up and heal'd'. It is not inappropriate, then, that in Adam's narrative of the birth of Eve her creation is followed immediately by a narrative of their sexual union.[128] However, in the 'literal' description of sex, Milton uses a deliberately, we might say chastely metaphorical method. Adam and Eve's sexual consummation is more directly rendered in the account of how they came to have bodies in the first place. As in Dürer's engraving, the brute fact of the bodies of Adam and Eve is the biggest puzzle of all.

Embodiment emerges perhaps as the deepest mystery in the poem, as intractable even as the problems of free will or of the existence of evil, which more obviously assail and threaten to overturn Milton's theology. Indeed it is perhaps the case that he finds the problem of embodiment a critical part of the questions of necessity and of ethics. This was a strong motive in his opposition to Hobbes's account of materialism. Hobbes denied the human being free will by making it dependent on the laws of mechanical motion, an automaton. For Milton, this is anathema. The human being is a living thing and therefore moves itself. The body is plastic and volatile. In this way, Milton can barely find a language to frame or contain it. The body in paradise is essentially ambiguous: poised between literal and figural, eros and agape, self and other, subject and object, it evokes from Milton both the most passionate of defences and the most embarrassed of disavowals. It creates insoluble difficulties of theology but inspires at the same time his most creative energies of poesis.

---

[128] Michael Schoenfeldt, '"Commotion Strange": Passion in *Paradise Lost*', in *Reading the Early Modern Passions*, 55.

Bibliography

PRIMARY SOURCES

A most pleasant comedie of Mucedorus (London: William Jones, 1598)

Alberti, Leon Battista, *On Painting*, trans. John R. Spencer (New Haven: Yale University Press, 1970)

Aristotle, *Nicomachean Ethics Books II–IV*, trans. C. C. W. Taylor (Oxford: Oxford University Press, 2006)

—— *Nicomachean Ethics*, ed. J. Bywater (Oxford: Clarendon Press, 1975)

—— *On the Soul, Parva Naturalia, On Breath*, ed. and trans. W. S. Hett, Loeb Classical Library (London: Heinemann, 1964)

—— *Rhetoric*, ed. and trans. John Henry Freese, Loeb Classical Library, (Cambridge, Mass.: Harvard University Press, 1994)

Arnold, Matthew, *Culture and Anarchy*, ed. John Dover Wilson (Cambridge: Cambridge University Press, 1971)

—— *The Poems of Matthew Arnold*, ed. Kenneth Allot (London: Longman, 1965)

Augustine, *Concerning the City of God against the Pagans*, ed. David Knowles and trans. Henry Bettenhouse (Harmondsworth: Penguin, 1972)

—— *Confessiones*, ed. L. Verheijen, Corpus Christianorum Series Latina, 27 (Turnholt: Brepols, 1981)

—— *Confessions*, trans. Henry Chadwick (Oxford: Oxford University Press, 1991)

—— *De civitate Dei*, Benedictine Edition (Paris: Gaume, 1838)

—— *De civitate Dei*, ed. B. Dombart and A. Kalb, 2 vols., Corpus Christianorum Series Latina, 47–8 (Turnholt: Brepols, 1955)

—— *De Genesi ad litteram, De Genesi contra Manichaeos, Opus imperfectus, Patrologia Latina*, 34

—— *De libero arbitrio, Patrologia Latina*, 32

—— *Retractiones, Patrologia Latina*, 32

Bastard, Thomas, *Chrestoleros Seuen bookes of epigrames* (London: Richard Bradocke, 1598)

Bayly, Lewis, *The practise of pietie directing a Christian how to walke that he may please God* (London: Iohn Hodgets, 1613)

Beard, Thomas, *The Theatre of Gods Iudgements: or, a collection of histories out of Sacred, Ecclesiasticall, and prophane Authours, concerning the admirable Iudgements of God vpon the transgressours of his commandements* (London: Adam Islip, 1597)

—— *The Theatre of Gods Ivdgements: Wherein is represented the admirable iustice of God against all notorious sinners, both great and small* (London: Adam Islip, 1612)

Beaumont, Francis, *The knight of the burning pestle* (London: Nicholas Okes, 1613)

Bernard of Clairvaux, *Sermones de diversis, Patrologia Latina*, 183

Beza, Theodore, *A briefe and piththie summe of the Christian faith made in forme of a confession, vvith a confutation of all such superstitious errours, as are contrary therevnto. Made by Theodore de Beza. Translated out of Frenche by R.F.* (London: Richard Serll, [1565?])

——*Iesu Christi Domini nostri Novum Testamentum, sive Novum foedus, cujus Graeco contextui respondent interpretationes duae* (Cambridge: Roger Daniel, 1642)

[Bible, Bishops'] *The holie Bible conteynyng the olde Testament and the newe* (London: Richard Jugge, 1568)

[Bible, Coverdale] *Biblia the Bible, that is, the holy Scripture of the Olde and New Testament, faithfully and truly translated out of Douche and Latyn in to Englishe* ([Cologne?: E. Cervicornus and J. Soter?]), 1535)

[Bible, Geneva], *The Bible and Holy Scriptures conteyned in the Olde and Newe Testament. Translated according to the Ebrue and Greke, and conferred with the best translations in diuers languages* (Geneva, 1561)

[Bible, Geneva] *The Bible, Translated according to the Ebrew and Greeke... With most profitable Annotations vpon all the hard places* (London: Christopher Barker, 1589)

[Bible, Geneva] *The Newe Testament of Our Lord Iesus Christ, Translated out of Greeke by Theod. Beza. Whereunto are adioined briefe summaries of doctrine... by the said Theod. Beza, and also short expositions of the phrases and hard places, taken out of the large Annotations of the foresaid Author and Ioach. Camerarius, by Loseler. Villerius. Englished by L. Tomson* (London: Christopher Barker, 1597)

[Bible, Great Bible], *The Byble in Englyshe that is to saye, the content of all the holye scrypture, bothe of the olde and newe Testament, truly translated after the veryte of the Hebrue and Greke textes* (London: Thomas Berthelet, 1540)

[Bible, King James Version] *The Holy Bible conteyning the Old Testament, and the New | newly translated out of the originall tongues, and with the former translations diligently compared and reuised, by His Maiesties speciall commandement* (London: Robert Barker, 1612)

[Bible, Matthew's] *The Byble which is all the holy Scripture: In whych are contayned the Olde and Newe Testament truly and purely translated into Englysh by Thomas Matthew* (Antwerp?: 1537)

[Bible, New Testament, Geneva], *The Newe Testament of our Lord Iesus Christ, translated out of Greeke by Theod. Beza. And also short expositions on the phrases and hard places, taken out of the large annotations of the foresayd Authour and Ioach. Camerarius, by P. Loseler Villerius. Englished by L. Tomson* (London: Christopher Barker, 1590)

[Bible, Old Testament, Tyndale], *The fyrst boke of Moses called Genesis* ([Antwerp: Martin de Keyser?], 1530)

Blackstone, William, *Commentaries on the Laws of England* (Oxford, 1769)

Bolt, Robert, *A Man for All Seasons* (New York: Vintage, 1962)

Bond, Ronald B. (ed.), *Certain Sermons or Homilies (1547)* (Toronto: University of Toronto Press, 1987)

Bonhoeffer, Dietrich, *Letters and Papers from Prison*, ed. Eberhard Bethge (London: SCM Press, 1972)

Bozio, Tommaso, *De signis ecclesiae*, 2 vols. (Rome: Ascanio, 1591)

Calvin, Jean, *Genesis*, ed. John King (Edinburgh: Banner of Truth, 1965)

——*Institutio Christianae religionis* (Geneva: Robert Estienne, 1559)

——*Institution de la religion chrestienne*, ed. Jean-Daniel Benoit, 5 vols. (Paris: Vrin, 1957)

——*The Institution of Christian Religion, wrytten in Latine by maister Ihon Caluin, and translated into Englysh according to the authors last edition* (London: Reinolde Wolfe & Richard Harison, 1561)

——*Ioannis Calvini opera quae supersunt omnia*, ed. Wilhelm Baum, Edvard Cunitz, and Edvard Reuss, Corpus Reformatorum (Braunschweig, 1891)

——*Opera selecta*, ed. P. Barth and W. Niesel, 5 vols. (Munich: Kaiser, 1928)

Cardano, Girolamo, *Hieronymi Cardani Mediolensis opera omnia* (Lyons: J. A. Huguetan and M. A. Ravaud, 1663)

Cecil, William, *Precepts, or, Directions for the well ordering and carriage of a mans life, through the whole course thereof: left by William, Lord Burghly, to his Sonne, at his death* (London: Thomas Jones, 1636)

Certayne sermons, or homelies appoynted by the kynges Maiestie, to be declared and redde, by all persones, vicars, or curates, euery Sondaye in their churches, where they haue cure (London: Richard Grafton, 1547)

Chapman, George, *Bussy d'Ambois a tragedie: as it hath been often presented at Paules* (London: William Aspley, 1607)

——Ben Jonson, and John Marston, *Eastward hoe As it was playd in the Blackfriers. By the Children of her Maiesties Reuels. Made by George Chapman. Ben: Ionson. Ioh: Marston* (London: George Eld, 1605)

Chaucer, Geoffrey, *The Riverside Chaucer*, ed. Larry D. Benson, 3rd edn. (Oxford: Oxford University Press, 1988)

Cicero, *Brutus, Orator*, ed. and trans. G. L. Hendrickson and H. M. Hubbell, Loeb Classical Library (London: Heinemann, 1962)

——*De finibus*, ed. and trans. H. Rackham, Loeb Classical Library (London: Heinemann, 1931)

——*De senectute, De amicitia, De divinatione*, ed. and trans. W. A. Falconer, Loeb Classical Library (London: Heinemann, 1964)

——*Tusculan Disputations*, ed. and trans. J. E. King, Loeb Classical Library (Cambridge, Mass.: Harvard University Press, 1960)

Coleridge, Samuel Taylor, *Collected Works*, 7 vols. ed. W. G. T. Shedd (New York: Harper, 1853)

Congreve, William, *The Complete Plays of William Congreve*, ed. Herbert Davis (Chicago: University of Chicago Press, 1967)

Cranmer, Thomas, *All the submyssyons and recantations of Thomas Cranmer, late Archbyshop of Canterburye: truely set forth both in Latyn and Englysh, agreable to the originalles, wrytten and subscribed with his owne hande* (London: John Cawood, 1556)

—— *Bishop Cranmer's Recantacyons*, ed. Richard Houghton with James Gairdner, Bibliographical and Historical Miscellanies, 15 (London: Philobiblon Society, 1854)

—— *Catechismus, that is to say, a shorte instruction into Christian religion for the synguler commoditie and profyte of childre[n] and yong people* (London: Nicholas Hyll, 1548)

—— *Miscellaneous Writings and Letters of Thomas Cranmer*, ed. John Cox, Parker Society (Cambridge: Cambridge University Press, 1846)

—— *The Remains of Archbishop Cranmer*, ed. Henry Jenkyns, Parker Society (Cambridge: Cambridge University Press, 1833)

Crespin, Jean, *Histoire des vrays tesmoins de la verité* (Geneva, 1570)

Cudworth, Ralph, *Collected Works of Ralph Cudworth*, ed. Bernhard Fabian, facsimile edition, 2 vols. (Hildesheim: Georg Olms, 1977–9)

Cummings, Brian (ed.), *The Book of Common Prayer: The Texts of 1549, 1559, and 1662* (Oxford: Oxford University Press, 2011)

Deguileville, Guillaume de, *The Pilgrimage of the Life of Man, English by John Lydgate, from the French of Guillaume de Deguileville*, ed. F. J. Furnivall and Katherine B. Locock, 2 vols. (London: Early English Text Society, 1899)

Descartes, René, *Meditationes de prima philosophia*, ed. Geneviève Rodis-Lewis (Paris: Vrin, 1978)

—— *Meditations on First Philosophy*, trans. Michael Moriarty, Oxford World's Classics (Oxford: Oxford University Press, 2008)

—— *Les Passions de l'âme*, ed. Geneviève Rodis-Lewis (Paris: Vrin, 1994)

—— *The Philosophical Writings of Descartes*, ed. John Cottingham, Robert Stoothoff, and Dugald Murdoch, 2 vols. (Cambridge: Cambridge University Press, 1984–5)

Donne, John, *ΒΙΑΘΑΝΑΤΟΣ a declaration of that paradoxe or thesis, that selfe-homicide is not so naturally sinne, that it may never be otherwise: wherein the nature and the extent of all those lawes, which seeme to be violated by this act, are diligently surveyed | written by Iohn Donne* (London: John Dawson, [1644])

—— *Biathanatos*, ed. E. W. Sullivan (Newark, Del.: University of Delaware Press, 1984)

—— *Deaths duell, or, A consolation to the soule, against the dying life, and liuing death of the body* (London: Thomas Harper, [1632])

—— *Letters to severall persons of honour written by John Donne Sometime Deane of St Pauls London. Published by John Donne, Dr. of the civill law* (London: J. Flesher for Richard Marriot, 1651)

Dürer, Albrecht, *Albrecht Dürer 1471 bis 1528: Das gesamte graphische Werk*, 2 vols. (Munich: Rogner & Bernhard, 1970)

Eliot, Thomas, *Bibliotheca Eliotae Eliotis librarie* (London: Thomas Berthelet, 1542)

—— *The dictionary of syr Thomas Eliot knight* (London: Thomas Berthelet, 1538)

Erasmus, Desiderius, *The first tome or volume of the Paraphrase of Erasmus vpon the Newe Testamente* ([London]: Edwarde Whitchurche, 1548)

—— *Nouum testamentum omne tertio ab Erasmo recognitum*, 3rd edn., 2 vols. (Basel: Johan Froben, 1522)

Ercker, Lazarus, *Fleta minor the laws of art and nature, in knowing, judging, assaying, fining, refining and inlarging the bodies of confin'd metals: in two parts* (London: Thomas Dawkes, 1683)

Fisher, John, *English Works of John Fisher, Bishop of Rochester: Sermons and Other Writings, 1520–1535*, ed. Cecilia A. Hatt (Oxford: Oxford University Press, 2002)

Foxe, John, *Actes and Monuments of these latter and perrilous dayes* (London: Iohn Day, 1563)

—— *Actes and Monuments*, 2 vols. (London: John Day, 1583)

—— *Christ Iesus triumphant A fruitefull treatise, wherin is described the most glorious triumph, and conquest of Christ Iesus our sauiour, ouer sinne, death, the law, the strength and pride of Sathan, and the world* (London: Iohn Daye, 1579)

—— *The Ecclesiasticall history contaynyng the Actes and Monumentes of thynges passed in euery kynges tyme in this Realme, especially in the Church of England* (London: John Daye, 1570)

—— *Rerum in ecclesia gestarum commentarii*, 2 vols. (Basel: N. Brylinger and J. Oporinus, 1559–63)

—— *The Unabridged Acts and Monuments Online* or *TAMO* (HRI Online Publications, Sheffield, 2011). <http//www.johnfoxe.org>

Furnivall, F. J. (ed.), *Political, Religious, and Love Poems*, Early English Text Society 15, repr. edn. (Oxford: Oxford University Press, 1965)

Gardiner, Stephen, *The Letters of Stephen Gardiner*, ed. J. A. Muller (Cambridge: Cambridge University Press, 1933)

Gataker, Thomas, *Of the nature and vse of Lots; A Treatise historicall and theologicall* (London: Edward Griffin, 1619)

Golding, Arthur, *A tragedie of Abrahams sacrifice, written in french by Theodore Beza* (London: Thomas Vautrollier, 1577)

Gouge, William, *The extent of Gods prouidence, set out in a sermon, preached in Black-fryers Church, 5. Nov. 1623, On occasion of the downe-fall of Papists in a Chamber at the said Black-fryers, 1623. Oct. 27* (London: George Miller, 1631)

Greene, Robert, *Mamillia. A mirrour or looking-glasse for the ladies of Englande* (London: Thomas Woodcock, 1583)

Haemstede, Adriaan van, *De geschiedenisse ende den doodt der vromer Martelaren, die om het ghetuyghenisse des Evangeliums haer bloedt ghestort hebben* (Emden, 1559)

Harpsfield, Nicholas, *The Life and death of Sr Thomas More, knight, sometimes Lord high Chancellor of England*, ed. Elsie Vaughan Hitchcock, Early English Text Society (London: Oxford University Press, 1932)

Hayward, John, *The first part of the life and raigne of King Henrie the IIII* (London: John Wolfe, 1601)

—— *The sanctuarie of a troubled soule written by I.H.* (London: John Wolfe, 1601)

Hegel, Georg Wilhelm Friedrich, *The Philosophy of History*, trans. Robert S. Hartman (Indianapolis: Bobbs-Merrill, 1953)

Heidegger, Martin, *The Question Concerning Technology and Other Essays*, trans. William Lovitt (New York: Harper and Row, 1977)

Heine, Heinrich, *Sämtliche Schriften*, ed. K. Briegleb (Darmstadt: Wissenschaftliche Buchgesellschaft, 1968–)

Hobbes, Thomas, *The Collected Works of Thomas Hobbes*, ed. Sir William Molesworth, 12 vols., repr. edn. (London: Routledge/Thoemmes Press, 1992)

——*Leviathan*, ed. Richard Tuck, Cambridge Texts in the History of Political Thought, rev. edn. (Cambridge: Cambridge University Press, 1996)

——*Man and Citizen (De Homine and De Cive)*, ed. Bernard Gert (Indianapolis: Hackett, 1991)

Holinshed, Raphael, *The Third volume of Chronicles, beginning at duke William the Norman, commonlie called the Conqueror* (London: Henry Denham, 1587)

Hooper, John, *A Declaration of Christe and of his offyce* (Zürich: A. Fries, 1547)

Huggarde, Miles, *The displaying of the Protestantes, [and] sondry their practises, with a description of diuers their abuses of late frequented* (London: Robert Caly, 1556)

Huloet, Richard, *Huloets dictionarie newelye corrected, amended, set in order and enlarged, vvith many names of men, tovvnes, beastes, foules, fishes, trees, shrubbes, herbes, fruites, places, instrumentes &c.* (London: Thomas Marsh, 1572)

Hume, David, *Essays on Suicide and the Immortality of the Soul, ascribed to the late David Hume, Esq., never before published* (London: M. Smith, 1783)

Hyperius, Andreas, *A speciall treatise of Gods prouidence and of comforts against all kinde of crosses and calamities to be drawne from the same With an exposition of the 107. Psalme. Heerunto is added an appendix of certaine sermons & questions, (conteining sweet & comfortable doctrine) as they were vttered and disputed ad clerum in Cambridge. By P. Baro D. in Diui.* ([London]: Iohn Wolfe, [1588?])

Jonson, Ben, *The alchemist. VVritten by Ben. Ionson* (London: Thomas Snodham, 1612)

——*Bartholmew fayre: a comedie, acted in the yeare, 1614 by the Lady Elizabeths seruants, and then dedicated to King Iames, of most blessed memorie* (London: Robert Allot, 1631)

——*The comicall satyre of euery man out of his humor. As it was first composed by the author B.I.* (London: Adam Islip, 1600)

Knewstub, John, *A sermon preached at Paules Crosse the Fryday before Easter, commonly called good Friday* (London: Thomas Dawson, 1579)

Letters and Papers, Foreign and Domestic, of the Reign of Henry VIII, ed. J. S. Brewer, J. Gairdner, and R. H. Brodie, 36 vols. (1862–1932)

Lipsius, Iustus, *Iusti Lipsii Epistolarum selectarum chilias* (Cologne: Antonius Meraldus, 1616)

——*Iusti Lipsii Manuductionis ad Stoicam philosophiam libri tres* (Antwerp: Officina Plantiniana, 1604)

Livy, *Ab urbe condita*, ed. and trans. B. O. Foster, Loeb Classical Library, 14 vols. (Cambridge, Mass.: Harvard University Press, 1961)

Loe, William, *Songs of Sion Set for the ioy of gods deere ones, vvho sitt here by the brookes of this vvorlds Babel, & vveepe vvhen they thinke on Hierusalem vvhich is on highe. By W.L.* ([Hamburg: n.p., 1620])

Lucretius, *Titi Lucreti Cari De rerum natura libri sex*, ed. and trans. Cyril Bailey, 3 vols. (Oxford: Clarendon Press, 1947)

Lupton, Thomas, *A persuasion from papistrie vvrytten chiefely to the obstinate, determined, and dysobedient English papists* (London: Henry Bynneman, 1581)

Luther, Martin, *Biblia: das ist, die ganze Heilige Schrifft Deutsch. Mart. Luth.*, 2 vols. (Wittenberg: Hans Lufft, 1534)

——*D. Martin Luthers Werke, kritische Gesamtausgabe*, 68 vols. (WA) (Weimar: Böhlau, 1883–1999)

——*D. Martin Luthers Werke, kritische Gesamtausgabe: Briefwechsel*, 18 vols. (WA Br.) (Weimar: Böhlau, 1930–85)

——*Lectures on Genesis*, ed. Jaroslav Pelikan, 4 vols. (St Louis, Mich.: Concordia, 1961)

Marlowe, Christopher, *Doctor Faustus and Other Plays*, ed. David Bevington and Eric Rasmussen, Oxford World's Classics (Oxford: Oxford University Press, 1995)

Martial, *Epigrams*, ed. and trans. D. R. Shackleton Bailey, Loeb Classical Library, 3 vols. (Cambridge, Mass.: Harvard University Press, 1993)

Milton, John, *Complete Prose Works of John Milton*, 8 vols. (New Haven: Yale University Press, 1953–82)

——*A Maske Presented at Ludlow Castle, 1634* (London: Humphrey Robinson, 1637)

——*Paradise Lost. A Poem in Twelve Books*, 2nd edn. (London: S. Simmons, 1674)

Montaigne, Michel de, *An Apology for Raymond Sebond*, trans. M. A. Screech (London: Penguin Books, 1987)

——*The Complete Works*, trans. Donald M. Frame (New York: Everyman's Library, 2003)

——[trans. John Florio], *Essays vvritten in French by Michael Lord of Montaigne, Knight of the Order of S. Michael, gentleman of the French Kings chamber: done into English, according to the last French edition, by Iohn Florio reader of the Italian tongue vnto the Soueraigne Maiestie of Anna, Queene of England, Scotland, France and Ireland, &c. And one of the gentlemen of hir royall priuie chamber* (London: Melchior Bradwood for Edward Blount and William Barret, 1613)

——*Les Essais*, ed. Jean Balsamo, Michel Magnien, and Catherine Magnien-Simonin (Paris: Gallimard, 2007)

——*The Montaigne Project: Villey edition of the Essais with corresponding digital page images from the Bordeaux Copy.* [ARTFL Project / Montaigne Studies, University of Chicago.] <http://www.lib.uchicago.edu/efts/ARTFL/projects/montaigne>

——*Oeuvres complètes*, ed. Albert Thibaudet and Maurice Rat, Bibliothèque de la Pléiade (Paris: Gallimard, 1962)

More, Thomas, *Complete Works of Thomas More*, 15 vols. (New Haven: Yale University Press, 1963–97)

More, Thomas, *The Correspondence of Sir Thomas More*, ed. Elizabeth Frances Rogers (Princeton: Princeton University Press, 1947)

——*A dialoge of comfort against tribulacion* (London: Richard Tottell, 1553)

——*A Dialogue of Comfort against Tribulation*, ed. Leland Miles (Bloomington: Indiana University Press, 1965)

—— *The Last Letters of Thomas More*, ed. Alvaro de Silva (Grand Rapids, Mich.: William B. Eerdmans, 2000)

—— *The vvorkes of Sir Thomas More Knyght, sometyme Lorde Chauncellour of England, wrytten by him in the Englysh tonge* (London: John Cawod, John Waly, and Richard Tottell, 1557)

Morice, James, *A briefe treatise of oathes exacted by ordinaries and ecclesiasticall iudges, to answere generallie to all such articles or interrogatories, as pleaseth them to propound And of their forced and constrained oathes ex officio, wherein is proued that the same are vnlawfull* (Middelburg: Richard Schilders, 1590)

Nashe, Thomas, *A pleasant comedie, called Summers last will and testament* (London: Simon Stafford, 1600)

——*Strange newes, of the intercepting certaine letters, and a conuoy of verses, as they were going priuilie to victuall the Low Countries* (London: John Danter, 1592)

Nietzsche, Friedrich, *The Gay Science*, trans. Walter Kaufmann (New York: Vintage Books, 1974)

Painter, William, *The palace of pleasure beautified, adorned and well furnished, with pleasaunt histories and excellent nouelles* (London: John Kingston, 1566)

Peele, George, *The araygnement of Paris a pastorall. Presented before the Queenes Maiestie, by the Children of her chappell* (London: Henry Marsh, 1584)

Perkins, William, *A golden chaine: or The description of theologie containing the order of the causes of saluation and damnation, according to Gods word* (Cambridge: John Legate, 1600)

—— *The Workes of that famous and worthie minister of Christ, in the Vniuersitie of Cambridge, M. W. Perkins*, 3 vols. (Cambridge: Iohn Legate, 1608–9)

Peter Lombard, *Sententiae in IV libris distinctae*, Bonaventuran edn., 2 vols. in 3 parts (Rome: Collegii S. Bonaventurae, 1971)

Philips, Edward, *The new world of English words, or, A general dictionary containing the interpretations of such hard words as are derived from other languages* (London: E. Tyler, 1658)

Pico della Mirandola, *Oratio de hominis dignitate* (Bologna: Benedetto Faelli, 1496)

Plato, *The Collected Dialogues of Plato*, ed. Edith Hamilton and Huntington Cairns (Princeton: Princeton University Press, 1982)

——*Euthyphro, Apology, Crito, Phaedo, Phaedrus*, ed. and trans. H. N. Fowler, Loeb Classical Library (London: Heinemann, 1977)

——*Laws*, ed. and trans. R. G. Bury, Loeb Classical Library, 2 vols. (London: Heinemann, 1926)

——*Lysis, Symposium, Gorgias*, ed. and trans. W. R. M. Lamb, Loeb Classical Library (London: Heinemann, 1961)

——*Phaedo*, ed. C. J. Rowe (Cambridge: Cambridge University Press, 1993)

——*Phaedo*, trans. David Gallop (Oxford: Clarendon Press, 1975)

——*Republic*, ed. and trans. Paul Shorey, Loeb Classical Library, 2 vols. (London: Heinemann, 1963)

——*Symposium*, ed. Kenneth Dover (Cambridge: Cambridge University Press, 1980)

Pliny, *Letters and Panegyricus*, ed. and trans. Betty Radice, Loeb Classical Library, 2 vols. (London: Heinemann, 1969)

Pordage, Samuel (?), *Mundorum explicatio, or, The explanation of an hieroglyphical figure wherein are couched the mysteries of the external, internal, and eternal worlds, shewing the true progress of a soul from the court of Babylon to the city of Jerusalem, from the Adamical fallen state to the regenerate and angelical* (London: Lodowick Lloyd, 1661)

Quintilian, *Institutio oratoria*, ed. and trans. Donald A. Russell, Loeb Classical Library, 5 vols. (Cambridge, Mass.: Harvard University Press, 2001)

Reynolds, John, *The Trivmphs of Gods revenge* (London: Felix Kyngston, 1621)

Ridley, Nicholas, *Certen godly, learned, and comfortable conferences, betwene…Rydley…Latymer during the tyme of their emprysonmentes* ([Strasbourg: heirs of W. Rihel], 1556)

Rogers, Richard, *Seuen treatises containing such direction as is gathered out of the Holie Scriptures, leading and guiding to true happines, both in this life, and in the life to come: and may be called the practise of Christianitie* (London: Felix Kyngston, 1603)

Roper, William, *The Life of Sir Thomas Moore, knighte*, ed. Elsie Vaughan Hitchcock, Early English Text Society (London: Oxford University Press, 1935)

St German, Christopher, *Doctor and Student*, ed. T. F. L. Plunkett and J. L. Barton, Selden Society, no. 91 (London, 1974)

——*A dyaloge in Englysshe, bytwyxt a Doctour of Dyuynyte, and a student in the lawes of Englande of the groundes of the sayd lawes and of conscyence* (London?: Robert Wyer, [1530?])

Sedulius, Henricus, *Praescriptiones Adversus Haereses* (Antwerp: Officina Plantiniana, 1606)

Seneca, *Ad Lucilium Epistulae Morales*, ed. and trans. Richard M. Gummere, Loeb Classical Library, 3 vols. (London: Heinemann, 1917–25)

——*Moral Essays*, ed. and trans. John Basore, Loeb Classical Library, 3 vols. (London: Heinemann, 1928–35)

——*Seneca his tenne tragedies, translated into Englysh* (London: Thomas Marsh, 1581)

Shakespeare, William, *The First Folio of Shakespeare* (New York: Norton, 1968)

——*Hamlet*, ed. Harold Jenkins, Arden Series 2 (London: Methuen, 1982)

——*Lucrece* (London: Richard Field, 1594)

——*Macbeth*, ed. Kenneth Muir, Arden Series 2 (London: Methuen, 1951)

——*Othello*, ed. M. R. Ridley, Arden Series 2 (London: Methuen, 1958)

——*Richard II*, ed. Peter Ure, Arden Series 2 (London: Methuen, 1956)

——*Richard III*, ed. Antony Hammond, Arden Series 2 (London: Methuen, 1981)

Shakespeare, William, *The Tragedy of Macbeth*, ed. Nicholas Brooke, The Oxford Shakespeare (Oxford: Oxford University Press, 1990)

Sidney, Philip, *Complete Works of Sir Philip Sidney*, ed. Albert Feuillerat, 4 vols. (Cambridge: Cambridge University Press, 1912)

Sophocles, *Oedipus the King, Oedipus at Colonus, Antigone*, ed. and trans. F. Storr, Loeb Classical Library (London: Heinemann, 1962)

Southwell, Robert, *An epistle of comfort to the reuerend priestes* [London: John Charlewood?, 1587?]

Speght, Rachel, *A Mouzell for Melastomus, the cynicall bayter of, and foule mouther barker against Evahs sex* (London: Nicholas Okes, 1617)

Spenser, Edmund, *Complaints Containing sundrie small poemes of the worlds vanitie* (London: William Ponsonbie, 1591)

Stanyhurst, Richard, *The First Foure Bookes of Virgils Aeneis, Translated into English Heroicall Verse, by Richard Stanyhurst* (London: Henrie Bynneman, 1583)

Stapleton, Thomas, *A counterblast to M. Hornes vayne blaste against M. Fekenham* (Louvain: John Fowler, 1567)

—— *Tres Thomae* (Douai: Borgard, 1588)

Starkey, Thomas, *A Dialogue between Pole and Lupset*, ed. T. F. Mayer, Camden Society, Fourth Series, 37 (London: Royal Historical Society, 1989)

Sutton, Christopher, *Disce mori. Learne to die A religious discourse, moouing euery Christian man to enter into a serious remembrance of his ende* (London: John Wolfe, 1600)

—— *Disce vivere* (London: E. Short, [1604?])

—— *Godly meditations vpon the most holy sacrament of the Lordes Supper With manie thinges apperteininge to the highe reuerenee [sic] of soe greate a mysterie.* (London: I[ohn] W[indet], 1601)

Tacitus, *Histories, Annals*, ed. and trans. C. H. Moore and J. Jackson, Loeb Classical Library, 4 vols. (London: Heinemann, 1962)

Thomas Aquinas, *Summa Theologica diligenter emendata*, ed. de Rubeis, Billuart et al., 6 vols. (Turin: Typographia Pontificia, 1860)

Thomas, A. H., and I. D. Thornley (eds.), *Great Chronicle of London* (London: Corporation of the City, 1938)

The true chronicle history of King Leir (London: John Wright, 1605)

Tudor Royal Proclamations, ed. P. Hughes and J. Larkin, 3 vols. (New Haven: Yale University Press, 1964–9)

Tyndale, William, *An Answer to Sir Thomas More's Dialogue*, ed. Henry Walter, Parker Society (Cambridge: Cambridge University Press, 1848)

—— *An Answere vnto Sir Thomas Mores Dialoge*, ed. Anne M. O'Donnell and Jared Wicks, The Independent Works of William Tyndale, 3 (Washington, DC: Catholic University of America Press, 2000)

—— *A compendious introduccion, prologe or preface vn to the pistle off Paul to the Romayns* ([Worms: P. Schoeffer, 1526])

—— *Doctrinal Treatises*, ed. Henry Walter, Parker Society (Cambridge: Cambridge University Press, 1848)

—— *Expositions of Scripture*, ed. Henry Walter, Parker Society (Cambridge: Cambridge University Press, 1849)

—— *The obedience of a Christen man and how Christen rulers ought to governe* ([Antwerp: Maarten de Kaiser, 1528])

Virgil, *Aeneidos: liber sextus*, ed. R. G. Austin (Oxford: Clarendon Press, 1977)

—— *Omnia opera: diligenti castigatione exculta: aptissimisque ornata figuris* (Venice: B. Zannis de Portesio, 1510)

Whitney, Geoffrey, *A Choice of Emblemes and other devises* (Leiden: Christopher Plantijn, 1586)

Wied, Hermann von, *Einfaltigs bedencken warauff ein Christliche in dem wort Gottes gegrünte Reformation an Lehrbrauch der Heyligen Sacramenten vnd Ceremonien Seelforge vnd anderem Kirchen dienst…verbesserung* (Bonn: Laurentius von der Müllen, 1543)

—— *Nostra Hermanni ex gratia Dei Archiepiscopi Coloniensis, et principis electoris, &c., simplex ac pia deliberatio* (Bonn: Laurentius von der Müllen, 1545)

—— *A simple, and religious consultation of…Herman by the grace of God Archebishop of Colone* (London: John Day, 1547)

SECONDARY SOURCES

Adams, Joseph Quincy, *The Dramatic Records of Sir Henry Herbert, Master of the Revels, 1623–73* (New Haven: Yale University Press, 1917)

Ajmar-Wollheim, Marta, and Flora Dennis (eds.), *At Home in Renaissance Italy* (London: V & A Publications, 2006)

Almond, Philip C., *Adam and Eve in Seventeenth-Century Thought* (Cambridge: Cambridge University Press, 1999)

Anzelewsky, Fedja, *Albrecht Dürer: Das malerische werk* (Berlin: Deutscher Verlag für Kunstwissenschaft, 1971)

Asad, Talal, Judith Butler, Saba Mahmood, and Wendy Brown, *Is Critique Secular? Blasphemy, Injury, and Free Speech*, Townsend Papers in the Humanities (Berkeley and Los Angeles: University of California Press, 2009)

Aston, Margaret, *England's Iconoclasts: Laws against Images* (Oxford: Clarendon Press, 1988)

—— *The King's Bedpost: Reformation and Iconography in a Tudor Group Portrait* (Cambridge: Cambridge University Press, 1993)

—— *Lollards and Reformers* (London: Hambledon Press, 1984)

—— and Elizabeth Ingram, 'The Iconography of the Acts and Monuments', in David Loades (ed.), *John Foxe and the English Reformation* (Aldershot: Ashgate, 1997)

Backus, Irena, *Life Writing in Reformation Europe: Lives of Reformers by Friends, Disciples and Foes* (Aldershot: Ashgate, 2008)

Baker, J. H., *An Introduction to English Legal History*, 3rd edn. (London: Butterworths, 1990)

Barber, Charles, '"You" and "Thou" in Shakespeare's *Richard III*', *Leeds Studies in English*, new series, 12 (1981), 273–89

Bartrum, Giulia, *Albrecht Dürer and his Legacy: The Graphic Work of a Renaissance Artist* (London: British Museum Press, 2002)

—— *German Renaissance Prints 1490–1550* (London: British Museum Press, 1995)

Bayet, Albert, *Le Suicide et la morale* (Paris: F. Alcan, 1922)

Baylor, Michael G., *Action and Person: Conscience in Late Scholasticism and the Young Luther* (Leiden: E. J. Brill, 1977)

Bellamy, Elizabeth Jane, Patrick Cheney, and Michael Schoenfeldt (eds.), *Imagining Death in Spenser and Milton* (Basingstoke: Palgrave Macmillan, 2003)

Belsey, Catherine, *The Subject of Tragedy: Identity and Difference in Renaissance Drama* (London: Methuen, 1985)

Berger, Peter L., *The Social Reality of Religion* (Harmondsworth: Penguin University Books, 1973)

—— (ed.), *The Desecularization of the World: Resurgent Religion and World Politics* (Grand Rapids, Mich.: Eerdmans, 1999)

Bethell, S. L., 'The Diabolic Images in Othello', *Shakespeare Survey*, 5 (1952), 62–80

Betteridge, Tom (ed.), *Sodomy in Early Modern Europe* (Manchester: Manchester University Press, 2002)

Bloom, Harold, *Shakespeare: The Invention of the Human* (Newark, Del.: University of Delaware Press, 1987)

Blumenberg, Hans, *The Legitimacy of the Modern Age*, trans. Robert M. Wallace (Cambridge, Mass.: MIT Press, 1983)

—— *Die Legitimät der Neuzeit*, 2nd edn. (Frankfurt: Suhrkamp, 1973–6)

—— *Paradigms for a Metaphorology*, trans. Robert Savage (Ithaca, NY: Cornell University Press, 2010)

Bobzien, Suzanne, *Determinism and Freedom in Stoic Philosophy* (Oxford: Clarendon Press, 1998)

Bradley, A. C., *Shakespearean Tragedy* (London: Macmillan, 1904)

Brigden, Susan, *London and the Reformation* (Oxford: Clarendon Press, 1989)

Brinkmann, Bodo, *Hexenlust und Sündenfall: Die seltsamen Phantasien des Hans Baldung Grien / Witches' Lust and the Fall of Man: The Strange Fantasies of Hans Baldung Grien*, Exhibition Catalogue, Städel Museum, Frankfurt am Main (Petersberg: Michael Imhof Verlag, 2007)

Brinkworth, E. R. C., *Shakespeare and the Bawdy Court of Stratford* (London: Phillimore, 1972)

Brody, B. (ed.), *Suicide and Euthanasia: Historical and Contemporary Themes* (Dordrecht: Kluwer, 1989)

Burckhardt, Jakob, *The Civilization of the Renaissance in Italy*, trans. S. G. C. Middlemore, 2nd edn. (Oxford: Phaidon Press, 1981)

—— *Die Kultur der Renaissance in Italien*, 2 vols., 11th edn. (Leipzig: E. A. Seeman, 1913)

Burrow, J. W., *A Liberal Descent: Victorian Historians and the English Past* (Cambridge: Cambridge University Press, 1981)

Camus, Albert, *Essais*, ed. R. Quilliot and L. Faucon, Bibliothèque de la Pléiade (Paris: Gallimard, 1965)

Cannon, Christopher, *The Making of Chaucer's English: A Study of Words* (Cambridge: Cambridge University Press, 1998)

Caputo, John D., and Gianni Vattimo, *After the Death of God* (New York: Columbia University Press, 2007)

Carruthers, Mary J., *The Book of Memory: A Study of Memory in Medieval Culture* (Cambridge: Cambridge University Press, 1990)

Cassirer, Ernst, P. O. Kristeller, and J. H. Randall, Jr. (eds.), *The Renaissance Philosophy of Man* (Chicago: University of Chicago Press, 1948)

Chambers, E. K., *William Shakespeare: A Study of Facts and Problems*, 2 vols. (Oxford: Clarendon Press, 1930)

Chambers, R. W., *Thomas More* (London: Jonathan Cape, 1935)

Chartier, Roger, 'The Practical Impact of Writing', in *A History of Private Life, iii: Passions of the Renaissance* (Cambridge, Mass.: Harvard University Press, 1989)

Chipps Smith, Jeffrey, 'Albrecht Dürer as Collector', *Renaissance Quarterly*, 54.1 (Spring 2011), 1–49

Cholbi, Michael, 'Suicide', in Edward N. Zalta (ed.), *The Stanford Encyclopedia of Philosophy* (Fall 2009 Edition) <http://plato.stanford.edu/archives/fall2009/entries/suicide/>

Clark, Andy, *Natural-Born Cyborgs: Minds, Technologies, and the Future of Human Intelligence* (Oxford: Oxford University Press, 2003)

Clemen, Wolfgang, *Shakespeare's Soliloquies* (London: Methuen, 1987)

Cobbett, William, *A History of the Protestant Reformation in England and Ireland* (London: Burnes, Oates and Washbourne, 1925)

Colley, Linda, *Britons: Forging the Nation, 1707–1837* (New Haven: Yale University Press, 1992)

Collinson, Patrick, *The Birthpangs of Protestant England: Religious and Cultural Change in the Sixteenth and Seventeenth Centuries* (London: Macmillan, 1988)

—— *The Elizabethan Puritan Movement* (London: Jonathan Cape, 1967)

—— *From Iconoclasm to Iconophobia: The Cultural Impact of the Second English Reformation* (Reading: University of Reading Press, 1986)

—— 'Literature and the Church', *The Cambridge History of Early Modern English Literature*, ed. David Lowenstein and Janel Mueller (Cambridge: Cambridge University Press, 2002).

—— Alexandra Walsham, and Arnold Hunt, 'Religious Publishing in England 1557–1640', in John Barnard and D. F. Mackenzie (eds.), *The Cambridge History of the Book in Britain*, vol. iv (1557–1695) (Cambridge: Cambridge University Press, 2002)

Compagnon, Antoine, *Nous Michel de Montaigne* (Paris: Éditions de Deuil, 1980)

Cottingham, John (ed.), *Descartes*, Oxford Readings in Philosophy (Oxford: Oxford University Press, 1998)

Cressy, David, *Literacy and the Social Order: Reading and Writing in Tudor and Stuart England* (Cambridge: Cambridge University Press, 1980)

Cummings, Brain (ed.),'Iconoclasm and Bibliophobia in the English Reformations, 1521–1558', in Jeremy Dimmick, James Simpson, and Nicolette Zeeman (eds.), *Images, Idolatry and Iconoclasm in Late Medieval England* (Oxford: Oxford University Press, 2002)

—— *The Literary Culture of the Reformation: Grammar and Grace* (Oxford: Oxford University Press, 2002)

—— and James Simpson (eds.), *Cultural Reformations: Medieval and Renaissance in Literary History* (Oxford: Oxford University Press, 2010)

Daniell, David, *Tyndale's Old Testament* (New Haven: Yale University Press, 1992)

Darlow, T. H., and H. F. Moule, *Historical Catalogue of Printed Editions of the English Bible 1525–1961*, ed. A. S. Herbert (London: British and Foreign Bible Society, 1968)

Davis, John F., *Heresy and Reformation in the South-East of England, 1520–1559* (London: Royal Historical Society, 1983)

de Grazia, Margreta, Hamlet *without Hamlet* (Cambridge: Cambridge University Press, 2007)

—— 'Soliloquies and Wages in the Age of Emergent Consciousness', *Textual Practice*, 9.1 (1995), 67–92

Derrett, J. D. M., 'The Trial of Sir Thomas More', *English Historical Review*, 79 (1964), 450–77

Derrida, Jacques, *Margins of Philosophy*, trans. Alan Bass (Chicago: Chicago University Press, 1982)

Dickens, A. G., *The English Reformation*, rev. edn. (London: Fontana, 1967)

Duffy, Eamon, 'Brush for Hire', *London Review of Books*, 26.16 (19 August 2004)

—— *The Stripping of the Altars: Traditional Religion in England, 1400–1580* (New Haven: Yale University Press, 1992)

Durckheim, Émile, *De la division du travail social* (Paris: Presses Universitaires de France, 1991)

—— *The Division of Labour in Society*, trans. W. D. Halls (London: Macmillan, 1984)

—— *Le Suicide: étude de sociologie* (Paris: Presses Universitaires de France, 1969)

Edgerton, William L., 'Shakespeare and the "Needle's Eye"', *Modern Language Notes*, 66 (1951), 549–50

Elton, G. R., *Policy and Police: The Enforcement of the Reformation in the Age of Thomas Cromwell* (Cambridge: Cambridge University Press, 1972)

Empson, William, *Seven Types of Ambiguity* (London: New Directions, 1930)

—— *The Structure of Complex Words* (London: Chatto & Windus, 1951)

Evans, J. M., *Paradise Lost and the Genesis Tradition* (Oxford: Clarendon Press, 1968)

Evenden, Elizabeth, and Thomas Freeman, 'John Foxe, John Day, and the Printing of the Book of Martyrs', in Robin Myers, Michael Harris, and Giles Mandelbrote (eds.), *Lives in Print* (London: British Library, 2002)

—— —— *Religion and the Book in Early Modern England: The Making of John Foxe's 'Book of Martyrs'* (Cambridge: Cambridge University Press, 2011)

Everett, Barbara, *Young Hamlet: Essays on Shakespeare's Tragedies* (Oxford: Clarendon Press, 1990)

Fallon, Stephen, *Milton among the Philosophers: Poetry and Materialism in the Seventeenth Century* (Ithaca, NY: Cornell University Press, 1991)

Fedden, Henry, *Suicide: A Social and Historical Study* (New York: Blom, 1972)

Fisch, Harold, *The Biblical Presence in Shakespeare, Milton, and Blake: A Comparative Study* (Oxford: Clarendon Press, 1999)

Fish, Stanley E., *Surprised by Sin: The Reader in Paradise Lost* (Berkeley and Los Angeles: University of California Press, 1971)

Fisher, John H., Malcolm Richardson, and Jane L. Fisher (eds.), *An Anthology of Chancery English 1417–1455* (Knoxville, Tenn.: University of Tennessee Press, 1984)

Flournoy, Théodore, *From India to the Planet Mars: A Study of Somnambulism with Glossolalia*, trans. Daniel Vermilye (New York: Harper, 1901)

Förster, M., 'Die altenglischen Verzeichnisse von Glücks- und Unglückstagen' in K. Malone and M. B. Ruud (eds.), *Studies in English Philology: A Miscellany in Honor of Frederick Klaebe* (Minneapolis: University of Minnesota Press, 1929), 258–77

Freeman, Thomas S., 'Foxe, John (1516/17–1587)', *Oxford Dictionary of National Biography* (Oxford: Oxford University Press, 2004), <http://www.oxforddnb.com/>

—— 'Harpsfield, Nicholas (1519–1575)', *Oxford Dictionary of National Biography* (Oxford: Oxford University Press, 2004)

—— 'A Library in Three Volumes: Foxe's "Book of Martyrs" in the Writings of John Bunyan', *Bunyan Studies*, 5 (1994), 48–57

—— 'Through a Venice Glass Darkly: John Foxe's Most Famous Miracle', *Studies in Church History*, 41 (2005), 307–20

Garber, Daniel, and Michael Ayers, *The Cambridge History of Seventeenth-Century Philosophy*, 2 vols. (Cambridge: Cambridge University Press, 1998)

Geisendorf, Paul-F., *Théodore de Bèze* (Geneva: Alexandre Julien, 1967)

Glover, Jonathan, *Causing Death and Saving Lives* (London: Pelican, 1977)

Grady, Hugh, *Shakespeare, Machiavelli, and Montaigne: Power and Subjectivity from Richard II to Hamlet* (Oxford: Oxford University Press, 2002)

Grafton, Anthony, *Bring Out Your Dead: The Past As Revelation* (Cambridge, Mass.: Harvard University Press, 2001)

—— *Cardano's Cosmos: The Worlds and Works of a Renaissance Astrologer* (Cambridge, Mass.: Harvard University Press, 1999)

Green, Felicity, *Montaigne and the Life of Freedom* (Cambridge: Cambridge University Press, 2012)

Greenblatt, Stephen, *Hamlet in Purgatory* (Princeton: Princeton University Press, 2001)

—— *Renaissance Self-Fashioning: More to Shakespeare* (Berkeley and Los Angeles: University of California Press, 1980)

—— *The Swerve: How the World became Modern* (New York: W. W. Norton, 2011)

Greene, Robert A., 'Instinct of Nature: Natural Law, Synderesis, and the Moral Sense', *Journal of the History of Ideas*, 58 (1997), 173–98

—— 'Synderesis, the Spark of Conscience, in the English Renaissance', *Journal of the History of Ideas*, 52 (1991), 195–219

Greg, W. W., *The Editorial Problem in Shakespeare*, 2nd edn. (Oxford: Clarendon Press, 1951)

—— *The Shakespeare First Folio: Its Bibliographical and Textual History* (Oxford: Clarendon Press, 1955)

Gregory, Brad S., *Salvation at Stake: Christian Martyrdom in Early Modern Europe* (Cambridge, Mass.: Harvard University Press, 1999)

Griffin, Miriam T., *Seneca: A Philosopher in Politics* (Oxford: Clarendon Press, 1976)

Guy, John, *The Cardinal's Court: The Impact of Thomas Wolsey in Star Chamber* (Hassocks: Harvester, 1977)

—— *The Public Career of Sir Thomas More* (Brighton: Harvester Press, 1980)

Haarløv, Britt, *The Half-Open Door: A Common Symbolic Motif within Roman Sepulchral Sculpture* (Odense: Odense University Press, 1977)

Hacking, Ian, *The Emergence of Probability: A Philosophical Study of Early Ideas about Probability, Induction and Statistical Inference* (Cambridge: Cambridge University Press, 1975)

Hadot, Pierre, *Philosophy as a Way of Life: Spiritual Exercises from Socrates to Foucault*, Eng. trans. ed. Arnold Davidson (Oxford: Blackwell, 1995)

Haigh, Christopher, *English Reformations: Religion, Politics and Society under the Tudors* (Oxford: Clarendon Press, 1993)

Haight, E. H., *The Symbolism of the House Door in Classical Poetry* (New York: Longmans, 1950)

Harbison, Craig, *Symbols in Transformation: An Exhibition of Prints in Memory of Erwin Panofsky* (Princeton: Princeton Art Museum, 1969)

Harrison, Peter, *The Bible, Protestantism, and the Rise of Natural Science* (Cambridge University Press, 1998)

Henry, Patrick, 'The Dialectic of Suicide in Montaigne's "Coustume de l'Isle de Cea"', *Modern Language Review*, 79 (1984), 278–89

Hess, Daniel, and Thomas Eser (eds.), *Der frühe Dürer* (Nuremberg: Verlag des Germanischen Nationalmuseums, 2012)

Hill, Christopher, *Society and Puritanism in Pre-Revolutionary England* (London: Secker & Warburg, 1964)

Hill, Geoffrey, *Collected Critical Writings*, ed. Kenneth Haynes (Oxford: Oxford University Press, 2008)

Hinz, Berthold, *Aphrodite: Geschichte einer abendländischen Passion* (Munich and Vienna: Hanser, 1998)

Hirsh, James, *Shakespeare and the History of Soliloquies* (Madison: Fairleigh Dickinson University Press, 2003)

Holdsworth, William, *A History of English Law*, 17 vols. (London: Methuen, 1903–72)

Hughes, Geoffrey, *Swearing: A Social History of Foul Language, Oaths and Profanity in English* (Oxford: Blackwell, 1991)

Hutson, Lorna, *The Invention of Suspicion: Law and Mimesis in Shakespeare and Renaissance Drama* (Oxford: Oxford University Press, 2007)

Inwood, Brad, 'Seneca on Freedom and Autonomy', collected in *Reading Seneca: Stoic Philosophy at Rome* (Oxford: Clarendon Press, 2005)

Jackson, James L., ' "They Catch One Another's Rapiers": The Exchange of Weapons in Hamlet', *Shakespeare Quarterly*, 41 (1990)

Jackson, Ken, and Arthur F. Marotti, 'The Turn to Religion in Early Modern English Studies', *Criticism*, 46.1 (2004), 167–90

Jensen, Michael, *Martyrdom and Identity: The Self on Trial* (London: Continuum, 2010)

Kaufmann, Thomas da Costa, 'Hermeneutics in the History of Art: Remarks on the Reception of Dürer in Sixteenth- and Early Seventeenth-Century Art', in J. C. Smith (ed.), *New Perspectives on the Art of Renaissance Nuremberg: Five Essays* (Austin: University of Texas Press, 1985), 22–39

Kenny, Anthony, *Thomas More* (Oxford: Oxford University Press, 1983)

Kermode, Frank, *Shakespeare's Language* (London: Penguin, 2000)

—— Anthony Holden, Robin Marris, Ken Follett, Linden Stafford, and Daniel Marciano, 'The Odds against Hamlet', *The Times Literary Supplement*, No. 5262 (6 February 2004), 11

Kilby, James A., 'The Odds on Sprinchorn's "The Odds on Hamlet" ', *Notes & Queries*, 16 (1968), 133–36

Knott, John R., 'John Foxe and the Joy of Suffering', *Sixteenth Century Journal*, 27.3 (Autumn 1996)

Koepplin, Dieter, 'Baldungs Basler Bilder des Todes mit dem nackten Mädchen', *Zeitschrift für Schweizerische Archäologie und Kunstgeschichte*, 35 (1978), 234–41

Koerner, Joseph Leo, *The Moment of Self-Portraiture in German Renaissance Art* (Chicago: University of Chicago Press, 1997)

—— 'The Mortification of the Image: Death as a Hermeneutic in Hans Baldung Grien', *Representations*, 10 (1985), 52–101

—— *The Reformation of the Image* (London: Reaktion Books, 2004)

Koselleck, Reinhard, *Begriffsgeschichten: Studien zur Semantik und Pragmatik der politischen und sozialen Sprache* (Frankfurt am Main: Suhrkamp, 2006)

—— *Futures Past: On the Semantics of Historical Time*, Studies in Contemporary German Social Thought (New York: Columbia University Press, 2004)

—— *The Practice of Conceptual History: Timing History, Spacing Concepts*, trans. Todd Samuel Presner (Stanford, Calif.: Stanford University Press, 2002)

Laneyrie-Dagen, Nadeije, *L'Invention du corps: la représentation de l'homme du Moyen Âge à la fin du XIXe siècle* (Paris: Flammarion, 2006)

Langer, Ullrich (ed.), *The Cambridge Companion to Montaigne* (Cambridge: Cambridge University Press, 2005)

Langley, Eric, *Narcissism and Suicide in Shakespeare and his Contemporaries* (Oxford: Oxford University Press, 2009)

Lea, H. C., *The Inquisition of the Middle Ages*, ed. Walter Ullmann (London: Eyre & Spottiswoode, 1963)

Leonard, John, *Naming in Paradise: Milton and the Language of Adam and Eve* (Oxford: Clarendon Press, 1990)

Lewis, C. S., *Studies in Words*, 2nd edn. (Cambridge: Cambridge University Press, 1967)

Luborsky, R. S., and E. M. Ingram, *A Guide to English Illustrated Books 1536–1603*, 3 vols. (Tempe, Ariz.: Medieval and Renaissance Texts and Studies, 1998)

Luborsky, Ruth, 'The Illustrations: Their Pattern and Plan', in David Loades (ed.), *John Foxe: An Historical Perspective* (Aldershot: Ashgate, 1999)

MacCulloch, Diarmaid, *Thomas Cranmer: A Life* (New Haven: Yale University Press, 1996)

MacDonald, Michael, and Terence R. Murphy, *Sleepless Souls: Suicide in Early Modern England* (Oxford: Clarendon Press, 1990)

McFarlane, I. D., and Ian Maclean (eds.), *Montaigne: Essays in Memory of Richard Sayce* (Oxford: Clarendon Press, 1982)

McGowan, Margaret, *Montaigne's Deceits: The Art of Persuasion in the Essais* (London: University of London Press, 1974)

Maclean, Ian, *Montaigne philosophe* (Paris: Presses Universitaires de France, 1996)

McMillan, Dougald, and Martha Fehsenfeld (ed.), *Beckett in the Theatre* (London: John Calder, 1988)

McNiven, Peter, *Heresy and Politics in the Reign of Henry IV: The Burning of John Badby* (Woodbridge: Boydell Press, 1987)

Manning, John J., 'Hayward, Sir John (1564?–1627)', *Oxford Dictionary of National Biography*, Oxford University Press, 2004; online edn., January 2008, <http://www.oxforddnb.com/>

Marius, Richard, *Thomas More* (London: Weidenfeld and Nicolson, 1993)

Martineau, Jane (ed.), *Andrea Mantegna* (Milan: Electa, 1992)

Maus, Katharine Eisaman, *Inwardness and Theater in the English Renaissance* (Chicago: University of Chicago Press, 1995)

Mauss, Marcel, and Henri Hubert, *Essai sur la nature et la fonction du sacrifice* (Paris: F. Alcan, 1899)

——*Sacrifice: Its Nature and Function*, trans. W. D. Halls (Chicago: University of Chicago Press, 1964)

Middle English Dictionary, <http://quod.lib.umich.edu/m/med/>

Minois, Georges, *History of Suicide: Voluntary Death in Western Culture* (Baltimore: Johns Hopkins University Press, 1999)

Miola, Robert, *Shakespeare and Classical Tragedy: The Influence of Seneca* (Oxford: Clarendon Press, 1992)

Monta, Susannah Brietz, *Martyrdom and Literature in Early Modern England* (Cambridge: Cambridge University Press, 2005)

Montagu, Jennifer, *The Expression of the Passions: The Origin and Influence of Charles le Brun's Conférence sur l'expression générale et particulière* (New Haven: Yale University Press, 1994)

Morford, Mark, *Stoics and Neostoics: Rubens and the Circle of Lipsius* (Princeton: Princeton University Press, 1991)

Murray, Alexander, *Suicide in the Middle Ages, vol. i: The Violent against Themselves* (Oxford: Oxford University Press, 1998)

Musson, Anthony (ed.), *Expectations of the Law in the Middle Ages* (Woodbridge: Boydell, 2001)

Nagel, Thomas, *The View from Nowhere* (New York: Oxford University Press, 1986)

Neale, J. E., *Elizabeth I and her Parliaments 1584–1601* (London: Jonathan Cape, 1957)

Neill, Michael, *Issues of Death: Mortality and Identity in English Renaissance Tragedy* (Oxford: Clarendon Press, 1997)

Noble, Richmond, *Shakespeare's Biblical Knowledge* (London: SPCK, 1935)

Nussbaum, Martha C., *The Fragility of Goodness: Luck and Ethics in Greek Tragedy and Philosophy* (Cambridge: Cambridge University Press, 1986)

Nyquist, Mary, and Margaret W. Ferguson (eds.), *Re-Membering Milton: Essays on the Texts and Traditions* (London: Methuen, 1988)

Oberman, Heiko A., *Luther: Man Between God and the Devil* (New Haven: Yale University Press, 1989)

O'Connell, Marvin, 'A Man for all Seasons: An Historian's Demur', *Catholic Dossier*, 8.2 (March–April 2002), 16–19

Ozment, Steven E., *Homo Spiritualis* (Leiden: E. J. Brill, 1969)

Panofsky, Erwin, *The Life and Art of Albrecht Dürer*, 4th edn. (Princeton: Princeton University Press, 1955)

Papy, Jan, 'Lipsius's Stoic Reflections on the Pale Face of Death: From Stoic Constancy and Liberty to Suicide and Rubens's Dying Seneca', LIAS: *Journal of Early Modern Intellectual Culture and its Sources*, 37.1 (2010), 35–53

Parshall, Peter, 'Lucas van Leyden's Narrative Style', *Nederlands Kunsthistorisch Jaarboek*, 29 (1978), 185–237

Paster, Gail Kern, Katherine Rowe, and Mary Floyd-Wilson (ed.), *Reading the Passions: Essays in the Cultural History of Emotion* (Philadelphia: University of Pennsylvania Press, 2004)

Patrides, C. A., *The Cambridge Platonists* (Cambridge: Cambridge University Press, 1969)

Petegree, Andrew, 'Illustrating the Book: A Protestant Dilemma', in Christopher Highley and John N. King (eds.), *John Foxe and his World* (Aldershot: Ashgate, 2002)

Poole, William, *Milton and the Idea of the Fall* (Cambridge: Cambridge University Press, 2005)

Potts, Timothy C., *Conscience in Medieval Philosophy* (Cambridge: Cambridge University Press, 1980)

Ratzinger, Josef, 'Conscience and Truth', *Conscience and Truth* (Braintree, Mass.: Pope John XXIII Medical-Moral Research and Education Center, 1991)

—— 'Conscience in its Age', *Church, Ecumenism and Politics* (New York: Crossroads, 1987), 165–79

Regosin, Richard L., *The Matter of My Book: Montaigne's Essais as the Book of the Self* (Berkeley and Los Angeles: University of California Press, 1977)

Rex, Richard, 'The New Learning', *The Journal of Ecclesiastical History*, 44 (1993), 26–44

Ricoeur, Paul, *Oneself as Another* (Chicago: University of Chicago Press, 1995)

Rist, John, *Stoic Philosophy* (Cambridge: Cambridge University Press, 1969)

Robinson, John, *Honest to God* (London: SCM Press, 1963)

Roh, Franz, 'Ein neues Selbstbildnis Dürers', *Reportorium für Kunstwissenschaft*, 39 (1916), 10–15

Roller, Matthew B., *Constructing Autocracy: Aristocrats and Emperors in Julio-Claudian Rome* (Princeton: Princeton University Press, 2001)

Russell, Conrad, *Parliaments and English Politics 1621–1629* (Oxford: Clarendon Press, 1979)

Russell, Diane H., *Eva/Ave: Woman in Renaissance and Baroque Prints* (Washington, DC: National Gallery of Art, 1990)

Saenger, Paul, 'Silent Reading: Its Impact on Late Medieval Script and Society', *Viator*, 13 (1982), 367–414

Sartre, Jean-Paul, *Literary and Philosophical Essays* (London: Rider & Co., 1955)

—— *Situations: essais de critique, I* (Paris: Gallimard, 1947)

Sayce, R. A., and David Maskell, *A Descriptive Bibliography of Montaigne's Essais 1580–1700* (London: Bibliographical Society, 1983)

Schoch, Rainer, Matthias Mende, and Anna Scherbaum (eds.), *Albrecht Dürer: Das druckgraphische Werk*, 3 vols. (Munich: Prestel Verlag, 2001–4)

Schoenfeldt, Michael, *Bodies and Selves in Early Modern England* (Cambridge: Cambridge University Press, 1999)

Schwartz, Heinrich, 'Schiele, Dürer and the Mirror', *Art Quarterly*, 30 (1967), 210–23

Screech, M. A., *Montaigne and Melancholy* (London: Duckworth, 1983)

—— *Montaigne's Annotated Copy of Lucretius: A Transcription and Study of the Manuscript, Notes and Pen-Marks* (Geneva: Librairie Droz, 1998)

Seigel, Jerrold D., *The Idea of the Self: Thought and Experience in Western Europe Since the Seventeenth Century* (Cambridge: Cambridge University Press, 2005)

Shaheen, Naseeb, *Biblical References in Shakespeare's Plays* (Newark, Del.: University of Delaware Press, 1999)

Sierhuis, Freya, 'The Rhetoric of Religious Dissent: Anti-Calvinism, Satire and the Arminian Controversy in the Dutch Republic', *Renaissance and Reformation Review*, 12 (2010), 307–27

Silver, Larry, and Susan Smith, 'Carnal Knowledge: The Late Engravings of Lucas van Leyden', *Nederlands Kunsthistorisch Jaarboek*, 29 (1978), 239–98

Sinfield, Alan, 'Hamlet's Special Providence', *Shakespeare Survey*, 33 (1980), 89–97

Skinner, Quentin, and Martin van Gelderen (eds.), *Freedom and the Construction of Europe: New Perspectives on Religious, Philosophical and Political Controversies* (Cambridge: Cambridge University Press, 2013)

Smith, Paul J. (ed.), *Een Ridder van groot oordel: Montaigne in Leiden* (Leiden: Universiteitsbibliotheek Leiden, 2005)

Sorabji, Richard, *Emotion and Peace of Mind: From Stoic Agitation to Christian Temptation* (Oxford: Oxford University Press, 2000)

Sprott, S. E., *The English Debate on Suicide from Donne to Hume* (La Salle, Ill.: Open Court, 1961)

Stachniewski, John, *The Persecutory Imagination: English Puritanism and the Literature of Religious Despair* (Oxford: Clarendon Press, 1991)

Starobinski, Jean, *Montaigne en mouvement* (Paris: Gallimard, 1982)

—— *Montaigne in Motion*, trans. Arthur Goldhammer (Chicago: University of Chicago Press, 1985)

Stock, Brian, *Augustine the Reader: Meditation, Self-Knowledge and the Ethics of Interpretation* (Cambridge, Mass.: Harvard University Press, 1996)

Strawson, Galen, 'Against Narrativity', *Ratio*, 17 (2004), 428–52

Taylor, Charles, *The Ethics of Authenticity* (Cambridge, Mass.: Harvard University Press, 1992)

—— *A Secular Age* (Cambridge, Mass.: Harvard University Press, 2007)

—— *Sources of the Self: The Making of the Modern Identity* (Cambridge, Mass.: Harvard University Press, 1989)

Taylor, Gary, "Swounds Revisited', in Gary Taylor and J. Jowett, *Shakespeare Reshaped* (Oxford: Clarendon Press, 1993), 51–106

Tilley, Morris Palmer, *Dictionary of Proverbs in England* (Ann Arbor: University of Michigan Press, 1968)

Tilmouth, Christopher, *Passion's Triumph over Reason: A History of the Moral Imagination from Spenser to Rochester* (Oxford: Oxford University Press, 2007)

Toynbee, J. M. C., *Death and Burial in the Roman World* (London: Thames and Hudson, 1971)

Trilling, Lionel, *Sincerity and Authenticity* (London: Oxford University Press, 1972)

Turner, James Grantham, *One Flesh: Paradisal Marriage and Sexual Relations in the Age of Milton* (Oxford: Clarendon Press, 1987)

Tutino, Stefania, *Law and Conscience: Catholicism in Early Modern England, 1570–1625* (Aldershot: Ashgate, 2007)

Usher, Brett, 'Gataker , Thomas (1574–1654)', *Oxford Dictionary of National Biography*, Oxford University Press, 2004; online edn, January 2008, <http://www.oxforddnb.com>

Vignaux, Paul, *Luther, commentateur des Sentences* (Paris: Vrin, 1935)

Villey, Pierre, *Les Sources et l'évolution des Essais*, 2 vols. (Paris: Hachette, 1908)

Viswanathan, Gauri, 'Secularism in the Framework of Heterodoxy', *PMLA*, 123.2 (March 2008), 466–75

Walker, Alice, 'The 1622 Quarto and the First Folio Text of Othello', *Shakespeare Survey*, 5 (1952), 16–24

Walker, Greg, 'Saint or Schemer? The 1527 Heresy Trial of Thomas Bilney Reconsidered', *Journal of Ecclesiastical History*, 40 (1989), 219–38

Wallace, Robert M., 'Progress, Secularization and Modernity: The Löwith/Blumenberg Debate', *New German Critique*, 22 (1981), 63–79

Walsham, Alexandra, *Providence in Early Modern England* (Oxford: Oxford University Press, 1999)

Watt, Jeffrey R., 'Calvin on Suicide', *Church History*, 66 (1997), 463–76

—— *Choosing Death: Suicide and Calvinism in Early Modern Geneva*, Sixteenth Century Essays & Studies (Kirksville, Mo.: Truman State University Press, 2001)

Watt, Jeffrey R. (ed.), *From Sin to Insanity: Suicide in Early Modern Europe* (Ithaca, NY: Cornell University Press, 2004)

Watt, Tessa, *Cheap Print and Popular Piety, 1550–1640* (Cambridge: Cambridge University Press, 1991)

Weber, Max, *From Max Weber: Essays in Sociology*, ed. H. H. Geerth and C. Wright Mills, new edn.(London: Routledge, 2009)

—— *Gesammelte Aufsätze zur Wissenschaftslehre*, ed. Johannes Winckelmann (Tübingen: J. C. B. Mohr, 1985)

—— *Wirtschaft und Gesellschaft: Grundriß der Verstehenden Soziologie*, 5th edn. (Tübingen: Mohr Siebeck, 1980)

Wegemer, Gerald, and Stephen Smith (eds.), *A Thomas More Sourcebook* (Washington, DC: Catholic University of America Press, 2004)

Wells, Stanley, and Gary Taylor, *William Shakespeare: A Textual Companion* (Oxford: Clarendon Press, 1987)

White, Christopher, *Rembrandt as Etcher: A Study of the Artist at Work*, 2 vols. (University Park, Pa.: Penn State University Press, 1969)

Williams, Arnold, *The Common Expositor: An Account of the Commentaries on Genesis* (Chapel Hill, NC: University of North Carolina Press, 1948)

Williams, Bernard, *Moral Luck* (Cambridge: Cambridge University Press, 1981)

Williams, Raymond, *Culture* (London: Fontana, 1981)

—— 'On Dramatic Dialogue and Monologue (Particularly in Shakespeare)', in *Writing in Society* (London: Verso, n.d.), 31–74

Wilpert, G., *I sarcofagi cristiani antichi*, 3 vols. (Rome: Ponteficio Istituto di Archeologia Cristiana, 1928–36)

Winkler, Friedrich, *Die Zeichnungen Albrecht Dürers*, 4 vols. (Berlin: Deutscher Verein für Kunstwissenschaft, 1936–9)

Index

Abbey of the Holy Ghost, The 76
absolution 133, 136, 140
accident(s) 207–8, 217, 223–4, 227,
    234–5, 259–60, 262–3, 268, 274
actor(s) 154, 169, 172, 174, 181, 185,
    203, 205–6, 226
Adam 23, 39, 49, 278–326
    Adamic language 304
Adorno, Theodor 10
adultery 158–9
Aeschylus 225, 235
    Oresteia 229
afterlife 17, 199, 251, 276
agency 208, 270
    and freedom 245, 255
    and language 181
    and self-authorship 92, 98–9
    divine in relation to human 2
    in suicide 258, 266
    moral 98, 228
    of the body 112
Alberti, Leon Battista *De pictura* 39, 296
Alciato, Andrea 129
Aldgate 116
Alington, Alice 89
Allin, Rose 110, 130–1
Alps 35, 318
altarpieces 30, 117–18, 280, 283
Althusser, Louis 186
Ambrose 136
Andrewes, Lancelot 194
angels 8, 35, 204, 298, 303, 311, 322–3
    bodies of 307
animal, animals 24, 282, 291, 304
    animal nature compared to human 8,
        9, 24, 281, 301, 320, 323
    ape 24
    camel 192–5
    cat 282, 289
    donkey 192
    elephant 320
    elk 282
    hare 291
    horse 180, 208, 290, 316
    monkey 291
    mouse 282, 289
    ox 282
    parrot 278, 282
    rabbit 282

serpent 278, 282, 291, 310, 313, 318,
    320–1
annihilation 200–1
anomie 3, 5, 243
apatheia 125
Apollo 49, 282, 285, 287, 289
appetite 73–4, 302, 321
Aquinas, Thomas 193
    on conscience 72–5, 78, 80, 84
    on suicide 241
    on the will 234
    works: *De veritate* 74
        Summa theologiae 241
Arabic 192
architecture 35, 39, 283
archive(s)
    and biography 99, 115
    as containers of selfhood 15, 44, 50–8,
        110
    collections: Bibliothèque Nationale,
        Paris 70, 104
        British Library 99, 104
        Corpus Christi College, Cambridge 99
        Lambeth Palace Library 100, 104–6,
            108
        National Archives 85, 135, 145
Aristophanes 193, 309
Aristotle 59, 72, 173, 234
    nature of the divine 281
    on motion 301
    on nature 59
    on the body 311
    on the passions 24
    on the soul 281
    on voluntary actions 246, 255
    works: *De anima* 301
        Nicomachean Ethics 246, 255, 281
        Physics 311
        Rhetoric 24
Arminianism 231–2
Arnold, Matthew 9, 169
art 15
    and death 34
    and iconoclasm 115
    and modernity 9
    and secularization 8, 115, 117–18
    and selfhood 53, 57
    and sexuality 293
    and the Reformation 117–18, 132, 280

art (*cont.*)
  as reflexive 44
  history, discipline of 29
  Renaissance theory of 39, 296, 318
  Roman 32–4, 282–3
artist 34–5, 39, 113, 122, 257, 280
  and authenticity 51, 53, 289 (see
    monogram, artist's)
  and nature of art 44
  as Christ 29
  as collectible 27, 45
  body of 27
  cult of 56, 290
  death of 316
  in relation to model 283–4
  naked 25, 40
  self as 15, 29–30, 32, 46, 53, 284,
    293–4
Asad, Talal 12
Aston, Margaret 110, 114, 117, 121–2,
    132
atheism 175
atoms 64, 198, 277
Audius 281
Audley, Thomas 71, 90
Augustine 47, 175–6, 232–3
  idea of the self in 47, 176–9
  on existence before and after
    death 198–9
  on man as image of God 281
  on martyrdom 102
  on private reading 136
  on suicide 259, 268
  on the passions 303
  works: *City of God* 178, 241–2, 251,
    268, 280, 281, 303
    Confessions 176, 178–9, 281
    De Genesi ad litteram 280
    De libero arbitrio 198–9
    De Trinitate 178, 281
    Retractiones 233
    Soliloquia 178–9
authenticity 94–6, 98–9, 101, 103–6,
    108–9, 124, 147–8
authorship 8
  and authority 58
  and biography 98, 101, 104, 260
  and secularity 14
  and selfhood 19, 29, 46, 53, 56, 92
  in the Bible 298–9
  theory of 18
autobiography 16, 30, 44–5, 51, 53, 99,
    178–9, 246–8, 269–70
autograph 15
  see also *monogram, artist's* and *signature*

autonomy 7, 16, 18, 67, 71, 75, 95,
    256–7, 267, 277

Badby, John 153, 156, 165
Baldung, Caspar 290
Baldung, Hans ('Grien') 30, 129, 310
  and death 314–18
  and sexuality 291, 293–4, 313, 316,
    318
  drawings by 294, 314
  follower of Dürer 56, 284, 290, 314
  images of witches 290
  self-portrait 30, 290
  works: *Bewitched Stable Groom* 316, **317**
    Death and a Woman (chiaroscuro
      drawing), 314, **315**
    Death and the Young Girl
      (paintings) 314
    Eve, the Serpent and Death 318
    Fall of Man (1511) 291, **292**, 293, 311,
      314
    (1519) 294, **295**, 311, 314
    Wild Horses 316
baptism 102, 114
Barbari, Jacopo de' 285
Barker, Christopher 194
Barthes, Roland 48
Bartrum, Giulia 29, 32, 293
Basle 7, 296, 314
Baxter, Richard 321
Bayet, Albert 244
Bayly, Lewis 177
Beard, Thomas 231–2, 234
Beaumont, Francis 168
Beckett, Samuel 225, 228
Begriffsgeschichte 17
Bellini, Giovanni 35
Belsey, Catherine 169
Berger, Peter 4, 10–11, 14
Berlin 284, 314
Bernard of Clairvaux 233
Beza, Theodore 191, 214, 246
  autobiographical narrative of 268–70
  death of 271
  works: *Abraham sacrifiant* 230
    Confessio christianae fidei 269–70
    Tractationes theologicae 269
  edition of New Testament 193–4
Bible
  as object 114
  commentary on 190, 192–5, 278–80,
    298–300
  documentary hypothesis (authorship of
    Genesis) 298–9
  patristic readings of 73, 78, 280–1

Rabbinic readings of 298–9, 310
scholastic readings of 73–4, 80
books of: Genesis 215, 217, 278,
  280–1, 283, 291, 293, 296,
  298–300, 304, 307–10, 320, 325
Leviticus 216, 222
Numbers 159
Judges 129, 214–15, 217, 220, 231
1 Samuel 222
1 Kings 233
Job 220
Psalms 80, 133, 140, 177, 221–2
Ecclesiastes 41, 232–3
Isaiah 88, 122
Ezekiel 73
Zechariah 151, 220
Matthew 151, 189–93, 212–13, 216,
  232, 234
Mark 191, 194
Luke 121, 191, 194, 223, 232
John 199
Romans 73, 81
2 Corinthians 97, 151
Philippians 196
1 John 190
Apocrypha 129, 215, 223
versions of: Bishops' 218, 223
Coverdale 114, 215, 218, 220–1
Geneva 97, 122, 191, 196, 212,
  215–16, 218, 222–3, 234–5
Geneva/Tomson 191, 193–4, 212, 222
Great 88, 215, 218, 222–3
King James 97, 215, 218, 223
Matthew's 214–15
New English Bible 215
Tyndale 214–20, 223
Vulgate 82, 97, 122, 137, 196, 200,
  222
Wycliffite 218
Bilney, Thomas 110, 122–5, 127, 132,
  146–7
  death of 133–43, 156, 161, 165
  trial of 83–4, 90
birth 16, 24, 323, 326
  and death 62
  and identity 266, 308
  memory of 298, 303, 306
Blackstone, William 240
blasphemy 61, 150, 158, 166, 188, 234,
  255
Bloom, Harold 213–14
Blumenberg, Hans 10–11, 17
Bocher, Joan 102
body 49, 313–16
  as contingent 61, 220

as mortal 17, 39, 41, 49, 51, 55–7,
  61–2, 199, 206, 248, 321–2
as sacred 124, 241, 281
cultural theory of vi, 17, 46, 120, 302
dignity of 307
female 49, 282–5, 289, 299, 308–9, 313
human (compared with angelic or
  divine) 280–1, 307
(philosophical meaning of) 16, 24, 32,
  278, 282–5, 294–310
male 24, 30, 35, 39, 41, 46, 49, 282–5,
  289, 299, 308–9, 313, 316
in death 27, 29, 32, 55, 121, 197, 214,
  220, 316, 322
in martyrdom 98, 104, 109, 112,
  119–27, 248
in pain and suffering 27, 29, 109, 112,
  119, 248, 257, 272
of saints 17, 35, 98, 104, 120–1, 124,
  127, 134
pleasures of 307
subjectivity of 323
parts of: abdomen 30, 278, 284, 294
bone 41, 43, 310, 314, 318
breast 41, 134, 284, 287, 291, 293,
  313, 316
chest 27, 40, 128, 278
elbow 27
face 27, 29, 30, 39–40, 49, 109, 112,
  129, 133, 285, 291, 297
fingers 110, 122–5, 127–8, 132, 278,
  291, 311, 313–14, 316, 320
genitals 24, 40, 283–4, 287, 289, 293
hair 27, 41, 56, 114, 212, 287, 290,
  314
hands 49, 92, 115, 118, 130, 133, 285,
  294, 297, 311, 313–14, 320–1, 325
head 27–9, 39, 76, 114, 120–1, 128,
  147, 166, 212, 234, 246, 263,
  281–2, 285, 302, 311, 316, 318
heart 108–9, 120–1, 149, 156, 160,
  189, 199, 224, 263, 272, 275, 281,
  310, 324
muscle 25, 30, 40–1, 278
navel 284
ribs 185, 299–300, 309–10, 323, 325
skin 22, 41, 43, 268–9, 289, 297, 314
skull 32–3, 40–1, 43, 226, 296
teeth 41, 168, 316
thumbs 291, 320
Boethius 234
Böhme, Jakob 321
Boleyn, Anne 85, 145
Bolt, Robert 67–70, 72, 88, 90–1
Bonaventure 72, 74

Bonhoeffer, Dietrich 6
Bonner, Edmund 105, 120, 125, 127–8
Bonvisi, Antonio 68
book(s)
    as image (of eternity) 204
    (of the self) 19
    as object 115–16
    compared with images 117
    illustrated 112, 284, 296
    kissing the 148
    'of creatures' 59
    of nature 59
    popular 116
Book of Common Prayer 94, 107, 210–11,
    214, 221–2
Bozio, Tommaso 270–1
Bradbrook, Muriel 209
Bradford, John 222
Bradley, A. C. 169–70, 236
Brinkmann, Bodo 293–4, 313–14, 318
Bruges 220
Bruno, Giordano 302
Brussels 129
Bucer, Martin 220
Bühler, Sebald 290, 294
Bultmann, Rudolf 6
Bunyan, John 93
Burckhardt, Jakob 1, 7–8, 15, 46–8
Burgkmair, Hans 291
Butler, Judith 12

Cain 73, 310–11
Calvin, Jean 12, 278
    death of 271
    on corporeality of God 281
    on providence 213–14, 234–5
    on suicide 241–2
    on the emotions 189, 281
    works: *Institutio* 213, 234–5
Calvinism 5, 99, 102, 112, 121, 194,
    212, 215–16, 220, 223
    and suicide 242, 254
    theology of providence 230–5, 268–71
Cambridge 113, 133, 230, 232
    Platonists 300, 302
Camus, Albert 245
Caninius 194
canon law 76, 84, 143, 242, 248, 266
Canterbury 69, 87
Capito, Wolfgang 271
Cardano, Girolamo 211–12
Carruthers, Mary 136
Cassianus, John 293
catholicism, European 3, 15, 17, 69, 88,
    95, 117–18, 141, 213, 232, 243–4,
    259, 278–9

catholics, English 14, 69, 87–8, 94, 97, 128,
    133, 153, 156, 176, 194, 213, 230, 232
Cave, Terence 59
Cawood, John 101, 104
Caxton, William 220
Cecil, William 116, 216
certainty 20, 34, 49, 60, 96, 209, 214,
    226, 229, 245, 261, 271
chance 15, 199, 207
    and Calvinism 215, 223, 232
    and mischance 208, 227–8
    and theology 210, 233–5
    games of 211, 233
    history of idea 208–10
    in Calvin 234–5
    in English Bible translations 227–33
    in the *Book of Common Prayer* 211
    in Gataker 233–4
    in *Hamlet* 226–8
    (Q1) 227
    mathematics of 209
    philosophy of 208
    word in relation to 'fortune', 'luck' 211
Chancery 77, 84–5
Chapman, George 168
Charles I (of England) 154
Charles V (Emperor) 80
Chartier, Roger 136
Chaucer, Geoffrey 218–19
Christ
    as interlocutor 177–8, 187
    as man of sorrows 49
    bodily love for 166
    corpse of 27, 35
    death of (as suicide) 267
    (as voluntary) 272
    face of 39
    flagellation of 130
    horoscope of 212
    image of 29, 40, 49
    imitation of 87, 177, 188, 221
    meeting with in death 196–7, 254–5
    name of 132
    on the Cross 121, 199
    sacramental body of 150
Cicero 128, 233
    as rhetorical model 197
    on death 50, 198
    on sensation 201
    on suicide 239
    on the passions 303
    De finibus 239
    Orator 39
    Tusculan Disputations 178, 202, 242, 276
Claesz, Pieter 41–3
    Vanitasstilleven **42**

Clark, Andy 325
Clemen, Wolfgang 183, 186
Clement, John 68
Cobbett, William 92
Cochlaeus, Johann 271
Coeffeteau, Nicolas 297
cognitive philosophy 21, 297, 325
col tempo 41, 53
Colchester 130
Cole, Henry 105
Coleridge, Samuel Taylor 169, 236
Colley, Lynda 93
Collinson, Patrick 93, 113, 115, 153, 165
Cologne 220, 280
common law 77, 85, 153, 158–9
communion 177, 210, 221
    table 114
confession
    legal 143, 153, 162, 164–5
    penitential 105, 248, 269
    confessionalism 17, 87, 101, 107
    confessional identity 94–5, 269
Congreve, William 172, 175
conscience 15, 17, 92, 124, 181–2, 259
    and individual freedom 68–9, 71, 75,
        152–3, 156, 159, 161, 166–7, 254
    and martyrdom 89–91, 94–5, 103,
        105–7
    as interior voice 86–7, 70, 90, 144,
        170, 271
    in scholastic thought 72–4, 86
    in legal sense 76–9, 83–5
    in theology 79–83, 87–8, 144–7
    meanings of 70, 86
    'prisoner of' 16, 68–9, 71, 132
consciousness 7
    and sensation 202–3, 321, 324
    and subjectivity 298, 304, 306, 318
    and unconsciousness 322
    historical 9, 40
    individual 14, 150
    intersubjective 41, 45, 51, 166, 183
    origins of 46–7, 174–5, 306
    political 67, 72, 86, 103
    stream of 21
    writing and 66
contingency vii, 15, 44, 61, 103, 106,
    219–20, 222, 233, 267, 277
Conway, Anne 302
Cornificius 22
cosmology 303, 307
Coventry 99
Cranach, Lucas 117–18, 314
    Adam and Eve 280, 291
    Venus 293
Cranmer, Thomas 124–5, 128, 147

and subjectivity 104, 106–8
biography of 92–4, 99, 102
death of 95, 98, 109–12, 121–2, 130, 132
recantation of 93, 101–2, 104, 107–8,
    112
trial of 100–1, 105–9
writing: *Book of Common Prayer*
    210–11, 221–2
    Catechism 114
creation artistic 27
    divine 59, 299–300, 320, 324
    myth 297
    as narrative 303
    of mankind 282, 298–9, 311, 322, 326
creed 107, 213
Crespin, Jean 102, 113, 119
Cromwell, Thomas 77, 84–5, 90, 146–7,
    166
crucifixion 121, 280
Cudworth, Ralph 302, 324–5
cultural history 1–3, 6–8, 15, 46–7
Curatt, John 135–6
Cureau de la Chambre, Marin 297

damnation 167, 188
Daniel, Samuel 184
danse macabre 318
Dante 193, 251
Davenant, William 154
Day, John 16, 93, 110, 112–13, 115–17,
    120–2, 125
de Grazia, Margreta 170, 174–5, 228,
    236–7
death 17, 213–14, 247, 254–65
    address to 183–4
    and freedom 253
    and limits of the imagination 186–7,
        205, 216, 248, 298, 321–2
    and the afterlife 17, 76
    as non-existence 196–202
    as sleep 174, 200
    boundary between life and 34
    desire for 253–5, 265–8, 274–6
    fear of 50, 106–9, 140, 198, 254, 256
    historiography of 49
    iconography of 40–1, 314–18
    imitation of 51
    of the author 58
    of the reader 58
    preparation for 57–8, 188, 255
    records of 55
    violent 119, 133, 227
    voluntary 227, 239, 246, 252, 267–72
Deguileville, Guillaume de 76, 86
deism 59
Derrida, Jacques 48, 117, 147

desacralization 3, 5, 7
Descartes, René 20, 47, 96, 296, 297, 300, 302, 308
  cogito in 20, 297
  res cogitans in 300, 301, 324
  works: *Description du corps humaine* 300
  Les passions de l'âme 297
  Meditationes de prima philosophia 297
desire 73, 133, 166, 177, 197, 201, 203, 247–8
  and appetite 306, 311, 313, 320–1
  and love 324
  for death 253–5, 265–8, 274, 276
  suppression of 127
determinism 210, 253
devils 35, 41, 164, 243, 270
dialogue
  between writer/reader or artist/viewer 46, 305
  dramatic 18
  (compared with soliloquy) 169, 176, 178–9, 197
  literary form 76, 83–4, 86, 89–90, 119, 178–9, 257–8, 309
dictionaries 76, 177
disenchantment (*Entzauberung*) 1–3, 5, 13
dissimulation 22, 96–7, 106
divination 212, 233
Dolomites 318
Donne, John 15, 50
  and autobiography 246, 248
  and paradox 248
  and providence 270–2
  on death 247, 268–9
  on martyrdom 267
  on natural law 248
  on suicide 238–9, 248–9, 254, 273
  works: *Biathanatos* 238, 246, 248–9, 267–72
  Death's Duel 248, 272
  Devotions upon Emergent Occasions 248
doorway 30
  as figure for death 32–41, 184
  (closed) 34
  (half-open) 34
doubt 61, 91, 97, 108, 137, 160, 172, 186, 250, 259, 261–3, 322
  doubting Thomas 102
Dover Wilson, John 9, 236
Drake, Sir Francis 93
dreams 155, 161, 174, 180, 199–200, 297, 305, 324
Dresden 129, 284, 291
Du Bartas, Guillaume Saluste 297
dualism 297, 300–1

Duffy, Eamon 13, 117–18, 214
Dürer, Agnes 55
Dürer, Albrecht 25
  annotation of images 29, 51, 53, 55
  coat of arms 30
  collecting of 25, 27
  copies of Mantegna 35
  death of 55
  drawings by 25, 27, 29, 32, 34, 51, 53, 55, 56
  hair of 56
  influence of 290–1, 310, 313–14, 318
  journey to Italy 34–5
  knowledge of classical sculpture 282–3, 286
  nude studies 25, 283–8
  portraits of family members 53–5
  preparatory studies by 49, 282, 287
  pupils of 284
  self-portraiture of 25, 29, 30, 46, 49, 51, 55
  use of colour ground 27
  works: *Adam and Eve* (engraving) 49, 278, **279**, 280, 282, 287, 289, 290, 293, 326
  (painting) 280
  Allegorie des Geistes 41
  'Anatomical Nude' 284
  Apollo and Diana (engraving) 285
  (drawing) 285, **286**
  Coat of Arms 30, **31**
  'Coat of Arms with a Skull' 32, **33**
  'Drawing of his Wife Agnes' 55
  'Geometrical Nude' 284
  'Head of Christ' 27, **28**, 29
  Knight, Death and the Devil 41
  Nemesis 285, 294
  'Nude Self-Portrait' 25, **26**, 29–30, 46, 49, 287, 316
  (?) *Portrait of Albrecht Dürer the Elder* 53
  Portrait of a Young Man 41
  Portrait of the Artist's Mother **54**, 55
  Portrait of Michael Wolgemut 29, 53
  St Jerome in his Study 40, 41
  Self-Portrait (Albertina) 29, 51, **52**
  (Munich) 29, 49, 284
  'Study of Eve' 287, **288**
  'Suffering Man' 27, 29
  Vier Bücher von menschlicher Proportion 296
  Young Girl threatened by Death 314
Dürer, Albrecht, the Elder 30
  (self(?)-)portrait of 53
Dürer, Barbara 53–5
Durkheim, Émile 3, 5, 243–4
Dutch 119, 220

Easter 39, 189
écorché 296
Edward VI, 68, 100, 102, 113–14, 118, 125
Egypt 32, 210, 217
Ekserdjian, David 39
election 99, 188–9, 216, 248
Eliot, Sir Thomas 76, 176
Eliot, T. S. 226
Elizabeth I, reign of 10, 87, 99, 156, 167
emblem books 129
embodiment 15–16, 41, 43, 46, 281–2,
    290, 296–8, 301–5, 320, 324–6
emotions 10, 22, 189, 257, 261, 281:
    see also *passions*
empiricism 61–2
Empiricus, Sextus 60
Empson, William 155, 206
Encyclopaedia Britannica 93
Enlightenment 2, 12, 16, 47, 240–1
Epictetus 257
Epicureanism 60, 276
Epicurus 201, 300
epistemology 44, 75, 88
equity 77, 80, 85, 87
Erasmus, Desiderius 115, 193, 242
eros 309, 326
Essex's rebellion 187
Eton 105
euthanasia 242, 245
Eve 39, 278–326
Evenden, Elizabeth 112–13, 116, 124–5
Everett, Barbara 225
excommunication 79, 133, 143, 158
executions, public 15, 18, 67–8, 100–1,
    104, 122, 124, 133–7, 139, 141,
    156, 158, 160–1, 215, 269
exegesis 115, 179, 190–5, 278
existentialism 6, 245
expurgation 154, 165
exstasis 310
Eyck, Jan van 29, 280

fall of man 40, 59, 278, 281, 283, 289,
    291, 293–4, 308–14, 316, 318,
    320–2
Family of Love 188–9
fideism 59, 269–70
figure study
    of human body: drawing (charcoal) 27,
        29, 55
    (pen/brush) 27, 29, 30, 35, 40, 51, 53, 55
    engraving 35, 40–1, 49
    fresco 35
    medal 32
    painting 29, 35, 53
    silverpoint 29, 51

woodcut 32, 112, 114, 121–30, 291,
    294, 316
figures of speech
    antanaclasis 181
    anthypophora 64
    catechresis 192
    ekphrasis 125, 183
    metalepsis 204–5
    metonymy 112, 127, 132
    parrhesia 22, 97
    synecdoche 57, 109, 281
finitude 24, 41, 44, 57, 63, 183–4, 204,
    276, 318, 322
First World War 6
Fish, Simon 84
Fisher, John 81–2
flesh 29, 40, 43, 63, 294
    as burden 249, 266
    as temporal 290, 313, 322
    burning 119, 125
    corruptible 196
    mortal 199, 314–18
    naked 280, 311
    organic 314
    in creation 299, 310
    in sexual union 310, 326
    versus spirit 289, 321
Florence 280, 282–3, 296, 314
Florio, John (Giovanni) 20, 200–2, 252
folly 39, 172
foreknowledge, divine 210
fortune 41, 173, 185, 197, 209, 211,
    215–16, 219, 221–3, 227, 232–4,
    236, 239, 256, 258, 274, 285
Foucault, Michel 7, 48, 179
Foxe, John 15–16, 134, 139
    humanism of 127–30
    iconoclasm of 113
    on Cranmer 101–4
    on iconoclasm 114–15, 117
    on oaths 153
    on sainthood 120
    on sincerity 103–4, 124, 140–1
    on suicide 238
    on writing 107, 132
    use of images in 110, 112, 115–16,
        118–19
    use of written sources in 98–9
    works: *Actes and Monuments* 69, 94, 98
        (1563 edition) 93, 110, **111**, 116, 122,
            123, 125, **126**, 130, **131**, 238
        (1570) 102, 103, 105, 107–9, 134,
            140, 156, (1583) 103, 222
    Christ Iesus triumphant 113
    *Rerum in ecclesia gestarum
        commentarii* 110

free will 23, 216, 245, 260–1, 270, 276, 326
freedom 21, 60, 95, 245, 276
  and political subjectivity 256, 274
  and slavery 251, 253, 255–6, 258 274
  from passions 255–6
  of choice 23, 73, 256, 266, 270
  of conscience 15, 69–71, 73, 80, 83, 88, 90, 95, 254
  of the individual 67, 69, 256–7
  of speech 22
  political 14–15, 67, 95, 253, 255–6, 260, 267
  religious 14, 88, 240, 255
Freeman, Thomas 68, 112–13, 116, 124–5
Freiburg im Breisgau 290
French 35–6, 51, 76, 96, 119, 177, 200, 213, 250
Freud, Sigmund 40, 72, 237, 306
Frith, John 96–7
future, the 64, 212, 214, 245, 269, 277, 313

gambling 208–9, 211–12, 220–1, 233
Gassendi, Pierre 300
Gataker, Thomas 212, 232–4
Gebel, Mathes 32
gender 14, 46
Geneva 113, 234, 242
Gennings, Edmund 156, 160, 165
German 10, 30, 180, 190, 220–1, 266
Germany 95, 280
Gerson, Jean 74, 78–80, 84
Gheeraerts, Marcus, the Younger 130
Ghent 280
Giorgione 41
Giovanni Antonio da Brescia 35, 40
  Descent into Limbo **38**, 39
Globe Theatre 174
Glossa ordinaria 192
Glover, Jonathan 244
God
  death of 5–6
  image of 178, 280–1, 307
  mind of 212, 307–8
Goes, Hugo van der 291
Good Friday 39, 188–9
Goodyer, Sir Henry 247
Gouge, William 216, 232
Gournay, Marie de 20, 56
grace 73, 79, 91, 124, 187–9, 214, 231, 235, 271
Grady, Hugh 186–7
Grafton, Anthony 212, 290
grammar 45, 180–1, 266

graves 199, 224, 226, 267, 314
  grave sculpture 32, 35
Greek 22, 60, 72, 82, 98, 141, 172, 191–4, 223, 228–9, 232, 239, 269, 310, 324
Green, Felicity 21, 201, 260
Greenblatt, Stephen 7–8, 169, 213
Greene, Robert 219
Gregory, Brad 95, 102
Griffin, Miriam 252, 257
Grindal, Edmund 99
Grynaeus, Simon 271
Gui, Bernard 143
Gurevich, Anton 13
Guy, John 85, 134

Hacking, Ian 209–11
Hadot, Pierre 178–9
Haemstede, Adriaan van der 113, 119
Hamburg 284
Hammond, Antony 181
Hampton Court Conference 165
handwriting 27, 51, 53, 55–6, 64, 99, 105, 107, 110, 112, 124, 127, 142
Harbison, Craig 289
Harpsfield, Nicholas 101, 106, 121, 124–5, 128
  Life of Thomas More 68–71, 86
Harrison, Peter 281, 308
Hayward, John 187–8
heaven 106
Hebrew 72, 129, 217–18, 232, 235, 309–10, 325
Hegel, Georg Wilhelm Friedrich 9, 117, 175, 186
Heidegger, Martin 9–10, 175
Heine, Heinrich 11
Hell 35, 39, 106–7, 164, 166, 200, 251, 303
Helvidius Priscus 255
Henry IV 143, 153
Henry VIII 85, 91, 96, 100, 114, 137, 140, 143, 145
Henry, Patrick 250–2
Herbert, Sir Henry 154–5
heresy 81, 83–4, 96–7, 100, 103–5, 130
  Anthropomorphism 281
  Epicureanism 276
  More's campaign against 133–8
  trial process 107, 141–6, 158, 160
hermaphrodites 289, 299
hermeneutics 191, 281, 320
Herodotus 223
Hill, Christopher 144, 148, 155
Hill, Geoffrey 156

Hirsh, James 172–4, 176, 183
Hobbes, Thomas
    and theology 300, 308
    on materialism 300, 326
    on mind 302
    on passions 303
    works: *De homine* 302
        Leviathan 300
Holbein, Hans, the Younger 114
Holinshed, Raphael 238
honesty 19, 22, 92, 96–7, 104, 144, 155, 160, 164
Hooker, Richard 188
Hooper, John 103, 119, 121
Hubert, Henri 3, 5
Huggarde, Miles 97
humanism 30, 34–5, 55–6, 122, 125, 128–9, 240, 242, 269, 274, 282
    late humanism 16, 256–7
Hume, David 239
humour theory 282
Hungary 30
hylozoism 302, 325

iconoclasm 115, 117–18, 120, 121
iconography 30, 32, 34, 41, 112
    Biblical 35
    mythological 35
    of death 40, 314
    of love 287
    of martyrdom 130
    of saints 121–2
    of sin 291, 293, 320
identity
    and sexual union 309
    as mirroring 289
    confessional 17, 94, 110
    human compared with divine 280–1, 307
    national 93
    outside of bodily existence 308
    personal 1, 4, 8, 15–18, 20, 29, 43, 48, 50, 92, 95, 98–9, 103, 108, 124, 169, 178, 186, 205, 272, 305–6, 308, 316
images
    and iconoclasm 113–16
    and idolatry 112
    as laymen's books 116–17
    burning of 115
    cult of 98
    in Protestantism 110–22
imagination 25, 205–6, 305, 325
immortality 23, 41, 255, 322
imperfection 24
incarnation 39, 102

individual, the 4, 9, 14, 17, 46, 60, 146–7, 150, 169–70, 243, 302
    and God 144
    and society 3, 5
    and the state 3, 8, 140, 159
    freedom of 7, 67, 256–7
    religion of 5, 7, 13, 68, 141
    rise of 8
individualism 1–2, 7, 13, 15, 46, 60, 96, 169
innocence, state of 289, 296, 313
Inquisition 8, 142, 212
insincerity 96–7, 103, 107–8
interior monologue 172
intersubjectivity 45, 320
inwardness 16, 20, 47, 78, 87, 95, 140–1, 161, 163, 305
Iphigenia 39
Italy 35

James I 152, 194, 215, 218, 223
James II 148
Jane, Queen of England 100
Jenkins, Harold 196, 209, 237–8
Jerome 40, 73, 78
Jerusalem 193–4
Jesuits 87, 128, 280
Jonson, Ben 230–1
    works: *The Alchemist* 231
        Bartholomew Fair 231
        The Devil is an Ass 231
        Eastward Ho 168
        Every Man in his Humour 231
        Every Man Out of His Humour 168, 230
justification, doctrine of 232

Katherine of Aragon 100, 145
Kaufmann, Thomas de Costa 318
Kenny, Anthony 67–9, 75–6, 80, 84
Kermode, Frank 170, 185, 209, 224
Kierkegaard, Søren 237
King Leir 168
Knewstub, John 188–9
Knochenmann, der 314, 318
Knox, John 116
Koepplin, Dieter 318
Koerner, Joseph Leo 27, 40, 117–18, 280, 290, 316
    on art in the Reformation 121–2, 132
    on self-portraiture 29–30, 44, 53
Koselleck, Reinhard 17
Kulmbach, Hans von 284

Lacan, Jacques 306
Lambert, John 102
Lambin, Denis 63–4

Langley, Eric 249
language 15
  and contingency 219, 223, 228–35
  and death 196–7, 272
  and figuration 186, 191–5, 204–6,
    310, 324–6
  and naming 304
  and necessity 209–11, 213–4
  and reflexivization 72, 266
  and subjectivity 17, 180–1
  as social 151, 155
  expletive 147, 156
  of conscience 81, 85–9
  of the passions 261
  of the self 20–1, 150, 170, 178, 185, 266
  origins of 304
  visual 34, 112, 120, 122, 132
Latimer, Hugh 100, 222
Laureti, Tomasso 129
law(s) 11–12, 19, 23
  and conscience 67, 76, 80
  and equity 78–9
  criminal 241
  divine 68, 71, 82, 87, 229, 241
  ecclesiastical 143, 188
  in English law courts 77, 84–5, 142
  Roman 32, 143
  of adultery 159, 165, 232
  of heresy 104
  of suicide 240
  of treason and sedition 148, 153
  secular 144, 244
  spiritual and temporal 85
  see also *canon law, common law,* and
    natural law
Le Brun, Charles 297
Leiden 129
Lennon, John 225
Leonardo da Vinci 283, 296
Lévi-Strauss, Claude 48
liberalism 2–3, 14, 67, 86, 88, 91, 169,
  240
life drawing vii, 25–7, 29–30, 40, 49,
  51–2, 53, 55–6, 283–8, 294, 310,
  314–16
life writing vii, 15, 21, 27, 44, 50–8, 60,
  63–6, 99, 104–9, 269–70
Ligeti, György 235
likeness 46, 178, 280, 308, 324
liminality 32, 40, 49, 107, 184, 187
Lincoln's Inn 232
Lipsius, Justus 239, 260, 263, 270
  and Tacitus 256, 265
  and paradox 258
  and tyranny 255

  letters of 255
  reading of Montaigne 259
  return to Catholic church 259
  works: *De constantia* 256–7
    Manuductio ad stoicam philosophiam 256,
    258–9
liturgy 94, 160, 210, 220–1, 310
Livy 127–30
Locke, John 96, 180, 266
Lodge, Thomas 225
Lollards 117, 143–4, 153, 156
London 99–100, 116, 127, 135, 230,
  269, 285
  Fulham Palace 120, 125
  Lambeth Palace 113, 230
  Tower of 67
  (writing in) 146, 187
  York Place 85
lottery 211
Louvain 68–9
Löwith, Karl 10
Lucan 274
Lucas van Leyden 280
  works: *Expulsion from Paradise*
    (1510) 310
    Fall of Man (1530) 311, **312**, 313, 320
    series of engravings on the Fall
    (1529) 310–13
Lucian 283
luck 214–23, 225, 228–31, 235
  bad 211, 214–15, 217, 225, 230
  moral 229
lucky days 216, 222
Lucretia 130, 238
Lucretius 17, 60–6, 197–8, 201, 255,
  275–7, 300
Lupset, Thomas 139, 192–3
Luther, Martin 12, 89, 101, 117–18, 321
  and art 121–2
  Biblical commentary of 190, 278, 281
  Biblical translation 220–1
  death of 270–1
  on conscience 79–82
  on grace 214
  on luck 220, 235
  'priesthood of all believers' 125

Macaulay, Lord (Thomas Babington) 93
MacCulloch, Diarmaid 92, 94, 104
Machiavelli, Niccolò 128, 187
Maclean, Ian 21, 44, 75
Madrid 280, 293
magic 3, 5, 12–13
Mahmood, Saba 12, 14
Malone, Edmond 181, 236

Mantegna, Andrea 34, 128
  influence on Dürer 35, 40
  works: *Descent into Limbo* 35, 37,
    39–40
  Entombment with Birds 35, 36
  Gaius Mucius Scaevola 129
Mantua 35
Manutius, Aldus 285
marginalia (manuscript) 63, 134
  (printed) 137, 119, 193–4, 216, 218,
    223, 242
Marlowe, Christopher *Doctor Faus-
    tus* 173–4, 200
marriage 145, 158, 167, 221, 232, 305,
    310
Martial 274
martyrdom 15, 18, 92–3
  and confessionalism 102
  and conscience 106, 153
  and doctrinal truth 104–5, 141
  and iconography 110, 119, 124–32
  and inwardness 95
  and narrative 98–9
  and suicide 238, 248, 267
Mary I, Queen of England 99, 100, 103,
    127
Mary, Virgin 35, 102, 113
Masaccio 280
Mass 106, 107, 125
materialism 16, 64, 300–2, 326
  'animist' 302
  anti-materialism 301–2
mathematics 209–11, 232, 284–5
Maus, Kathleen Eisaman 95
Mauss, Marcel 3, 5
meditation 43, 136, 175, 177–8, 182,
    184, 186, 199–200
  on death 187–9, 192, 247–8
melancholy 40, 254, 282, 296
Melanchthon, Philipp 271
memory 29, 63, 162, 171, 273, 277, 281,
    305–6, 323
Menander 233
Merleau-Pony, Maurice 48
metaphor 56, 186, 189, 191–2, 195–7,
    204, 314, 324–6
metaphorology 17
Michelangelo Buonarroti 129, 280
Michelet, Jules 7
Middle Ages
  drama of 172
  idea of 7, 10, 46, 99, 117–18, 120,
    124, 130
Middleton, Thomas 231
Milton, John 15, 50

  and materialism 300–2, 324–5
  and metaphor 324–6
  and mortality 321–2
  and narration 323
  and Ovid 306
  and Plato 310
  and *res cogitans* (Descartes) 301
  as reader of the Bible 299
  controversy with Hobbes 301
  dualism of 301–3
  on creation 298, (human) 303–7,
    323–6
  on death 322
  on embodiment 297, 302, 306–10,
    321, 324–6
  on origins of language 304
  on sexual difference 308–9
  on suicide 238
  on the passions 282, 309–10
  works: *Comus* 301
  De doctrina Christiana 301, 308
  Paradise Lost 238, 297–9, 302–10,
    321–6
mind
  and memory 63
  and sense impressions 62
  and subjectivity 22, 89–91, 140–1,
    158–62, 244, 255, 262, 265
  and the passions 274
  as container of thoughts 45, 88, 101
  as human faculty 188, 213, 281, 307,
    325
  as location of conscience 69, 74, 81, 180
  as reflection of self 29, 56, 64, 90, 137,
    169, 171–3, 203
  boundary of mind and body 297,
    300–3, 324–5
  in relation to writing 56, 63–5, 179
  material substance of 300–2
  of God 212, 307–8
Miola, Robert 181
miracles 120, 124, 141
mirrors 25, 45, 51, 171
mischance 208, 227–8
modernity vi–vii, 1, 4, 7, 9–11, 16, 20,
    59, 67, 71–2, 75, 88, 91, 92–5, 99,
    132, 138, 146, 169, 175, 238–40, 290
  historiography of 46–8
monogram, artist's 25, 27, 29, 287, 291,
    293–4, 314, 316
Monta, Susannah 95
Montaigne, Michel de 15–16
  and Aristotle 246
  and Cicero 50, 197, 201, 201–2, 242,
    276

Montaigne, Michel de (*cont.*)
  and Épicureanism 276
  and freedom 21–3, 60, 246, 251,
    253–6, 260–1, 274, 276
  and Lipsius 255–60
  and Lucretius 60–6, 197, 201, 255,
    275–7
  and modernity 48
  and mortality 23–4, 43, 51, 56–8, 63
  and natural law 16, 249
  and non-existence 200–2
  and paradox 251–2, 260
  and Plato 202, 252–3, 257, 276
  and sex 24
  and stoicism 50–1, 179, 242, 252–3,
    255–65, 274–5
  and suicide 249–65
  and Tacitus 263, 265
  and theology 62
  annotations in copy of Lucretius 63–4,
    65, 277
  birth of 57
  body of 19–20, 24, 57
  'book of the self' in 19–20
  death of 56–7
  idea of the self 16, 20, 21, 45, 48,
    57, 267
  on death of Cato 250, 261–2
  of Seneca 252–65
  philosophical method of 43–4, 60–1
  revising of book 56
  scepticism of 44, 58–62, 197, 202,
    259, 274
  writing, idea of 21, 44, 51, 56–7, 60,
    63, 179, 250, 259–60, 262, 276
  works: *Essais* 19–20, 22, 43–4, 60
    (1580 edition) 19–20, 56, 253
    (1588) 20, 56, 58, 255
    ('Bordeaux copy' of 1588) 20, 50,
      56–8, 63
    (1595) 20, 56, 253
    'Apologie de Raimond Sebond' 23–4,
      58, 61–3, 197, 200–2, 238, 254–5,
      259–60
    'Au lecteur' 19–20
    'Coustume de l'isle de Cea' 246,
      250–1, 253, 255–6, 259–60, 262,
      268, 274–6
    'De l'art de conferer' 262
    'Des boyteux' 262
    'De la cruauté' 250, 261
    'Des livres' 21
    'De la physionomie' 200–3
    'Des trois bonnes femmes' 262–5
    'De la vanité' 259
    'Du repentir' 22

'Philosopher c'est apprendre à
    mourir' 50, 56–8, 248, 253, 276
moral philosophy 5, 20, 22, 47, 50, 51,
    74–6, 79–80, 87, 94–8, 129, 179,
    206, 217, 229–35, 239–44, 248–9,
    253, 262, 265, 274
morality play 174
morbidity 29, 40, 290
  of the flesh 310–21
More, Henry 302
More, Thomas 16
  as figure of conscience 67–8, 70–1
  as Lord Chancellor 77, 84–5, 134–7
  death of 92, 145, 166
  in prison 86, 146
  on conscience 88–91
  on heresy 137, 142, 145–7, 166
  on law 76–7, 84–5
  on the Oath 70, 88, 145
  on suicide 242–3
  practice in Star Chamber 84, 134–7,
    140–2, 162
  practice of Chancery law 84–5
  practice of common law 77
  reputation under Mary 69
  under Elizabeth 87–8
  resignation of 85
  trial of 68, 71, 94, 145–7
  works: *Apology* 76
    Confutation of Tyndale 133
    Debellation of Salem and Bizance 84
    Dialogue Concerning Heresies 83–4,
      137, 146
    *Dialogue of Comfort against
      Tribulation* 86, 243
    The workes of Sir Thomas More 69, 89
    Utopia 242
Morice, James 153, 159, 165
Morice, Ralph 99
mortality 16–17, 23–4, 259
  and autobiography 248
  and contingency 61, 318, 322
  and reflectivity 206, 226
  and self-portrait 41
  and subjectivity 43, 183, 185, 188–9,
    195, 211, 305, 318
  as boundary 17, 32, 49, 51, 274, 321
  in idea of art 53, 55, 290
  in classical philosophy 63, 197, 276
  in idea of writing 56–8, 275
  of Christ 39
Mucedorus 168
Muir, Kenneth 205–6
Munich 1–2, 29, 283
  Alte Pinakothek 49, 129, 262, 284
Murano 25

Murray, Alexander 254
mysticism 2, 74, 104, 214, 310, 321
mythology 35, 287, 291, 309

Nagel, Thomas 44
nakedness 34, 39
    Adam and Eve 49, 278, 280, 283, 287,
        291, 318, 321
    and shame 293
    artist as naked 25, 32, 40
    self as naked 19, 21, 24, 296
narcissism 22, 40, 45, 186, 306–7, 309
narration
    first-person 18
    multiple 323
narrative
    and contingency 260–5
    conveying meaning 97–8, 226–7
    in painting and art 39, 132, 313, 316
    of creation 322–3, 326
    of martyrdom 95, 99, 102, 104, 106,
        119, 134, 139–41
    of providence 260
    of selfhood 16, 108–9, 177, 187, 298
Nashe, Thomas 219, 225
natural law 19, 23, 62, 74, 239, 241, 244,
    248–9
natural science 2, 61, 281
nature 59, 171, 239, 252, 272, 291, 293,
    324
    animal 320
    human 20, 23–4, 62, 95, 197, 281, 282–7
    laws of 35, 208, 241, 244, 248–9, 275,
        308
necrophilia 316
necropolis 32
Neill, Michael 49
neo-stoicism 253, 257–64, 267
Nero 240
New Historicism 8
Nietzsche, Friedrich 5–7, 48, 118
Noble, Richmond 192, 194
non-existence 40, 57, 62, 199, 200–2,
    266, 305
Norton, Thomas 234–5
Norwich 99, 122, 133–5, 143, 147
nothingness 18, 201
nude study 25–6, 29–30, 46, 49, 278,
    282–7, 290, 311, 316
Nuremberg 30, 53, 55, 284, 289, 290
    Chronicle 34
Nussbaum, Martha 228–9, 235
Nyquist, Mary 299

O'Connell, Marvin 68–9, 75–6, 84
oaths 18

bans on 152–4
censorship of 150–1
ex officio 82, 142–3, 145–6, 153,
    164–5, 167
foul 148–52, 155, 162, 165
minced 151–2
of allegiance 70, 88, 145–8, 165
of Succession 70
of Supremacy 71
Oberman, Heiko 80
Oecolampadius, Johannes 271
Oporinus, Johannes 296
original sin 39, 72, 278, 282, 290–1, 293,
    313
Orpheus 35
Ouldsworth 113
Ovid 306–7, 310
Oxford 68, 92, 99, 100, 110, 128
    Balliol College 100
    Christ Church 101
    Oxford Movement 94

pain 24, 27, 30, 119, 122, 124–5, 127,
    130, 201, 254, 258, 276, 322
Painter, William 128
Panofsky, Erwin 27, 29–30, 35, 48, 278,
    282–3, 285 , 287, 289
paper as
    figure for mortality 41, 47, 61–6, 106–9
    for selfhood 105, 136, 161–2
Papy, Jan 257
Paraeus, David 278
Paris 35, 56, 70, 246, 269
Parker, Matthew 113, 134
parliament 76, 114, 145, 148, 152–3
    Act of Succession 145
    Act of Supremacy 71, 96–7, 145
    repeal of *ex officio* oath 165
    Suicide Act 240
    Treason Act 145
Parr, Katherine 222
passions 17, 22, 24, 50, 177, 189, 253, 256,
    274, 281, 282, 297, 302–3, 320, 326
Paul's Cross 188
Paulina, Pompeia 263–5
Peele, George 219
Pelles, Thomas 135–6, 141–2, 161
penance 105, 133, 137, 159
Pererius, Benedictus 280
periodization 10, 12, 46–7
perishability 41, 43, 55, 248, 322
    of flesh 112, 314
    of ink and pencil 55
    of paper 41
perjury 142–3, 146, 164
Perkins, William 5, 213

persecution 92, 119, 129, 222, 267
person see *identity, individual, self,*
    subjectivity
personhood 4, 8–9, 16, 46, 55, 57, 60,
    64, 74, 80, 103, 109, 138–40, 147,
    150, 169, 178, 188–9, 228, 253,
    266, 276, 305, 308
Persons, Robert 87–8, 176
Peter Lombard *Sententiae* 72, 74, 79
Petronius 233
phenomenology 45, 88, 141, 271
Philip of Macedon 251
philosophy
    idea of 6, 11, 43–5, 51, 178–9, 238,
    251, 277, 296
Pico della Mirandola 23, 49
Pirckheimer, Wilibald 55
plague 29
Plato 217, 234
    on death 89, 202, 276
    on knowledge 308
    on love 309–10, 323
    on moral luck 217
    on suicide 239, 242, 252–3, 257–8
    on the soul 73
    works: *Apology* 202
    Crito 89
    Laws 258
    Phaedo 239, 242, 252–3, 276
    Republic 73
    Symposium 309–10
    Timaeus 308
Plautus 172
pleasure 24, 44, 64, 188, 202, 249, 261, 307
Pliny the Elder 193, 283
Pliny the Younger 39, 129
Plutarch 62, 128, 233
Poliziano, Angelo 285
pope, papacy 5, 80–2, 93, 100
    Innocent III 143
    Paul IV 88
Pordage, John 321
Porras, Stephanie 27
Porsenna 127
post-Christianity 7
post-colonialism 12
postmodernism 6, 48
Praxiteles 283
prayer 79, 94, 105, 107, 133, 140, 164,
    166, 177, 179, 187, 210–11, 214,
    221–2, 247–8, 271, 314
predestination 17, 213, 214, 229, 234,
    254, 269–70
prison 16, 67, 79, 100–1, 125, 143, 145
    as metaphor of selfhood 184–6, 189,
    270, 272

writing in 85–6, 89
private (the) 72
    boundary of 171, 205
    in relation to public 137–41, 144–5,
    149, 151–2, 156–7, 195
    'invention of' 15, 138–40
    conscience 86–7, 144, 153
    dissidence 148
    meaning 145–6, 150, 158
    opinion 144
    prayer 133
    reading 136–7
    religion 14
    rights 67–8
    self 27, 146, 245
    thought 162, 166, 170, 174
    sexual privacy 287
Privy Council 116, 216
probability 208–11, 232
proclamations 137–8, 211
pronouns 171, 181, 266
    first person 18, 57, 84, 110, 174,
    180–2, 298
    le moi 19, 21
    shift 171
prophecy 2, 93, 102, 151, 205
Protagoras 257
providence 121
    divine 210, 212, 214, 215–16, 220,
    229, 231, 233
    and chance 18, 230
    special providence 213
public 15, 69, 92, 104
    good 67
    interpretation 124
    knowledge 72
    law 11
    meaning 150–1, 156–7
    reading 133–5
    space 15, 153–4, 157–8
    speech 136
    'sphere' 137
    witness 144
    meaning in relation to 'private'
    137–41, 145–8, 163, 166, 195
    'public scandal' 142
    res publica 139
puritanism 12, 144, 152–3, 155, 159,
    165, 211–12, 216, 230, 232, 306
Pythagoras 257

Quakers 144
Quintilian 22, 39

randomness 210, 228–9
Rastell, John 84

Rastell, William 68, 69
Ratzinger, Josef (Benedict XVI) 3, 75
Rawlins, Erkinald 222
reading
    aloud 135–7
    and death 58
    and interiority 136–7
    and selfhood 19, 132
    and visual representation 122, 125
    examples of Renaissance practice 63–6,
        251, 253, 275–7
    of the Bible 82, 221
    representation of 99, 110
recantation 92–3, 143
    of Bilney 133–8, 140, 161
    of Cranmer 101–2, 104, 107–8, 112,
        124, 132
Rede, Edward 135–6, 141–2, 161
reflectivity 45, 48, 51, 181
reflexivity 20, 23, 44–6, 72, 175, 316
Reformation, the 3, 12–13, 17, 50, 72,
        75, 97–9, 196, 278
    and art 115, 117, 280
    Catholic 15, 118
    counter-Reformation 69
    Edwardian 118
    English 94, 134
    Henrician 87, 89
    Protestant 5, 15, 102, 104, 107
Reigate 113
relativism 3, 44, 75
religion 2
    and art 9, 290
    and literature 9, 12, 13, 15
    and modernity 2, 12–13, 15
    and natural knowledge 58, 254–7
    and politics 16, 148
    and the Reformation 94, 103, 107
    and the secular 4, 17, 255
    and scepticism 60–1, 240
    and science 1–3
    decline of 3, 8
    historiography of 4–5, 12, 87
    of the body 13
    of the literate 124–5
    popular 117
    private 14, 141
Rembrandt van Rijn 280
    Adam and Eve 318–20, **319**
Renaissance 1, 39, 283, 318
    and selfhood 49
    art 7, 278
    idea of the 4, 7–9, 11–12, 15, 18,
        46–9, 175, 240
    reception of classical sculpture 32, 34,
        282–3

revisionist history of 48
    theory of art 318
    symbolism of 34, 283
reproduction
    of identity 309
    sexual 291
revelation, divine 59, 61, 68, 84
Reynolds, John 231
rhetoric 11, 15–16
    classical 22, 24, 197
    forensic 158
    humanist 56, 251, 253, 258, 318
    theatrical 170, 175–6, 178–9, 182
Rich, Sir Richard 70, 86, 145–6
Richardson, Ian 181
Ricoeur, Paul 98
Ridley, Nicholas 88, 99–100
Rist, John 257
ritual 3, 5, 10, 13, 16–17, 107, 118, 140,
        159, 164
    of death 17, 41, 55, 241
    of penance 133, 149
Robinson, John 6
Rogers, John 215
Rome 100, 129, 230, 280
    ancient 32, 34, 130
Roper, Margaret 89
Roper, William 68, 70–1, 86
Rousseau, Jean-Jacques 95
Rowley, William 231
Rubens, Peter Paul 257
    Death of Seneca 262–3, **264**
Russell, Dianne 311, 313, 318, 320

sacraments vi, 3, 5, 84, 102, 114, 118,
        130, 133, 140–1, 143, 149, 177
sacrifice 5
saints 35, 98, 115, 118, 141
    cult of 17, 98, 120, 122
sanctification 17
sarcophagus 32, 34, 35
Sartre, Jean-Paul 245
Satan 76, 293, 305, 322
Scaevola, Gaius Mucius 125, 127–30
scepticism 44, 58–60, 62, 90, 197, 202,
        240, 259, 274
    Pyrrhonist 60
Schäuflein, Hans 284
Schedel, Hartmann 34
Schiele, Egon 25
Schiller, Friedrich 1
Schmitt, Carl 10–11
Schoenfeldt, Michael 307, 321, 326
scholasticism 72–81, 84, 86–7, 117, 241,
        248
Schopenhauer, Arthur 237

science 1–3 see *natural science*
Screech, Michael 23, 60–1, 63–4, 66
scripture 58–9, 80, 84, 124, 215–18,
    222–3, 235, 308
Sebond, Raimond 58–60
Second World War 4
secular, the 92, 94, 96, 175, 179, 195,
    198–9, 210, 214, 231
  and the religious 4, 13, 16, 18, 255
  law 71, 79, 142, 144, 158
  society 2–3
  'secular theology' 6
  virtues 129
secularity 4, 8–9, 12, 17, 254
  and literature 9, 210, 214
  and modernity vi, 4, 198–9, 255
  and politics 11–12, 87, 99
  and Shakespeare 8, 16, 175, 236
secularization vi, 60–1, 94, 118, 158,
    169, 175, 178, 240, 287
  of ecclesiastical property, 3
  origin of word 10
  secularization thesis: 1–18, 187, 240
Sedulius, Henricus 270
Seigel, Jerrold 44–5, 47–8, 181, 266
self, the
  as incomplete 171, 178, 186, 203–4
  as other 289
  noun derived from pronoun 19,
    180–1, 238, 266, 303
  history of 14, 46–50
  idea of 14, 19–20, 181
  language of 22, 181
  limits of 23, 44, 49, 51, 57, 60–1, 91,
    180, 184, 244, 267, 274–7
  naked 24
self-address 12, 15, 172, 182
self-cancellation 60, 172
self-incrimination 143–4
self-mutilation 101
self-portraiture 15, 16, 25–30, 40, 43–5,
    49, 53, 284, 287, 289, 290, 316
self-reflection 30, 45, 63, 171, 247, 265, 318
Seneca 128, 231, 241, 257, 267
  death of 262–5
  on suicide 239–40, 253, 258, 274
  works: *Ad Lucilium Epistulae
    Morales* 252, 255–6, 260
  De ira 61
  Hippolytus 230
senses, the 59, 61–2, 188, 202, 262, 281
sermons 81, 133, 146, 150, 189, 193,
    196, 213
sexuality 14, 162, 290–1, 311
  and death 158, 318
  and sin 293, 313

animal 316, 320
sexual act 166, 293–4
difference 46, 287, 289, 308
organs 24
union 308, 326
violence 130
Shaheen, Naseeb 210–11
Shakespeare, William vi–vii, 6, 8
  and Augustine 198–9
  and Cicero 197–8
  and Lucretius 197–8
  and Montaigne 197, 200–3
  and psychoanalysis 236–7
  and the Reformation 50
  and Virgil 231
  as Catholic 14, 194, 213
  as iconic Renaissance author 8, 10–11
  as secular 14–6
  biography of 14
  chance in 207–8, 226–8
  citation of Bible in 189, 194–5, 212–4
  coincidences in 208, 226
  conscience in 180
  death in 166, 182–3, 186–7, 196–8,
    200, 203, 207
  figure of Christ in 187
  forensic process in 158, 160–2, 164
  imagination in 205–6
  inwardness in 163, 184–6, 205–6
  kingship in 184, 186–7
  kneeling in 161
  lying in 162, 182
  memory in 171
  music in 185
  pronouns in 171, 181
  problem of metaphor in 186, 189–95,
    203–6
  prayer in 187
  public and private space in 157–8
  religious meditation in 182, 186–91,
    203–4
  sense of mortality in 183, 186–7, 189,
    195–6, 204–6, 226–7
  sexual act in 166
  sincerity in 97
  suicide in 198, 228, 236–8
  swearing in 155–6, 162, 164–6
  theology of providence in 220, 229,
    231
  thought process in 170, 184–6, 203,
    224
  voyeurism in 157, 161
  wagers in 208–9
  use of: asides 205
  beds 157–8
  confession 164

dialogue 156–7
hearsay 161
scene-changing 157
soliloquy 168–75, 180–91, 195–7, 199–200, 206, 236–8
stage directions 168, 174, 180, 184
Works: First Folio 155
plays: *Antony and Cleopatra* 211, 267, 272–3
Cymbeline 199, 266
Hamlet 8, 43, 169–72, 174–5, 179–82, 185, 195–200, 202–5, 207–14, 220, 224–35, 236–8, 241, 256, 266–8, 270–1, 276
Henry V 168
Julius Caesar 272–3
King Lear 200
Macbeth 5–6, 203–6
Measure for Measure 197–8
Merchant of Venice 211
Othello 152–67
Richard II 184–91, 194–5, 203–4
Richard III 168, 170–1, 180–2
Romeo and Juliet 182–4
poems: *Lucrece* 238
shame 24, 185, 239, 251, 283, 293–4
sickness 27, 29, 30, 55, 130, 196, 201, 246, 248, 258, 268, 269
Sidney, Sir Philip 238
Sierhuis, Freya 22, 256
signature 109, 112, 124, 147, 289
silence 88, 124, 133, 136, 145, 160, 163–4, 170, 179, 182, 223, 265
Silver, Larry 311
sincerity 17, 21–2, 92, 94–8, 103–8, 110, 124–7, 260
meaning of 'sincere' 103–4
sleep 27, 161, 174, 197, 199–200, 224, 247, 282, 299–300, 303, 305–6, 311, 322, 324–5
Smith, Susan 311
social sciences 2–4, 14, 17
sociology 1, 3, 11
Socrates 89, 202, 276
death of 239, 255
Sol 285
soliloquy 15, 18
and death 195–203
and interiority 169–70, 174–5
and religious meditation 177–80
as colloquium with God 179, 182
compared with internal dialogue 176–80
history of 172–5
in Augustine 178–9
in Greek tragedy 172

in Elizabethan drama 172–4
in Roman comedy 172
in Shakespeare 168–75, 180–91, 195–7, 199–200
origins of word 172, 175–6
solipsism 62, 71, 91, 182, 248, 305
Sophocles 229, 235
soul 34, 39, 51, 64, 73–4, 76, 78–9, 90, 160, 177–8, 191, 204, 244, 249, 261, 281, 299–301, 308, 310
immortality of 255
mortality of 276
union of with body 196, 201, 206
Southwell, Robert 128, 176
Spain 93
Speght, Rachel 299
Spenser, Edmund 128
Sprott, S. E. 240
St German, Christopher 76–81, 83–6
Stachniewski, John 254
Stanyhurst, Richard 229–30
Stapleton, Thomas 87
Star Chamber 84, 90, 135, 142, 162
Starkey, Thomas 139
Starobinski, Jean 249, 261–2
statute, in English law 69, 100, 138, 143, 148,
on oaths 153, 154
on suicide 240
still life 41–3
Stock, Brian 178
stoicism 50–1, 125, 127, 179, 197, 214, 274–5, 303
on suicide 237, 240, 242, 252–3, 255, 257–65, 267
Strasbourg 290–1
Stratford-upon-Avon 11, 158
Studley, John 230
subjectivity 6–7, 17, 60, 201, 226
and emotion 189
autonomy of 75, 267, 274–7
history of 46–7, 186
in art 318
literary 15, 108, 174, 298–305
political 256
religious 16, 110
'subjective turn' 94
suffering 27, 29, 95, 112, 119, 121, 130, 132, 248, 257–8, 262, 269, 272, 276
suicide 15
and friendship 272
and insanity 240, 244
and political freedom 249, 256–8
and religious burial 228, 240–1
and secularization 240, 244

suicide (*cont.*)
  and sociology 243–4
  as medical condition 244–5
  as psychological condition 239
  as release from suffering 258
  assisted 245, 273
  decriminalization of 240
  in ancient philosophy 239–40
  in Christian thought 241–2, 245–6, 254
  in existentialism 245–6
  in humanist thought 242–3
  in stoicism 252–65
  origins of word in English 238–9
supernatural 34
superstition 3, 103, 118
Sutton, Christopher 177, 188
swearing see *oaths*
Sylvester, Joshua 297
synderesis 72–6, 78, 79–80, 84, 89

Tacitus 187, 256, 263, 265
Talmud 194
tapestry 129
Taylor, Charles 1, 4, 20–1, 23, 47–8, 94,
    96–8, 246
  works: *A Secular Age* 17, 20
    Ethics of Authenticity 110–12
    Sources of the Self 20, 97
Taylor, Gary 154
temporality 34, 41, 43, 183, 224–8, 290,
    310–11, 320
Terence 128, 172
theatricality 173, 186
theology
  and secularity 3, 6, 240–1, 244, 274
  and demythologization 6
  and literature 10, 210, 212–13
  history of 210, 271, 308
  natural 58–61, 73–4, 241, 254, 281
  political 10–11
  sacramental 118
  see also *Calvinism scholasticism*
Theophylact 193
thinking
  a priori 74
  as communicative 21
  as incomplete 204–5
  as mortal 43, 57–8, 63, 183, 322
  as non-material 302
  as perfect form of knowledge 308
  as process 44, 50–1, 170, 184–6, 203,
    224, 265, 302, 320
  as private or secret 107, 109, 112, 162,
    166, 174, 189
  as self-referential 179

as treasonable 145, 160
  content of 90
Thomas, Keith 13
Thrasea, Publius Clodius 256–7, 263–4
tombs 32, 34, 71–2, 182–3
Tomkins, Thomas 110, 125–8, 130
Tomson, Laurence 193–4
torture 69, 109, 120, 125, 128
transcendence 2, 9, 44
transience 41, 43–4, 63, 267
treason 100, 130, 145–6, 158, 185
trials, legal
  adultery 158–9
  heresy 100, 104–5, 107, 134, 137,
    142–3, 145–6, 158, 160
  treason 100, 145–6, 158
Trilling, Lionel 96–7
Trinity 307
Trubowitz, Rachel 322
truth conditions 68, 84, 87, 94, 95, 258
Turner, William 116
Tyndale, William 134, 235
  biblical translations of 215–20, 223
  death of 119
  on conscience 81–3, 86–8, 144
  on luck 214–18
  on oaths 144, 151
  on scripture 86
  works: *Answer to More* 83, 144
    Obedience of a Christen Man 81–2, 84,
      144
Tyrrell, Edmund 130

uncertainty 20, 49, 61, 95, 214, 217,
    259, 261, 265, 268, 316
unconscious, the 47
United Nations 71
Ure, Peter 194

Valerius Maximus 283
vanitas 41–3, 53
Venice 34, 296
Venus 282, 287, 289, 293–4, 314
Vermigli, Peter Martyr 278
Vesalius, Andreas 296
Vienna 41
  Albertina 29, 55, 287, 290
viewer 121, 178, 291, 293
  as reflection 289
  implied presence of 25, 30, 32, 39, 43,
    46, 284, 294
Villagarcia, Juan de 101, 112
violence 50, 114–15, 128, 130, 144, 150,
    156, 163–4, 227–8, 251, 262
Virgil 230–1, 251

Viswanathan, Gauri 9, 12, 14
Vitruvius 283, 296
voluntary, voluntarism 23, 72, 233, 241,
    246, 255, 259–61, 265–72
voyeurism 112, 157, 161, 291

Walsham, Alexandra 115, 215
Warburton, William 236
Weber, Max 1–2, 5, 10, 13
Webster, John 232
Weimar 25
Wheeler, Elizabeth 158
White, Christopher 320
Whitgift, John 153, 165, 194
Whitney, Geoffrey 129
Wied, Hermann von 220
will, the
    and agency 252
    and desire 268
    and external constraints 260–1, 270
    and human limitation 23, 267–8
    and moral choice 216
    and the body 301, 313, 326
    as faculty 81, 250, 281
    control of 50
    divine 234, 250, 270, 307

philosophy of 71–4, 79, 81
    sovereign 276
Williams, Bernard 229, 235
Williams, Raymond 169, 174
Wilson, Nicholas 91
witches 205, 216, 290, 316–17
Wittenberg 117, 213, 234, 283
Wolfe, John 187
Wolgemut, Michael 29, 34, 53, 55
Worms, Diet of 80
writing
    and being 21
    and death 51
    and subjectivity 20–2, 44, 105, 107–9,
        124, 178
    as reflection 44
    hand 112, 124, 127
    idea of 99
Wyclif, John 97

Xenophon 223

York 116

Zanchius, Hieronymus 278
Zwingli, Huldrych 12, 121, 271